Patti Blundell

CHADRON STATE COLLEGE
1000 Main Street
Chadron, NE 69337-2690
(308) 432-6000

TO: Patti Blundell
Hildreth 305C

Educational Governance
and Administration

Fourth Edition

Educational Governance and Administration

Thomas J. Sergiovanni
Trinity University, San Antonio

Martin Burlingame
Oklahoma State University

Fred S. Coombs
University of Illinois, Urbana-Champaign

Paul W. Thurston
University of Illinois, Urbana-Champaign

Allyn and Bacon
Boston • London • Toronto • Sydney • Tokyo • Singapore

Series Editor: Ray Short
Editorial Assistant: Karin Huang
Director of Education Programs: Ellen Mann Dolberg
Marketing Manager: Brad Parkins
Production Administrator: Annette Joseph
Production Coordinator: Holly Crawford
Editorial-Production Service: Lynda Griffiths, TKM Productions
Composition Buyer: Linda Cox
Manufacturing Buyer: Suzanne Lareau
Cover Administrator: Jenny Hart
Cover Designer: Brian Gogolin

Copyright © 1999, 1992, 1987, 1980 by Allyn & Bacon
A Viacom Company
160 Gould Street
Needham Heights, MA 02194

Internet: www.abacon.com
America Online: keyword: College Online

Library of Congress Cataloging-in-Publication Data

Educational governance and administration / Thomas J. Sergiovanni . . .
   [et al.]. -- 4th ed.
      p.   cm.
   Includes bibliographical references and index.
   ISBN 0-205-28496-5
   1. School management and organization--United States.
I. Sergiovanni, Thomas J.
LB2805.E346   1998
371.2'00973--dc21   97-47393
                                            CIP

Printed in the United States of America

10 9 8 7 6 5 4 3 2 1   03 02 01 00 99 98

Contents

Preface   xi

PART I The Context for Schooling in the United States

1   **Public Values and School Policy: The Roots of Conflict**   **1**
Defining the Context   2
Policy Instruments   4
Public Values and School Policy   6
Competing Values and Images of Schooling   11
Three Theories of Leadership   13
The School as a Moral Community   14
Appendix 1.1   15
References   19

2   **Issues Shaping School Policy and Administration**   **20**
School Autonomy and Governmental Control   21
Legislated Learning and Bureaucratic Teaching   24
Balancing Democratic and Professional Authority   27
Different Theories of Change   31
Maintaining Public Confidence   34
Managing Public Confidence   36
References   38

3   **Demographics and the Challenge to Education in the United States**   **40**
Persistent Problems   42

Equality and Equity   43
Population Changes   45
Educational Attainment and Achievement   47
Questions for Education   50
A Viewpoint   52
Summary   54
References   54

PART II Introduction to Educational Administration

4   Educational Administration: An Overview   55
Policy and Policy in Use   56
Administration Defined   58
Critical Responsibilities of Administrators   60
Evaluating Administrators   65
Dimensions and Measures of School Effectiveness   66
Critical Administrative Processes   66
Critical Administrative Skills   70
Educational Administration as Educational Leadership   72
Managerial, Political, and Educational Roles   72
Qualitative Aspects of Leadership   74
The Substance of Leadership in Education   76
References   78

5   Educational Administration as an Emerging Profession   80
Background   81
Recent Pressures to Reform   86
The Dark Side of Professionalism   91
The Changing Focus   94
Pursuing a Knowledge Base   97
Women in Administration   98
Women and the School Principalship   100
Appendix 5.1   106
References   112

6   The Development of Thought in Educational Administration   115
Models of Administrative Practice   115
Setting the Stage: Managers of Virtue   116
Major Strands of Thought in Administration   120
Educational Administration as an Applied Science   145

A Reflective-Practice Perspective 147
Educational Administration as a Moral Craft 148
References 152

7 **Theories and the Practice of Educational Administration** **155**
Theory and Practice 156
Challengers 159
What Is to Be Learned? 165
References 167

8 **Administrative Work, Roles, and Tasks** **168**
The Work-Activity School 168
The Nature of Managerial Work: Mintzberg 169
Variation in Administrators' Work 177
Characteristics of Administrative Work 179
Time as a Scarce Resource 181
References 184

PART III A Cultural View of Schooling and Administration

9 **The Everyday Life of Students and Teachers in Schools** **185**
The Concept of Culture 186
Student Life in Schools 188
Teacher Life in Schools 191
Reforms and Teachers' Lives 192
References 197

10 **The Everyday Life of the School Principal** **198**
Ed Bell and His School 198
Portraits of Good High School Principals 200
Principals as Instructional Leaders 202
What Should Principals Do? 203
What Should Principals Not Do? 206
References 210

11 **The Everyday Life of the School Superintendent** **211**
Historical Overview of the Superintendency 212
Superintendents and Conflict 217
The Future of the Superintendency 222
References 223

PART IV Introduction to Governance in Education

12 The School as a Political Organization   224
The Four Values Revisited   225
Reconciling Interests: The Problem of Collective Choice   227
A Closer Look at Policy   230
Influence, Power, and Authority Patterns   234
Community Power Structure   236
The Interests of Students and Parents   237
Teachers and Their Organizations   239
Minority Interests   243
Business Interests   243
Other Education Interests   244
The Role of the Public   245
Summary   246
References   247

13 Policymaking in the Local School District   248
The Locus of Authority at the Local Level   249
Policymakers at the Local Level   251
School-Board Politics   254
Three Versions of the Policy Process   260
Collective Bargaining   262
Site-Based Management   263
Referenda   264
Summary   267
References   268

14 The Influence of the Federal Government   269
The Early History of Federal Involvement   270
The Federal Role after World War II   271
Categorical Aid for Economic and Social Problems   274
Exit Equity, Enter Excellence   274
Presidential Politics and School Reform   275
The Federal Education Establishment Today   278
Summary   283
References   284

15 The New State Role in Education   285
Who Makes State Education Policy?   286
The Emergence of a New State Role   290
Interest Groups at the State Level   291
Federal, State, and Local Relations   293

The Centralization-Decentralization Issue   295
Summary   297
References   298

PART V Legal and Financial Considerations

16 **Public Schools and the Law   299**
Understanding the Legal System   299
Sources of School Law   300
Administrative Responsibility   304
State and Federal Judicial Structures and Jurisdictions   305
Litigation and Preventive Law   309
Summary   311
References   312

17 **Legal Considerations in Public-School Administration   313**
Legal Sources and Specializations   313
State Legal Considerations   314
Torts (Negligence)   320
Contracts   324
Limitations of Authority by the Federal Constitution   324
Legal Standards of Liability   348
Developing a Policy Regarding Sexual Misconduct among Students   354
References   355

18 **School Finance: Equitably Funding Schools for Excellence   359**
Revenue Generation and Distribution   360
Income, Sales, and Property Taxes   360
Criteria for Evaluating Taxes   364
Nontax Sources of Revenue   367
Distribution of State Revenues   368
Constitutional Challenges to Funding Public Education:
      Three Waves of School Finance Litigation   372
Striving for Equity and Excellence: Financing Schools
      in the Twenty-First Century   378
References   383

Index   387

Preface

This book introduces readers to administration and governance in education. Its main audience is those who aspire to be educational administrators and supervisors. For them, the book will provide an overview of the field and a preview of the more specialized courses and experiences they are likely to encounter later in their professional lives. In addition, the book is designed to help administrative aspirants assess the suitability of their own capabilities, dispositions, and interests to a career in educational administration. Other audiences include teachers and teacher-organization leaders, legislators and legislative assistants, and nonprofessionals who want to be better informed about the nature and structure of administration and governance in education. Prior knowledge of this field is not assumed of readers.

We believe that it is best to view the issues of educational administration as connected to those of educational governance. Educational administration is involved not only with the process of administering schools, but also with the execution of public affairs in educational organizations; the performance of executive functions; the guiding, controlling, and directing of educational organizations; and the judicious use of means to accomplish educational ends. Educational governance is concerned with the organization and machinery through which political units such as federal agencies, state departments, and local school districts exercise authority and perform functions and the complex political institutions, laws, and customs that are the basis of the performance of administrative functions and responsibilities. In practice, the two are dynamic and interdependent.

The Context for Schooling in the United States

Demands, constraints, and choices have always shaped the decision-making character of educational administration. Only the content of demands, constraints, and choices changes with the times. Chapters 1 through 3 of this book examine the environment in which schooling in the United States exists. Enduring public values such as equity, efficiency, choice, and excellence are examined historically and currently as prime influences on school policy. The expression of these values changes with the times, but the values themselves are both formidable and stable. Indeed, conflicts among the four values are responsible for much of the current debate about the adequacy of U.S. schools and the reforms needed to improve them. The values are examined within the context of several issues now influencing administrative practice: school autonomy and governmental control; the influence of state-legislated learning on teaching as a profession; balancing democratic and professional authority; and understanding different theories of change. The environment of schooling in the United States is further defined by the presentation of demographics that detail the scope and scale of teaching and schooling and provide a forecast of future trends. Throughout the first three chapters, the emphasis is on school administrators bringing balance and reason to the issues at hand as they become involved in the politics of education.

Introduction to Educational Administration

Chapters 4 through 8 introduce readers to educational administration as a profession and as a field of study. The purpose of these chapters is to provide readers with perspectives on the emergence of the field and on its professional and intellectual roots. This appraisal is necessarily critical, for, as a relatively young field, educational administration is characterized by progress and promise, by problems and dim prospects. Special attention is given to the emerging cultural perspective in educational administration. Leadership within the cultural perspective and school culture building are discussed, along with the more traditional bureaucratic, human-relations, and political views of school organization and functioning.

These chapters also introduce readers to the substantive aspects of administration. Using a theory-to-practice perspective, emphasis is given to understanding administrative theory and the ways that it can be used to gain insights about administrative practice. Emphasis is also given to the issue of how educational administrators actually spend their time on the tasks they accomplish. This descriptive analysis is then examined in light of prescriptions found in the literature of organizational, administrative, and supervisory leadership. Such scrutiny should help readers determine "the way it is" and contrast this with the best thinking on "the way it should be."

A Cultural View of Schooling and Administration

Chapters 9 through 11 provide a cultural view of schooling and administration by relying heavily on descriptive studies of schools that emphasize ethnographic and anthropological ways of knowing. The purpose of these chapters is to increase the reader's cultural understanding of life in schools, the school superintendency, and the school principalship through a search for the powerful themes that help the individual define a personal reality, steer sensible courses of action, and find meaning in life.

Introduction to Governance in Education

Chapters 12 through 15 introduce readers to governance structure and issues in education. These chapters include discussions of policymaking in local school districts, state and federal influences on education, and the broad policymaking structure of schools in the United States. Important changes are taking place in the governance of education in this country. The state seems to be emerging as the dominant force not only in establishing school policy but also in providing the administrative structures and arrangements for the day-by-day operation of schools. Should this trend continue, the historically dominant local school districts will find themselves with diminished authority.

Is the United States moving toward a system of state education with fifty school districts? What are the consequences of such an event should it materialize? Is the next logical step a move from fifty school districts to one? At the same time, there is unprecedented interest in such ideas as site-based management, site councils, and the introduction of marketing concepts to the governing of schools. These developments challenge centralized governing structures. It is difficult to predict which way the winds will blow with respect to changes in the governance of schooling, but clearly the ancient Chinese curse "May you live in interesting times" fits today's educational scene.

Legal and Financial Considerations

Chapters 16 through 18 are concerned with legal and financial considerations in the operation of schools. Supreme Court and federal constitutional standards, as well as state-level legal considerations, are explored, and their influence on public-school administration is assessed. The public values of equity, efficiency, choice, and excellence are revisited within the legal context with regard to schooling and issues of school finance.

A Time of Renewal

Much progress has been made toward understanding the process of schooling and school administration since the first edition of this book was published. An avalanche of research has provided a fairly refined and highly useful image of what a successful school is and how administrators can work to bring about school improvements. Schools are being understood from the cultural perspective, providing new and rich insights to be used in developing promising school policies at the state level and more effective administrative practices at the local level. Heightened interest in viewing schools as learning, caring, and inquiring communities adds still another push to redefine how schools should be organized and led. This edition chronicles not only the difficulties to be faced but also the excitement that is now emerging as educational administration seeks to renew itself as a profession committed to teaching and learning, building better schools, and creating a better society. The need for *more* administrators may not be great, but the need for *new* administrators is pressing—men and women who understand the complexities of modern administration and can cope with its new dimensions. This book is intended to be a first step in that direction.

A book such as this requires a collaborative effort over a considerable period of time. We were privileged to share our insights with each other as plans for the book developed and individual chapters were prepared. In this sense, the book is the result of a team effort.

Educational Governance
and Administration

Chapter *1*

Public Values and
School Policy

The Roots of Conflict

If limited to three words to describe the world of school administration and the nature of managerial work, Rosemary Stewart (1982) would choose *demands, constraints,* and *choices.* She suggests that managerial jobs comprise "an inner core of *demands,* an outer boundary of *constraints* and an in-between area of *choices*" (p. 14). *Demands* come from the forces and pressures that school administrators cannot ignore—things they must do to avoid sanctions for their schools that ultimately could imperil their jobs. *Constraints* are the factors internal and external to the school that limit what school administrators can do. Sometimes demands and constraints are imposed externally by legal mandates and requirements, budgetary limitations, community pressures, school outcome specifications, and role expectations of important others such as school board members, members of the business community, and parents. Sometimes demands and constraints come from within the school in the form of work rules, expectations of teachers, school organizational arrangements, union contracts, and the norms, mores, unwritten rules, and standard operating procedures that reflect the school's culture.

Choices exist within any demand-and-constraint set. Choices are opportunities for school administrators in similar jobs to do different things or to do the same things in different ways. One of the hallmarks of a successful school administrator is the ability to expand the area of choice by deft handling of demands and constraints. However, there are limits. Further, as the nature of demands and constraints changes, choice options change also. The context and nature of demands and constraints is, therefore, a good starting point in trying to understand what educational administration is and is not, and what school administrators can and cannot do.

In recent years, the configuration of demands and constraints has undergone dramatic changes. Schooling in the United States today is characterized by a new politics of education and a fundamental shift in the basic governance structure for organizing and administering schools. Much of what has happened is only now being sorted out, and the implications for administrative practice in the decades ahead are only beginning to be understood.

Defining the Context

The general pattern for defining the context for schooling in the United States was set politically at this nation's inception. The Constitution and its amendments decreed that education would be a state responsibility; the states handed the responsibility off to local jurisdictions. For the next 182 years, despite shortterm variations in this pattern, local government and local educational agencies reigned supreme in governing schools. The Soviet launch of *Sputnik* in 1957 posed the first serious challenge to the legacy of local control in matters of schooling. The United States appeared at risk as the Soviets pulled ahead in the space race. The schools were judged to be at fault, and the proposed solution was for the federal government to protect the public interest by initiating and paying for massive reforms. A major change had begun to take place in how the schools of this nation were to be governed and administered.

Some applauded the change, claiming that local control was, at best, a romantic and inefficient vestige of an earlier time. After all, the size and scale of the republic at its inception bears little resemblance to its present state.

> *Consider, first, the matter of numbers. It is startling to recall that when the constitution which still guides American society was ratified, there were less than four million persons in the thirteen states of the Union. Of these, 750,000 were Negro slaves outside society. It was a young population—the median age was only sixteen—and at that time fewer than 800,000 males had reached voting age. When George Washington was inaugurated as the first President of the United States, New York City, then the capital of the country, had a population of only 33,000. (Bell, 1973, pp. 69–70)*

At that time, the nation was considered to be an agricultural society. Cities were defined as having 2,500 or more people, and only a few cities existed. A highly decentralized school system was ideally suited to the times. Life is much more complex today, and the governance and administration of schools must reflect this complexity.

The United States was judged to be at risk again in 1983, only about 25 years after the "risk" caused by the launching of the Soviet *Sputnik*. This time, it was the Japanese and the South Koreans who were pulling ahead, warned *A Nation at Risk*

(National Commission on Excellence in Education, 1983). New reforms were the answer, but this time the states would surge forward to challenge the authority of local educational agencies. There had been a steady growth of state control in the decade of the seventies, "when states began to get involved in such matters as accountability, school finance reform, categorical programs, school improvement efforts, minimum competency testing, and civil rights regulations" (Kirst, 1989, p. 65). But *A Nation at Risk* was a challenge to state governments to "gather in" their authority in unprecedented ways from local agencies, to initiate reforms on a massive scale.

The language of the report was such that the governors of our states dared not to ignore its message:

> *Our nation is at risk. Our once unchallenged preeminence in commerce, industry, science, and technological innovation is being overtaken by competitors throughout the world.... If an unfriendly power had attempted to impose on America the mediocre educational performance that exists today, we might well have viewed it as an act of war. As it stands, we have allowed this to happen to ourselves. We have squandered the gains in student achievement made in the wake of the Sputnik challenge. Moreover, we dismantled essential support systems which help make those gains possible. We have, in effect, been committing an act of unthinking, unilateral educational disarmament. (National Commission on Excellence in Education, 1983, p. 5)*

In 1979, for the first time in the history of the nation, state and federal funding of schools exceeded that derived from local sources. *A Nation at Risk* coaxed the states to increase their contribution further. Pocketbooks were opened wide as funded mandates for improvement (such as minimum competence testing, the career ladder for teachers, stipulated curriculum requirements, and providing for school achievement auditing) emerged from our state capitals.

For this "first wave" of reform in the eighties, the favored policy instruments were mandates and inducements. By 1986, the reform reports that appeared began to take on a different flavor. Three of these "second wave" reports were particularly influential: *Tomorrow's Teachers: A Report of the Holmes Group*; the Carnegie Forum on Education and the Economy's report *A Nation Prepared: Teachers for the 21st Century*; and *What Next? More Leverage for Teachers*, a publication of the Education Commission of the States. These reports addressed bringing about changes in teachers, their work conditions, and their preparation.

The Holmes Group report emphasized increasing the standards for entry into teaching, strengthening the liberal arts foundation of teacher preparation, raising standards of entry into the teacher profession, and strengthening the connections between departments and schools of education and the public schools. The Education Commission of the States report was a plea for reforms to be more responsive to the expertise that exists among teachers. In the foreword, then New Jersey governor and Commission chairman Thomas H. Kean stated:

> *The conversation reported in this book sustains my belief that we are on the edge of a second phase of teacher reform, one that builds upon and extends what we did earlier but brings in many new themes. For example, our friends tell us that we should be more careful in what we regulate about teaching. Set firm, clear standards for the results we expect, but let educators have more leeway in deciding how to meet the standards. They say that the kind of people we want in the classroom just won't stay without this kind of professional responsibility. And they warn us that we must attend to the way schools are organized, and we should avoid state sanctions that add to an already bureaucratic quality in schooling.... They tell us that the profession itself must take up the fight we began for higher professional standards. (Green, 1986, inside cover)*

Similarly, the Carnegie Forum's report emphasized the importance of upgrading the preparation of teachers and teaching and of providing teachers more autonomy on the one hand and holding them more accountable on the other. They proposed, for example, creating a National Board for Professional Teaching Standards, upgrading the liberal arts education of teachers, providing incentives for teachers linked to schoolwide performance, and restructuring teacher and administrative roles to give teachers greater access to decision making. Though the emphasis was on teaching, a basic formula was beginning to emerge of tightly connecting the educational establishment to standards and outcomes but loosely connecting them to means.

Policy Instruments

Reforms of the first and second waves can be distinguished by the ways in which policymakers sought to make changes. McDonnell and Elmore (1987) group various instruments for changing school policies into four categories: mandates, inducements, capacity-building strategies, and system-changing strategies (p. 134). *Mandates* are rules and regulations designed to govern directly the choices and actions of educators and schools; *inducements* are the exchange of money and other benefits to educators and schools in return for desired choices and actions; *capacity building* is the use of money and other benefits for the purpose of investing in human resources by building up educators' capacities to choose and act in desired ways; and *system changing* seeks to bring about desired choices and actions by the "reallocation of power and authority among those involved in the process of schooling" (p. 134).

Each of the policy instruments is based on different assumptions and has different consequences for the educational system. These assumptions and consequences are summarized in Table 1.1. The first wave of reform emphasized mandates and inducements. For example, mandates require action regardless of whether schools are ready or able to comply. Failure to comply results in penalties. System changing, by contrast, assumes that present structures and operating pro-

TABLE 1.1   Policy Instruments—Assumptions and Consequences

	Assumptions	Consequences
Mandates	Action required regardless of capacity; good in its own right	Coercion required
	Action would not occur with desired frequency or consistency without rule	Create uniformity, reduce variation
		Policy contains information necessary for compliance
		Adversarial relations between initiators, targets
		Minimum standards
Inducements	Valued good would not be produced with desired frequency or consistency in absence of additional money	Capacity exists; money needed to mobilize it
	Individuals, agencies vary in capacity to produce; money elicits performance	As tolerable range of variation narrows, oversight costs increase
		Most likely to work when capacity exists
Capacity-building	Knowledge, skill competence required to produce future value; or	Capacity does not exist, investment needed to mobilize it
	Capacity good in its own right or instrumental to other purposes	Tangible present benefits serve as proxies for future, intangible benefits
System-changing	Existing institutions, existing incentives cannot produce desired results	Institutional factors incite action; provokes defensive response
	Changing distribution of authority changes what is produced	New institutions raise new problems of mandates, inducements, capacities

Source: L. M. McDonnell & R. Elmore, "Getting the Job Done: Alternative Policy Instruments," *Educational Evaluation and Policy Analysis, 9*(2), 1987, p. 141. Copyright 1987 by the American Educational Research Association.

cedures are simply not able to produce the desired results and must, therefore, be restructured.

As waves push forward and then recede, they create a mixed undercurrent. In the nineties, for example, it became apparent that the second wave of reform never replaced the first. Instead, both waves together were applied to schools, creating an undercurrent that provided schools with conflicting and often irreconcilable expectations. The second wave placed more emphasis on capacity building and system changing. The intent of a particular reform proposal and the choice of a favored implementing policy instrument have consequences that determine the mix of demands and constraints facing school administrators and the choices available to them as they act. Intents and instruments represent value statements as do demands and constraints. In this sense, the world of school government and administration represents a struggle over values as administrators seek to find and expand choices.

Part I of this book (Chapters 1–3) examines the present context for schooling in the United States at two levels: the underlying basic values of American education that compete for attention and the examples of issues that dominate the agendas of educational policymakers and school administrators. How these issues are resolved and the nature of the balance that is struck between competing values will determine the future of U.S. education for the decades ahead. Among the issues to be considered are the crisis in educational quality, who the schools will serve and who will decide, legislated learning and creeping bureaucracy in the classroom, mandated testing of teachers and students, and equity in the provision of schooling to all Americans. Equality, efficiency, excellence, and choice are identified as four competing values that represent the undercurrent for debates on the issues. The concept of "flow of images" is then examined in the context of schools' attempts to maintain public confidence.

Public Values and School Policy

Even though the values of equity, efficiency, choice, and excellence are deeply embedded in this country's heritage, they exist in a constant state of tension, so that too much emphasis on any one hinders expression of each of the other three. At various times in America's history, one or another of these values has been overemphasized, with predictable consequences. For example, during the Great Society years of Lyndon Johnson's presidency, the value of equity was targeted for special emphasis. To achieve equity in schooling, the federal government initiated a number of school programs and passed laws that many felt circumscribed the discretion of local educational agencies. Affirmative-action laws provided school districts with quotas and with specific selection processes to follow, lest they be disqualified from receiving federal funds. Many observers of that scene felt that federal initiatives with respect to teaching programs resulted in a watering down of education that seriously compromised the value of excellence in schooling. Nearly everyone agrees that the overall cost of the Great Society's educational programs seriously endangered the value of efficiency. Inflation and interest rates were high, and excess federal spending was considered the cause. The reforms resulted in increases in the bureaucracy at all levels of school governance.

The first wave of reform of the eighties, some would argue, represented a mirror image of the seventies. In the eighties, the emphasis seemed to be on excellence at the expense of equity, efficiency, and choice. The negative effects of uniform standards and standardized testing, rigid "no pass, no play" laws, competency tests for teachers, standardization of details of the curriculum, and one-best-way teaching evaluation systems seemed to be disproportionately felt among minorities. Further, the reforms were costly, with benefits in student achievement and school improvement elusive. The use of mandates and inducements as the prime policy instruments led to the kind of centralization and standardization that provided enough overload in demands and constraints to seriously compromise choices for individual school districts, schools, teachers, and administrators. Local school boards and parents were similarly overwhelmed. The four values and their influence on school policy are considered next.

Equity

Equity means fairness in sharing the resources available for schooling. This educational value corresponds to a general societal value honoring fair play and equal opportunity. Equity does not always mean providing identical resources to each student or school or providing the same access to every educational program. Sometimes identicalness and sameness are considered unfair. In a golf match, for example, some players are given an advantage, a handicap, to offset some advantage in natural or other talent others may have. Admittedly, one often struggles to identify just what constitutes a fair handicap, but the objective is to give each golfer an equal chance to win. Students with special needs or with disadvantaged opportunities for coming to school ready to learn are examples of students who are often given more resources in an attempt to level the learning field for all students.

Often, equity suffers at the hand of excellence. Some policymakers, for example, argue that incentives should be provided to motivate schools to strive for excellence. In states with statewide testing, these policymakers recommend that schools with high test scores be rewarded with increased autonomy or cash bonuses or both. In Texas, for example, schools are sorted into one of four performance categories—exemplary, recognized, acceptable performance, or low performance—based on student scores on the Texas Assessment of Academic Skills. Low dropout rates and high attendance rates of exemplary schools are rewarded with generous cash bonuses from the state. Low-performing schools, by contrast, are threatened with loss of autonomy and endure public shame as the school rankings are posted in local newspapers. Low-performing schools do receive extra resources in the form of state help with the development of school improvement plans, but many teachers and local school officials equate this help with attempts to reduce their discretion. Although the distribution of state resources on the basis of merit has appeal to advocates of excellence in schools, equity advocates argue for the distribution of resources based on need.

One way to balance concerns for equity and excellence is by adopting a value-added approach to accountability. This approach provides recognition based on effectiveness gains that are not uniformly benchmarked. Instead, benchmarking is done individually on a school-by-school basis. In effect, instead of schools competing with each other, they compete with their own previous performance levels. An example of such an approach and a discussion of the issues surrounding the equity/excellence controversy are provided in Appendix 1.1 in the form of a position paper prepared by Texas superintendents of schools.

Equity often conflicts with the values of excellence, efficiency, and choice. Adjusting the allocation of resources by formula and enforcing such adjustment through external controls can restrict the freedom of school districts, compromise their basic liberties, and thus pose a threat to local control. As local control is compromised, the argument continues, school districts lack the incentives to strive for excellence. Further, external control typically leads to standardization and uniformity, thus stifling local initiative and reducing the ability of local educational agencies to provide responsive schooling.

Efficiency

Benjamin Franklin's lessons of thrift and getting one's money's worth have traditionally been part of the cultural legacy of the United States. Americans have a historic predisposition for getting their money's worth when it comes to public spending, and the closer this spending is to home, the greater their concern. Our system of local control and local tax support creates a problem as school costs continue to rise. Schools are labor intensive; despite the potential offered by technological advances, technology has not brought about great cost savings. Chrysler can cut costs by using robots. Other production-oriented enterprises fight inflation with advances in technology. Teacher salaries are the greatest costs in any school budget; however, they have risen without measurable increases in productivity, thus raising questions of efficiency in the minds of the public.

This efficiency question is also raised by the apparent increase in the administrative costs of running schools. Former Secretary of Education William J. Bennett notes:

> *While total instructional expenditures per pupil went up 64 percent between 1960 and 1980, spending on administration and other noninstructional matters rose 107 percent. The number of non-classroom instructional personnel in our school systems grew by 400 percent between 1960 and 1984. And during those years, money spent on teacher salaries dropped from over 56 percent to under 41 percent of total elementary and secondary school spending. Too much money has been diverted from the classrooms; a smaller share of the school dollar is now being spent on student classroom instruction than at any time in recent history. It should be the basic goal of the education reform movement to reverse this trend toward administrative bloat and to reduce the scale of the bureaucratic "blob" draining our school resources. (Bennett, 1988, p. 46)*

Many policy analysts and educational administrators dispute Bennett's claims. Berliner and Biddle (1995), for example, point out that "across the country, central-office professionals constitute only 1.6 percent of the staffing of public school districts" (p. 79). Eliminating all of the central office professionals in the nation, Berliner and Biddle explain, would enable the reduction of class size by only one student. They note further that in the business world and in the non-school public administration world, the average ratio of employees to administrators is 7.1 to 1. In schools, the figure is 14.5 to 1. Regardless of who is right in this debate, the image of inefficiency in running our schools remains strong in the minds of the public.

The efficiency value is the undercurrent for the nation's concern for accountability. Accountability is manifested in the form of product testing (students), program budgeting (objectives), and adoption of systems-analysis management designs (emphasizing efficiency in operations). The concern for "fiscal containment" is a political manifestation of the efficiency value. Spurred by California's Proposition 13, passed in 1968, advocates of fiscal containment sought to limit government spending and promote a balanced budget, advocating across-the-board tax reductions (Timar & Guthrie, 1980). Sometimes efforts to promote more efficient schools backfire. For example, regulating accountability by standardizing the curriculum and introducing student testing programs and standardized teacher evaluation systems brings with it increases in administrative and monitoring staffs that can lead to more bureaucratic "blob" in state education departments and school district central offices. Current research confirms the view that although standardized teaching and testing may be more efficient for achieving basic increases in a student's performance, they are less effective and therefore less efficient for achieving higher-level student performance (Newman, Marks, & Gamoran, 1995; Elmore, 1995).

Excessive concern for efficiency compromises the choice value by seriously constraining what local jurisdictions, local communities, and the professional educational establishment are able to do; makes the goal of equity difficult by reducing the amount of resources generally available; and results in a relative decrease in spending, which compromises the value of excellence. Some seek to promote efficiency and excellence by advocating an elitist approach to education. They would spend much more of our resources on the best and brightest students and much less on the rest. This position compromises the values of choice and equity.

Choice

There is a bit of the New England town meeting in all Americans, and a strain of Jacksonian democracy permeates our collective personality. Some claim that such images are more myth than reality, perpetuated by a desire to preserve the romantic on the one hand and the necessity to maintain some semblance of control in an age of bureaucracy and impersonality on the other. Whether such images are symbolic or real, schools are particularly significant in maintaining the value of choice, for they represent the last vestige of local control in the tradition of the town meeting and the local tax referendum.

In recent years, local control has been slipping away to state and federal levels. Efficiency in schooling requires that decisions be made at higher and more remote levels of government. This centralization is manifested in regulations prescribing a certain sameness, which often compromises one's right to do what she or he thinks is best for students locally. Even the concept of excellence is thought by many to be defined in a universalistic way. The local standard of excellence, so much a part of this nation's tradition in schooling, is giving ground to one defined by the state and perhaps the nation.

Centralists believe that many of the ills of schools resulted from too much choice given to local educational agencies. "They have had their chance, and what is the result?" is the lament often heard. At the other extreme are those who believe that parents and teachers know best and that the best education results from giving these groups the power to decide. Suspicious even of central office control within local school districts, they would advocate school-site management, strong parent councils, and fiscal as well as curricular autonomy for individual schools. Many people of this persuasion choose to leave the public-school system, feeling that these ideals are more easily realized in private schools.

Embedded in this controversy are the tensions between those who advocate market choice and those who advocate democratic choice. *Market choice* is decidedly more efficient, requiring neither bureaucratic machinery nor large investments in leadership. The key motivating factor is individual self-interest. *Democratic choice,* by contrast, involves lengthy, complex, and often combative processes of participation as issues are discussed and decisions are made. Advocates of democratic choice believe that some issues in society are too important to be left to the whims of the market. Market choice, they point out, is based on the tendency of individuals to make decisions that maximize self-interest. Democratic choice, by contrast, requires that self-interest be sacrificed for the common good. This theme will be explored further in Chapter 2.

Excellence

Of the four values, excellence is the most difficult to define. This difficulty stems in part from the political rhetoric with which the word *excellence* is used by special-interest groups who favor one or another of the other values. Advocates of equity, for example, are quick to define excellence in terms of an educational program's ability to respond to the issues they consider important. Similar definitions of excellence emerge in the rhetoric of advocates of liberty and efficiency. Excellent programs are those locally determined in response to unique local needs, or excellent programs are those that result in higher test scores.

For most, excellence is considered to have something to do with a school's ability to achieve its objectives in a high-quality way. On the one hand, it refers to the school's ability to have students measure up to standards of good work. But as the noted evaluation expert Robert Stake (1985) points out, "Outstanding performance on a trivial task is not excellence" (p. 3). This observation adds still another dimension to the definitional problem. Those who strive for excellence by emphasizing only achievement test scores would not measure up to Stake's standards. He believes that "excellence . . . means students have keen understanding and the ability to perform well. Excellent performance includes the intellectual powers of recall, reasoning, problem solving, and interpretation" (p. 3).

Newman, Marks, and Gamoran (1995), for example, view excellence in education as expressions of authentic pedagogy. Their extensive research leads them to define *authentic pedagogy* using three criteria: construction of knowledge, disciplined inquiry, and having value beyond high school. Though many educators agree that this definition is valid, many policymakers disagree. Assessing authentic pedagogy by applying these standards to the work that teachers give students to do, the teaching that takes place in the classroom, and the work that students actually do is both complex and time consuming. As an alternative, these policy-makers propose a more efficient definition of excellence, such as high student scores on standardized tests.

Whether excellence conflicts with efficiency, it appears, depends on the definition of excellence that is used. This reality raises the question of which value drives the other. Do advocates of standardized testing, for example, choose this standard for reasons of excellence or for reasons of efficiency? For reasons of excellence or for reasons of tradition? For reasons of excellence or for reasons of simplicity?

Competing Values and Images of Schooling

Though none of the four values alone represents a sufficiently strong banner under which to launch school reform, value pairs seem to have enough credibility and strength for this purpose. Particularly powerful are pairs that combine either excellence or equity with one of the other values. Four such pairs are illustrated in Figure 1.1.

The value of equity combined with efficiency, for example, aptly captures the great push for educational reform that accompanied President Johnson's Great Society programs. The federal government loomed large in this effort as dollars and accompanying regulation strings were freely distributed to local school districts. This was an era of bureaucratic-centralized liberalism in schooling.

The value of equity combined with choice has provided a persistent mind-set for schooling highly favored by the educational establishment, taught in the nation's schools of education, and striven for by many liberal groups. The strategy in this case is to empower parents and teachers through site-based management, the building of professional community, and similar means to revive the system. This combination of equity and choice represents the egalitarian ideal that is so much a part of America's cultural legacy.

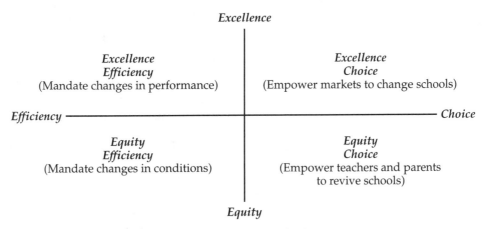

FIGURE 1.1   Competing Values and School Ideals

Excellence combined with efficiency seemed to characterize the thrust of the school-reform movement in the mid-1980s and still persists today. *A Nation at Risk* made the case for this viewpoint that schools must toughen up, students must measure up to tougher standards or leave, more emphasis must be placed on maintaining the nation's competitive edge, and the best and the brightest students must be identified and nurtured. Unlike the situation under the federal centralization of the Johnson years, the states were to set the standards, provide the regulations, and hold the local schools accountable to these standards. Considering each state one at a time, this combination of excellence and efficiency does seem to be more efficient. But when all the states are viewed collectively, this strategy may well be inefficient. The supremacy of the state in matters of school policy resulted in the growth of state education bureaucracies, increases in state educational legislation, and additional costs of doing educational business in the nation's 50 state capitals. Bureaucratic bloat, it appears, may have actually increased with the consolidation of power at the state level.

Excellence combined with choice describes the values of those who subscribe to elitist images but are not willing to give up control over their own destinies. What will be taught, who will be taught, and how schooling will be funded are decisions that they are unwilling to relinquish. The alternative they choose is either to leave the public schools for private schools or to convert their own public schools into the form and shape of private schools. In either case, the value of equity is subordinate, for it interferes with the struggle for excellence.

Many policy experts put all their eggs in the parental and school-choice basket as they seek to reform the schools. Allowing parents to choose schools from among others within the school district or the state introduces market forces that advocates believe will drive out the bad and encourage the good (excellence). For market forces to operate, they point out, schools must provide genuine choices. This kind of diversity requires that school administrators and teachers be given wide discretion in deciding matters of schooling. For this to happen, the schools will have to be deregulated. Further, expensive evaluation systems with costly administrative monitoring will no longer be necessary. Parents will simply vote with their feet by moving their children from schools that are not working to those that are. Deregulation, they maintain, promises to deflate the bureaucratic bloat and create more efficient schooling.

Critics maintain, however, that parents who are more knowledgeable and who can move their students from one school to another easily are the ones who are likely to benefit. Families from middle and upper socioeconomic status (SES) are likely to be overrepresented in this group, with lower SES families underrepresented. This situation, critics maintain, will compromise the value of equity. Proponents counter by suggesting that incentive systems be developed that will encourage schools to recruit lower SES students through information programs and other means. Schools, for example, might be given bonus money for each lower SES student they recruit. Proponents argue, as well, that lower SES families living in inner cities seem to express the most interest in school choice. The support for this movement, in other words, is generally stronger in inner cities than it is in the suburbs.

　　Life would be simple if educational administrators found a placid school environment within which to work—if they found a *tabula rasa,* so to speak. Then all they would need to do is to provide the necessary reason and sense of purpose, and all else would follow in harmonious bliss. But the world of school governance and administration is both turbulent and complex. The pulls and tugs of the four dominant values that provide the undercurrent for school policy and administration liken the job of school administration to that of juggler and tightrope walker as values are deftly handled and balanced. Reason and sense of purpose are important too, particularly if they are combined with a certain passion. Educational leaders, for example, are often able to bring about enough balance among key competing values to make things work for teaching and learning because the qualities of reason, balance, purpose, and passion are embodied in their leadership.

Three Theories of Leadership

The third edition of this book pointed out that what appears to be a more balanced view of school reform emerged from studies of highly effective business organizations (Peters & Waterman, 1982) and schools (Sergiovanni, 1991). This view is embodied in a new theory of management and organization—high-performance theory—that guides the practice of educational policy at the state level and is now creeping into the literature of educational administration. This new theory is offered as a progressive alternative to the more traditional pyramid and railroad theories.

　　The *pyramid theory* assumes that the way to improve schools is to have one person assume responsibility for others by providing directions, supervision, and inspection. But as the number of people to be supervised increases, and as separate work sites develop, management burdens must be delegated to others, and a hierarchical system emerges. Rules and regulations are developed to ensure that all the managers think and act the same way. This managerial structure provides the protocols and guidelines used for planning, organizing, and directing schooling.

　　The *railroad theory* assumes that the way to improve schools is by standardizing the work processes. Instead of relying on direct supervision and hierarchical authority, a great deal of time is spent anticipating all the questions and problems that are likely to come up. Then answers and solutions are developed that represent tracks people must follow to get from one goal or outcome to another. Once the tracks are laid, all that needs to be done is to train people how to follow them and to set up monitoring systems to be sure that they are followed. When the railroad theory is applied to schools, it creates an instructional delivery system in which specific objectives are identified and tightly aligned to an explicit curriculum and a specific method of teaching. Teachers are supervised and evaluated, and students are tested to ensure that the approved curriculum and teaching scripts are being followed. Critics argue that, as a result, principals and teachers use fewer skills and student work becomes increasingly standardized.

The *high-performance theory* differs from the others by deemphasizing both top-down hierarchies and detailed scripts that tell people what to do. Decentralization is key. Workers are empowered to make their own decisions about how to do things. Schools are advised to take control by connecting people to outcomes rather than rules or work scripts. Borrowing from the practices of efficient business organizations, the high-performance theory assumes that the key to effective leadership is to connect workers tightly to ends, but only loosely to means (Gerstner, Semerad, Doyle, & Johnston, 1994). When the high-performance theory is applied to schools, the ends are measurable learning outcomes. Though outcomes themselves are standardized, schools are free to decide how to achieve them. Principals and teachers can organize schools and teach in ways that they think will best enable them to meet the standards. The theory emphasizes collecting data to determine how well workers are doing and encouraging them to figure out ways to continuously improve their performance.

In all three theories, schools are perceived as formal organizations, like corporations or transportation systems. At issue for many educators, however, is whether the formal organization metaphor fits the nature of a school's purpose, the work that it does, the relationships needed for serving parents and students, the context of teachers' work, and the nature of effective teaching and learning environments.

Both the pyramid and railroad theories, for example, separate the planning of how work will be done from its actual performance. "Managers" (state or central-office officials) are responsible for the former, and "workers" (principals and teachers) are responsible for the latter. This separation may work in running a chain of fast-food restaurants, but not, so the argument goes, in schools where professional discretion is essential to success.

In high-performance theory, workers are provided with outcomes and other standards and then they decide how to do the work. But because planning what to do is separated from planning how to do it, problems of isolation, fragmentation, and loss of meaning remain. The danger is that when means and ends are separated, professional discretion may be reduced and democratic principles may be compromised. An important question is whether parents, principals, and teachers will feel sufficiently empowered by being involved in decision-making processes that are limited to the issue of *how* but not *what*—in other words, means but not ends.

The School as a Moral Community

An alternative to pyramid, railroad, and high-performance theories is to view the school as a moral community (Sergiovanni, 1991; Glickman, 1993; Lieberman, 1988). This theory, advocates argue, has two important advantages over the others: It provides for moral connections among teachers, principals, parents, and students, and it helps all of them to become self-managing. This theory will be discussed further in Chapter 6.

All theories of leadership emphasize connecting people to each other and to their work; not all theories emphasize the same kinds of connections, however. The pyramid, railroad, and high-performance theories emphasize contractual connections and assume that people are primarily motivated by self-interest. To get things done, extrinsic or intrinsic rewards have to be traded for compliance, and penalties are threatened for noncompliance. Leadership inevitably takes the form of bartering between the leader and those being led. Moral connections are stronger than extrinsic or intrinsic connections because they come from commitments to shared values and beliefs that teachers, parents, and students accept, and from the obligations they feel toward each other and their work. Moral connections are grounded in cultural norms rather than in psychological needs.

Which of the theories—pyramid, railroad, high-performance, or moral community—will dominate the educational scene as we cross into the next millennium is an issue yet to be resolved. The struggle over which theory makes sense for the nation's schools provides the undercurrent for the array of more surface issues, which will be discussed in Chapter 2.

Appendix 1.1
Getting Accountability and School
Improvement on Track in Texas:
A Report by the School Superintendents of Bexar County*

Beginning in the Fall of 1993, the Texas Education Agency, in response to a new law passed by the state legislature, placed every school in the state into one of four performance categories: exemplary, recognized, acceptable performance and low performance. The ratings were based on student scores on the Texas Assessment of Academic Skills Test, attendance rates and on the number of students who have dropped out.

What Is Wrong with This System?

- This system makes the assumption that a high achieving school and a value-adding school are the same.
- This system implies a cause and effect relationship between the rating a school receives and the performance of teachers and administrators who work in that school.
- This system rewards some teachers, principals and schools who should not be rewarded and punishes other teachers, principals and schools who should not be punished.
- These flaws in the state's accountability system raise serious scientific and moral questions.

Source: Center for Educational Leadership, Trinity University, San Antonio, TX.

An Example

Are high achieving schools and value-adding schools the same? Let's take the Knightsbridge community schools[1] as an example. Knightsbridge is located north of Houston. According to an advertisement that appeared in a recent edition of the *Houston Chronicle,* "Knightsbridge's students attend one of the best high schools in Texas. Student scores on the Texas Assessment of Academic Skills (TAAS) are equal to or exceed those of students in every district in the Houston area. College statistics are staggering. Ninety-six percent of the high school students plan to attend college. The high school is just one example of the excellent education Knightsbridge's students enjoy. Public grade schools, pre-schools, Montessori schools, church-affiliated schools and day care centers in Knightsbridge also provide outstanding learning environments."

Needless to say, the schools that serve the Knightsbridge community were rated favorably by the state's accountability system. Student attendance rates are high, thanks to parents who insist that they go. Very few students drop out of Knightsbridge's schools, due to parents who insist that they stay. Further, about ninety percent of the families with school-aged children in Knightsbridge have both parents present in the home and virtually all of the families can be considered middle or upper income. These statistics are linked to lower dropout rates, less gang activity, and higher student achievement. Most of the students who enter Knightsbridge's schools speak English fluently; already know their letters and sounds with many already knowing how to read; come from homes that are filled with books and computers; have community agencies committed to serve their needs; go to summer camp; take lessons in piano, dance, karate, etc.; see doctors regularly, and eat and sleep well. Knightsbridge's students are brought up at home to respond favorably to the competitive environment of the school, to sit quietly, to be studious, and to otherwise respond to the values of the typical school.

If Knightsbridge's scores are linked to these factors rather than to what teachers and principals are doing, then questions have to be raised about how much value its schools are adding to the education of their students. Would students do just as well on the state's indicators if the existing principals and teachers were replaced with new ones? What would happen if large numbers of students were suddenly home-schooled, transferred to private schools, or even transferred to schools that are labeled "low performing" by the state's system? Would they do just as well as before? If they did just as well, then no significant cause and effect relationship would exist between what teachers and principals in Knightsbridge are doing and student scores, dropout rates and attendance statistics. We would be able to exchange the principals and teachers of Knightsbridge with a random sample of principals and teachers from schools rated in the lower categories of the state's accountability system without seeing much of a change in the accountability indicators. Since a significant cause and effect relationship would not exist between what the schools are doing and the showing of their students on the state's effectiveness indicators, the schools might be considered high achieving but not value-adding.

Adding Value

Many schools who serve communities similar to Knightsbridge manage to *add value* to the advantages that the students bring. As a result, the performance of their students is not just up to par but extraordinary. These schools are *both* high achieving and value-adding. Unfortunately, the state's new accountability system is not able to differentiate between the "Knightsbridges" that are high achieving but not value-adding and the "Knightsbridges" that are *both* high achieving and value-adding.

Nor is the state's new accountability system able to differentiate between schools with scores lower than Knightsbridge's that manage to add value and those that don't. The scores of such value-adding schools might remain modest on an absolute scale, but would still represent significant gains in student performance. A school that *adds value* in this way is a good school, and should be celebrated rather than labeled low performing.

What Does Research Tell Us about School Improvement?

What are the conditions that are needed for every student to learn to be competent in the basic skills, to master important subject matter, to function in the modern workplace, to accept citizenship responsibilities, and to become a person of character? Educational research tells us that the answer to this question, while difficult to achieve, is easy to understand.

Simply put, the conditions for effective teaching and learning are best when the ecology for learning is in balance.[2] The ecology for learning consists of the family and neighborhood, the community and its institutions, and the schools. All three parts of the ecology for learning contribute to the *development of human capital*. Beginning with birth, each child begins to deposit funds of knowledge into his or her human capital development savings account. These funds of knowledge increase in quantity and kind as the child's interactions increase within the family and the neighborhood, and within the community and its institutions. When children arrive in kindergarten, they bring these human capital savings accounts with them.

The funds of knowledge that children bring to school, however, differ in kind and in quantity. Some children have learned how to "sit quietly and wait their turn." Other children have learned to assert themselves. Some children have learned to respond to the school's competitive environment. Other children have learned to avoid competition. Some children have visited small towns and farms and have learned a great deal about how they work, how they contribute to the economy, and what life in them is like. Other children have never visited a farm or small town, nor have they seen a book or a serious television program about farms and rural life.

Students who bring the "right" funds of knowledge from home and community are better able to accumulate the funds of knowledge that schools offer. For them the ecology for learning is in balance. These students are likely to be high achievers regardless of what the schools do.

The more connected the family is to the community, and the family and community to the school, the more likely the funds of knowledge from these sources are to be properly balanced. Where the ecology for learning is out of balance, the school must help the family and community adjust to the school. And the school must accept its responsibility for adjusting its values to the family and community parts of the learning ecosystem. A good accountability system takes into account ecological factors.

What Should Be Done?

We believe that the state should hold schools accountable for *adding value* to the human capital that students accumulate in the areas of academic development, adult socialization and character development. Since success will depend on whether the family and neighborhood, the community, and the school dimensions of the ecology for learning are in balance, the state should develop an accountability system that includes benchmarking of relevant indicators. We need to know where a school is at time one and what progress it has made at time two. We need to know the nature and size of the human capital savings account that each student brings to school and maintains throughout his or her school career. Once this information is available, schools should be asked to develop report cards that include not only test data and dropout statistics, but also information about efforts to improve other dimensions of the learning ecosystem. Report cards would provide answers to such questions as: How well are students achieving? How do test scores and other performance indicators compare with where students were at an earlier time? Given the nature and condition of the school's learning ecology, does this information indicate that the school has added value to the development of students' human capital? If not, what must be done to help this school to become more productive—to increase its contribution to student learning?

A Fair and Just System

Most Texans agree that holding schools accountable is not only reasonable, but necessary, if we want quality schools. Most Texans also believe in the traditional American values of fairness and justice. These values are embodied in the way we play. We devise handicap systems to ensure that golfers and jockeys compete fairly. We invent "draft" systems to ensure that over time, teams are able to compete fairly. We believe that most Texans want to apply these same values of fair play to our schools. To play fair we need a more valid definition of school productivity and a value-added approach to school accountability.

Endnotes
1. Knightsbridge is a pseudonym, but the events are based on fact.
2. For example, see John I. Goodlad, *A Place Called School* (New York: McGraw-Hill, 1984).

References

Bell, D. (1973). *The coming of post-industrial society.* New York: Basic Books.

Bennett, W. J. (1988). *American education: Making it work.* Washington, DC: U.S. Government Printing Office.

Berliner, D. C., & Biddle, B. J. (1995). *The manufactured crisis: Myths, fraud and the attack on America's public schools.* Reading, MA: Addison-Wesley.

Carnegie Forum on Education and the Economy. (1986). *A nation prepared: Teachers for the 21st century.* New York: Carnegie.

Elmore, R. (1995). Structural reform and educational practice. *Educational Researcher, 24*(9), 23–26.

Gerstner, L. V., Jr., Semerad, R. D., Doyle, D. P., & Johnston, W. V. (1994). *Reinventing education entrepreneurship in America's public schools.* New York: Dutton.

Glickman, C. (1993). *Renewing America's schools: A guide for school-based action.* San Francisco: Jossey-Bass.

Green, J. (Ed.). (1986). *What next? More leverage for teachers.* Denver: Education Commission of the States.

The Holmes Group. *(1986). Tomorrow's teachers: A report of the Holmes Group.* East Lansing, MI: Author.

Kirst, M. W. (1989). Who should control the schools? Reassessing current policies. In T. J. Sergiovanni & J. H. Moore (Eds.), *Schooling for tomorrow. Directing reforms to issues that count.* Boston: Allyn and Bacon.

Lieberman, A. (Ed.). (1988). *Building a professional culture in schools.* New York: Teacher's College Press.

McDonnell, L. M., & Elmore, R. F. (1987). Getting the job done: Alternative policy instruments. *Educational Evaluation and Policy Analysis, 9*(2), 133–152.

National Commission on Excellence in Education. (1983). *A nation at risk.* Washington, DC: U.S. Government Printing Office.

National Education Association. (1883). *Report of the Committee on Secondary School Studies* (U.S. Bureau of Education Bulletin 205). Washington, DC: U.S. Government Printing Office.

Newman F., Marks, H., & Gamoran, A. (1995). Authentic pedagogy: Standards that boost student performance. *Issues in Restructuring School* (Report no. 8, Spring). Madison: Center on Organization and Restructuring of Schools, University of Wisconsin.

Peters, T. J., & Waterman, R. H. (1982). *In search of excellence.* New York: Harper and Row.

Seattle Post Intelligence. (1985, July 18).

Sergiovanni, T. J. (1991). *The principalship: A reflective practice perspective* (2nd ed.). Boston: Allyn and Bacon.

Stake, R. (1985). *The essential individualization of excellence and equity.* Unpublished manuscript.

Stewart, R. (1982). The relevance to some studies of managerial work and behavior to leadership research. In J. G. Hunt, U. Sekaran, & C. A. Schriesheim (Eds.), *Leadership beyond establishment views.* Carbondale: Southern Illinois University Press.

Timar, T. B., & Guthrie, J. W. (1980). Public values and public policy in the 1980s. *Educational Leadership, 38*(2), 112–115.

Chapter 2

Issues Shaping School Policy and Administration

Links between school policies and the public values of excellence, equity, efficiency, and choice are deeply embedded in the process and politics of schooling and remain persistent over time, though specific issues for their expression change. During the sixties and early seventies, the push was for more education for more people in an effort to reduce inequality among individuals and groups; improve economic opportunity by raising the nation's supply of intelligence and skill; spread capacity for personal fulfillment by developing talents, skills, and creative energies; improve cultural life in the nation; reduce prejudice and misunderstanding by fostering contact among diverse groups; and improve the quality of civic and political life (Ravitch, 1985, p. 32). This was a national agenda, and the federal government played a major role in prodding local educational agencies to change by providing financial incentives and legal mandates. The values of equity and efficiency loomed large as a basis for educational policymaking.

Educational policymaking in eighties, by contrast, was influenced by demands for excellence and efficiency, with state governments assuming direct and highly regulatory responsibility for change. During the decade of the nineties, choice was added to this mix as an important factor in school reform. Many states, for example, began experimenting with charter schools. Also, magnet schools and schools within schools have enjoyed popularity in many local school districts. From this context, issues emerge that shape the present and future governance and administration of America's schools. Three are selected for discussion in this chapter to illustrate the interplay between school policy and the three basic public values: school autonomy and governmental control; legislated learning and bureaucracy in the classroom; and the struggle between democratic and professional authority. The future of schooling will be determined by how these issues are shaped and resolved. Throughout this process, school administrators will need to maintain the confidence of their many constituents and publics. The "flow of images" they communicate to their publics will determine whether such confidence is maintained. This chapter concludes with a discussion of how school administrators manage the flow of images.

School Autonomy and Governmental Control

Is the increased consolidation of power and authority for schooling at the state level a reversible trend? Constitutionally, the states have always had the major share of responsibility for schooling but delegated this responsibility to local jurisdictions. During the seventies and early eighties, much of this authority was recaptured. Increases in the state share of school funding as a result of school finance reform were accompanied by state efforts to extract greater accountability from local schools. Categorical grant programs of various kinds exchanged money for compliance with state and federal agendas. Civil rights regulations also helped in the erosion of local authority by increasing the demands and constraints on local school administrations, thus limiting choices. Kirst (1989) maintains that since 1950, the trend has been toward decreasing the influence of school boards, local superintendents, and local central administration and increasing the influence of federal and state governments, the courts, private business and foundations, and teacher unions. The height of this shift of influence seems to have manifested itself in the reforms of the early 1980s. To the question of why that wave of reform took such a centralized course, Kirst (1989) answers, "Basically, state governments do not believe that local authorities pay sufficient attention to curriculum quality, teacher evaluation, and academic standards" (p. 66).

Though there appears to be a widespread loss of confidence in local authorities, some contradictory trends are apparent. For example, many experts who study school-improvement efforts are convinced that despite the importance of both federal and state efforts, the battle for excellence must be won school by school. This reality requires that not just local school districts but schools within them become sufficiently autonomous for needed and responsive action to take place (Goodlad, 1984; Sizer, 1985). These experts are convinced that though adoption of school-improvement ideas can be mandated, sustained implementation and institutionalization of changes must be school site based. John Goodlad, for example, notes that "for a school to become the key unit for educational change requires a substantially different stance at the district level than now exists" (quoted in Quinby, 1985, p. 17). He maintains that too often school-improvement efforts are conceived at the district level and implemented uniformly by all schools in a district at the same time. As a result of his research, Goodlad concludes that districts should encourage individual schools to develop their own plans based on their own analysis of school problems. School improvement, he maintains, requires district support and sponsorship, but success depends on the extent to which the principal, teachers, students, and parents associated with individual schools participate in thinking about their problems and conceiving of their own school-improvement efforts.

Despite trends toward increased centralization in schooling, an extensive movement toward site-based management (SBM) has developed. One way that site-based management works is for each principal in the school district, representing her or his school community, to propose individual school-improvement plans to the superintendent. Together, the principal and the superintendent develop a school-improvement contract that details planned changes, links plans to specific time lines, and specifies what the superintendent and the central office will do to help the school succeed. When fully implemented, SBM recognizes the importance of the school to effective school improvement and the criticalness of the principal's management and leadership to that school. The principal is responsible for working with teachers, staff, students, and parents to determine the school's objectives and educational program.

Site-based management is not viable in school districts where centralized policies and regulations are elaborate and detailed. Responsibilities delegated to the school typically include the development, supervision, and evaluation of an educational program that fits needs determined by the school and its community; the selection, orientation, supervision, and continuing professional development of all staff assigned to the school; the development, supervision, and evaluation of guidance and counseling services, discipline codes, and regulations, including record keeping and reporting of academic progress; the establishment of a parent advisory committee that works closely with the principal and the management team in deciding school policies; and the general management of the buildings and grounds.

Site-based management also requires that schools be given a degree of financial independence. Individual schools, for example, might receive a lump sum determined by formula but linked to the number of students being served. Once the sum is received, the principal and the management team, perhaps in consultation with a parent advisory group, develop the school's own budget based on the decision makers' perceptions of its problems and needs and the goals and objectives it wishes to pursue. In many respects, the individual school site functions much as does a school district.

How will the future balance be struck between movements toward a stronger state presence in education on one hand and SBM on the other? Both movements have appeal. Part of the American tradition has long held that individuals should be self-governed, subject only to the general mores and rules of society as expressed in legislation and social norms. This basic value is held in common by liberals, conservatives, and moderates (Shirley, 1984). Defining the appropriate balance between individual and school autonomy and government control, however, is not so easily done. With respect to individuals, the Bill of Rights, the Declaration of Independence, and the Constitution define appropriate protections both formally and informally. Shirley (1984) suggests that what may well be needed is a bill of rights for institutions, such as schools, that would provide guidelines for their freedoms and their responsibilities. Among the freedoms that would be guaranteed to institutions by such a bill of rights would be:

1. The freedom within general guidelines to define institutional mission, goals, and strategies
2. The freedom to manage internal fiscal affairs subject to only two limitations: living within the total dollars appropriated by the state and refraining from transferring funds between operating and capital budgets
3. The freedom to determine organizational arrangements and individual workloads and to select and promote personnel

Shirley joins many other observers in suggesting that these three freedoms are now being denied public institutions, such as schools, in many states. What were once general guidelines for helping schools to define their missions are now becoming fairly detailed master plans complete with control devices (testing, for example) to ensure that plans are implemented in specific ways.

The freedom to manage internal affairs may well have been lost with the linking of funds to specific educational programs. Many states regulate, rather extensively, certification requirements and promotion requirements for teaching personnel. This is especially true in states that have mandated career ladders to the point of providing specific criteria for advancement. When this is the case, local schools do not have the freedom to determine their own organizational and personnel actions as they relate to workload distribution, promotions, and so forth.

The institutional bill of rights proposed by Shirley would include the responsibilities that institutions have to the public and to state governments, which appropriately function as the public's watchdog. Among these responsibilities would be reporting the degree to which goals and priorities are being accomplished and the extent to which public funds are managed responsibly.

As a result of his analysis of dozens of commissions and reports examining the quality of schooling in the United States and his examination of the research on effective schools, Harold Howe II (1983), a former U.S. commissioner of education, concludes, "Schools are more likely to change for the better if central office and school board directors allow individual schools to seek their own definitions of excellence.... Individual school initiatives can be strongly encouraged by providing each school with some funds and allowing the staff to decide how this money will be spent" (p. 170).

Both Shirley and Howe may prove to be educational prophets. At this writing, it appears that the trend toward greater centralization has crested. As the balance between efficiency and choice and between excellence and equity becomes increasingly upset, it is likely that there will be a strong and widespread movement toward local school autonomy. Nonetheless, this movement will remain unfulfilled as long as high-performance theory remains the decision-making framework for policymakers. High-performance theory, as noted in Chapter 1, gives schools and their communities autonomy over means but not ends, over process but not substance, and over management concerns but not policy concerns.

Legislated Learning and Bureaucratic Teaching

In 1975, when Georgia became the first state to require competency testing of teachers, few experts would have predicated that within 10 years, 37 other states would enact similar legislation or rules (Sandefur, 1985, p. 22). State-mandated testing of students has also swept the country. The southeastern part of the country, with its tradition of larger school districts and more centralized school-government arrangements, took the lead in mandating such testing. In many other parts of the country, states reacted with disinterest. In Illinois, for example, with more than 1,000 independent school districts and a tradition of strong local control, there was little notice of this movement. Ohio and other midwestern states that shared Illinois's school-government tradition reacted with similar disinterest. But 1985 would reveal a different tale for Illinois, Ohio, and many other states. For example, Illinois passed the Education Reform for the State of Illinois Bill (SB370), which provided for staged testing of students, beginning in elementary school, in the areas of reading and mathematics. By state policy, promoting students for social or other nonacademic reasons was to be discouraged.

Uniformly applied state-standardized tests require agreements with respect to what will be taught and what is to be learned. To buttress its student-testing program, in 1983, Texas passed HB246, which detailed the essential elements thought to characterize the well-balanced curriculum. Covering 247 pages, the elements were arranged by grade level and subject for the elementary school and by subject matter for the high school. Recommended teaching times for each essential element were provided as part of the package. The state's testing program is designed to assess the extent to which appropriately designated elements are mastered by students at various levels. Individual schools, as was noted in Appendix 1.1, are sorted by the state into one of four categories (exemplary, recognized, acceptable performance, and low performance) based on student test scores as well as student attendance and dropout rates.

Wise (1979) has coined the term *legislated learning* to describe what is going on in Texas and many other states. Legislated learning provides for uniform and tight alignment between student-performance outcomes and the curriculum, between the curriculum and teaching, and between teaching and testing. The beginning and end of this legislated-learning chain are crucial. It is assumed that by specifying in detail what is to be accomplished and then by testing to ensure that objectives are met, greater state control is attained over the school curriculum and how it is taught. In this sense, both the railroad theory and the high-performance theory described in Chapter 1 advocate the practice of legislated learning. The railroad theory specifies both the means to be used and the ends to be accomplished. High-performance theory provides only the ends. But standardized ends for everyone wind up creating standardized means by everyone.

As one might expect, the legislation of learning is viewed differently by different interests. Politicians and the public at large generally support the concept (or at least their understanding of the concept). State mandates of this kind promise to raise expectations for learning and to toughen standards, with the result being better schooling. This is an attractive platform in the eyes of the public. Excellence, however, is left undefined. The public responds not to the substance of such mandates but to the rhetoric of excellence within which the substance is embedded. Excellence, like motherhood, is readily subscribed to, whether defined adequately or not.

The impetus for legislated learning is an effort by state legislators to take control of schools away from local jurisdictions in an effort to respond to the general public's dissatisfaction with what it considers to be the lowering of academic standards. Advocates view legislated learning as a means to enhance accountability, a way to stop the downward slide of test scores, and an insurance policy in providing students with the competencies they need for functional participation in society. As Casteen (1984) points out:

> *Governments regulate schooling because they see education as an essential public service. Since poor schools and poor teachers threaten the public welfare while good ones enhance it, there must be effective "quality control mechanisms." Historically, it has fallen to the states to provide them. In recent decades, teachers' organizations have frequently called for transfer of quality control from the state to the members of the occupation. "Professionalism" is the banner under which this call is issued. Education is too important to the public welfare for the public, acting through the state, to relinquish responsibility for its quality. (p. 214)*

Many experts from within the professional community, by contrast, predict imminent and long-range negative consequences of legislated learning on the quality of teaching and learning and on the profession of teaching. As the alignment between outcomes and curriculum, curriculum and teaching, and teaching and testing becomes tighter, a more rigid educational system emerges. This system is unable to respond to highly idiosyncratic student needs or to society's political, economic, and social changes that define the context of schooling. Further, alignment introduces a high degree of predictability and reliability to the educational system; this influences decision making, makes teaching an schools "teacher and administrative proof," and encourages "pawn" rather than "origin" (DeCharms, 1968) feelings among all those involved.

Wise (1979) maintains that legislated learning unavoidably leads to bureaucratization in the U.S. classroom. In elaborating on this theme, Darling-Hammond (1984) observes,

> *Unfortunately the approach to improving education reflected in most of the policy initiatives of the past decade has done little to increase the attractiveness of teaching; it may, in fact, have exacerbated the problem. Based on a factory model of schooling in which teachers are semiskilled low-paid workers, at least two thirds of the states have enacted policies in the nineteen seventies that sought to standardize and regulate teacher behaviors. Elaborate accountability schemes . . . and other efforts to develop a teacher proof curriculum were imposed in the belief that if teachers do exactly as they are told, students will learn exactly as they are sup-*

posed to. Bureaucratic controls on teaching behavior were used as an alternative to upgrading the quality of teachers or of professional decision making (pp. 13–14)

Darling-Hammond and Wise (1983) maintain that teachers and other professionals oppose bureaucratic attempts to constrain classroom decisions, not because they are opposed to accountability, but because they believe that standardized teaching prescriptions reduce their ability to teach effectively. The result is not only less effective teaching and learning, these professionals say, but a dissatisfied teaching force as well.

In sum, those who express concern about the legislation of learning fear that teaching will become increasingly bureaucratic and that the occupation will retreat from its present posture as a fledgling profession. Professionals and bureaucrats function quite differently at work. The work of bureaucrats is programmed for them by the system of which they are a part. The work of professionals emerges from an interaction between professional knowledge and individual client needs. A standard definition of a *bureaucrat*, for example, is an official following a rigid, narrow and formal routine. By contrast, a *professional* is assumed to be in command of a body of knowledge that enables him or her to make informed judgments in response to unique situations and individual client needs.

Essential to professionalism is that sufficient freedom exists so that professionals are able to use informed judgments as they practice. Bureaucratic knowledge, on the other hand, is more routine and standardized to enable systematic application by bureaucrats. The emphasis is on standard treatment of standard practical problems. Bureaucrats are expected to respond exactly the same way to specific classes of problems; this way of working is antithetical to the concept of professional work. Further, the argument goes, patterns of teaching practice are actually characterized by instability, complexity, and variety, and thus uniform answers to problems are not likely to be helpful to teachers as they teach. The argument concludes with the observation that as teaching and learning decisions are programmed, the teacher's role changes from that of professional diagnostician and decision maker to bureaucratic follower of directions (Sergiovarnni, 1991).

How the issue of legislated learning is played out will influence the new politics of education and will demand attention from policymakers and school administrators alike. Some advocates of legislated learning, for example, recommend that states go even further: "States should consider undertaking an even more active and direct role in education reform. Specifically, from our experience in California, we contend that states should take the lead in defining and controlling educational content. . . . States should also establish clear expectations for schools in terms of required allocations of time to all subjects at the elementary level and graduation requirements at the high school level" (Murphy, Mesa, & Hallinger, 1984, p. 24). Although this position has political appeal to many, a plea for even more legislated learning is not likely to be well received within the educational establishment.

For the most part, the educational establishment feels more comfortable with John Goodlad's view: "Cosmetic changes can be legislated and mandated; the ways children and youth acquire knowledge and ways of knowing cannot. These depend on the knowledge and creativity of teachers. Better preparation of principals and teachers, along with help and time for designing school programs at the site are necessary ingredients of school improvement" (quoted in Quinby, 1985, p. 16).

The educational establishment would agree as well with Michael Kirst's observation that "centralization may be better for naval units, steel mills and state highway departments," but when it comes to teaching and learning, research shows that effective school reform takes place "when those responsible for each school are given more responsibility rather than less" (*Sunday Express News*, 1984). Research, however, rarely informs the development of policy. Typically, politicians do not behave in response to evidence or other rational sources—they act on behalf of preferences and beliefs. The development of policy is a subjective process that seeks to maximize certain values, goals, and interests thought to be important, a point often overlooked by school administrations and other members of the educational establishment.

Balancing Democratic and Professional Authority

Wise (1988), a leading spokesperson for increased professional authority in matters of schooling, notes:

> *In a profound sense, it doesn't matter who controls education, as long as every young citizen is fully prepared to exercise the rights and duties of citizenship in the democratic, free enterprise tradition of America.... The question of who should control education is a pragmatic ... one. Central control is to be deplored not because it represents the shift of power ... among the three branches and the three levels of government. Rather central control is to be deplored because with the technology currently available for managing schools, it reduces the responsiveness of schools to their clientele and so reduces the quality of education. (p. 331)*

Advocates of increasing professional authority in the control of schools build their case around the premise that quality teaching requires on-the-spot decisions by highly trained teachers—decisions that cannot be preprogrammed or otherwise legislated. The case for professional authority can be summed as follows: "Professionalism assumes that because the members of a particular profession possess a specialized body of knowledge and have been judged competent to practice that profession they should be free to decide how best to serve their individual clients. In other words, accountability should be based on norms and standards collectively defined and enforced by peers" (McDonnell, 1989, p. iv).

Though advocates of professional authority provide compelling arguments for its legitimacy, another form of authority seems equally legitimate—the authority of democratic or popular control. According to McDonnell (1989), "Popular or democratic control requires that schools, as public institutions, be held accountable to the citizenry and its elected representatives. This form of accountability assumes that public officials have the right to impose on schools and those who work there a set of performance standards consistent with the norms and expectations of the larger community" (p. iv). Advocates of democratic authority provide equally compelling arguments that lead to the conclusion that the educational establishment is faced with two legitimate values. Both democratic and professional authority are important in U.S. society and should be reflected in school policies. They are contrasted in Table 2.1.

At the heart of this conflict is whether decisions about how schools should be organized and run, how teachers should be prepared and employed, how administrators should function, how teachers and students should be evaluated, and what will be taught should be made by laypersons on the basis of majority preferences either directly through local school councils or indirectly through the electoral process or by professional educators on the basis of their experience and special expertness. Given our system of government, the public enjoys the prerogative to set policy and to evaluate the extent of school compliance with policy. But every professional group enjoys prerogatives of its own as well. In education, these include setting standards, determining the nature of teaching practice, and honoring such values as academic freedom.

TABLE 2.1   Two Approaches to Governing Public Education

	Popular Control	Professional Control
Practitioners Are Accountable to	Electorate and its representatives	Professional norms, and through them, to clients and the public
Interests Served	Constituents Political parties Organized groups Public interest as defined by political ideology Personal	Client welfare as defined by professional norms and standards Personal
Basis of Authority	Consent of the governed	Expert knowledge and judgment
Implementing Mechanisms	Elections Executive and legislative policymaking Courts Public bureaucracies	Training and licensing Professional associations Teacher involvement in school budgetary, personnel, and curriculum decisions

Source: Lorraine M. McDonnell, *The Dilemma of Teacher Policy.* Joint report issued by The Center for Policy Research in Education and the Center for the Study of the Teaching Profession (Santa Monica: The RAND Corporation, 1989), p. 8.

If the values of both democratic authority and professional authority are legitimate, how might they be balanced in such a way that the public gets the controls it wants over school quality and the profession gets the discretion it needs to provide that quality? One approach is to tightly connect the schools to a set of professional process and performance outcome standards and then loosely connect them to means for achieving these standards. Professional standards would include requirements for preparing, inducting, and licensing teachers, and performance standards would specify what is expected qualitatively from the schools. In both cases, standards need to be general enough to allow principals, teachers, and schools discretion over their professional lives, but specific enough to provide for direction and accountability.

A second approach is to rely on the market forces that come into play in a choice system of education. The professional establishment, in partnership with parents, would be given considerable autonomy over the nature and functioning of each individual school site. Advocates of this approach maintain that professional autonomy needs to be real if schools are to differ with respect to what they are about and how they seek to accomplish their goals. Subject to market forces, parents will choose to send their children to schools that they consider to be working. Democratic and professional authority, so the reasoning goes, would be achieved through the mechanism of choice as options are developed.

Many policy experts (e.g., Chubb & Moe, 1989) believe that choice is not only the answer to resolving the dilemma of democratic versus professional authority but may be the secret to providing the balance between and among excellence, equity, and efficiency as well. Their reasoning is that school-choice plans offering a variety of teaching and learning options will require substantial deregulation of the existing bureaucracy (efficiency). Market forces inherent in choice will drive out the bad schools and encourage the good (excellence). Undaunted by critics who worry that families that are privileged economically and more knowledgeable about schooling will benefit the most, advocates believe that in the end, all schools will get better (equity).

But some experts doubt whether enough political momentum presently exists to support school choice. Kirst (1990). for example, points out that "vouchers have never been voted on in any state, and federal tuition tax credits were defeated during the Reagan presidency. Consequently, it is hard to see choice as a major reform at this juncture. The period of 1986–1988 appears to be one of digesting the reforms from an earlier era" (p. 28). His comments are speculative at best. In 1990, for example, Wisconsin passed a limited voucher plan allowing about 1,000 Milwaukee public-school students the option of attending a nonsectarian private school at state expense. Voucher advocate John E. Coons (quoted in Snider, 1990, p. 1) called the plan "a very historic day for the poor and for civil rights." He explained, "People who have been pretty much entombed in segregated public schools will have a chance to get their civil rights vindicated in the private sector."

In recent years, choice has become a permanent theme on the policy agenda but understood in a more diversified way. Diversity has changed the nature of the debate from "for school choice" or "against school choice" to "for some kinds of choice but against other kinds of choice." Cookson (1994), for example, provides 12 different definitions of *choice* as follows:*

> Intradistrict-choice. *A plan that allows students to choose schools within one public school district. Depending on the specific plan, the range of choice may include a few to all schools in a district.*

> Interdistrict-choice. *A plan in which students may cross district lines to attend school. Tuition funds from the state follow the student, and transportation costs are usually provided. Unlimited interdistrict choice is equivalent to statewide open enrollment.*

> Intrasectional-choice. *A plan that is limited to public schools.*

> Intersectional-choice. *A plan that includes both public and private schools.*

> Controlled-choice. *A student assignment plan that requires families to choose a school within a community, but choices can be restricted to ensure the racial, gender, and socioeconomic balance of each school. Often, such plans reflect a strategy to comply with court-ordered desegregation.*

> Magnet schools. *Public schools that offer specialized programs, often deliberately designed and located so as to attract students to otherwise unpopular areas or schools. Magnet schools are often created to promote racial balance.*

> Postsecondary options. *Programs that enable high school students to enroll in college courses at government expense. The courses they take may contribute to high school graduation requirement as well as to their college programs.*

> Second-chance programs. *Alternative schools and programs for students who have difficulties in standard public school settings. Most often these students have either dropped out of school, are pregnant or are parents, have been assessed as chemically dependent, or have been expelled from their previous school.*

> Charter schools. *Publicly sponsored autonomous schools that are substantially free of direct administrative control by the government but are held accountable for achieving certain levels of student performance (and other specified outcomes).*

> Work place training. *Apprenticeship programs to teach students a skilled trade not offered through present vocational training. Costs are divided between the employer and the school district.*

> Voucher plans. *Any system of certificate or cash payments by the government that enables public school students to attend schools of their choice, public or*

---

*Peter W. Cookson, Jr., *School Choice: The Struggle for the Soul of American Education* (New Haven, CT: Yale University Press, 1994), pp. 14–16. Copyright © 1994 by Yale University Press. Reprinted by permission.

private. Vouchers have a fixed value and are redeemed at the time of enroll-ment.

Tuition tax credits. *A system of funding choice that allows parents to receive credit against their income tax if their child attends a nonpublic school. Such a system is, by definition, intersectional. (pp. 14–16)*

Different Theories of Change

Why do people who share the same goals and who have the same information wind up on different sides when issues of how to improve schools are debated? One explanation is they bring to the debate different theories of human nature. Theories of human nature are at the center of prescriptions, legal systems, constitutions, contracts, socialization patterns, norm systems, and other attempts to define human action and to codify human behavior. They determine how we treat others and others treat us, and they determine what is just and good and what is unjust and evil (e.g., see Sergiovanni, 1997).

Hobbes believed that human nature has both a *reasonable* side rooted in moral conceptions of goodness and a *passionate* side rooted in psychological egoism. The reasonable side includes our *capacity* to embody such virtues as altruism, moral bearing, self-sacrifice, and cooperation aimed at the enhancement at what we believe to be the common good. The passionate side recognizes our *propensity* to satisfy our physical and psychological needs, to compete to win, and to accumulate wealth aimed at enhancing our own pleasure. Hobbes (1950) believed that humankind's passionate side is a natural condition. The rational side, by contrast, is artificial, having been achieved by committing to covenants that are culturally determined.

In the ideal, the two sides of human nature exist in reasonable balance. Despite this complexity, most policymakers operate from more simple theories of human nature, believing that people are inclined toward good or inclined toward evil. The first inclination represents the unconstrained view of human nature and the second inclination represents the constrained view (Sowell, 1987). Though constrained and unconstrained views are ends of the same continuum, with people positioned at different places, it is useful to think about two clusters comprised of people with similar enough views to be considered as holding either constrained or unconstrained theories.

Change agents who hold the *unconstrained* view believe that teachers, for example, can be trusted to act morally, and therefore must be provided with the freedom to optimize their moral propensity to do what is right. They have both the capacity and the need to sacrifice their self-interests for valued causes and for conceptions of the common good that they value. As professionals, they are willing to accept responsibility for their own practice, and they commit themselves to the learning needs of their students above other concerns. When teachers do not respond to this ideal, it is thought not to be because of their human nature but because of factors that they do not control.

Within the *constrained* view, it is believed that teachers will act selfishly if given the chance. Their primary concern is to maximize their self-interests. Thus, constraints in the form of incentives and penalties must be provided to force them to do the right thing. Advocates of this view believe that the moral limitations of human nature must be accepted, but can be manipulated in favor of the common good by the proper use of checks and balances such as rewards and punishments (Smith, 1937). Teachers may have the capacity to do the right thing, they reason, but this capacity is motivated only if constraints are provided.

Constrained Change Strategies

Both constrained and unconstrained views of human nature influence the strategies that policymakers use to improve schools. Those with constrained views rely on bureaucratic "leadership" and market strategies. *Leadership* in this discussion is defined as relying on the leaders' interpersonal styles and motivational skills to "motivate" change by trading psychological gratification and other forms of need fulfillment for compliance with proposed changes. Those with unconstrained views rely on professional, cultural, and democratic strategies. Both bureaucratic and leadership strategies offer teachers and schools trades of rewards and punishments, incentives and disincentives, for their compliance with change directions. In the first instance, these trades are managed by rules, mandates, and direct supervision. In the second instance, these trades are managed by the styles and interpersonal skills of leaders as they motivate and inspire change. Market forces also rely on trades. But these trades do not require intensive administration or intensive leadership. Instead, they rely on rational choice theory linked to the propensity of people to function as individuals who seek to maximize their gains and cut their loses in an open marketplace. The "invisible hand" of the market is depended on to motivate change.

Rational Choice Theory

Bureaucratic, leadership, and market change strategies rely on versions of rational choice theory to motivate change. The origins of rational choice theory are found in the fields of economics, evolutionary biology, and behavioral psychology. From economics comes the image of the person as one who is always in pursuit of self-interest and who is never satisfied with what has been accumulated. He or she operates alone, meaning that the drive to maximize gains and cut loses is pursued without regard for the welfare of others (Simon, 1950; Samuelson, 1947).

Darwin's (1985) theories of natural selection expanded the emphasis on competition that plays a major role in market change force strategies. Competition, he argued, weeds out the weak players, thus making the pool of survivors and new replacement for the weak stronger over time. Self-interest motivates competitive play. Darwin's theory provides the script for many school-choice proposals that are based solely on free-market principles.

Behavioral psychology contributed the law of effect (Skinner, 1953) to the market change force equation. According to the law of effect, human behavior is controlled by past consequences. Thus, having received a reward or punishment in the past, the individual is conditioned to repeat the behavior again and again to get the reward and to avoid the punishment in the future.

One particular variation of rational choice theory is agency theory (Moe, 1984). *Agency theory* assumes that the interests of managers and workers are not the same. Workers are interested in the best deal for the least effort. Managers are interested in the best performance at the least cost. Managers are dependent on workers who have more information about how to do the job. Given the choice, workers will take advantage of this situation. Thus, managers must use checks and balances as well as rewards and punishments to control and motivate workers (Bimber, 1993). Agency theory fits school change by substituting change agent for manager and teacher for worker, or the state for manager and the school site for worker.

Unconstrained Change Strategies

Professional, cultural, and democratic change strategies embody the unconstrained view of human nature. Professional strategies, for example, rely on professional training, standards of practice, and norms for behavior that, once internalized, are believed to compel change. Change behavior, advocates of this view argue, is motivated by professional virtues that function as substitutes for bureaucratic, personal, and market change forces (Sergiovanni, 1994). One professional virtue is a commitment to practice teaching in an exemplary way by staying abreast of new developments, researching one's own practice, trying out new approaches, and otherwise accepting responsibility for one's own development. Another professional virtue is to accept responsibility not only for one's own individual practice but also for the practice of teaching itself that exists in the school. Embodiment of this virtue transforms teaching from a collection of individual teaching practices to a single and shared practice of teaching. As teachers come to share the same practice, the argument continues, a third virtue comes into play: *colleagueship,* defined as teachers being connected together by morally held webs of obligations and commitments. Taken together, advocates believe, the professional virtues enable the development of professional community.

Change agents who rely on cultural change strategies believe that schools can become covenantal learning communities with cultures that compel changes among teachers and students that result in better teaching and learning. Cultural change strategies rely on community norms, values, and ideals that, when internalized, speak to everyone in a moral voice. Teachers, students, and other members of this community, it is argued, will then be motivated by felt obligations that emerge from the shared values and norms that define the school as a covenantal community (e.g., see Etzioni, 1988; Sergiovanni, 1994).

Democratic change strategies rely on commitment to democratic social contracts that function as the source for values to guide school decision making and as the source for patterns of obligations and duties that compel change. Advocates of this strategy seek to transform teachers and students into "citizens" committed to civic virtue. *Civic virtue* is defined as the willingness to sacrifice one's self-interest for the common good.

Not only do professional, cultural, and democratic change strategies all embody the unconstrained view, they all share the purpose of building community in schools as a means to leverage deep changes. When used together, the three change strategies seek to transform schools from organizations or markets to professional, learning, and democratic communities.

The six strategies for bringing about change in schools, along with their characteristics and likely consequences, are summarized in Table 2.2. Note that when bureaucratic, leadership, and market strategies are used, schools are likely to change just enough to avoid penalties, get rewards, or win in the marketplace. But once the prospects for penalties, rewards, or winning are removed, changes are likely to disappear. Professional, cultural, and democratic forces, by contrast, compel change from within and are thus likely to be more enduring.

Educational administration as both a discipline and a practice is in a constant state of evolution. During the twentieth century, both pyramid and railroad theories first dominated and were then challenged by high-performance theory. Despite this new vision's progressive features, all three of the theories share the constrained view of human nature. The theory of school as a moral community embodies the unconstrained view. During the nineties, advocates of schools as learning communities have been successful in establishing a beachhead assault on the three theories based on the constrained view. It is too early to tell, however, whether the new movement will be successful.

Maintaining Public Confidence

It should be clear from this discussion that easy solutions to fundamental value differences will not be forthcoming and that whatever answers do emerge will not result from simplistic and rational conceptions of the process of decision making. Instead, the destiny of schools is and will continue to be in the hands of various interests, each seeking advantage over others. Though state and local educational agencies, professionals in schools, politicians, and laypersons all appeal to the same rhetoric (excellence in schooling, improving teaching and learning, and so on), the real world of schooling is a creation of how this rhetoric is interpreted by interests and how these meanings are exchanged as a highly political process unfolds. Simply put, what is best for pupils, teachers, and schools is perceived differently by different groups.

Throughout the process, school administrators must maintain an adequate degree of public confidence at the local level in order for schools to function reasonably well. Without such confidence, the necessary material, political, and moral

TABLE 2.2   Change Strategies, Characteristics, and Consequences

Change Strategies	Change Practices	Theories of Human Nature	Change Consequences
Bureaucratic	1. Rely on rules, mandates, and requirements to provide direct supervision, standardized work processes, and/or standardized outcomes to prescribe change.	*Constrained*: The visible hand of rational choice theory linked to penalties is necessary to motivate change.	School changes just enough to avoid sanctions. Change stops when sanctions are removed.
Leadership	2. Rely on personality, leadership style, and interpersonal skills of change agents to motivate change.	*Constrained*: The visible hand of rational choice theory linked to psychological rewards is necessary to motivate change.	School changes just enough to receive gratification of needs. Change stops when rewards are not available.
Market	3. Rely on competition, incentives, and individual choice to motivate change.	*Constrained*: The invisible hand of rational choice theory linked to individual self-interest is necessary to motivate change.	School changes just enough to win in the marketplace. Winning becomes less important after repeated losses.
Professional	4. Rely on standards of expertise, codes of conduct, collegiality, felt obligations, and other professional norms to build professional community.	*Unconstrained*: The visible hand of professional socialization provides standards of practice and norms that compel change.	School internalizes norms of competence and virtue that compel change.
Cultural	5. Rely on shared values, goals and ideas about pedagogy, relationships, and politics to build covenantal community.	*Unconstrained*: The invisible hand of community norms, values, and ideas speak in a moral voice to compel change.	School internalizes community norms that compel change.
Democratic	6. Rely on democratic social contracts and shared commitments to the common good to build democratic community.	*Unconstrained*: The invisible hand of democratic traditions and internalized norms compel change.	School internalizes democratic norms that compel change.

Source: Adapted from Thomas J. Sergiovanni, "Organization, Market and Community as Strategies for Change: What Works Best for Deep Changes in Schools?" In Andy Hargreaves and Ann Lieberman (Eds.), *International Handbook of Educational Change* (Vol. 5) (Boston: Kluwer Academic Publishers, 1997).

support will not be forthcoming. Carol and Cunningham (1984) define *confidence* as "belief in, faith in, understanding of, willingness to support, pride in, loyalty to and willingness to defend a school or school system" (p. 111).

This definition is significant in the sense that it speaks to confidence in a particular school rather than in the institution of schooling. The annual Gallup survey of public opinion with respect to schooling, for example, typically reveals that the public differentiates between schooling in general and schools with which they are familiar. Schools as institutions rate a report grade of C, whereas schools close to home or attended by children of respondents rate a high B. This difference in how schooling, in general, and known schools are viewed suggests that public support can be maintained by local school officials.

Many policy experts and organizational theorists point out that though schools are dependent on outside forces for legitimacy and support, they are somewhat disconnected in operation from influence as they engage in day-to-day activities. The states require and the public expects that achievement test data be collected, but such data are rarely used to evaluate teachers in schools or to otherwise inform the decision-making process. School committees are chartered to study problems and make recommendations in support of decisions already made but unannounced. This is often the case with respect to school closings. Administrators conduct elaborate information searches and data-gathering efforts not to inform but to justify their decisions (see, e.g., Meyer & Rowan, 1978; Meyer, 1984).

In light of these findings, it is reasonable to ask, Why go through the expensive and elaborate motions of rational planning? Why collect information to guide decisions already made? The answer is that despite the ways in which schools and other organizations actually operate, they need to communicate a flow of images to important constituencies to maintain their legitimacy in the eyes of such constituencies. For example, the public expects schools to operate in a rational, logical manner, and legitimacy in the eyes of the public requires that such an image be communicated clearly and decisively.

Laswell (1971) uses the term *flow of images* to refer to the aggregate of perceptions an organization communicates to the public that results in the forming of an impression. This impression is shaped over time as the public experiences a "multitude of small, individual experiences acquired personally through direct contact with schools or with children, learned through the media, heard from one's neighbors, or gained perhaps from an acquaintance who works in the school" (Carol & Cunningham, 1984, p. 114). The problem is complicated by the reality that schools serve many publics and that contradictory flows of images must often be communicated.

Managing Public Confidence

The management of public confidence requires deft handling of the flow of images communicated to various constituencies. Since the needs, requirements, and interests of constituencies differ, image flows must differ and thus often contradict each other. Contradictory flows are possible because of the loose structuring or coupling that characterizes schooling. For examples, despite efforts of states to create a tight alignment between school goals and objectives and curriculum, between curriculum and teaching, and between teaching and testing to ensure control over the process, this alignment is difficult to accomplish within the actual process of schooling. As Cusick (1983), foe example, points out, the reality is that in most schools, each classroom operates independently of all others, as if it were a separate school.

To the extent that this argument is valid, public confidence can be managed by paying close attention to the flow of images that counts the most—images closest to home. And this seems to characterize what school administrators actually do. They typically express a healthy concern for public debates regarding schooling in the nation and participate in those debates. But they are far more concerned about the flow of images communicated in their own schoolyards.

Carol and Cunningham (1984) surveyed parents in an attempt to identify those perceived school characteristics that led to increased public confidence. Not surprisingly, they found that dedicated and competent teachers headed the list, tied for top rank with special instructional and extracurricular programs. These investigators comment, "Of equal importance was the availability of 'special programs.' Such programs might address the needs of handicapped youngsters, those with learning disabilities, or those in need of specialists, they might provide excellent music classes, field trips or travel. Together with other extracurricular programs (particularly sports programs) the inclusion of 'special programs' contributed significantly to confidence in the school" (Carol & Cunningham, 1984, p. 115).

Next in the rankings were perceptions that the school was effectively administered and pride in the buildings and grounds. Respondents commented on the importance of administrators being leaders of teams of teachers and on their capacity to be problem solvers on behalf of parents and students. When the school was perceived as having a caring, student-centered atmosphere and as having positive attitudes toward students and staff, public confidence was enhanced. These two qualities enjoyed fifth and sixth rank. Student discipline, curriculum, and achievement ranked seventh, eighth, and ninth, respectively, among the 25 items identified. The ranks are summarized in Table 2.3.

Though the findings from this study are preliminary, they do provide an indication of why school administrators spend more time projecting images of confidence and effectiveness, pride, and climate than they spend on curriculum, student achievement, and other characteristics included in Table 2.3. It suggests further that despite the public debates and intense policy deliberations that characterize the national agenda, school administrators focus primarily on the affairs of schooling in their own backyards.

TABLE 2.3   Ranking of Responses Leading to Confidence at a School Building Level

Rank	Reasons	No. of Responses
1.5	Dedicated, competent teachers	75
1.5	Special instructional and extracurricular programs	75
3.5	Administrator(s) effectiveness	61
3.5	Buildings and grounds	61
5.	Student-centered, "caring" atmosphere	51
6.	Positive attitudes of students/staff	40
7.	Student discipline	38
8.	Curriculum	36
9.	Student achievement	30
10.	Parent participation	28
11.	Communication with parents	22
12.	Public image	22
13.5	High standards, goals, expectations	15
13.5	Board/superintendent relations, policies, decisions	15
15.	Administrator/staff community service	13
16.	Courteous office staff	12
17.	Linkages with other institutions, sectors	11
18.	Successful graduates	10
19.33	Student awards, honors	9
19.33	Testing, guidance, and counseling programs	9
19.33	Community involvement with school	9
22.	Adequate funding	5
23.	Students' dress	4
24.5	Equity	3
24.5	Community education	3

Source: L. N. Carol & L. L. Cunningham, "Views of Public Confidence in Education," *Issues in Education,* 2(2), 118, 1984. Copyright 1984 by the American Educational Research Association. Reprinted by permission of the publisher.

References

Bimber, B. (1993). *School decentralization lessons from the study of bureaucracy.* Institute of Education and Training. Santa Monica, CA: Rand Corporation.

Carol, L. N., & Cunningham, L. L. (1984). Views of public confidence in education. *Issues in Education 11*(2), 110–126.

Casteen, J. T. (1984). The state's responsibility for teacher quality. In C. E. Finn, Jr., D. Ravitch, & R. T. Fancher (Eds.), *Against mediocrity. The humanities in America's high schools.* New York: Holmes and Meier.

Chubb, J. E., & Moe, T. M. (1989). A report to the people of Connecticut. *Educational Choice.* Norwalk, CT: The Yankee Institute.

Cookson, P. W. (1994). *School choice: The struggle for the soul of American education.* New Haven, CT: Yale University Press.

Cusick, P. A. (1983). *The egalitarian ideal and the American high school.* New York: Longman.

Darling-Hammond, L. (1984). *Beyond the commission reports: The coming crisis in teaching.* Santa Monica, CA: Rand Corporation.

Darling-Hammond, L., & Wise, A. E. (1983). Teaching standards or standardized teaching? *Educational Leadership, 41*(2), 66–69.

Darwin, C. (1985). *The origin of species by means of natural selection.* Harmondsworth, NY: Penguin.

DeCharms, R. (1968). *Personal causation: The internal affective determinants of behavior.* New York: Academic Press.

Etzioni, A. (1988). *The moral dimension: A new economics.* New York: The Free Press.

Goodlad, J. I. (1984). *A place called school.* New York: McGraw-Hill.

Hobbes, T. (1950). *Leviation.* New York: E. P. Dutton.

Howe, H., II. (1983). Education moves to centerstage: An overview of recent studies. *Phi Delta Kappan, 65*(3), 167–172.

Kirst, M. (1989). Who should control the schools? Reassessing current policies. In T. J. Sergiovanni & J. H. Moore (Eds.), *Schooling for tomorrow: Directing reforms to issues that count.* Boston: Allyn and Bacon.

Kirst, M. (1990). The crash of the first wave recent reform in the U.S.: Looking forward and backward. In S. Bacharach (Ed.), *Education reform: Making sense of it all.* Boston: Allyn and Bacon.

Laswell, H. D. (1971). *A pre-view of policy sciences.* New York: American Elsevier.

March, J. G., & Olsen, J. P. (1976). *Ambiguity and choice in organizations.* Oslo, Norway: Universitel Sforlaget.

McDonnell, L. M. (1989). *The dilemma of teacher policy.* Center for the Study of the Teaching Profession. Santa Monica, CA: Rand Corporation.

Meyer, J. (1984). Organizations as ideological systems. In T. J. Sergiovanni & J. E. Corbally (Eds.), *Leadership and organizational culture.* Urbana-Champaign: University of Illinois Press.

Meyer, J. W., & Rowan, B. (1978). The structure of educational organizations. In M. W. Meyer (Ed.), *Environments and organizations.* San Francisco: Jossey-Bass.

Moe, T. (1984). The new economic of organizations. *American Journal of Political Science, 28*(4), 739–777.

Murphy, J., Mesa, R. P., & Hallinger, P. (1984). A stronger state role in school reform. *Educational Leadership, 42*(2), 20–26.

Quinby, N. (1985). Improving the place called school: A conversation with John Goodland. *Educational Leadership, 42*(6), 16–19.

Ravitch, D. (1985). The *schools we deserve.* New York: Basic Books.

Samuelson, P. (1947). *Foundations of economic analysis.* Cambridge, MA: Harvard University Press.

Sandefur, J. R. (1985). State assessment trade. *AACTE Briefs, 6*(2), 21–23.

Sergiovanni, T. J. (1991). *The principalship: A reflective practice perspective* (2nd ed.). Boston: Allyn and Bacon.

Sergiovanni, T. J. (1994). *Building community in schools.* San Francisco: Jossey-Bass.

Sergiovanni, T. J. (1997). Organization, market and community as strategies for change: What works best for deep change in schools? In A. Hargreaves and A. Lieberman (Eds.), *International Handbook of Educational Change* (Vol. 5). Boston: Kluwer Academic.

Shirley, R. C. (1984). Institutional autonomy and government control. *Educational Forum, 48*(2), 217–222.

Simon, H. A. (1950). *Administrative behavior: A study of decision-making processes in administration organization.* New York: Macmillan.

Sizer, T. R. (1985). Common sense. *Educational Leadership, 42*(6), 21–22.

Skinner, B. F. (1953). *Science and human behavior.* New York: Macmillan.

Smith, A. (1937). *An inquiry into the nature and causes of the wealth of nations.* New York: Modern Library.

Snider, W. (1990, March 28). Voucher system for 1000 pupils adopted in Wisconsin. *Education Week, 9*(27), 1, 14.

Sowell, T. (1987). *A conflict of visions.* New York: Morrow.

Sunday Express News (San Antonio). (1984). Interview with Michael Kirst, December 16.

Wise, A. E. (1979). *Legislated learning: The bureaucratization of the American classroom.* Berkeley: University of California Press.

Wise, A. E. (1988). Legislated learning revisited. *Phi Delta Kappan, 69*(5), 329–332.

Chapter *3*

Demographics and the Challenge to Education in the United States

Consider the following three scenes:

Scene 1: Westside Elementary School is an old brick building that sits on a two-city-block site. Surrounded by an eight-foot chain link fence, the playground is asphalt covered and features several sets of swings. The parking lot has a gate to keep out everyone but faculty. Within six blocks of Westside are two low-income housing projects, the city schools' bus barn, and several small manufacturing plants. There is one convenience store two blocks from Westside but the nearest grocery store or department store is over three miles away. Students who live north of the school use a pedestrian overpass over a main arterial street to get to campus. Those who come from the south must pass through the two housing projects. Census tract data indicate that some 30 percent of adults over age 25 in the area have not completed high school. Police records indicate the area has a high level of petty crimes, abuse, and drug trafficking.

The children who attend Westside come from homes that are generally headed by single mothers. Nearly 80 percent of these families headed by a single mother are below the poverty line, even though 60 percent of these mothers are employed full time. Nearly 60 percent of Westside's families have an income level less than $15,000 and almost 90 percent of Westside's students qualify for the free lunch program. Only one-third of the students who start the school year in September will be in the school when it closes in June. Some students who enroll at Westside later in the year will report that it is the third school they have attended that school year; many of them will not finish the year at Westside. Approximately 50 percent of the students are African American, 45 percent are White, and 5 percent are Hispanic.

Test scores for Westside sixth-grade students indicate that most achieve at the third-grade level in reading and mathematics. About one-third of all third-graders cannot read. Teachers report many behavioral problems in their classes and continually ask for smaller class sizes and more parental involvement.

Scene 2: A husband and wife sit in their comfortable chairs in their family room watching the national evening news and sipping their coffee. During the course of that newscast, there are stories on

- Speculations about whether "the race card" will be played in the murder trial of a former professional athlete
- Factors that contributed to the successful passage of a state referendum that ended affirmative action as an element in admission to state-supported institutions of higher education
- Threats of a boycott of products of a national company, unless a suit dealing with discrimination in promotions and hiring was settled by the weekend
- A member of Congress proposing a bill to increase cuts in welfare spending
- Sex scandals in basic training sites in a branch of the military (as well as a report that another branch of the military had established a hot line for sex-related incidents)
- An interview with a woman who claimed a car rental company had denied her a rental car because of her race and age

Scene 3: Northwest High School sits on a site that includes an all-brick, two-story building built in the late 1920s. The edifice has carved columns and intricately carved statues. The large double doors open on a seal in the floor that proclaims "Northwest High—Home of the Wildcats"; students do not step on this seal. The trophy case near the entry doors is jammed; an inspection of the trophies indicates that most come from the 1930s and 1940s; the last trophy in the case is dated 1973.

The neighborhood surrounding Northwest is made up of single-family houses, most built in the 1930s. Most are well maintained. Census tract data on the neighborhood suggests that it has become racially mixed over the last 40 years and the level of education and income have been constant over this period. About 85 percent of all adults over age 25 in the area have completed at least two years of high school; income levels are above the federal poverty level but as that level rises, more and more families will fall into poverty. Northwest enrolls 1,230 students from the neighborhood—55 percent are White, 25 percent African American, 12 percent Hispanic, 5 percent Native American, and 3 percent Asian. When the school opened, it was 100 percent White.

The halls are patrolled by security guards who are off-duty police officers who wear their uniforms and carry their side arms. All are equipped with walkie-talkies, as is the assistant principal. Each classroom has a panic button that alerts the office to trouble. Fights are common in the halls and cafeteria; security guards often are forced to physically restrain combatants. Gang dress and symbols are not allowed; strangers coming to campus are interrogated by guards and often asked to leave. Students sneak off the school grounds to smoke and are herded back to the school by the guards and assistant principal. Teachers complain to the assistant principal that guards are often very physical with students; guards complain that teachers do not assist them in maintaining the security of the building. Guards patrol the teachers' parking lot to ensure that no vandalism is done to their cars. They check the students' parking lot for smokers, those sneaking out of class, and amorous students seeking privacy in a car.

Student achievement scores are low; most students read at least two grade levels below their current grade; mathematics achievement is even less. Only about 15 percent of the student body intends to go to college but nearly 60 percent plan on attending local technical schools or community colleges. Teachers who have been at the school for over 10 years are resigned to working with "good kids who come from poor backgrounds"; new teachers assigned to the school seek transfers to other schools as quickly as they can.

Persistent Problems

These scenes suggest persistent problems in American society and in American education. Those problems will be examined partially in this chapter as the link between demography (the science of the determinants and consequences of human population change) and gender, race/ethnicity, and social class. Over the last 50 years, population change and these issues have confronted U.S. education; they will continue to challenge U.S. education well into the twenty-first century. The problem of education in this country can be stated simply: As a people, we have promised to all children that their educational experiences in schools will not be influenced by gender, race/ethnicity, and social class. All will receive equal educational opportunity. We have not fulfilled that promise; what must be done?

During the last half of the twentieth century, courts and federal and state governments have acted in ways that have sought to ensure this promise. For example, in 1954, the Supreme Court declared that racially separate schools were unequal and should be ended with all deliberate speed. In 1964, Congress enacted laws that provided special funds for students from low-income families. In that same year, Congress enacted laws that sought to end discrimination based on gender and race, and to require affirmative action to correct these discriminations.

These actions produced major debates within our society about issues such as reverse discrimination, quotas, and unfair practices. Some suggest that any such remedies are inherently wrong; others believe that the remedies have succeeded and now need to end; some believe that the remedies are helping but still need to be applied; others suggest that things have not changed.

This chapter will not resolve this conflict. Instead, it suggests distinctions about equality and equity that may help sharpen this debate, then it discusses how changes in our population over the next years may well intensify the debate. Evidence is presented about the possible impact of gender, race/ethnicity, and social class on school attainment and achievement. The chapter then considers the continuing importance of three questions about equality and equity, and it concludes by suggesting a viewpoint for educational administrators.

Equality and Equity

To understand the importance of demographics in terms of society, we must understand how the determinants and consequences of human population change may create rewards and benefits for some individuals and not for others. A series of questions about equality and equity must be asked. Once these questions are clear, we may turn to how population differences may influence decisions made in areas such as education.

The principle of equality can be stated simply: All people should be treated exactly alike. There are no acceptable moral reasons for treating people differently. If one person receives $100 or 100 lashes, all individuals in society should receive $100 or 100 lashes. There are no relevant differences among people.

Many suggest that strict equality is not possible in society. They maintain that people are different and should receive different amounts of money or punishment. Rather than equality, they argue for the notion of equity, which involves two principles: formal justice and material justice. The principle of formal justice can be stated as follows: Society ought to treat individuals morally alike, unless there is a morally good reason for treating these individuals as different. In contrast to the notion of equality, there may be differences that exist that should be taken into account. For example, a typical classroom assignment in U.S. history might ask students to write a report on World War I. Students who are able to use the computer or a typewriter may type their report; those who do not have these skills may write the report in long hand. Reports will be graded similarly. In this example, differences between individuals are considered. An analysis suggests that students should be treated alike in terms of grading because typing or handwriting is not a good moral reason for treating these students as different.

If analysis suggests that the difference should be taken into account, a second set of questions becomes important: What ought to be considered a difference? and How can a difference be remedied to provide justice to all? Again, simplistically, imagine that four individuals are asked to run a race of 100 yards. One is a sprinter who was on the Olympic team, the second is an individual with only one leg who must use a crutch to run, a third is an individual who has a cast on a broken ankle, and the fourth has an inflamed big toe. The principle of formal justice would suggest that these individuals are different; the principle of material justice would suggest, first, that physical differences exist that influence their ability to race. The second question of material justice would be, How should these physical differences be weighed to create a fair race? For example, the race could have a staggered start—some further down the track than others—if it is to be fair. A discussion of material justice would suggest particular ways of determining how much head start each individual should have when the race starts. For example, one suggestion for a relevant principle of material justice might be that each individual run the 100 yards and be timed for the distance. The staggered start given each individual would be determined by the distance the person covers in a particular time period.

Consider one last simplistic example. Suppose three students enroll in an English literature class. All students have been given a test measuring aptitude for studying English literature. One student scored 50 (the lowest on the test), the second scored 100 (the mean on the test), and one scored 150 (the highest on the test). Proponents of equality would see the test results as not relevant. The question of formal justice would be, Should these students be treated the same in this class? The test results indicate there are differences in their aptitude for the class. Should aptitude be treated as a relevant moral reason for treating students differently? If the answer is no, then students should be treated exactly alike (equality). If the answer is yes, then the question of formal justice has been answered. The discussion of material justice would ask, Since aptitude is a morally relevant reason for treating students differently, then how should allowances be made so that students are remedied but fairly so? Should the student who receives the lowest grade, for example, be given extra tutoring and have points added to tests? Should the student who received an average score receive no tutoring and have no points deducted or added to tests? Should the student who receives the highest grade have no tutoring and have points deducted from tests? The principle of material justice asks, Are these remedies fair in the sense that although differences are acknowledged, "unfair" advantage is given to none?

These examples suggest two points. First, the question of formal justice is often answered in a way that also includes an answer to the first question of material justice. For example, we ask, What can be done to remedy discrimination against athletes by professors? The question suggests that we already know that differences exist that are relevant and we know what those differences are. Second, what happens if natural events or remedies "correct" the difference? Returning to the runners, if the cast is removed and the inflamed toe is cured, what happens to the staggered start of those two runners? What happens to the English literature student if, after several exams and quizzes, it is determined that there is no relation between aptitude test scores and achievement in class? Should we stop tutoring and adjusting tests at that moment, after we have given the midterm exam, or should we continue to the end the term? Principles of material justice that are applied to situations may need to be adjusted over time as events and remedies change the situation for the better or the worse.

In sum, discussions about equality and equity involve three important questions:

1. Is the discussion about strictly equal treatment for all regardless of differences?
2. Is the discussion about whether individuals should be treated differently (equity/formal justice)?
3. Is the discussion about what differences are relevant and the magnitude of remedy (equity/material justice)?

Population Changes*

It is important to remember that if all politics is local, so is all population change. Average change for the nation or for a region of the nation masks great diversity within the nation or the region. With that in mind, three questions will be examined: (1) What can be said about general population changes in terms of growth and race/ethnicity by the year 2000? (2) What is known about the conditions of children? and (3) What can be said about where Americans live?

U.S. Population Changes by the Year 2000

The following projections were selected by dividing the nation into five regions and using two states from each region as representatives:

- In the Northeast, neither Maine nor New York will increase in population much by the year 2000. (Maine's 1 percent growth will result in 1.26 million residents and New York's 0 percent growth will result in 18.15 million residents.) In 2000, Maine will be largely White (98.4 percent), whereas New York will be diverse (5.7 percent Asian, 18.2 percent African American, 15.5 percent Hispanic, and 60.8 percent White).
- In the South, Alabama will increase in population by the year 2000 by 5 percent (4.45 million in 2000), whereas Florida will increase 8 percent (15.23 million). Alabama in 2000 will be 25.5 percent African American and 73.3 percent White, whereas Florida will be 15.3 percent African American, 15.7 percent Hispanic, and 70.6 percent White.
- In the Midwest, Illinois will increase in 2000 to 12.05 million people (a 2 percent increase). Wisconsin will increase 4 percent to 5.33 million. Illinois in 2000 will be 3.5 percent Asian, 15.5 percent African American, 10.5 percent Hispanic, and 70.8 percent White. Wisconsin will be 6.1 percent African American, 2.6 percent Hispanic, and 91.1 percent White.
- In the Southwest, Texas will grow 7 percent from 1995 to 2000; it will be 2.8 percent Asian, 12.6 percent African American, 29.2 percent Hispanic, and 56.1 percent White. Oklahoma will grow to 3.37 million (3 percent) and be 8.4 per-

---

*The U.S. Census Bureau has a World Wide Web site: http://www.census.gov; all information in this section was generated from tables available at the time of writing.

cent African American, 3.7 percent Hispanic, 8.3 percent Native American, and 79.8 percent White.

- In the West, California will grow to 32.52 million in 2000 (a 3 percent increase from 1995), whereas Washington will grow 8 percent (5.43 to 5.86 million). California will be 13.2 percent Asian, 7.5 percent African American, 32.7 percent Hispanic, and 47.5 percent White in 2000. Washington will be 6.1 percent Asian, 3.3 percent African American, 6.1 percent Hispanic, 1.8 percent Native American, and 82.8 percent White.

These figures suggest that growth in population and in terms of race/ethnicity vary considerably by state. Within the same regions, neighboring states such as Oklahoma and Texas often indicate differences in growth and race/ethnicity composition. The figures do not reveal that school enrollments will increase from 1995 to 2000. Predictions for school enrollments must be made by examining the distribution of population within states by age. Such an examination reveals that increases of 11 to 19 percent will occur in 8 states, increases of 5 to 10 percent in 13 states, increases of less than 5 percent in 12 states, and decreases in 17 states and the District of Columbia (*Tulsa World*, 1996). For example, California and Washington will have enrollment increases of more than 10 percent, Texas will increase between 5 and 10 percent, but Oklahoma will decrease 0.7 percent. Illinois will increase less than 5 percent, whereas Wisconsin will decrease; Alabama will increase more than 10 percent, yet Florida increases less than 5 percent. Maine will decrease and New York will increase by less than 5 percent.

The Condition of Children

Census information can be examined to explore such issues as the condition of children. For example, the Annie E. Casey Foundation in KIDS COUNT provides an annual data book of national and state information based on census information. Included in this data book are indicators such as percent of low birth-weight babies, infant mortality rate, juvenile violent crime arrest rate, and information on school dropout and not attending school rates. According to the *KIDS COUNT Data Book 1995*, "The percent of children in poverty is perhaps the most global and widely used indicator of child well-being" (p. 14).

Turning to the states previously reviewed and using the single indicator of percent of children in poverty, note the following statistics:

- In New York 23.3 percent and in Maine 19.3 percent of children live in poverty.
- In Alabama 23.6 percent and in Florida 24.4 percent of children live in poverty.
- In Illinois 21.1 percent and in Wisconsin 14.0 percent of children live in poverty.
- In Texas 24.2 percent and in Oklahoma 21.8 percent of children live in poverty.
- In California 22.7 percent and in Washington 12.9 percent of children live in poverty.

The nationwide average percentage of children living in poverty is 20.6. Put another way, one in five children in the United States lives in poverty. In New York, Alabama, Florida, and Texas, nearly one in four children lives in poverty.

Urban/Rural Areas

It is true that there is great diversity among Americans, but there are also some similarities. Americans are increasingly living in urban areas: In 1900, 39.6 percent of the country's population lived in urban areas; in 1990, 75.2 percent lived in urban areas. Specifically, in 1900, Oklahoma was 92.6 percent rural; in 1990, Oklahoma was 32.3 percent rural. In 1900, New York was 27.1 percent rural; in 1990, New York was 15.7 percent rural. Again, there is some diversity by state, but it seems clear that the United States has become an urban nation. By 1930, 56.1 percent of Americans lived in urban settings and that percent continues to increase decade by decade.

In sum, we are of a culturally diverse nation whose diversity continues to increase, one in five children lives in poverty, and we are more and more urban.

Educational Attainment and Achievement

This section examines educational attainment and educational achievement in light of equality and equity. *Educational attainment* refers to levels of education; it is measured by years of school attended and degrees obtained. *Educational achievement* refers to mastery of certain learning outcomes; it is measured by tests.

Educational Attainment

Table 3.1 provides a snapshot of educational attainment for persons age 25 and over as of March 1996. Of the 168 million persons, less than 0.06 percent had no schooling, 17.7 percent had completed less than four years of high school, 33.6 percent had completed four years of high school, 15.8 percent had completed a bachelor's degree, and 0.96 percent had completed a doctorate. Put another way, 51.4 percent of this population had four years or less of high school attainment and 48.6 percent had attainment beyond high school.

Table 3.2 provides a different perspective on educational attainment. It provides information on the percentage of persons age 25 and older who have completed four years of high school or more for selected years from 1965 to 1995 by race/ethnicity and gender. An inspection of this table suggests that attainment has increased for all race/ethnicity groups. The most dramatic increase has been for Blacks. However, attainment is related to race/ethnicity. Whites have attained at rates much higher than Blacks or Hispanics. Moreover, Hispanic attainment rates in 1995 are comparable to White rates of attainment in 1965 and Black rates in 1980. Attainment is also related to gender but these differences are much smaller than the relationship to race.

TABLE 3.1   Persons Age 25 and Over by Educational Attainment: March 1996

Both Sexes—Education		Total (in thousands)
Total Persons 25+		**168,323**
None		966
Elementary:	1–4	2,061
	5–6	3,479
	7–8	7,116
High School:	1	4,133
	2	5,808
	3	7,161
	4	56,559
Some college, no degree		29,201
Associate Degree, Vocational Program		6,495
Associate Degree, Academic Program		5,676
Bachelor's Degree		26,540
Master's Degree		9,101
Professional School Degree		2,416
Doctorate Degree		1,611

Source: U.S. Census Bureau (March 1996) *Current Population Survey.*

TABLE 3.2   Percent of Persons 25 Years Old and Over Who Have Completed High School or More, by Race, Hispanic Origin, and Gender: Selected Years 1965 to 1995

	White		Black		Hispanic Origin	
Year	*Male*	*Female*	*Male*	*Female*	*Male*	*Female*
1965	50.2	52.2	25.8	28.4	NA	NA
1970	57.2	57.6	32.4	34.8	NA	NA
1975	65.0	64.1	41.6	43.3	39.5	36.7
1980	71.0	70.1	51.1	51.3	46.4	44.1
1985	76.0	75.1	58.4	60.8	48.5	47.4
1990	79.1	79.0	65.8	66.5	50.3	51.3
1995	83.0	83.0	73.4	74.1	52.9	53.8

Source: U.S. Census Bureau, World Wide Web site: http://www.census.gov

If we were to discuss attainment in terms of equality, equity, and material principles of justice, it seems clear that attainment differs by gender and by race/ ethnicity. A strict equality argument would suggest that gender and race should not be considered as relevant differences; differences are found because individuals who do attain or who do not attain do so for individual characteristics unrelated to gender or race. Those who attain may have more ability and more tenacity, whereas those who do not attain have less ability and less tenacity. These are characteristics on which individuals may differ, but they are not the sorts of things that can be corrected by the notion of justice.

Those arguing for equity would agree that individuals might differ on ability and tenacity but that social conditions influence ability and tenacity; in turn, ability and tenacity influence educational attainment. Such social conditions as proper nutrition and the ability to see opportunities as equal may influence ability and tenacity of individuals; improving the ability of others and their sense of their ability to influence their future should lead to increases in educational attainment. Moreover, the debilitating social conditions that dampen ability and tenacity are related to gender and race/ethnicity. Social remedies can be applied to these social conditions; change in these conditions will change the characteristics of individuals and the level of educational attainment.

This line of reasoning already suggests material principles—nutrition and a sense of efficacy about the future. Developing this line of reasoning would require determining the relationship of nutrition and ability, of efficacy and discrimination. Once these relationships were determined, social programs could be constructed to remedy these circumstances.

Table 3.2 also suggests that over time the levels of educational attainment for Blacks and Hispanics have increased sharply. Some might suggest that social programs aimed at producing remedies based on race/ethnicity are still needed, but that it may soon be time to reduce or discontinue such remedies.

Educational Achievement

One source of educational achievement materials is provided by the National Educational Goals Panel, which came into being in 1990 as part of Goals 2000 legislation.* Beginning in 1990, the National Education Goals Panel organized test information generated by the National Assessment of Educational Progress (NAEP) tests. Begun in 1969, the NAEP tests were expanded to include goals besides academic achievement and now include voluntary participation by 44 states and territories.

Table 3.3 presents information on the percentage of students by grade, gender, and race/ethnicity who met the National Educational Goals Panel performance standards in reading in 1994 and mathematics in 1992. An inspection of the table suggests that in reading, about 25 percent of males and slightly more than 37 percent of females reached these standards. There are great differences in achieve-

*The National Education Goals Panel has a World Wide Web site: http://www.ncrel.org/ncrel/sdrs/ areas/issues/envrnment/go/go4panel.htm

TABLE 3.3   **Percent of Students Who Met the National Education Goals Panel Performance Standard by Year, Test, Grade, Gender, and Race/Ethnicity**

	Reading 1994			Mathematics 1992		
Grade	4	8	12	4	8	12
Male	26	23	29	20	23	18
Female	34	36	43	17	24	14
Asian	48	44	33	30	44	31
Black	9	9	13	3	3	3
Native American	18	20	20	10	9	4
Hispanic	13	14	20	6	8	6
White	37	36	43	23	32	19

Source: National Education Goals Panel, *1995 National Goals Report: Volume One: National Data* (Washington, DC: U.S. Government Printing Office, 1995), various pages with materials abridged.

ment by race/ethnicity. For example, Asian and White students achieve at a much higher rate than Black students. In mathematics, males and females perform about the same. However, there are major differences in achievement by race/ethnicity. Black, Hispanic, and Native American students consistently perform less well than Asian and White students.

Questions for Education

Issues such as equality and equity permeate U.S. education. Much has been discussed about that topic; the information provided in the preceding section suggests population changes will not end, and, in fact, may exacerbate that debate. If the promise of American education is to provide equal educational opportunity for all students, how that promise is kept requires ongoing discussions considering questions of equality and equity in light of an increasing racially and ethnically diverse population—a population that has a large percent of children living in poverty and an increasingly urban population. Moreover, educational attainment and achievement appear influenced by gender, race/ethnicity, and social class as reflected by income level.

This section suggests that there are three important questions that should be discussed: (1) Where are equality and equity measured? (2) How should equality and equity be measured? and (3) When are remedies no longer needed? The answers to these questions rest in part on demographic information and in part on beliefs about American life.

Where Are Equality and Equity Measured?

Equality and equity can be measured in terms of inputs, processes, or outcomes. *Inputs* refers to resources that are made available, such as dollars spent for teachers' salaries, facilities, and textbooks. *Processes* refers to resources applied in classrooms and schools, such as teacher time, instructional materials, and teacher in-service training. *Outcomes* refers to student achievements, such as scores on standardized tests, admission to postsecondary education institutions, and job placements.

In general, as a people, we are leery, of great disparities in any of these areas. Courts, for example, continue to hear suits arguing against great differences in terms of inputs as these are related to the wealth of districts. School districts seek to provide some similarities in terms of process by providing training for all the teachers of a district. Sharply different scores on achievement tests by schools raises questions about what can be done to improve such schools and raise their scores. But being leery does not lead us to argue for equality. As a people, we would reject the notion that all districts have to have the same facilities or teacher salaries, that all classes in Algebra 1 have to be taught the same way, or that all students should score exactly the same on a mathematics achievement test.

Rather than equality, we have sought to argue for a floor for inputs, processes, and outcomes. We have argued that inputs should meet minimum standards. We are generally unwilling to provide "caps" on the efforts of schools, districts, and states in efforts to provide input resources. In the few cases that caps have been imposed, the level of such caps has been many times the level of minimums in these areas. We also have argued that processes should meet minimum standards. We have guaranteed the minimums using teacher certification, state-approved curriculum guidelines, and approved textbooks. Processes have rarely, if ever, been capped. Outcomes, again, are most often stated in minimums. The National Educational Goals Panel, for example, sets a minimum performance standard, hoping that all students reach this level.

Those pressing for equity suggest that in these three areas we have not done well as a people. They argue that equality of input presumes that students are treated "as if" they come to school similarly situated. The obvious disparities among the backgrounds of children necessitate that equity be considered when resources concerning inputs are examined. Children who are raised in poverty may need additional resources to be successful in schools. Equity of processes also should pertain; teachers should be assigned to classes in ways that give students who require special treatment the opportunity to get instruction that takes into account special needs. Equity of output means that any differences found on test scores should be unrelated to differences students bring to school and should be related to their behaviors in schools that could not be remedied.

In short, the debate about equality and equity in terms of inputs, processes, and outcomes often deals with equality by creating minimums. Proponents of more equity have not seen minimums as a good remedy.

How Should Equality and Equity Be Measured?

Issues of how equality and equity should be measured have floundered. On the one hand, equality in terms of strict numeric equivalents makes little sense in comparing school, districts, states, or nations. Such comparison is invalid because of the dissimilarities of schools, districts, states, and nations.

Equality as a concept suggesting exact alikeness also has been troubled by diversity. Equity has had the same fate. There are so many possible sources of difference that could be remedied that finding common ground for those seeking more equity has been difficult, if not impossible.

We have used the proxies of gender, race, and social class to begin the exploration of the issue. Differences on these issues have served as ways of thinking about equity at large; they are not that helpful in thinking about equity in a specific context. For example, gender bias against women can be seen at the level of a school district but might not be evident at a particular school within that district. It is difficult to untangle the specific details that require remedies in specific situations. Often, proponents of equity have been forced to argue for equality of damage (all women are discriminated against) and equality of remedy (all women should be remedied). Such a strategy seems inconsistent with material principles of justice.

When Are Remedies No Longer Needed?

If the first two question seem difficult to answer, it is this third one that most perplexes citizens. At what point does a remedy become an advantage? If we believe that individuals are disadvantaged by race, and if remedies are applied, at what point do we believe these remedies should be ended, and if they are not ended, at what point do those individuals become advantaged?

If remedies seem reasonably clear when major disadvantages exist, they are far less clear when minor and insignificant disadvantages exist. In Table 3.3, for example, it seems clear that Black students are disadvantaged in comparison to Asian students. If we were to remedy Black students in terms of Asian students, how much percentage difference would we accept in order to say that the remedy was successful—0 percent, 1 percent, 2 percent, 3 percent, or some other figure? Would we seek a remedy, for example, in terms of mathematics achievement in eighth grade for males (disadvantaged) when compared to females?

In sum, these three questions illustrate the continuing discussion about equality and equity in U.S. education that will continue because of anticipated demographic changes.

A Viewpoint

As we approach the relationship among equality and equity and demography, three points seem clear. First, educational administration in a pluralistic society requires educational administrators to think clearly about these relationships. Second, school administrators have firsthand knowledge that suggests the need for equity more than equality. Third, school administrators must think most deeply about when a remedy is successful.

Thoughtfulness

The gist of this chapter is a plea for present and future school administrators to think deeply and carefully about equality and equity in light of the changing population of schools. All must come to understand their own views about equality and equity, about formal and material justice. Nieto (1992), for example, argues that school administrators need to affirm diversity. Such an affirmation will aid most students. In contrast, Capper (1993) argues that school administrators in a pluralistic society need to use multiple perspectives (paradigms) to think about the paradoxes and promises of education. The authors have no such solution in mind; rather, the competing values of American life provide many different ways of working to create equality and equity.

Apparent Diversity

The daily lives of many school administrators, particularly as the United States becomes more and more urban, include more and more encounters with the diversity and pluralism of our society. In some ways, it is difficult for school administrators to believe in the equality of American life. Without the benefits of an overview in demography, the students who cross the threshold of U.S. schools are living proof of the nation's pluralism and diversity. Finding equality is much harder than noticing differences that suggest the need for equity.

Such a recognition, however, does little more that raise the questions of material justice. That differences exist, and that differences should be targeted for remedy, does not produce answers about the remedy and its fairness. Is it enough to provide children of poverty with a free breakfast and lunch? Should they be provided medical assistance in the form of free checkups for vision problems? Vitamin supplements? Chest x-rays? And on and on. It is the questions of material justice and of fair remedy that come to mind as everyday life exposes administrators to diversity and pluralism.

Such issues require administrators to revisit their own experiences, to rethink their views of what classrooms should be like, to reconsider the ways that schools can provide multiple services to children, and to ponder anew what American education is all about. Such tasks are not easy in days filled with crisis after crisis, problem after problem. Yet they are what is required as administrators stand by the door and watch students enter the school.

Returning to this chapter's opening scenes, What could be done by an administrator at Westside Elementary? A principal might confront the problems of Westside by a multipronged attack, including retooling teachers to work with students who have special needs; providing baby-sitters for mothers so they can come to school and meet with teachers; seeking corporate partners interested in providing equipment and expertise to the building; writing grants to state and federal government agencies, seeking funding for special programs; and working with students to improve their test-taking skills. What might your husband or wife do after listening to the news? Or what might the principal of Northwest High do?

Successful Remedies

If school administrators see on a daily basis the diversity of American life, they also need to be most alert to when changes have taken place that remedy situations. As noted earlier, this may be the most vexing of all problems created by demographic change. As new groups continue to come to the United States, as economic changes create major shifts in the income levels of families, and as earlier programs produce changes in pools of job applicants, administrators must be sensitive to success or the need to continue programs. Such assessments require much discernment. Is it enough, for example, to seek a new principal in a school and have one African American applicant for the position? Contemplating such questions often requires a careful rethinking of principles of material justice.

Summary

This chapter has provided information on demographic changes in the United States that have and will continue to affect schools. Over the last 50 years, administrators have faced some of these changes. As a society, we have debated the importance of equality and equity. At times, these debates have produced laws that sought to produce more equity; at times, these debates have affirmed the belief in equality.

For those who seek to be or who are school administrators, diversity and pluralism are often facts of life. As administrators help create and shape the climates for our schools, issues of equality and equity are not far from the surface. Often, the everyday life of schools leads administrators to stress equity. But such a stress requires careful attention to issues of material justice and of the need to assess remedies to see if they should end or continue. These are not easy tasks; they require school administrators to think about their own perspectives and to weigh them carefully against the opinions of others in society.

References

Annie E. Casey Foundation. (1995). *KIDS COUNT data book 1995.* Baltimore, MD: Author.

Capper, C. A. (Ed.). (1993). *Educational administration in a pluralistic society.* Albany: State University of New York Press.

Nieto, S. (1992.) *Affirming diversity: The sociopolitical context of multicultural education.* New York: Longmans.

Tulsa World (Oklahoma). (1996). August 26, p. A-13.

C h a p t e r **4**

Educational Administration

An Overview

Who are administrators? What are their responsibilities? How do they obtain and exercise authority? How can their authority be checked? Are they leaders or managers? Are they really necessary? Can schools function successfully without them? Parents and teachers often ask such questions, as do members of the general public. Occasionally, the questions are asked skeptically. Administrators are not always portrayed in a favorable light. But few will deny that ours is a complex society with difficult problems that are hard to solve by relying solely on informal administrative arrangements.

In his classic treatment of the art of administration, for example, Tead (1951) invites readers to journey with him on a mythical voyage designed to illustrate the complexity of organization and administration in U.S. society.

> *Fly over New York City imaginatively in an airplane, and remove the roofs from successive buildings in your mind's eye. What do you see? You see people, tens of thousands of them, at work. You see top executives in quiet offices thinking, planning, conferring, issuing orders which affect people in distant localities where their companies have plants. You see boards of directors hearing reports and adopting policies which may mean more or less employment in Akron, Detroit, Pittsburgh. You see department store heads in conference with merchandise managers. You see office managers in insurance companies, banks, investment houses, wholesaling firms, facilitating the labors of many. You see huge hospitals in which doctors, nurses, and auxiliary staffs are working to restore health. You see universities, colleges, and schools in which administrators and teachers are providing education. You see governmental bureaus—Federal, state and municipal—in all of which some phase of the public welfare is being served.*

> *Everywhere there are people managing and there are people being managed.*
> *This is taking place in organizations, large or small, and for all kinds of purposes.*
> *(p. 1)*

The governance and administration of education provide a good example of the nature and importance of administrative activity in our society. The educational establishment ranks among the largest of public and private enterprises. More than 2 million teachers and roughly 53 million students in thousands of public and private schools throughout the nation function daily. Fifty state departments of education, several departments of federal government, as well as dozens of private and semiprivate organizations assume responsibility for the analysis and development of broad policy to guide this vast enterprise. Thousands of school boards and tens of thousands of administrators function in the development and administration of policies that govern the day-by-day operation of schools.

The United States is committed to universal education through the high school and in some communities through the junior college. Much progress has been made toward this goal but much more needs to be done. Past accomplishments and future success have relied on and will continue to rely on the quality of educational leadership and governance available to local schools: Educational administration at all levels, from superintendent to department chairperson, assume key roles in the process of building quality education. No one would deny the importance of enacting sound education policy at the state and federal levels, but sound policy in itself is not the answer to school problems and issues. One cannot legislate or mandate superior teaching and learning or other aspects of quality education. These result from the efforts of competent and committed professionals who work with youngsters day after day, the commitment and support a school enjoys from its community, and organizational and other logistical support provided to the school—characteristics that are the domains of educational leadership, governance, and administration.

Policy and Policy in Use

Some experts argue that too much emphasis is given to the educational policy development process and not enough to the articulation of policy into administrative designs and structures and the embodiment of policy into school practice. Others take the opposite position. Both positions assume that policy and administration are separate. The classical literature in administration and public policy, for example, makes a fairly clear distinction between the policy-development process (establishing mission statements, guidelines, general regulations, and mandates) and the articulation of policies into administrative rules and professional practices. The first modern distinction between policy and administration appears in Frank J. Goodnow's book *Politics and Administration*, published in 1900.

Earlier distinctions were made by Woodrow Wilson (1887) in "The Study of Administration": "Public administration is detailed and systematic execution of public law. Every particular application of general law is an act of administration. . . . The broad plans of governmental action are not administrative. . . administration lies outside the proper sphere of politics. Administrative questions are not political questions" (p. 97). Approximately 100 years earlier, Alexander Hamilton had written in *The Federalist: "The Administration of Government,* in its largest sense, comprehends all the operations of the body politic . . . but in its most usual, and perhaps its most precise significance, *it is limited to executive details,* and falls peculiarly within the province of the executive department" (italics added) (Rossiter, 1961, p. 435). In his later writings, Goodnow (1905) would emphasize again that "politics has to do with policies and expressions of the state will. Administration has to do with execution of these policies" (p. 15).

Traditionally, the policy process was presumed to be the arena for shaping our future by providing the decision-making structures designed to harness the implementing decisions of administrators and professionals. Policymakers create policy, and professionals articulate policy in practice. Policymakers decide, and professionals do. This time-honored distinction may serve as a source of legitimacy and rationality. Separating the two may be ideal, but in practice it is more myth than reality.

In 1945, Nobel laureate Herbert A. Simon commented on the distinction between policy and administration as follows: "Yet, neither in Goodnow's study nor in any of the innumerable distinctions that have followed it have any clear-cut criteria or marks of identification been suggested that would enable one to recognize a "policy question" on site, or to distinguish it from an "administrative question" (p. 54). And in 1949, Paul H. Appleby, then dean of the Maxwell School of Public Administration at Syracuse University, commented, "Congress and legislators [state education departments and school boards] make policy for the future, but have no monopoly on that function. . . . Administrators are continually laying down rules for the future and administrators are continually determining what the law is, what it means in terms of action, what the rights of parties are with respect both to transactions in process and transactions in prospect. Administrators make thousands of such decisions to one made by the courts. . . . Administrators also . . . formulate recommendations for legislation, and this is a part of the function of policy-making" (pp. 6–7). He noted further, "Executives do not sit at different desks, treating policy as one and administration as the other. . . they more often deal with whole problems than they deal with them as exclusively problems of policy or problems of administration" (p. 19).

A more realistic view of the policy process in practice reveals a distinction between policy as stated and policy in use. *Policy in use* refers to policy that is created as guidelines are interpreted, mandated characteristics are weighed, differential priorities are assigned, action theories are applied, and ideas come to life in the form of implementing decisions and professional practice. Policy in use is the policy that is felt by students and teachers as schooling takes place. It results from the interpretation of policy statements. For these reasons, in the real world the line between policy and administrative practice is fragile.

The role of research in developing policy and in creating policy in use is important. But research rarely informs the development of stated policy. Typically, politicians don't behave as a result of objective research findings. They act on behalf of preferences and beliefs. The *stating of policy* is a subjective process that seeks to maximize certain values and aspirations thought to be important. Since these values are often not shared in identical ways by various groups, decisions are made as special interests seek to maximize gains according to their held beliefs. Though research plays an important role in political process of policymaking, the findings of research are rarely considered to be privileged by policymakers. Administrators often lament this situation. "Research shows that small schools and multiage classrooms make sense. Why doesn't the school board pay attention to this research?" they might reason and ask. But administrators, too, are inclined to make decisions more on the basis of values and perspectives than research findings. Perhaps the answer is that research findings should not substitute for decisions that policymakers or administrators make. Instead, interpretation of stated policies into administrative designs and actions, or the creation of policy in use, can and should be informed by the best available research. It is at this level that stated policy becomes sensible and reasonable practice.

Administration Defined

Administration is generally defined as the process of working with and through others to accomplish organizational goals effectively and efficiently. There is a performance quality to most definitions of administration, and since resources are always limited and decisions must be made as to how best to allocate these resources, efficiency becomes an additional quality.

Typically, a distinction is made between administration and leadership. The school principal, for example, is responsible for a number of teachers and other employees, each with specific tasks to do. The principal's job is to coordinate, direct, and support the work of others by defining objectives, evaluating performance, providing organizational resources, building a supportive psychological climate, running interference with parents, planning, scheduling, bookkeeping, resolving teacher conflicts, defusing student insurrections, placating the central office, and otherwise helping to make things go. Hemphill (1958) and Lipham (1964) would consider these administrative, rather than leadership, activities. Administration, according to this view, refers to the normal behaviors associated with one's job. To Hemphill and Lipham, the differences between the two can be seen in the behavior of leaders who initiate new structures, procedures, and goals. Leadership, they would suggest, emphasizes newness and change.

Zaleznick (1977), for example, describes leaders as follows:

> *They are active instead of reactive, shaping ideas instead of responding to them. Leaders adopt a personal and active attitude toward goals. The influence a leader*

exerts in altering moods, evoking images and expectations, and in establishing specific desires and objectives determines the direction a business takes. The net result of this influence is to change the way people think about what is desirable, possible, and necessary. (p. 1)

Though this distinction between administration and leadership has become widely accepted in the literature and has a number of advantages, on balance, negative consequences seem to dominate. Administration comes to be seen as a less essential, lower-status activity, whereas leadership is viewed as superior. Further, the glamour of the leadership concept results in its receiving far more attention in the literature than may be warranted. As a result, administration is viewed as the straw concept as writers glamorize leadership. This leads to a prescriptive literature that is often out of kilter with reality. This literature encourages unreasonable expectations for change for administrators; causes feelings of inferiority, anxiety, and guilt among them; and provides the public with unrealistic images of what administrators can actually do. Though administrators are important, for example, the fate of schools depends on teachers and others sharing the responsibility for leadership. In a sense, leadership is a form of social capital. The more this capital is shared, the more new capital is created.

Leadership and administration are so interrelated that, practically speaking, both behavior modes should be considered necessary and important variations in administrative style. The choice is not either leadership or administration, but a better balance between the two and a more realistic view of the possibilities for each. Important also are issues of education and the significance of educational leadership. Later in this chapter, leadership qualities, missions, and roles in *education* are examined as a set of concepts distinct from leadership and administration in general.

In business and other settings, the terms *management* and *management behavior* are used to refer to administration and sometimes to both administration and leadership. As many of the references in this book suggest, much of the management literature is appropriate to educational administration. In recent years, the term *management* has become more popular in educational circles. But sometimes it is used in a derogatory sense. Popular articles, for example, often ask, "Should a principal be a manager or an educational leader?" implying that the first choice is demeaning. Perhaps one reason for this is a desire by many to keep the administration of schools separate from that of business and industrial organizations (Sergiovanni, 1996).

In many respects, educational administration is a first cousin to public administration and carries with it some of the same traditions. In that field, the term *administration* is preferred over *management* because of the acknowledged intermingling of administration with policy. Administration is a "broad term involving policy-making as well as execution.... 'Management' involves the same intermingling of policy-making and execution but it is here assigned arbitrarily to a lower level and used to signify executive action with least policymaking significance" (Appleby, 1949, pp. 24–25). To many, the separation from policy makes management a form of script-following rather than script-writing. Script-following emphasizes doing things right rather than being concerned with what one ought to do. This emphasis compromises the school administrator's governance and stewardship responsibilities (Selznick, 1957; Sergiovanni, 1990). The following sections review critical responsibilities of administrators, generally accepted administrative processes, and necessary administrative skills in an attempt to provide a basic overview, definition, statement of purpose, and conception of educational administration. Later, more specific attention is given to the educational administrator's responsibilities for providing educational leadership to his or her school community.

Critical Responsibilities of Administrators

At a basic level, schools and other kinds of organizations engage in similar activities. Argyris (1964) refers to these as organizational-core activities that guarantee their survival. The core activities are *attainment of organizational goals, maintaining integration of the organizational system, and adapting to forces in the organization's external environment* (Argyris, 1964, p. 315). Each of the core activities comprises a set of organizational imperatives for the school, to which administrators and school boards must attend. To these three can be added an additional imperative particularly suited to the school—*maintaining cultural patterns* (Parsons, 1951, 1960). To Parsons, the four activities define the survival and growth requirements of social systems such as groups, organizations, communities, and societies. As core activities for schools, the four can be viewed as composed of many subactivities, and these, in turn, result in behaviors called administrative functions.

Function might include, for example, planning, organizing, controlling, coordinating, teaching, communicating, and evaluating. Functions are directed toward particular intended consequences. The consequences, in turn, are defined by the core activities of achieving goals, internal maintenance, external adaptation, and maintaining cultural patterns. The core activities represent organizational imperatives because the neglect of any one can threaten the survival of the school. Schools must experience certain levels of success in achieving goals, in maintaining themselves internally, in adapting to their external environments, and in maintaining their cultural patterns. Each core activity will now be discussed in more detail.

Maintaining Cultural Patterns

Maintaining the school's cultural pattern is concerned with protecting and nurturing school and community traditions and cultural norms. School administrators and school-board members typically are sensitive to the salient motivational and cultural patterns that exist in the community over time, and these patterns are an important part of the school's official and hidden curricula. School traditions emerge, images are fabricated and nurtured, and accepted ways of operating become established in a system of written and unwritten norms that provide a given school or school community with a distinct personality. Graduation ceremonies, football games, holiday programs, newsletters, and public-relations programs are some of the more visible ways of fabricating and maintaining cultural-pattern images, as are student-conduct codes, policy handbooks, and other public attempts to control the behavior of students. Often, the symbols of cultural-pattern maintenance are more important than actual conditions. Some schools are known for their athletic prowess, others foster an elite academy image, and still others are thought of as well-rounded traditional schools where the ideal student is viewed as having a B average and being a cheerleader or an athlete, taking an active role on the yearbook, being prom king or queen, and later attending the local state university. Some of the most critical times for school administrators occur when cultural-pattern demands are in transition, often as a result of population shifts, desegregation mandates, or other abruptions in the normative character of the school community.

Cultural patterns are expressed in the formal written and unwritten rules or codes that provide teachers, students, administrators, and others with expectations, norms, assumptions, and beliefs. They define the acceptable way of school and community life and give meaning to this life.

Attaining Goals

Goal attainment suggests administrative and school-board responsibilities that are direct and well understood—defining objectives and mobilizing resources to attain them. Because of its visibility, goal attainment becomes the public agenda for recruiting and evaluating administrators and board members, though in reality, judgments of ineffectiveness result most frequently from deficiencies in other responsibility areas, such as maintaining the school's cultural pattern.

Peshkin's (1977) account of the hiring of a new school superintendent in "Mansfield" illustrates the public acknowledgment of goal attainment criteria by the school board, but the actual concern for maintaining a school/community cultural pattern is in making the hiring decision. Consider, for example, the following excerpts from school-board discussions in Mansfield following interviews of several candidates:

> *Should we talk about Hagedorn to see why we don't want him?*
> *Yes, let's get the feeling of the board on him. I believe we have better men. Not quality-wise, though. He could handle the job and the P.R. (Public Relations). I don't think he's the type we're looking for.*
> *I hate to say it, but his physical appearance is against him. You need to call a spade a spade.*
> *He's not stable like some of the others.*
> *I'm afraid he'd be the brunt of behind-the-back jokes.*
> *He's carrying far too much weight. That's a strain on the heart.*
> *He was tired. A man that size gets physically tired. We shouldn't kid ourselves. Image is very important. That size is against him.*
> *The next one is Dargan.*
> *I was impressed, but I feel he is too big for our town and school. His ideas are for the city, for bigger schools. We're not ready for all that.*
> *I felt he would probably be anxious to start a lot of things I don't know if we're*

ready for. He's definitely for a nongraded system. He said he'd start slow, but he wanted it pretty bad. Knocking down walls scares you just a bit.

I was impressed, but then we had more fellows in. We learned more about this nongraded idea. He would be a pusher, I'm sure.

He had too many ideas to start off with. You need to see what a school has before jumping in.

I thought he might be a little slow with discipline problems.

I saw dollar signs clicking around in my head when he talked. He may be too intelligent for this community. He may talk over the heads of the community.

Another thing. He was emphatic about four weeks vacation.

Salary-wise he asked for the most.

Well, this Dargan, he said he wanted to come to a small community. I think he may want to bring too many ideas from the city with him. He may be more than we want.

What did you like about Morgan? These next three are a hard pick.

He gave a nice impression here, I believe, of getting along with the public and the kids. This impressed me more than anything.

To me he talked generalities.

He had a tremendous speaking voice. He's young.

His voice got very nasal at the end when he got relaxed.

He wouldn't stay.

I believe he'd be a forceful individual.

Take this other man, Rogers. I had a feeling about him. He said, "If you hired me and I accepted it." I don't think he's too anxious for the job.

I can see why he was offered a job selling real estate. He's got the voice. He'd have your name on the line. I'm inclined to believe he'd talk himself out of most situations. Getting down to brass tacks, he spoke in generalities. He admitted he didn't know too much about new things in education. We need more specific answers.

More or less, this leaves us with Vitano.

He's the man to put on top.

I'd hate to pick any of the top three over the others.

Both Vitano and Rogers said that they have no hours. They work by the job. Vitano worked his way through college.

He was on ground floor as far as salary goes.

And he's country. (pp. 187–188)*

Though the board had established public selection criteria around the theme of goal attainment, its actual criteria revolved around the cultural-pattern theme. Dargan, for example, was considered by the board to be overqualified and too cosmopolitan, though his goal-attainment qualifications were acknowledged. Hage-

---

**Source:* A. Peshkin, "Whom Shall the Schools Serve? Some Dilemmas of Local Control in a Rural School District," *Curriculum Inquiry,* 6(3), 186–188. Copyright 1977. Reprinted by permission.

dorn, despite goal-attainment qualifications, just did not "look right" to the board. He did not fit their image of a good superintendent. Morgan and Rogers are rejected for similar reasons. As Peshkin (1977) notes, "Perhaps it should have been self-evident that no one could be chosen Superintendent of Schools in Mansfield who did not appear 'country,' the board's short-hand term to describe a person who would be suitable for their rural dominated, traditionally oriented school" (p. 188). Vitano was the candidate who best fit Mansfield's cultural pattern.

Adapting to External Environment

A third area of critical responsibility for school administration reflects the need for schools and communities to adapt to their external environments. Communities change and schools change with them. The advance of technology and the evolution of political processes place enormous pressures on schools. Coping with environmental demands for change as a result of declining enrollments, for example, has required substantial changes in finance formulas, personnel policies, organizational structures, facility usages, district boundary lines, teacher-association–board contracts, and educational-program designs. The challenge for school administrators and boards is to adapt externally in a fashion that preserves some sense of internal identity, continuity, and balance. A growing literature deals with adaptation problems of schools from the perspectives of politics and public policy, the sociology and politics of innovation, and the social psychology of change.

Maintaining Internal Integration

Maintaining internal maintenance requires the coordination and unification of units, departments, and schools into a single entity. Psychologically, internal maintenance refers to the building of a sense of identity and loyalty to the school among teachers and students and providing them with a sense of satisfaction and well-being in return. Some theorists have defined administrative effectiveness around the internal-maintenance theme by suggesting that effectiveness is the integration of individual and organizational needs; indeed, this social-systems theme dominated the literature of educational administration during the 1950s and 1960s (e.g., Getzels, Lipham, & Campbell, 1968). More recently, studies of successful schools reveal the presence of a strong culture that bonds teachers to a common purpose and provides them with increased opportunities for finding meaning in work (Sergiovanni, 1984). These schools are highly successful in tending to cultural patterns and the maintenance of internal integration.

Balancing Core Areas

Different schools and school districts can be expected to emphasize different patterns of core activities in response to their unique situational characteristics, but all four areas must be provided for to some degree by all schools and school districts. Following Parsons, Bales, and Shils (1953) and Deutsch (1963), Mills (1967) suggests that core-activity patterns under conditions of survival are different from those under conditions of growth. The *survival pattern* will look something like the following:*

1. Adaptation—*when external resources are cut off, the group must be able to find new ones; when current techniques become obsolete or ineffective, it must invent new ones.*
2. Goal attainment—*when blocks appear before the goal, it must be able to circumvent them; when members become confused or frustrated or distracted, it must be able to reorient them and remobilize their resources.*
3. Integration—*when one part of the group threatens to destroy other parts, the group must be able to check, protect, and coordinate them; it must bridge differences between the strong and the weak, the competent and the inept, the active and the passive, and so on; it must create concepts or symbols of itself as a collective unit that unites its sub-parts.*
4. Pattern-maintenance—*in the face of contrary pressures, the group must be able to sustain its standard procedures, reinforce members' feelings and affective relations, enforce its rules, confirm its beliefs and affirm its values; and it must, for example, be able to "remember" its customs from one meeting to the next. (Mills, 1967, p. 17)*

By contrast, the *growth pattern* will resemble the following:*

1. Adaptation
    a. *"An increase in openness—that is, an increase in the range, diversity, and effectiveness of [a group's] channels of intake of information from the outside world" (Deutsch, 1963, p. 140)*
    b. *Capacity to extend the scope of the group's contacts and obligations beyond current boundaries*
    c. *Capacity to alter the group's customs, rules, techniques, and so on, to accommodate new information and new contacts*
2. Goal attainment
    a. *Capacity to hold goal-seeking effort in abeyance while alternative goals are being considered*
    b. *Capacity to shift to, or add, new goals*
3. Integration
    a. *Capacity to differentiate into sub-parts while maintaining collective unity*
    b. *Capacity to export resources without becoming impoverished and to send emissaries without losing their loyalty*
4. Pattern-maintenance and extension
    a. *Capacity to receive new members and to transmit to them the group's culture and capabilities*
    b. *Capacity to formulate in permanent form the group's experience and*

---

*Both patterns are from Theodore M. Mills, *The Sociology of Small Groups.* © 1967, pp. 17, 21. Reprinted by permission of Prentice Hall, Inc., Englewood Cliffs, New Jersey.

learning and to convey them to other groups and to posterity (Mills, 1967, p. 21)

The problem becomes more complex with the realization that too much emphasis in one area can often jeopardize the other areas. For example, an overemphasis on internal maintenance may actually jeopardize goal attainment, and an overemphasis on external adaptation can often upset the maintenance of cultural patterns. In the first instance, consider a school that agrees to a policy of teacher supervision and evaluation that emphasizes the development of good human relationships and high morale (internal maintenance) at the expense of providing teachers with sufficient responsibility, evaluative feedback, and other performance incentives (goal attainment). A "happy teacher" emphasis does not in itself ensure high-quality teacher performance. (Adopting the inverse strategy is also problematic. Imagine a school with "effective" supervision and evaluation that destroys morale.) In the second instance, consider a school that responds to its perception of societal needs by implementing an educational program characterized by individualized instruction and an abundance of student alternatives (external adaption) but in so doing projects an image of permissiveness and anarchy to a community with a more traditional conception of schooling (maintaining community cultural patterns). Here, adapting to the perceived needs of society in general is at odds with the prevailing value system of the local community.

As even a brief study of educational administration will reveal, progress is slow and incremental. Administrative activity takes place within time constraints. Typically, administrators are not able to wait until everything is perfect before making or implementing decisions. Compromises are more the rule. Satisfactory solutions that are agreeable under current circumstances are accepted in favor of better or ideal solutions that are not possible at the moment. Each of the core activities that comprise critical administrative responsibilities are, therefore, better seen as having qualities of elasticity that enable stretching and contracting. By capitalizing on this elastic quality, administrators seek to balance one critical responsibility area against another without forcing one or neglecting another to the point where survival of the school is endangered.

Evaluating Administrators

The four critical responsibility areas to which school administrators are expected to respond provide the basis for their evaluation. Superintendents are evaluated by their school boards and communities based on perceptions of their performance in all four areas, though goal attainment is likely to be the public standard and other areas more implicitly considered. Superintendents evaluate principals similarly (Peterson, 1984). Principals, in turn, use the same general pattern to evaluate teachers (Cusick, 1983).

Principals, as an example, are presumed to be evaluated primarily on the basis of goal-attainment criteria. Much attention is given to educational goals and objectives they are expected to pursue and to evaluation designs attendant to the quality of teaching and learning and to student learning outcomes. The intent is to link what principals do to various dimensions of successful student learning and other goal-attainment indicators. Peterson (1984), however, finds that principals generally perceive goal attainment to be secondary to criteria that emerge from cultural patterns, maintaining internal integration, and the external environment. He notes, for example, that half of the 120 elementary principals studied believed that the central office relied heavily on the community and impressions of parents as sources of evaluation information (p. 592). Indeed, "public reaction, parents are happy, no complaints, and public relations" accounted for 207 of the items mentioned. By contrast, "student performance and progress: test scores, academic performance" and "instructional programs: innovation, good programs, instructional leadership" accounted for only 9 percent and 8 percent, respectively (Peterson, 1984, p. 593). The full array of evaluation criteria as perceived by principals is shown in Table 4.1. The fourth column in Table 4.1 indicates which of the critical responsibility areas are most associated with each criterion. The table suggests that goal attainment alone is too simplistic an indicator of what constitutes the typical school administrator's agenda.

Dimensions and Measures of School Effectiveness

The criteria used to evaluate administrators and the four critical responsibility areas to which they must attend suggests that despite simplistic definitions of school effectiveness that focus on student outcomes, many dimensions actually exist. Schools, for example, must not only attain teaching and learning goals but must do so efficiently and in a manner that keeps faculty morale high, order in the school, and peace in the community. In light of this reality, school measurement and evaluation experts and organizational sociologists who specialize in studying effectiveness in organizations concentrate on many dimensions as they conduct their studies and make their calculations (Goodman & Associates, 1977). Most experts agree that school effectiveness is multidimensional. Table 4.2 illustrates some of the criteria and measurements that are often used in determining how effective a school is. Note that only 7 of the 24 measures are classified as goal attainment (GA).

Critical Administrative Processes

Administration has been broadly defined as the process of working with and through others to accomplish organizational goals effectively and efficiently. This definition was supplemented by identifying four broad areas of administrative responsibility: maintaining the school's cultural pattern, goal attainment, internal maintenance of integration, and external adaptation. *Administration* can also be defined as a process of functions. *Planning, organizing, leading,* and *controlling* are

TABLE 4.1 Criteria Perceived to Be Important When Central Office Evaluates Principals

Criteria	Number of Times Category Mentioned by Respondents ($N = 360$)	Percentage of Respondents Listing Item ($N = 112$)	Percentage of All Items Mentioned	Critical Responsibility Areas
1. Public reaction: parents are happy, no complaints, public relations	72	64	30	CP, EA
2. Teacher reaction: good morale, no grievances, teacher-principal relations	54	48	15	II
3. Principal and teacher compliance to district rules and procedures; includes meeting attendance and paperwork	44	39	12	CP, II
4. Not making waves: smooth running, few problems taken to central office, keeping superintendent informed, not raising difficult questions	37	33	10	CP, EA, II
5. Student performance and progress: test scores, academic performance	31	28	9	GA
6. The instructional program: innovation, good programs, instructional leadership	29	26	8	GA
7. Overall school operation: includes atmosphere and climate	21	19	6	II
8. Relations with students, student compliance, and discipline	14	12	4	CP
9. Good working relations with central office	7	6	2	CP, EA
10. Miscellaneous 1: includes plant management, leadership style, peer relations	25	22	7	
11. Miscellaneous 2: all single items	26	23	7	
Critical responsibility areas:	Cultural patterns (CP) External adaptation (EA) Maintaining internal integration (II) Goal attainment (GA)			

Note: The critical responsibility areas are added to Peterson's table.

TABLE 4.2   Dimensions and Measures of School Effectiveness

Dimensions	Measures	Critical Responsibility Areas
1. *Productivity*	The extent to which students, teachers, groups, and schools accomplish outcomes or services intended.	GA
2. *Efficiency*	The ratio of individual and school performance to the costs involved for that performance. Costs are calculated not only in terms of time and dollars but in objectives or outcomes neglected so that other objectives or outcomes might be emphasized or accomplished.	II
3. *Quality*	The level and quality of accomplishments, outcomes, performance, and services of individuals and the school.	GA
4. *Growth*	Improvements in quality of offerings, responsiveness and innovativeness, talent, and general competence, when a school's present status is compared with its own past state.	GA
5. *Absenteeism*	The number of times not present and frequency of nonattendance by teachers, students, and other school workers.	II
6. *Turnover*	The number of voluntary transfers and terminations on the part of students, faculty, and other workers.	II
7. *Teacher job satisfaction*	The extent to which teachers are pleased with the various job outcomes they are receiving.	II
8. *Student satisfaction*	The extent to which students are pleased with the various schooling outcomes they are receiving.	II
9. *Motivation*	The willingness and drive strength of teachers, students, and other school workers as they engage in the work of the school.	II
10. *Morale*	The general good feeling that teachers, parents, students, and others have for the school, its traditions, and its goals and the extent to which they are happy to be a part of the school.	CP
11. *Cohesion*	The extent to which students and teachers like one another, work well together, communicate fully and openly, and coordinate their efforts.	CP
12. *Flexibility-adaptation*	The ability of the school to change its procedures and ways of operating in response to community and other environmental changes.	EA
13. *Planning and goal setting*	The degree to which the members plan future steps and engage in goal-setting behavior.	GA
14. *Goal consensus*	The extent to which community members, parents, and students agree that the same goals exist for the school.	CP

TABLE 4.2 *(Continued)*

Dimensions	Measures	Critical Responsibility Areas
15. *Internalization of organizational goals*	The acceptance of the school's goals and belief by parents, teachers, and students that the school's goals are right and proper.	CP
16. *Leadership-management skills*	The overall level of ability of principals, supervisors, and other leaders as they perform school-centered tasks.	GA
17. *Information management and communications*	The completeness, efficiency of dissemination, and accuracy of information considered critical to the school's effectiveness by all interested parties, including teachers, parents, and the community at large.	II
18. *Readiness*	The probability that the school could successfully perform some specified task or accomplish some specified goal if asked to do so.	EA
19. *Utilization of the environment*	The extent to which the school interacts successfully with its community and other arenas of its environment and acquires the necessary support and resources to function effectively.	EA
20. *Evaluation by external entities*	Favorable assessments of the school by individuals, organizations, and groups in the community and in the general environment within which it interacts.	EA
21. *Stability*	The ability of the school to maintain certain structures, functions, and resources over time and particularly during periods of stress.	CP
22. *Shared influence*	The degree to which individuals in the school participate in making decisions that affect them directly.	II
23. *Training and development emphasis*	The amount of effort and resources that the school devotes to developing the talents of teachers and other school workers.	GA
24. *Achievement emphasis*	The extent to which the school places a high value on achieving existing and new goals.	GA
Critical responsibility areas:	Cultural patterns (CP) External adaptation (EA) Internal integration (II) Goal attainment (GA)	

Source: Adapted from J. P. Campbell et al., *The Measurement of Organizational Effectiveness: A Review of Relevant Research and Opinion.* Final Report, Navy Personnel Research and Development Center Contract N00022-73-C-0023. (Minneapolis: Personnel Decisions, 1974), pp. 38–133.

the four functions most often mentioned by theorists (e.g., Gulick & Urwick, 1937; Koontz & O'Donnell, 1972; Sears, 1950).

Planning involves setting goals and objectives for the school and district and developing blueprints and strategies for their implementation. *Organizing* involves bringing together human, financial, and physical resources in the most effective way to accomplish goals. *Leading* has to do with guiding and supervising subordinates. Plans of organizations are implemented by people, and people need to be motivated, expectations need to be defined, and communication channels need to be maintained. *Controlling* refers to the administrator's evaluation functions and includes reviewing, regulating, and controlling performance, providing feedback, and otherwise tending to standards of goal attainment and internal-maintenance responsibilities of administration, with some attention to external adaptation. Maintaining the school's cultural-pattern responsibilities is typically neglected by those who write about administrative processes.

Critical Administrative Skills

Still another way in which administration can be examined is by identifying competencies and skill areas necessary for carrying out the processes of administration. Katz (1955) has identified three basic skills upon which, he feels, successful administration rests—technical, human, and conceptual.

Technical skill assumes an understanding of and proficiency in the methods, processes, procedures, and techniques of education. Noninstructional technical skills include specific knowledge in finance, accounting, scheduling, purchasing, construction, and maintenance. Technical skills are more important to administrative and supervisory roles lower in the school hierarchy. The department chairperson or grade-level supervisor, for example, needs far greater command of technical skills relating to teaching and learning in a particular field than does the principal. The business manager needs a more technical command of accounting procedures and computer uses than does the superintendent.

Human skill refers to the school administrator's ability to work effectively and efficiently with others on a one-to-one basis and in group settings. This skill requires considerable self-understanding and acceptance as well as appreciation, empathy, and consideration for others. Its knowledge base includes an understanding of and facility for leadership, adult motivation, attitudinal development, group dynamics, human needs, morale, conflict management, and the development of human resources. Human skills seem equally important to administrative and supervisory roles throughout the school hierarchy. Regardless of position, all administrators work through others; that is, they use human skills to achieve goals.

Conceptual skill includes the school administrator's ability to view the school, the district, and the educational program as a whole. This skill includes the effective mapping of interdependence for each of the components of the school as an organization, the educational program as an instructional system, and the functioning of the human organization. The development of conceptual skill relies heavily on a balanced emphasis of administrative theory, knowledge of organizational and human behavior, and educational philosophy. Conceptual skills are considered more important to roles further up the organizational hierarchy. The superintendent, for example, may not know much about the technical aspects of teaching youngsters with learning disabilities to read but must know how this piece of the puzzle fits and interacts with other aspects of operating the school district.

Figure 4.1 summarizes the dimensions of educational administration. The four critical responsibility areas are listed on the left margin, and the four critical processes on the bottom margin. Together, they form a 16-cell, two-dimensional grid for mapping administrative activity. The shaded area, which marks the intersection of maintaining cultural patterns with the controlling functions, might be illustrated by an administrator who is surveying community attitudes toward a particular school policy or program. The grid becomes three dimensional when the three critical administrative skills are added. In surveying community attitudes, for example, the administrator needs to know the technical rudiments of survey conducting and reporting. Human skills will be needed in obtaining public participation in the project and in resolving disputes that might be evident in the survey. Conceptually, the administrator needs to understand the implications of the intended and unintended consequences of the survey on educational program planning, the school's public relations program, and other factors. Additional

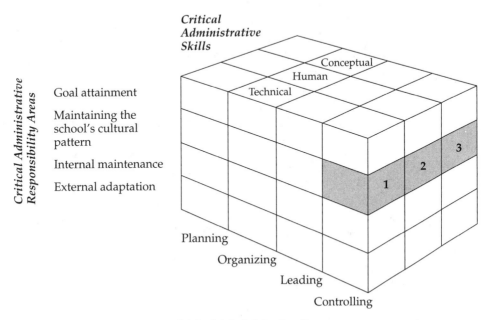

Critical Administrative Processes

FIGURE 4.1 Mapping Educational Administration

insights into the role and function of educational administrators—which highlight needed competencies, specific tasks, and descriptions of how administrators actually spend their time—are provided in later chapters.

Educational Administration as Educational Leadership

Before proceeding further, the important topic of educational leadership and its relationship to administration will be considered. It will become increasingly clear that administrative responsibilities are vast and encompass a variety of roles and an array of problems and issues—many of which seem not to be clearly or directly related to education.

Increasingly, for example, educational administrators are portrayed as managers. School boards and community publics demand sound fiscal management and expect the school to be run in a businesslike fashion. Indeed, such topics as cost-effectiveness, accountability, fiscal integrity, efficiency, wage administration, and personnel policy capture increasingly large shares of the headlines in education. Rivaling the manager image of education administration is that of politician. On the local scene, for example, communities are more diverse, expectations and demands for resources are more ambiguous and vocal, power and authority are more diffuse, and public participation in the affairs of the schools is more intense. At a broader level, the strengthened role of state education departments—through mandated legislation, the federal government, and the courts—and the shifts in school-funding patterns that afford greater responsibility to federal and state levels are further reinforcers of the politician image for educational administration.

Managerial, Political, and Educational Roles

Though many decry the emergence of managerial and political roles in educational administration, the inescapable realities of modern educational administration require that administrators understand and articulate these roles. But to borrow a metaphor from management, the "bottom line" for educational administrators remains *educational leadership*. Management roles, therefore, though critically important, are not central. Indeed, they exist only to support and complement educational leadership roles.

By the same token, political roles are supplements to and supporters of educational governance roles. Both leadership and governance have qualities beyond what presently is; they suggest a vision of what is desirable and good and a determination to marshal organizational energy in this direction. Leaders and statespersons, however, cannot neglect managerial and political roles. Still, good management and good politics are not in themselves sufficient.

Perhaps the point can best be made by focusing in detail on the leadership aspects of educational administration and contrasting these with good management. Levitt (1976), for example, describes management as follows:

Management consists of the rational assessment of a situation and the systematic selection of goals and purposes (what is to be done?); the systematic development of strategies to achieve these goals; the marshalling of the required resources; the rational design, organization, direction, and control of the activities required to attain the selected purposes; and, finally, the motivating and rewarding of people to do the work. (p. 73)

The administrator as manager, according to this view, is concerned with such questions as, What should be accomplished? and How are best results achieved? Certainly these are important considerations in the effective operation of schools and school districts. But as Zaleznik (1977) points out, "It takes neither genius nor heroism to be a manager, but rather persistence, tough-mindedness, hard work, intelligence, analytical ability and, perhaps most important, tolerance and good will" (p. 68).

Educational leadership, by contrast, is a more expansive concept that includes concern for the worth of objectives and their impact on school and society. The administrator as manager suggests a utilitarian quality (What are the best means to achieve given ends?); educational leadership suggests a normative quality (How adequate are the ends themselves?). Beyond concern for the value of objectives and the overall mission of the school, leadership evokes a quality of living and attractiveness that moves individuals and organizations beyond the ordinary in their zeal, commitment, and work habits. As Zaleznik (1977) suggests, leaders

are active instead of reactive, shaping ideas instead of responding to them. Leaders adopt a personal and active attitude toward goals. The influence a leader exerts in altering moods, evoking images and expectations, and in establishing specific desires and objectives determines the direction. . . . The net result of this influence is to change the way people think about what is desirable, possible, and necessary. (p. 71)

In sum, and following Starratt (1990), it might be helpful to view the educational administrator as being an actor with two parts to play. Each of the parts, educational leader and manager, comes with its own and very different script. When following the managerial script, the professional administrator is concerned with instrumental and process matters articulated in accordance with the values of bureaucracy:

(a) Students and teachers should be treated uniformly; (b) policies and rules are applied uniformly for all specific instances; (c) because of scarce resources, the school must get the most for every dollar by concentrating on efficiency; (d) the school-wide results are what counts (improving test scores, lowering overall truancy and vandalism, achieving overall budgetary balance); (e) in order to assess overall results, there is a need for maintaining extensive records and information banks and reports; (f) loyalty to the school, rather than to individuals or groups is

important; (g) one's sense of authority derives from the wider governing body, and is based on the organization's charter and by-laws. (p. 47)

When following the educational leader script, by contrast, the professional administrator is concerned with matters of purpose and substance, and with struggling to identify the right thing to do. The administrator strives to bring to the forefront the kind of rationality that is based on what makes sense educationally and what is morally right. It makes sense, for example, to treat teachers and students differently, to provide teachers with discretion so that they are able to make informed decisions in light of the situations that they face, and so on. Though some overlap exists, for the most part, the two scripts are antithetical. As with the actor, sometimes the professional administrator is able to bring the scripts into harmony. At other times, they tug at each other and often one becomes dominant.

Qualitative Aspects of Leadership

Having established that educational leadership requires good management but that good management is not sufficient, the nature of leadership will now be examined more closely. Starratt (1977), for example, suggests that, in addition to management skill, the leader brings to her or his work extra qualities of vision, intensity, and creativity. Leaders are concerned with a vision of what is possible and desirable for them and others to achieve and a vision of the significance of what they are presently doing. The leader engages in organizational activities with great energy and brings to the job an intensity of desire, commitment, and enthusiasm that sets him or her apart from others. The leader brings to the organization and its work a certain freshness of thought, a commitment to new ideas, and a belief in creativity change. Concentrating on the qualities of vision, intensity, and creativity, Starratt (1977) believes that leaders can be distinguished from others as follows:

1. *Leaders work beneath the surface of events and activities, seeking a deeper meaning and deeper value. They are able to identify the roots of meaning in the ebb and flow of daily life in schools and, as a result, to provide students, teachers, and community members with a sense of importance, vision, and purpose above the seemingly ordinary and mundane.*
2. *Leaders bring to the school a sense of drama in human life that permits one to surface above the dulling routine which often characterizes day-by-day activity. They see the significance of what a group is doing and could be doing. They have a feel for the more dramatic possibilities inherent in most situations and are able to urge people to go beyond the routine, to break out of the mold into something more lively and vibrant.*
3. *Leaders are able to communicate their sense of vision by words and examples. They use language and symbols which are easily understood but which also communicate a sense of excitement, originality, and freshness.*

4. *Leaders provide opportunities for others to experience their vision and sense of purpose so that others come to share in their ownership.*
5. *Leaders are able to transform their vision, intensity, and creativity from idiosyncratic or personal meanings into goals, structures, and processes for the school. Ideas become programs, visions become goals, and senses of commitment from others become operating structures. Indeed the leader translates qualities of leadership into characteristics of the school as an organization.* (p. 5)

Bennis (1984) finds that compelling vision is the key ingredient of leadership among heads of highly successful organizations he studied. *Vision* refers to the capacity to create and communicate a view of the desired state of affairs that induces commitment among those working in the organization. Vision becomes the substance of what is communicated as symbolic aspects of leadership are emphasized. Lieberman and Miller (1984) refer to this as the power of "moral authority." The school administrator makes symbolic statements by his or her actions, statements, and deeds. In describing this power from case-study notes involving a student discrimination incident, they state:

Principals can maintain neutrality and let things progress as they always have; even that is a moral statement. Or they may take an active stance, threatening the assumptions of staff members and moving the school in more progressive or more regressive directions. Principals condone or condemn certain behaviors and attitudes; they model moral precepts as they go about their job. When the administrators at Albion took the side of minority students in the lunchroom radio incident, they gave a clear message to faculty that discrimination by race was not to be tolerated. A powerful message was transmitted. Had there been administrative apathy, an equally powerful point would have been made. (p. 76)

Principals and other school administrators are cast into powerful symbolic roles whether they intend it or not and whether they like it or not. Taking no action, in certain circumstances, can be as powerful a symbolic statement as taking any action.

Bennis (1984, p. 64) and Bennis and Nanus (1985, p. 17) view leadership as a form of power that represents one's capacity to translate intention into reality and sustain it. This is the idea of transformative leadership described in Burns's seminal *Leadership* (1978). This is also what Follett (1941) had in mind when she wrote, "The most successful leader of all is one who sees another picture not yet actualized. He sees the things which belong in his present picture, but which are not yet there.... Above all, he should make his co-workers see that it is not *his* purpose which is to be achieved, but a common purpose, born of the desires and activities of the group" (pp. 143–144).

Studies of leadership in highly successful and effective schools provides support for the importance of vision and other qualitative aspects of leadership. The work of Edmonds (1979) and of Brookover and Lezotte (1979) reveals that effective

schools are characterized by high agreement among staff regarding goals and purposes and a clear sense of mission. Similarly, studies by Bossert and colleagues
(1982) and Greenfield (1982) reveal that goal orientation and the articulation and
modeling of school purposes by principals are important characteristics. The
research of Blumberg and Greenfield (1980) reveals that effective principals show
active and direct behaviors at building and articulating a vision of what the school
is. Lipsitz (1984), in her case studies of successful middle schools, observes:

> *The schools made powerful statements both in word and in practice, about their
> purposes. There is little disagreement within them and little discrepancy between
> what they say they are doing and what they are actually doing. As a result every-
> one can articulate what the school stands for. . . .*
>
> *Each of the four schools has or had a principal with a driving vision who
> imbues decisions and practices with meaning, placing powerful emphasis on why
> things are done as well as how. Decisions are not made just because they are prac-
> tical but for reasons of principle. (pp. 172, 174)*

In sum, leaders are able to grasp the deeper meaning and value of seemingly
common events, translate these into a dramatic sense of purpose and vision, con-
vincingly communicate both meaning and purpose to others, obtain their commitment and sense of partnership, and articulate these qualities into organizational
goals, structures, and programs (Sergiovanni, 1990). Managerial skills remain
important, for once programs are identified, they need to be effectively and efficiently articulated.

The Substance of Leadership in Education

Some qualities of leadership are universal to all types of organizations. Hospital,
business, military, governmental, and educational administrator-leaders, for
example, bring to their respective organizations common qualities of vision, intensity, and creativity. The substantive aspects of leadership, on the other hand, have
to do with the unique and central context of the work of a particular organization.
Educational program, curriculum and instruction, teaching and learning, and
supervision and evaluation are the central concerns of schools, and these comprise
the substance of educational leadership.

One problem with recent trends toward pressuring educational administrators to assume more managerial and political roles is that these have become central, displacing educational roles. Goodlad (1978) describes this problem as
follows:

> *Recent years have been harrowing ones for school administrators. We have yielded
> to the pressures and temptations of becoming experts in fiscal and personnel man-
> agement, public relations, collective bargaining, and the political process. Few of
> us are trained or experienced in any of these, even though we must take responsi-
> bility for them. . . . It is now time to put the right things at the center again. And*

the right things have to do with assuring comprehensive, quality educational programs in each and every school under our jurisdiction. (p. 322)

Continuing, Goodlad (1978) feels that serious steps need to be taken to reverse this trend.

One step is to check our present perspectives regarding what is central to our work. If, in so doing, we conclude that collective bargaining, balancing the budget, and informing the public are central, something has gone amiss. These are the conditions surrounding, complicating and, perhaps, endangering our jobs. We ignore them at our peril; we would be well advised to attend special institutes or workshops so as to be thoroughly updated on the issues and our role in dealing with them. But to put these matters at the center, often for understandable reasons of survival and expediency, is to commit a fundamental error which, ultimately, will have a negative impact on both education and one's own career. Our work, for which we will be held accountable, is to maintain, justify, and articulate sound, comprehensive programs of instruction for children and youth. (p. 326)

Certainly Goodlad's arguments are persuasive, but keeping matters of educational program central to one's roles will not be easy. A first step is to make a commitment to educational leadership, viewing managerial and political roles as important to educational leadership but not as ends in themselves.

What can one expect from making a commitment to educational leadership? Some evidence exists that such a commitment is at the heart of noticeable differences between effective and ineffective educational administrators. In a study of effective and ineffective elementary school principals conducted by Goldhammer and associates (1971), principals of effective schools had the following characteristics in common:

1. *Most did not intend to become principals. Most indicated that they had intended to teach, but were encouraged to become principals by their superiors.*
2. *Most expressed a sincere faith in children. Children were not criticized for failing to learn or for having behavioral difficulties. The principals felt that these were problems that the school was established to correct; thus the administrators emphasized their responsibilities toward the solution of children's problems.*
3. *They had an ability to work effectively with people and to secure their cooperation. They were proud of their teachers and accepted them as professionally dedicated and competent people. They inspired confidence and developed enthusiasm. The principals used group processes effectively; listened well to parents, teachers, and pupils; and appeared to have intuitive skill and empathy for their associates.*
4. *They were aggressive in securing recognition of the needs of their schools. They frequently were critical of the restraints imposed by the central office and of the inadequate resources. They found it difficult to live within the con-*

> *straints of the bureaucracy; they frequently violated the chain of command, seeking relief of their problems from whatever sources that were potentially useful.*
> 5. *They were enthusiastic as principals and accepted their responsibilities as a mission rather than as a job. They recognized their role in current social problems. The ambiguities that surrounded them and their work were of less significance than the goals they felt were important to achieve. As a result, they found it possible to live with the ambiguities of their position.*
> 6. *They were committed to education and could distinguish between long-term and short-term educational goals. Consequently, they had established philosophies of the role of education and their relationship within it.*
> 7. *They were adaptable. If they discovered something was not working, they could make the necessary shifts and embark with some security on new paths.*
> 8. *They were able strategists. They could identify their objectives and plan means to achieve them. They expressed concern for the identification of the most appropriate procedures through which change could be secured. (p. 233)*

These characteristics suggest that effective principals were certainly concerned with good management and politics, but clearly, educational leadership was their paramount concern. This observation is supported by numerous studies of effective and successful schools. A fundamental assumption underlying this book is that managerial and political roles, no matter how important, must be judged on the basis of how they serve educational-leadership aspirations of administration. Indeed, this is the yardstick by which one assesses the usefulness and appropriateness of further administrative study in such areas of law, finance, facilities, politics, organizational behavior, and other topics.

References

Appleby, P. H. (1949). *Policy and administration.* Tuscaloosa: University of Alabama Press.

Argyris, C. (1964). *Integrating the individual and the organization.* New York: John Wiley.

Bennis, W. (1984). Transformative power and leadership. In T. J. Sergiovanni & J. E. Corbally (Eds.), *Leadership and organizational culture* (pp. 64–71). Urbana: University of Illinois Press.

Bennis, W., & Nanus, B. (1985). *Leaders.* New York: Harper and Row.

Blumberg, A., & Greenfield, W. (1980). *The effective principal. Perspective on school leadership.* Boston: Allyn and Bacon.

Bossert, S. T., Dwyer, D., Rowan, B., & Lee, G. (1982). The instructional management role of the principal. *Educational Administration Quarterly, 3*(18), 34–64.

Brookover, W. B., & Lezotte, L. W. (1979). *Changes in school characteristics coincident with changes in school achievement.* East Lansing, MI: Institute for Research on Teaching, Michigan State University.

Burns, J. M. (1978). *Leadership.* New York: Harper and Row.

Cusick, P. A. (1983). *The egalitarian ideal and the American high school.* New York: Longman.

Deutsch, K. W. (1963). *The nerves of government.* New York: The Free Press of Glencoe.

Edmonds, R. (1979). Some schools work and more can. *Social Policy, 9*(2), 28–32.

Follett, M. P. (1941). *Dynamic administration.* New York: Harper and Row.

Getzels, J. W., Lipham, J., & Campbell, R. (1968). *Educational administration: A social process.* New York: Harper and Row.

Goldhammer, K., Becker, G., Withycombe, R., Doget, F., Miller, E., Morgan, C., DeLoretto, L., & Aldridge, B. (1978). *Elementary school principals and their schools.* Eugene, OR: University of Oregon, Center for the Advanced Study of Educational Administration.

Goodlad, J. I. (1978). Educational leadership: Toward the third era. *Educational Leadership, 35*(4), 319–323.

Goodman, P. S., & Associates. (1977). *New perspectives on organizational effectiveness.* San Francisco: Jossey-Bass.

Goodnow, F. J. (1900). *Politics and administration.* New York: Macmillan.

Goodnow, F. J. (1905*). The principles of administrative law in the United States.* New York: G. P. Putnam.

Greenfield, W. (1982). *A synopsis of research on school principals.* Washington, DC: National Institute of Education.

Gulick, L., & Urwick, L. (Eds.). (1937). *Papers on the science of administration.* New York: Institute for Public Administration.

Hemphill, J. K. (1958). Administration as problem-solving. In A. Halpin (Ed.), *Administrative theory in education.* Chicago: Midwest Administration Center, University of Chicago.

Katz, R. L. (1955). Skills of an effective administrator. *Harvard Business Review, 33*(1), 33–42.

Koontz, H., & O'Donnell, C. (1972). *Principles of management* (5th ed.). New York: McGraw-Hill.

Levitt, T. (1976, Summer). Management and the post industrial society. *The Public Interest.*

Lieberman, A., & Miller, L. (1984). *Teachers, their world and their work.* Arlington, VA: Association for Supervision and Curriculum Development.

Lipham, J. (1964). Leadership and administration. In National Society for the Study of Education yearbook, *Behavioral science and educational administration* (pp. 119–141). Chicago: University of Chicago Press.

Lipsitz, J. (1984*). Successful schools for young adoles-* cents. New Brunswick, NJ: Transaction Books.

Mills, T. M. (1967). The *sociology of small groups.* Englewood Cliffs, NJ: Prentice-Hall.

Parsons, T. (1951). *Toward a general theory of social action.* Cambridge, MA: Harvard University.

Parsons, T. (1960). *Structure and process in modern society.* Glencoe, IL: The Free Press.

Parsons, T., Bales, R. F., & Shils, E. A. (1953). *Working papers in the theory of action.* New York: The Free Press of Glencoe.

Peshkin, A. (1977). Whom shall the schools serve? Some dilemmas of local control in a rural school district. *Curriculum Inquiry, 6*(3), 181–204.

Peterson, K. D. (1984). Mechanisms of administrative control over managers in educational organizations. *Administration Science Quarterly, 29*(4), 573–597.

Rossiter, C. (Ed.). (1961). *The federalist papers: Alexander Hamilton, James Madison, and John Jay.* New York: New American Library.

Sears, J. B. (1950). *The nature of administrative process.* New York: McGraw-Hill.

Selznick, P. (1957). *Leadership in administration: A sociological interpretation.* Berkeley: University of California Press.

Sergiovanni, T. J. (1984). Leadership and excellence in schooling. *Educational Leadership, 45*(5), 4–13.

Sergiovanni, T. J. (1990). *Value-added leadership: How to get extraordinary performance in schools.* San Diego: Harcourt Brace Jovanovich.

Sergiovanni, T. J. (1996). *Leadership for the school house: How is it different? Why is it important?* San Francisco: Jossey-Bass.

Simon, H. A. (1945). *Administrative behavior: A study of decision making processes in administrative organizations.* New York: The Free Press.

Starratt, R. J. (1977, June). *Apostolic leadership.* Jesuit Commission on Research and Development Workshop, San Jose, CA.

Starratt, R. J. (1990). *The drama of schooling, the schooling of drama.* Bristol, PA: Falmer Press.

Tead, O. (1951). *The art of administration.* New York: McGraw-Hill.

Wilson, W. (1887). The study of administration. *Political Science Quarterly, 2.*

Zaleznick, A. (1977). Managers and leaders: Are they different? *Harvard Business Review, 55*(3).

Chapter 5

Educational Administration as an Emerging Profession

The virtues of creating a strong and admired profession of school administration are spoken widely and loudly by both the academic and professional administration communities. Suggestions otherwise are considered heresy. As a result, no serious conversation exists within educational administration that addresses the unanticipated negative consequences. One reason for this silence is that the present leadership of our schools has the most to gain by pushing for increased professionalism. Thus, this leadership is likely to resist considering other possibilities, and is more likely to gloss over unanticipated problems associated with professionalism. Professors of educational administration, for example, have a vested interest in what has been taught and written over the years. Practicing administrators, too, have vested interests themed to power and job security that might be threatened if professionalism was slowed down or if its direction changed.

Professionalism in educational administration is an issue worth discussing critically (Sergiovanni, 1991). Nearly everyone agrees, for example, that some special preparation is needed for school administrators, but the question of how much is not as easily resolved. For example, will increases in professional preparation and standards for admission and training further divide teachers and administrators? Is too much specialized professional preparation a threat to democratic authority? Will increased professionalism restrict access of women and minorities to positions in educational administration? What is the long-term effect on teacher professionalism as the professionalization of educational administration increases? Could it be, for example, that increased professionalization of administrative roles is a form of hidden hierarchy that further subordinates teacher roles? If more and better study in educational administration is desirable, what specifically should be studied? Does a common knowledge base exist? If so, whose interests does it serve?

Before putting these issues squarely on the table for discussion, it will be helpful to back up and examine the events that have led to today's situation.

Background

Educational administration has a short history. Only since World War II has it shown signs of establishing itself as a fully organized and distinct profession. Though much groundwork was done during the early decades of the twentieth century in building a "science" of education and administration, the years 1946 and 1947 are considered critical. During this period, the American Association of School Administrators (AASA) received a report from its planning committee urging a long-range commitment to the professionalization of educational administrators. This committee recommended that AASA work to improve preparation programs in administration at colleges and universities, to encourage school boards to develop more adequate standards for the selection of superintendents, and to become more active as an organization in the general professional affairs of education. The 1947 annual AASA conference was characterized by initial planning for the formation of the National Conference of Professors of Education Administration (NCPEA). Its members, professors, and others involved in the preparation of administrators at colleges and universities, met that summer in Endicott, New York, and produced a landmark report titled *Educational Leaders: Their Functions and Preparation.*

Three years later, the emerging profession of educational administration received an important boost—the development of the Cooperative Program in Education Administration (CPEA). Founded as a result of a Kellogg Foundation grant and of planning by the AASA, the National Association of Rural Superintendents, and the Council of Chief State School Officers, CPEA resulted in the establishment, by 1951, of regional centers at eight American universities (University of Oregon, Stanford University, University of Texas, University of Chicago, Ohio State University, George Peabody College for Teachers, Columbia University, and Harvard University). An account of CPEA activities can be found in Moore (1947). The purposes of these centers were:

1. *to improve preparation programs for preservice training of potential administrators and in-service training of administrators already in the field.*
2. *to develop greater sensitivity to large social problems through an interdisciplinary approach involving most of the social sciences.*
3. *to disseminate research findings to practicing administrators.*
4. *to discover new knowledge about education and about administration.*
5. *to develop a continuing pattern of cooperation and communication among various universities and colleges within a region and between these institutions and other organizations and agencies working in the field of educational administration. (Kellogg Foundation, 1961, p. 13)*

A significant outgrowth of CPEA activity was the establishment in 1956 of the University Council for Educational Administration (UCEA). The initial membership nucleus consisted of 33 major universities with doctoral-level preparation programs in educational administration. The purposes of UCEA were to improve the preservice and in-service education of school administrators, stimulate and conduct research, encourage innovation through development projects, and disseminate materials growing out of research and development activities. Originally located at Teachers College, Columbia University, UCEA moved its headquarters staff to Ohio State University in 1959, to Arizona State University in 1984, to Pennsylvania State University in 1992, and to the University of Missouri in 1996, where it remains today with a membership of 54 universities.

The UCEA had a significant effect on building an identity among professors of educational administration and on improving their training. Further accomplishments included beginning the task of developing a knowledge base in the social and management sciences for preparing administrators. The UCEA has also served as a public forum on behalf of the academic community in influencing federal and state policy decisions relating to educational administration. Other landmark developments during this formative period were the publication in 1964, by the National Society for the Study of Education, of a yearbook devoted to the relationship of the behavioral sciences to educational administration (Griffiths, 1964) and the establishment of the Center for the Advanced Study of Educational Administration (CASEA) in 1964 at the University of Oregon. In recent years, the UCEA has been a leader in working for equity in educational administration, particularly with respect to women. During the 1980s, the organization took the lead in pushing for reform in the preparation of educational administration and in standards for admission and reestablished itself as a leader in developing the knowledge base of the profession through a series of annual conferences begun in 1987. This latter theme, as will be discussed later in this chapter, remains prominent today.

In 1968, the AASA established the National Academy for School Executives (NASE). Modeled after similar advanced in-service arms of other professions, the academy offers intensive workshops, seminars, and other activities designed to keep superintendents in touch with current developments and issues and up to date in current concepts and skills. Activities of the academy are highly regarded, as evidenced by wide attendance, expanding programs, and the awarding of academic credits by several universities to administrators who participate in academic programs.

During the 1970s and 1980s, preparation programs for school administrators were under increased scrutiny by licensing agents of state departments of education and by universities. This was a period of restlessness within the profession and of dissatisfaction by policymakers and others on the outside. Calls for reform were common. Some policy experts doubted whether the school administration establishment has either the will or the ability to initiate needed changes. Peterson and Finn (1985), for example, state:

It may be that piecemeal reform is simply inadequate to the task of overhauling the training, licensure, and professional standards of school administrators. It may also be that the profession lacks the fortitude or the perspective for a thoroughgoing, self-induced overhaul. Perhaps governors, business leaders, and blue ribbon commissions will need to bring school administration under the kind of intense scrutiny that they have applied to school teaching. Maybe one state needs to burst from the pack with a radically different model of training, licensure, selection, evaluation, and recruitment into this field. Perhaps the universities need a modern day Flexner to map their route through a systematic—and system wide—reformulation of the precepts and practices of administrator training. (p. 62)

During the sixties and seventies, university preparation programs for school administrators emphasized the curious blend of administrative and organizational theory on the one hand and management technicalities on the other. This resulted in a curriculum that in some ways was more academic than professional, as it mimicked the basic social science disciplines, and in other ways resembled vocational curriculum with emphasis on the nuts and bolts of buildings, bonds, and budgets. Far less emphasis was given to schooling as an institution, to its philosophical, social, and historical basis, and to the knowledge and skills needed for administrators to function as leaders able to enhance teaching and learning. As Peterson and Finn (1985) point out:

The required courses in such programs—closely tracking those spelled out in state certification requirements—commonly emphasized building management rather than instructional leadership, paying far closer attention to such subjects as school law and school finance (sometimes even to such minutiae as "facilities and transportation" or "scheduling") than to understanding what makes good teaching, what constitutes an outstanding history textbook, or how to determine whether a youngster is learning up to the level of his ability. (p. 62)

These analysts refer to a study by James Guthrie and associates (Peterson & Finn, 1985) that concluded, after examination of programs approved by the California State Education Department, that they "give great attention to human relations and public relations courses and skills" (p. 50). Recognizing that these techniques may be worth pursuing, the Guthrie study concludes that "the knowledge and skills needed to become an effective educational leader and school manager are generally not those provided" (Peterson & Finn, 1985, p. 50).

In 1978, Lawrence A. Cremin, then president of Teachers College, Columbia University, urged that the preparation and dissertation for professional educators not mimic that required for the Ph.D. in traditional academic areas. Among his many recommendations was that professional studies include a well-organized and closely supervised clinical or apprentice experience and that the dissertation be much more professional in its focus and orientation.

The problem of piecemeal part-time study at the doctoral level has been addressed by a few smaller "established" universities and by a handful of "innovative" universities. In 1974, for example, Jesuit-run Seattle University developed a doctoral program in educational leadership that featured identifiable cohorts who studied together on the university campus over a period of three years by engaging in intensive weekend and summer sessions. Nova Southeastern University of Fort Lauderdale, Florida, introduced its now famous external doctoral program that featured identifiable groups, or "clusters," of students who studied together in intensive sessions for fixed periods (weekends and summers). Nova awarded more than 1,300 doctorates between 1972 and 1979 (*Kappan* editors, 1979, p. 565). Nova has continued this productivity pace over the years and today is a leader in the number of educational administration doctorates awarded. Current active enrollment is about 1,000 students, with over 30 percent being students of color. Since 1989, 730 students have graduated from Nova's doctoral program, with 22 percent of these being students of color.

In many respects, these programs resembled the pattern of study provided for experienced executives seeking MBA degrees in business schools throughout the country. The University of Chicago, Northwestern University, and other prestigious schools feature executive programs that do not require traditional full-time study, and this pattern has become accepted throughout the business schools of the country. Though considered odd, and even criticized a few years ago, the part-time intensive study designs of innovators such as Seattle University and Nova Southeastern University are now being used by such established institutions as Teachers College, Columbia University, Texas A&M University, and the University of Illinois at Urbana-Champaign. Further, doctoral programs are becoming more clinically focused—emphasizing the everyday problems of schools and school leadership as opposed to extensive academic study in the various social science disciplines. Greater emphasis is also given to ethical issues and to developing a critical stance consistent with democratic norms and traditions. This is true not only for the universities experimenting with new time frames for study but for others as well (e.g., Miami University, Oxford Ohio, Vanderbilt University, Fordham University, and Texas A&M University).

In discussions of school administration programs, most of the emphasis is given to study at the doctoral level. This is curious since the vast majority of students who become certified to practice study at the master's level. Further, they typically study part time. With this reality in mind, many universities are seeking to strengthen master's-level programs by requiring cohort study within a fixed and compact time frame and by offering programs that focus on the problems of school practice (e.g., Stanford University and Trinity University).

Stirrings of change can also be heard from professional organizations such as the AASA and academic organizations such as the UCEA. In 1983, the AASA issued *Guidelines for the Preparation of School Administration*, which called for school administration training to encompass seven critical knowledge and skill areas: "School climate and how to improve it, critical theory and how to apply it, the curriculum and how to construct it, 'instructional management systems' and how to run them, staff members and how to evaluate them, school resources and how to allocate them, educational research and how to utilize it" (Peterson & Finn, 1985, p. 55). In 1985, the executive committee of UCEA passed a resolution to establish the National Committee on Excellence in Educational Administration, charged with studying and making recommendations concerning the preparation of school administrators for the future (discussed in the next section).

AASA, with approximately 20,000 members, remains the most influential professional organization for administrators. Superintendents dominate this organization. Though principals and other administrators are not excluded, they typically identify with more specialized professional groups such as the National Association of Secondary School Principals (NASSP), the National Elementary School Principals Association (NESPA), the Association of School Business Officials (ASBO), and similar organizations for supervisors, personnel administrators, and others.

Unlike teachers, who are bound together in the over 2-million-member National Education Association (NEA) or the smaller but influential American Federation of Teachers (AFT), educational administrators lack a strong national voice and strong rallying organization. Changes can be expected in this situation as administrators feel the need to maintain a strong, unified, professional interest in the face of increased concentration of power over education at the state and federal levels, and of increased influence of teachers on school boards at the local level. This is now occurring in many states, with the development of all-inclusive administrative organizations (e.g., the Association of California School Administrators and the Colorado Association of School Executives). In recent years, the Association for Supervision and Curriculum Development (ASCD) has grown to an organization of approximately 180,000 members by appealing to all to join together around a common interest—improved teaching and learning and better schooling. Perhaps their success is a harbinger of further efforts to unite not only administration but all educational professionals in a common cause.

During the last 10 years, the UCEA has increased its efforts to become a community of scholars committed to building up the knowledge base of educational administration and to be a potent voice in the reform of the profession. Under the leadership of executive director Patrick Forsyth, the organization has been in the forefront of women's rights, has commissioned a number of policy studies on the future of educational administration, and has rededicated itself to scholarly inquiry focusing much more on the problems of schooling, thus correcting its historically unbalanced emphasis on the social science disciplines. The University of Michigan, Auburn University, and the University of Illinois, 3 of the original 33 members who left the UCEA, rejoined the council. Though losing such prestigious members as Stanford, Harvard, and Chicago points in one direction, the return of those 3 and the addition of such newcomers as Boston, Buffalo, Cincinnati, Fordham, Hofstra, Illinois State, Northern Illinois, Toledo, and Miami of Ohio adds fresh perspectives and new energies on behalf of the council's agenda.

Recent Pressures to Reform

Since the publication of *A Nation at Risk* in 1983 (National Commission on Excellence in Education), dozens of reports from blue-ribbon committees have appeared, seeking to reform teaching and schooling. The reports of the Carnegie task force on teaching as a profession (Carnegie Forum, 1986) and of a group of about 100 leading research-oriented universities that comprise the Holmes Group were particularly influential. They recommended radically restructuring the way that teachers are prepared and licensed. Instead of relying on mandates and inducements as policy instruments to bring about change, Carnegie and Holmes based their recommendations on building up the capacities of teachers to function more effectively on the one hand and on changing the structure of the profession itself on the other (McDonnell & Elmore, 1987). The Carnegie task force worked to establish a national board for professional standards that would "board certify" teachers. Board certification is strictly voluntary. The board issued a report, *Toward High and Rigorous Standards for the Teaching Profession,* which sketched out its initial policies and perspectives in 1989. The Holmes Group agenda included requiring five years of university study to qualify as a teacher (Holmes Group, 1986). During the first four years, the prospective teacher would study in the liberal arts; the fifth year would include intensive clinically focused study in a Professional Development School (Holmes Group, 1990). The Holmes plan loosely follows the general pattern now in place for medical doctors.

In both cases, the reforms were successful in strengthening the general and professional education of teachers. Better preparation, the reformers reasoned, would increase the teacher's professional standing in society. As this standing increased, states, school boards, and the general public would grant more autonomy to teachers. The emphasis would shift from regulating what teachers do to what results schools are getting. The reformers were confident that increased and better preparation combined with on-the-job autonomy would result in better teaching and learning.

For the most part, the reforms of the early and mid-1980s were silent on the preparation of educational administrators. Teachers got all the attention. Moves to increase the professionalization of teaching have the potential to threaten the standing of the educational administration establishment. The creation of a national board for teachers, for example, raised more than a few anxious eyebrows. Not to be outdone, in 1986, the UCEA created the National Commission on Excellence in Educational Administration. The commission was funded by a number of foundations, including Danforth, Ford, and MacArthur, and included among its 27 commissioners then Arkansas governor Bill Clinton, Atlanta superintendent Alonzo Crim, California State University system chancellor W. Anne Reynolds, and Michigan State education dean Judy Lanier. Albert Shanker, the president of the American Federation of Teachers, was also a member. Of the 27 commissioners, 12 represented the academic educational administrator community, 3 were school superintendents, 4 represented professional associations for school administrators, and among the 8 others, only Shanker represented teachers. The commission was chaired by Daniel E. Griffiths, a highly respected professor of educational administration and former dean of education at New York University.

The commission issued a 60-page report, *Leaders for Tomorrow's Schools*, in March of 1987. The report called for sweeping changes in the recruitment, preparation, regulation, and evaluation of school administrators. According to Griffiths (*UCEA Review*, 1987):

> *This commission was asked to examine the quality of educational leadership in this country and I must say that our research reveals troubling aspects through the field including: lack of definition of good educational leadership; lack of leadership recruitment programs in the schools; lack of collaboration between school districts and universities; the discouraging lack of minorities and women in the field; lack of professional development for school administrators; lack of quality candidates for preparation programs; lack of preparation programs relevant to the job demands of school administrators; lack of sequence, modern content, and clinical experiences in preparing administrators; lack of licensure systems which promote excellence; and lack of a national sense of cooperation in preparing school leaders. (p. 1)*

The eight major recommendations of the commission were:

1. *Educational leadership should be redefined.*
2. *A national policy board on educational administration should be established.*
3. *Administrative preparation programs should be modeled on those in professional schools.*
4. *At least 300 universities and colleges should cease preparing educational administrators.*
5. *Programs for recruitment and placement of ethnic minorities and women should be initiated by universities, school boards, state and federal governments, and business and industry.*
6. *The public schools should become full partners in the preparation of school administrators.*
7. *Professional development activities should be an integral component of the careers of professors and practicing administrators.*
8. *Licensure programs should be substantially reformed.* (UCEA Review, 1987, p. 1)

The report was greeted with enthusiasm by the educational administration establishment though murmurs of dissent could also be heard. Commissioners Shanker and Lanier refused to endorse the report, claiming it did not go far enough in recommending the restructuring of the roles of school administrators and teachers and of how schools should be organized and operated.

Some academics were concerned that the report merely repackaged traditional conceptions of administrators in a way that repositioned the educational administration establishment to ensure its survival in the light of new pressures. Gibboney's (1987) views reflect some of these reservations:

How can it [the report] speak seriously about reform when it resurrects and builds on the same trivial courses in management and administration that have been taught for several decades? . . . The commission . . . reveals its management obsession—for example in the concern for "skills." The word "skills" abounds in the report, while the word "idea" as an energizing force in leadership is barely apparent. The commission urges districts to set up "assessment centers" that would identify and improve the skills of potential school principals and practicing administrators. Why not, I wonder, have idea-assessment centers as well? . . . It is no accident that such questions do not arise in reform talk cast in the image of good management, because managerial skills, by their very nature, cannot deal with issues of educational substance. (p. 28)

Gibboney believes that the report emphasizes managerial processes and skills in the preparation of school administrators at the expense of educational purposes and substance.

As a result of the commission's recommendations, in 1988, the UCEA took the lead in establishing the National Policy Board for Educational Administration (NPBEA). David Clark, another well-known professor of educational administration and former education dean at Indiana University, was its first executive director. Member organizations included the American Association of Colleges of Teacher Education, the American Association of School Administrators, the Association for Supervision and Curriculum Development, the Council of Chief State School Officers, the National Association of Secondary School Principals, the National Conference of Professors of Educational Administration, the National School Boards Association, and the UCEA. The Danforth Foundation joined the sponsoring organizations in providing funding.

In 1989, the NPBEA issued a report titled *Improving the Preparation of School Administrators: Agenda for Reform* that detailed existing shortcomings in the preparation of school administrators and provided a bold blueprint for change. *Agenda for Reform* recommended that preparation programs follow a professional studies model rather than one that either mimics the academic disciplines or resembles a series of ad hoc and disconnected staff-development workshops. An executive summary of their recommendations appears in Exhibit 5.1.

A number of commission recommendations sparked considerable controversy. Requiring a core educational administration faculty of at least five persons, eliminating study at the master's-degree level completely, requiring that the doctorate in educational administration be a prerequisite for national certification, and requiring state licensing for line administrators, for example, would very likely result in the closing of several hundred administrative preparation programs. Small liberal arts colleges and universities would be particularly affected, as would many state university colleges. In all, the report was not viewed as being practical enough to accommodate to the realities that face educational administration students as they study and to the political realities of turf competition among colleges and universities.

EXHIBIT 5.1   Executive Summary: An Agenda for Reform

The National Policy Board for Educational Administration is committed to the improvement of educational leadership. This report specifies a nine-item agenda for improving the preparation of administrators who will lead our nation's elementary and secondary schools and school districts. These nine items are grouped into three categories of necessary change addressing people, programs, and assessment.

People
The National Policy Board advocates the improvement of preparation programs by modifying the quality, diversity, and numbers of people involved in those programs and specifically recommends that:

1. Vigorous recruitment strategies be mounted to attract
    • The brightest and most capable candidates, of diverse race, ethnicity, and sex.
    • A minority enrollment at least comparable to the region's minority public school enrollment.
2. Entrance standards to administrator preparation programs be dramatically raised to ensure that all candidates possess strong analytic ability, high administrative potential, and demonstrated success in teaching[1] including
    • Assessment of analytic ability and administrative aptitude by a standardized national test, with admission to preparation programs limited to individuals scoring in the top quartile.
    • Assessment of teaching excellence by state licensure, master's degree in teaching, and evidence of successful teaching in a classroom setting.
3. The quality of faculty in administrator preparation programs be ensured by
    • Strengthening faculty recruitment, selection, and staff development programs.
    • Maintaining a critical mass of at least five full-time faculty members.
    • Providing the bulk of teaching, advising, and mentoring through full-time faculty who have demonstrated success in teaching, clinical activities, and knowledge production in the field.
    • Ensuring a student-faculty ratio comparable to other graduate professional degree programs on campus.

Programs
The National Policy Board advocates strengthening the structure, duration, and content of the pre-service preparation of educational administrators and specifically recommends that:
4. The doctorate in educational administration (EdD) be a prerequisite to national certification and state licensure for full-time administrators who are in charge of a school or school system.[2]
    • Sixth year or specialist degree programs in educational administration be abolished for this level of position.
    • Programs in educational administration terminating in a master's degree be abolished altogether.
5. One full-time year of academic residency and one full-time year of field residency be included in the EdD preparation program. Modifications in the type or duration of the clinical residency are permitted for candidates with full-time administrative experience in education. Additional appropriate program requirements are to be determined by the faculty of the graduate school or graduate division in education at each institution.

(Continued)

EXHIBIT 5.1   *(Continued)*

6. The elements of the curriculum be developed to transmit a common core of knowledge and skills, grounded in the problems of practice, including
   • Societal and cultural influences on schooling.
   • Teaching and learning processes and school improvement.
   • Organizational theory.
   • Methodologies of organizational studies and policy analysis.
   • Leadership and management processes and functions.
   • Policy studies and politics of education.
   • Moral and ethical dimensions of schooling.
7. Long term, formal relationships be established between universities and school districts to create partnership sites for clinical study, field residency, and applied research.

Assessment

The National Policy Board advocates the development and implementation of quality assurance mechanisms and specifically recommends that:

8. A national professional standards board consisting primarily of practicing school administrators be established to develop and administer a national certification examination and that states be encouraged to require candidates for licensure to pass this examination.
9. National accreditation of administrator preparation programs be withheld unless the programs meet the standards specified in this report and that criteria for state accreditation and program approval include these standards.

Source: "Improving the Preparation of School Administrators: An Agenda for Reform," *UCEA Review,* 30(3), 1989, 3–9. Copyright 1989 by University Council for Educational Administration. Reprinted by permission.

[1]The teaching requirement should be considered optional in the case of the position of chief school business administrator.

[2]Although a chief school business administrator may be prepared in a doctoral program for educational administration, alternative routes to this specialization are appropriate including, for example, an MBA, a sub-doctoral program in education, or a joint education-business program.

In November of 1989, the National Policy Board for Educational Administration incorporated as an independent organization. Scott D. Thompson, former executive director of the NASSP, became the new executive secretary in January of 1990, replacing Clark. The board issued a new report, *The Preparation of School Administrators: A Statement of Purpose,* in March 1990. Though reiterating the knowledge base recommendations that appeared in the first report, this report softened its recommendations for full-time study, for eliminating the master's degree, and for a required critical mass of educational administration faculty. It provided for two levels of certification as follows: "An entry level certificate would require a master's degree in teaching or a content field, plus 30 semester hours in school leadership including clinical experiences, followed by an assessment of competence. The advanced level would require a doctorate which includes one academic year of full-time study and successful field experiences beyond the entry level certification requirements, followed by an assessment of competence" (NPBEA, 1990).

Since the appearance of the 1990 report, the UCEA, the NPBEA, and the various school administrator professional associations have been working together to change the emphasis in preparation programs for school administrators away from generic management concerns and away from a direct leadership by giving more emphasis to teaching and learning concerns and by advancing the view that school administrators should be leaders of leaders. Both changes reflect the progress that is being made in the professionalization of teaching.

The Dark Side of Professionalism

Americans tend to feel that the professionalization of anything makes it better. Beneath the glamour and material benefits associated with educational administration's achieving status as a recognized profession, however, are a number of possible unanticipated negative consequences for schools and communities. (This section closely follows Sergiovanni [1991].)

Emergent professions, for example, attempt to develop a definition, role, and function distinctly different from those of other occupations working in the same area, particularly those with lower organizational status. To do otherwise may endanger their claim to distinctiveness and special importance. Professionals, after all, are presumed to be experts in something that others are not. It is this expertness that gives them authority over others. Educational administrators as "experts are presumed to deliver their services to the limits of their competence, to respect the confidences granted them by their clients [teachers, parents, students], and not to misuse for their own benefit the special powers given them within the boundaries of their relationship. In return, clients are expected to accept the professional's authority in specific areas of expertise, to submit to the professional's ministrations. . . . In short, clients are expected to behave as though they accept and respect the professional's autonomy as an expert" (Fischer, 1990, p. 358). One could argue, however, that being an expert requires having a monopoly over specialized knowledge and skill.

If having a knowledge and skill monopoly is key, then for educational administrators to enjoy full status, their knowledge and skill monopoly needs to be different from that of teachers. Expertness as an educator may not do, since it is common to both teachers and administrators. In the past, educational administration has relied on management themes as it sought to build a distinctive knowledge monopoly. And, since administrators are hierarchically superior to teachers, one unanticipated consequence has been that managerial expertise became hierarchically superior to educational expertness. Such an arrangement has never been acceptable in medicine, law, or other more established professions and should not be acceptable in education.

One alternative to managerial expertness is to build the educational administrator's knowledge monopoly around interpersonal themes and leadership abilities. Intensive study would be required in organizational behavior, human relations, and similar topics. The purpose would be to beef up her or his psychological authority instead of or in combination with the bureaucratic authority. Doing so, however, may place process over substance, thus reinforcing the "managerial mystique" that seems now to be entrenched in the cultures of both corporate and schooling America. Zaleznik (1989) points out that "the managerial mystique is only tenuously tied to reality. As it evolved in practice, the mystique required managers to dedicate themselves to process, structures, roles, and indirect forms of communication and to ignore ideas, people, emotions, and direct talk" (p. 2).

To Haller and Strike (1986), building the educational administrator's expertness around interpersonal themes in an effort to bolster psychological authority raises serious ethical questions.

> *We find this an inadequate view of the administrative role. . . . Its first deficiency is that it makes administrative success depend on characteristics that tend to be both intangible and unalterable. One person's dynamic leader is another's tyrant. What one person sees as a democratic style, another will see as the generation of time-wasting committee work . . . our basic concern with this view, however, is that it makes the administrative role one of form, not content. Being a successful administrator depends not on the adequacy of one's view, not on the educational policies that one adopts and how reasonable they are, and not on how successful one is in communicating these reasons to others. Success depends on personality and style, or on carefully chosen ways for inducing others to contribute to the organization. It is not what one wants to do and why that is important; it is who one is and how one does things that counts. We find such a view offensive. It is incompatible with the values of autonomy, reason and democracy, which we see as among the central commitments of our society and our educational system. Of course educational administrators must be leaders, but let them lead by reason and persuasion, not by forces of personality. (p. 326)*

Walton (1969) provides three scenarios for building the knowledge base of educational administration: (1) a common profession of administrators and teachers with shared educational expertness as the authority, (2) a profession built on generic management skills, and (3) a policy-politics–based profession. In his words:*

> *1. The first of these arises from the assumption that the administrative function cannot be abstracted from the other functions of the educational organization. From this assumption it follows that the educational administrator must be a teacher, a scholar, or an educator. While he has administrative duties and responsibilities, these are so closely related to the purposes and processes of education that they cannot be understood or performed adequately apart from the intrinsic educational activities of the organization. As an educator, the educational administrator is not and cannot be restricted to purely administrative tasks, but he*

---

*John Walton, *Administration and Policymaking in Education* (rev. ed.) (Baltimore: Johns Hopkins University Press, 1969), pp. 41, 42, 43. Reprinted by permission.

engages in the same professional activities as the teacher, the counselor, the scholar, and the researcher. He is primarily a specialist in education, or in some academic discipline, rather than in administration per se; and he is on part, or full-time, assignment to attend to the administrative aspects of his profession, which involve primary considerations of education. (p. 41)

2. The second ... centers around the regard for administration as a function that can be abstracted from the other functions of an organization and the belief that its nature is essentially the same in all organizations. This type ... would provide ... for an administrative class, specialists in administration rather than in education, who conceivably would be interchangeable from one type of institution to another. (p. 42)

3. A third ... Education, along with other institutions in society, has become tremendously complex, heterogeneous, unwieldy and competitive. This state of affairs has given rise to the need for administrators who conceive the various components in relationship to one another and, also, can ensure the survival of educational organizations. So important is this function for the prevention of chaos and disintegration that the person who knows how to run an educational enterprise should also have, and, as a matter of fact, will have, a great deal to say about the purposes for which it is run. The specialist may provide the administrator with facts and technical information, but decisions about the purposes of education and the methods required to accomplish these purposes should be left to the administrator, whose mind can encompass the complex and far-reaching effects of such decisions. (pp. 42–43)

The second scenario resembles the model now in place in hospitals. In general, a professional management team runs the hospital as a complex organization and a separate professional medical team runs the hospital as a healing organization. Though both hierarchies coexist, when push comes to shove, the latter hierarchy is the more powerful. Further, those associated with the medical hierarchy enjoy higher average salaries and greater prestige than their management counterparts. Opting for scenario 2 in education would require that the present educational hierarchy be radically restructured.

The third scenario has the potential to compromise the value of democratic authority in running our schools. It would bring to the administrative role the kind of policy clout that is now heavily shared with local school boards, state legislators, state departments of education, and other stateholders. Neither education nor management would comprise the "core technology" of profession of educational administration, but politics and policy instead.

To the authors, scenario 1 deserves consideration as the metaphor of choice for an emerging profession of educational administration. But scenario 1 suggests that we may need to rethink the present direction in building the profession of educational administration. For this scenario to work, a more modest view of administrative training and certification may be needed—one that does not compete with teaching but complements it. Educational administration would simply be an extension of teaching. Educational expertness in this scenario would be shared with teachers. Shared expertness is key, for the knowledge of teachers always rivals the educational knowledge of administrators.

Some specialized knowledge of management and organization and some skill in organizational matters would be added to this shared educational expertness. But the question is, How much? Too much "expertness" in management may compromise shared educational expertness. Further, though highly specialized management expertness may be appropriate for large corporations and other vast bureaucracies, the typical school is comparatively small.

The Changing Focus

Recent studies of the effectiveness of formal training in educational administration raise important questions about the present and future direction of preparation programs. Zheng (1996), for example, found that an inverse relationship exists. The more preparation in educational administration the 12,000 administrators in his sample had, the less effective they were perceived to be by their teachers. In his words:

> Most states require principals to have a degree in Educational Administration in order to qualify for a principal license. Nevertheless, statistical evidence from this study fails to provide support to the logic of this requirement. While having a degree in Educational Administration makes no difference for private school principals in terms of their perceived effectiveness of instructional leadership, it decreases the rating of principals in public schools. Public school principals who have a degree in Education Administration are rated 0.101 points ($p < 0.001$) lower than other principals when other factors are being held constant. (p. 19)

Related to the question of formal preparation in educational administration is the value of administrative experience. Zheng (1996) found that principals with more experience were actually perceived as being less effective: "The longer a principal stays in school administrative positions, the more negatively he/she is perceived by teachers" (p. 20). These findings raise the question of whether what is now being studied as one prepares to be a principal is actually helpful or harmful. Further is the question of whether there is something inherent about the ways in which schools are presently organized and run that, over time, encourages principals to behave in ways that they are perceived as being less effective by their teachers.

Despite this and other studies that point to negative effects of preparation in educational administration, some bright spots may be on the horizon. Since the mid-1980s, the trend has been for school administrators, particularly school principals, to emphasize instructional leadership tasks and to view themselves once again as principal-teachers. Indeed, in many schools, it is becoming fashionable for administrators to teach (albeit part time) once again. The emphasis today on building school cultures, enhancing collegiality and empowerment, and renewing a commitment to shared decision making suggests that the two professions may be coming back together again. Indeed, one optimistic forecast is that the two professions of educational administration and teaching will be brought together as one common profession bonded by a shared commitment to teaching and learning on the one hand but allowing for differentiated roles on the other. Recent efforts to redefine the "core technologies" of both professions gives this forecast a chance. For example, the National Association of Elementary School Principals has recently revised its document *Proficiencies for Principals: Kindergarten through Eighth Grade*, first issued in 1986. The proficiences they identify for principals are remarkably similar to those required of expert teachers:*

> *Summing up, among the numerous characteristics and skills and proficiencies that mark the effective K–8 principal, four areas are basic:*
>
> *Child growth and development: The principal must bring to the position expert knowledge in the field of child growth and development, preferably fortified by extensive practical experience in teaching children, and must be capable of guiding the staff toward assuring the curriculum is relevant and appropriately challenging.*
>
> *Teaching and learning processes: The principal must similarly be soundly grounded in the teaching and learning processes, in both contemporary and traditional patterns of instruction and in validated instructional techniques and strategies.*
>
> *General knowledge: The principal must bring to the position a basic liberal arts foundation productive of a firm grasp of basic curriculum content and an understanding of the relationship between the body of knowledge and the elementary/middle school curriculum.*
>
> *School climate: The principal must be a caring person who knows how to create a school climate or "culture" that is based on mutual trust and respect, is productive of high morale, and places strong emphasis on children's social and academic development. (NAESP, 1986, pp. 3–4)*

Professional Standards for Superintendents, published by AASA in 1993, and the 1996 NASSP report *Breaking Ranks: Changing an American Institution* make similar overtures to a new kind of leadership that would be more suitable for an increasingly professionalized teaching force. *Breaking Ranks*, for example, stands out for its emphasis on teaching and learning and on the conditions that enhance both as the central focus of the principalship. Arguing that "high school is, above all else, a learning community and each school must commit itself to expecting demonstrated academic achievement for every student in accord with standards that can stand up to national scrutiny" (p. 2), the report recommends that "every student have a personal adult advocate; the Carnegie Unit be replaced or redefined; student anonymity be banished; teachers meet no more than 90 students per day; every stu-

*National Association of Elementary School Principals, *Proficiencies for Principals: Kindergarten through Eighth Grade* (Alexandria, VA: Author, 1986), pp. 3–4. Reprinted by permission.

dent have a Personal Plan of Progress; imaginative flexible scheduling be the order of the day; every principal and teacher have a Personal Learning Plan" (p. vi).

Signs of change are evident not only from the various educational administration professional associations but also many state departments of education. In a dramatic departure from its usual managerial perspective on school administrators as bureaucratic functionaries, for example, the Texas Education Agency adopted a new set of proficiencies for school administrators in 1994. The new proficiencies call for administrators who will guide "the learning community and the development of a vision that reflects students' needs for academic achievement and success in life and makes that vision tangible for others through positive action. The administrator encourages the collaborative planning, implementation, assessment, and ongoing modification of strategies to achieve this mission. While continually striving to expand the base of support for the learning community, the administrator also creatively allocates resources such as money, time, facilities, technology, and volunteers. In addition, the administrator uses innovative governance structures and methods to further the mission of the learning community" (Texas Education Agency, 1994, p. 11). Other proficiencies include establishing a climate of mutual trust, facilitating a sound curriculum and effective teaching and learning, communicating the learning community's vision, demonstrating a commitment to learning for all students and staff, and promoting equity and diversity within a common framework that bonds people together.

Since the establishment of the NPBEA in 1988, significant steps have been made in developing new standards for the preparation of educational administrators. Working closely with the UCEA, the American Association for Colleges of Teacher Education (AACTE), the NCPEA, the ASCD, the AASA, the NAESP, and the NASSP, the policy board developed a set of curriculum guidelines that included 11 knowledge and skill areas grouped into five broad categories; strategic leadership, instructional leadership, organizational leadership, political and community leadership, and the internship. The guidelines provide standards that specify the leadership skills needed for school administrators "to generate a culture for effective teaching and learning in restructured schools where teachers are viewed as professionals" (NCATE, 1995). The curriculum guidelines were approved by NCATE in 1995 and now comprise the standards that universities must follow as they seek to have their school administration preparation programs accredited by the association. The guidelines are provided in Appendix 5.1.

The new NCATE/NPBEA standards are noteworthy for the emphasis they give to teaching and learning, to building inclusive learning communities, and to providing leadership within an emerging culture of teacher professionalism. This emphasis is in contrast to the more generic view of leadership themed to organizational and management issues of a more decontextualized variety that has characterized school administration preparation programs in the past. Arthur Wise, president of NCATE, describes the new standards as follows: "For the first time we have a set of standards which begin to envision a role for administrators consistent with the emerging conception of the new professional teacher.... The new vision is one in which the teacher is an independent professional who bases instructional decisions on knowledge of research and the wisdom of practice rather than a semi-skilled professional who must be told what to do" (NCATE, 1995).

Pursuing a Knowledge Base

Though it appears that a consensus is emerging among practicing professionals as to what the knowledge base of educational administration is, much less consensus can be found in the academic world. In 1989, the theme of the UCEA annual convention was "The Knowledge Base of Educational Administration: Moving Beyond the Theory-Practice Dilemma," reflecting once again the council's continued interest in the knowledge base question. In 1991, the council established the "identification of an appropriate knowledge base" as its primary goal and appointed a committee charged with planning the necessary work and reporting its findings by 1994. Under the chairmanship of Wayne K. Hoy, the committee divided into seven teams, each pursing a domain of knowledge as follows:

Societal and Cultural Influences on Schooling

Teaching and Learning Processes

Organizational Studies

Leadership and Management Processes

Policy and Political Studies

Legal and Ethical Dimensions of Schooling

Economic and Financial Dimensions of Schooling

For each knowledge domain, five documents were to be produced: a domain taxonomy, a narrative overview of the domain's content, an annotated bibliography, a portfolio of 10 illustrative articles, and the development of a representative case study. The task force issued the report *Educational Administration: The UCEA Document Base* in 1993. The results of this effort remain unclear. Much controversy exists over what was included and what was left out of this document base. Despite some progress, it appears that a rigorously grounded and objective consensus as to what constitutes the knowledge base in educational administration does not exist.

Pohland (1992) believes that confusion within the academic community about the knowledge base is both predictable and consistent with what should be expected in a "pre-paradigm" field. Pohland points out that unlike the natural sciences, pre-paradigm fields are characterized by a lack of cohesion among members, a strong practice orientation, a nonstandardized literature, low collegiality, and little consensus as to what should be included in preparation programs. As a result, the knowledge base is debated and even contested. Many schools of thought exist; standard solutions to problems do not exist.

It is not likely that this difference between the academic community and the professional associations that represent practicing school administrators will be easily resolved. At this writing, it appears that the professional view that emphasizes leadership processes directed toward improving learning is getting the most attention in the standards for school administration preparation debate.

Women in Administration

To date, it appears that efforts to professionalize educational administration have not served women very well. Teaching is heavily staffed by women and administration is heavily staffed by men. Traditionally, educational administration has emerged as a male profession concerned with male themes of bureaucracy, control, and power. Women, by contrast, have traditionally held strong commitments to teaching. Campell and Lam (1993), for example, point out that "there is no other profession or field in the United States which has an equivalent history of numerical domination by women coupled with a continuing legacy of exclusion of women from key decision-making roles" (p. 205).

The status of women in the superintendency during the 1969–1970 school year was bleak, indeed. Fully 98.7 percent of the superintendents who participated in the AASA study were men. No women were represented among the 137 superintendents of school districts with student enrollments above 25,000, and only 20 percent of the remaining 1,266 superintendent participants were women. In a 1975 statistical report issued by the U.S. Department of Health, Education and Welfare (HEW), only 65 of the 13,037 superintendents in the country were identified as women (p. 173). In 1988, a report issued by the National Center for Educational Information pointed out that women comprised 65 percent of the teaching force but accounted for only 4 percent of the school superintendents, 10 percent of the secondary school principals, and 30 percent of the elementary school principals (Feistritzer et al., 1988). Shakeshaft (1987) reported that the 1972 figures were 1 percent, 1.4 percent and 19.6 percent, respectively. When compared with the 1972 and 1988 data, the more recent figures suggest some modest improvements. Using data provided by the American Association of University Women, Campbell and Lam (1993) note that approximately 5 percent of superintendents are women, the majority employed in suburban districts, and that a large number of school board members were women. Bell and Chase (1993) put the figure at 5.6 percent, and a 1992 American Association of School Administrators survey (Glass, 1992) reports that 6.6 percent of all superintendents nationwide are women.

The general distribution of women across all roles in education continues to suggest staffing patterns that discriminate against women. Figure 5.1, for example, shows that though more than 60 percent of teachers are women, they account for only a negligible percentage of junior and senior high principals and assistant principals. Note also the domination of women in stereotyped roles such as librarian and nurse. Comparatively, women fare better in elementary school administrative positions—but that figure may be deceptive, as will be discussed in the next section.

If educational administration and teaching are brought closer together rather than separated along rigid professional lines, then teaching can become a natural springboard for women to administration and the number of potential female

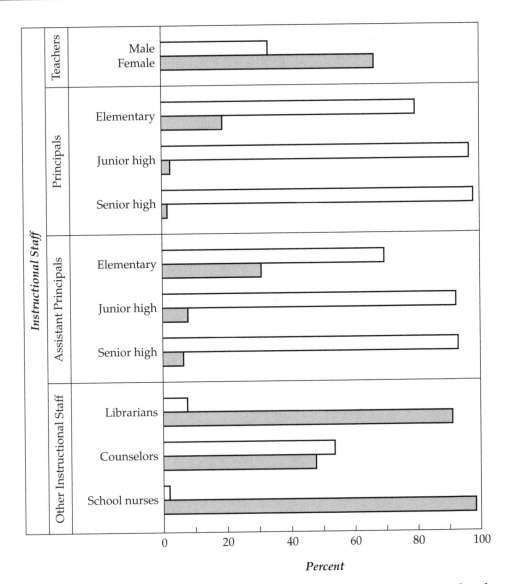

FIGURE 5.1 Percentage Distribution of Full-Time Public School Instructional Staff, by Sex: 1972–1973

Source: U.S. Department of Health, Education, and Welfare (1975), p. 71.

administrators would increase dramatically. By mystifying administration, however, and by changing its center from issues of substance (school purposes, etc.) to issues of process (the most efficient and effective means to get things done) and its core technology from teaching and learning to something called management, administration is placed squarely into the male world.

Shakeshaft (1987) explains that the problem is androcentrism—"the practice of viewing the world and shaping reality from a male perspective. It is the elevation of the masculine to the level of the universal and the ideal and honoring of men and the male principle above women and female" (p. 94). She continues, "In an androcentric world, hierarchy of status exists. Men and women must do different things; women and what women do are less valued than are men and what men do [and thus teaching is less valued than administration] . . . discrimination on the basis of sex is necessary for the existence of an androcentric (male-defined) world to exist. . . . Thus it is this ideology . . . that explains why men, and not women, occupy the formal leadership positions in school and society" (p. 95). In recent years, and on a comparative basis, women have made significant gains in educational administration. Some women with a foot in the door are strong advocates of increased professionalization of educational administration as traditionally defined, feeling that their own roles will be enhanced as they embody traditional management values and leadership styles. The authors have doubts. There is little reason to believe that androcentricity will be reduced in a highly professionalized educational administration simply because of increases in the number of women. The problem is that the process of professionalization itself—themed to bureaucratic, organizational, and managerial values—may be androcentric. For androcentricity to be reduced, the substance of educational administration will need to shift to teaching and learning and to caring (see, e.g., Noddings, 1992; Beck, 1994; Marshall, Patterson, Rogers, & Steele, 1996). Also, *community* will need to replace *organization* as the metaphor for the school (Sergiovanni, 1994).

Women and the School Principalship

Approximately every 10 years, the National Association of Elementary School Principals and the National Association of Secondary School Principals conduct studies of the status of the principalship (see, e.g., Pharis & Zakariya, 1979; McCleary & Thomson, 1979). From these studies, a portrait of principalship characteristics can be charted over time. In 1928, for example, 55 percent of the elementary school principals surveyed by NAESP were women. This figure decreased to 41 percent in 1948, 38 percent in 1958, 22 percent in 1968, and 18 percent in 1978. The 1988 NAESP study (Doud, 1989) shows a slight increase by estimating the percentage of women in the principalship to be 20 percent. It appears from these figures that women are a vanishing breed among principals of elementary schools. This assertion is also supported by age statistics. In 1968, for example, 71 percent of the male principals were under 50 years of age, and their median age was 43. During this same year, 77 percent of the female principals were 50 years of age or older, and their median age was 56. These figures are particularly interesting in light of the fact that during this period only 15.4 percent of the teachers in public elementary schools were men. In a 1976 study of Illinois administrators, Carver found that though there were 102 women elementary principals age 56 or older, fewer than 100 women teachers with administrative certificates were available from the prime age group (under age 36) to replace these women principals upon retirement.

The 1978 NAESP study of the principalship (Pharis & Zakiriya, 1979) revealed some improvements in age balance among the sexes. About 35 percent of the men principals were over age 50, as compared to approximately 50 percent of the women principals. The median ages for men and women principals reported in the 1988 NAESP study (Doud, 1989) were 47 and 50, respectively. Nonetheless, one can still conclude that among elementary school principals, women are fewer in number, the number is declining, and the few who are in this role are, on the average, older than their male counterparts.

Statistics for the secondary school principal are even less encouraging. Comprising 10 percent of the principalship force in 1965, women accounted for only 7 percent in 1977. In 1981, the typical junior high or middle school principal could be described as a White male between the ages of 45 and 54. Only 6 percent of this group were women. According to a 1993–1994 survey conducted by the National Center for Educational Statistics (1995), the typical school principal could be described as a White male between 45 and 48 years old. Roughly 80,000 principals were included in this survey—52,000 males and 27,000 females. The male principals averaged about 20 years of experience in education with 10 of those years being in the principalship. Female principals averaged about 18 years of experience, with 5 of those years being in the principalship.

When asked why they chose the principalship, 20 percent of the principals who participated in the 1968 national study indicated that they preferred administration and supervision over classroom teaching, 17 percent indicated that they needed a larger income, 30 percent considered the principalship to be especially important, and 30 percent had been encouraged to take the principalship by the superintendent's office. Some 56 percent of the female supervisory principals (as opposed to 16 percent of the men) took the principalship because they were encouraged to do so by the superintendent's office. Recent studies of the principalship find that the most highly effective principals are very much oriented to teaching and learning rather than to an administrative "career" in an executive sense.

Where one does find female principals, one also finds smaller schools. Approximately one-third of the women elementary school principals, for example, head schools with enrollments of 100 or fewer students. More than half of all female principals can be found in schools with enrollments of less than 400. At the secondary school level, 75 percent of the women head schools of 745 students or fewer, as compared with 37 percent of the men. Only 1 percent of the women head schools of 2,000 or more students, as contrasted with 14 percent of the men. To the extent that size of school can be considered as an indicator of prestige, one can conclude that the least prestigious principalships are more likely to be filled by women. Opportunities for women who aspire to the principalship seem to be greater in larger cities. The National Council of Administrative Women in Education (1973) reports that in the largest cities of the United States, women occupy about 30 percent of the principalships.

The general underrepresentation of women in the ranks of educational administration cannot be attributed to lack of supply. According to a New York State Education Department report issued in 1988, women accounted for 4 percent of

New York state's superintendents, 13 percent of its high school principals, and 28 percent of its elementary principals during the 1987–1988 year. But during the 1984–1987 period, women in New York state earned half of the doctoral degrees awarded in educational administration, earned over half of the master's degrees, and accounted for half of all of the administrative certificates issued. It appears that the number of women certified each year well exceeds the number employed, leading some experts to conclude that the supply of qualified women is plentiful but they are not being hired in equitable numbers (Sadker, Sadker, & Klein, 1991).

More than sex equity is at stake as one examines these figures. The evidence suggests that, though in the minority, women principals are *overrepresented* in schools considered to be highly effective. This assertion is based, in part, on an examination of articles describing successful schools that have appeared in *Educational Leadership* and other journals in the last 10 years, on the case study literature of successful principals (see, e.g., Dwyer et al., 1985; Lipsitz, 1984; Sergiovanni, 1990), and on the burgeoning literature that contrasts the leadership effectiveness of male and female principals. Reasons for the success of women can be traced, in part, to their greater commitment to the values of teaching and learning as opposed to the values of bureaucratic management and control and to a more democratic and value-oriented leadership style that serves school rather than organizational purposes. On the first count, Meskin (1979) explains:

> *The woman principal begins her working years strongly committed to the occupation of teaching. Her eye is rarely on career advancement, and she concentrates instead on knowing the ins and outs of her profession. When, often by a fluke, she is promoted to a principalship in later life, her long years as a basic service professional in an organization stand her in good stead. She shows greater ability and self-confidence in directing the instructional program than men do simply because of her deeper understanding of the art of teaching, and she also demonstrates a high degree of ability in administering the school, the milieu in which she worked so long. Because again she is not seeking promotion from her present rank, she commits herself wholeheartedly to the role of principal and is able to master the job in a highly competent fashion. (pp. 336–337)*

Of course, a fair number of men serve as principals of successful schools, too. Though the research is skimpy, a reasonable assertion is that these men bring to their practice a disposition, set of priorities, and leadership style that resembles their women counterparts. They view themselves, for example, more as "servants" to school purposes and to those who struggle with them to achieve these purposes. This is in contrast to the style of "superiors" who expect others to serve them. This assertion raises the thorny question of whether differences do indeed exist in the ways men and women manage and lead. The evidence for school administrators suggests that the answer to this question is yes. Moreover, the differences have something to say about the nature and content of educational administration preparation programs and about the whole issue of just how professionalized educational administration should become. As noted earlier, for example, professionalization, as now understood, may not serve women very well.

Meskin (1979) reviewed a number of studies that compared the behaviors of men and women principals. Her analysis of the Florida Leadership Project conducted in the 1950s led her to conclude that women tended to use both democratic behaviors and effective administration practices more frequently than men.

Meskin reviewed as well the landmark leadership research of Hemphill, Griffiths, and Fredericksen (1962). These investigators gave principals "in-baskets" filled with typical school problems to solve. Solutions were then evaluated by panels of experts. When solutions were evaluated by teachers and by the principals' superiors, both groups displayed more positive attitudes toward the performances of women than those of men. With respect to specific categories of problems, women were judged better than men in "exchanging information," "maintaining organizational relationships," and "responding to outsiders." Men, on the other hand, fared better in "complying with suggestions made by others" and "analyzing the situation." Meskin (1979) observes that "women seem to be more thorough in their in-basket, use more information from the background materials, and discuss information more with superiors and subordinates. Men, on the other hand, made concluding decisions and followed pre-established structures to a greater degree in problem-solving and took more terminal actions" (p. 333).

It appears from this study that women outperformed men in interpersonal and informational aspects of leadership but that men were better bureaucratic managers. Other data from this study indicated that women were more concerned with the objectives of teaching, pupil progress, and the evaluation of learning than were men. Further, superiors rated women as being better in evaluating the performance of new teachers and as more willing and able to provide instructional leadership. "In the important role of instructional leaders, women principals seem to far outshine their male colleagues" (Meskin, 1979, p. 331).

Another study reviewed by Meskin was that of Gross and Trask (1964). The indicators or effectiveness used in this study were teacher ratings of the principal's performance, teacher morale, and student academic performance. These investigators concluded that women's performance as elementary school principals was superior to that of men. In commenting on the study, Meskin (1979) states, "When educational values are considered, women principals showed a greater concern with individual differences and with the social and emotional development of the child than men principals. When evaluating teachers, women place greater stress on the teachers' technical skill and their responsibilities to the school organization than men. Women also tended to exert more supervisory control in their work and to worry less than male principals about their responsibilities" (p. 335). In a more recent study, Shakeshaft and Perry (1995) found that women principals gave teachers more feedback about their teaching performance than did men principals. Further, this feedback included more detail about teaching and provided more specific recommendations for improvements.

Lee, Smith, and Cioci (1993) investigated how high school principals' gender affects teachers' evaluations of their leadership. Men and women teachers assessed the leadership of male principals as being almost equally effective. By contrast, women teachers assessed the leadership of female principals as being very effective but men considered female principals to be largely ineffective. The researchers suggest that men may be evaluating female principals poorly because they resist what is unfamiliar, are threatened by their more open and participatory style, are unsettled by the push to become more of a team player, and feel uncomfortable with the idea that one's teaching practice should be more visible. Further, men may feel that they have been well served by the present system that seems to favor them. Despite these differences in how men and women teachers evaluate male and female principals, both groups report higher levels of locus of control, self-efficacy, and staff influence over policy when working with female principals (Lee, Smith, & Cioci, 1993).

Using statistics from the 1993–1994 schools and staffing survey, Zheng (1996) examined teacher perceptions of the instructional leadership effectiveness of their principals. Roughly 12,000 public and private school principals and 55,000 teachers were included in his sample. Instructional leadership was measured by the extent to which teachers reported that their principals evaluated them fairly, let them know what was expected, were supportive and encouraging, included them in important educational decisions, provided resources to support teaching and learning, enforced school rules, talked to them about their teaching practice, communicated a vision, and developed clear goals and priorities for the school. Female principals were more positively rated as educational leaders by their teachers than were male principals.

From these and other studies, it seems appropriate to conclude that, as a group, female principals are more effective in providing instructional leadership than are male principals. To put it another way, if all that was known about two candidates competing for the same principalship position was that one was male and the other female, these studies suggest that the female would be a better bet.

The definitive work on the topic is Shakeshaft's (1987) *Women in Educational Administration.* She covers much of the same ground just presented but extends the discussion by providing a historical analysis and a biting critical commentary based on an examination of over 200 dissertations and 600 research articles. With respect to the question of whether differences exist in male and female styles, Shakeshaft concludes:*

1. Relationships with others are central to all actions of women administrators. *Women spend more time with people, communicate more, care more about individual differences, are concerned more with teachers and marginal students, and motivate more. Not surprisingly, staffs of women administrators rate women higher, are more productive, and have higher morale. Students in schools with women principals also have higher morale and are more involved with student affairs. Further, parents are more favorable toward schools and districts run by women and thus are more involved in school life. . . .*

2. Teaching and learning are the major foci of women administrators. *Women administrators are more instrumental in instructional learning than men and they exhibit greater knowledge of teaching methods and techniques. Women*

administrators not only emphasize achievement, they coordinate instructional programs and evaluate student progress. In these schools and districts, women administrators know their teachers and they know the academic progress of their students. Women are more likely to help new teachers and to supervise all teachers directly. Women also create a school climate more conducive to learning, one that is more orderly, safer, and quieter. Not surprisingly, academic achievement is higher in schools and districts in which women are administrators.

3. Building community is an essential part of a woman administrator's style. *From speech patterns to decision-making styles, women exhibit a more democratic, participatory style that encourages inclusiveness rather than exclusiveness in schools. Women involve themselves more with staff and students, ask for and get higher participation, and maintain more closely knit organizations. Staffs of women principals have higher job satisfaction and are more engaged in their work than those of male administrators. These staffs are also more aware of and committed to the goals of learning, and the members of the staffs have more shared professional goals. These are schools and districts in which teachers receive a great deal of support from their female administrators. They are also districts and schools where achievement is emphasized. (p. 197)*

More recently, Lee, Smith, and Cioci (1993, p. 156) found that, as a group, female principals use a more democratic and participatory style and evidence a style that is more personalized. Male principals, by contrast, were inclined to be more direct than autocratic and to use styles that were more impersonal and structured. Further, female principals focused more of their efforts on teaching and learning and on other academic concerns. Male principals were more inclined to be management oriented.

Shakeshaft (1995) found that gender seems also to be related to operational definitions of ethical behavior. Although both male and female superintendents value competence and trust (Garfinkel, 1988, cited in Shakeshaft), they give each a different priority. Female superintendents look for competence first in a team member. Male superintendents identify trust as their number-one priority, viewing competence as being much less important. In Shakeshaft's words, "Women saw things differently. Not only did women not code 'telling something' as disloyal, they said they expected subordinates to tell unless specifically instructed otherwise. They expected people to discuss conversations, actions and feelings with others" (p. 152). Men, by contrast, "said they assumed that if they told a subordinate something, the subordinate would not tell others unless he or she had been instructed to do so" (p. 152). Further, male team members reported that the way to show loyalty was not to disagree with the superintendent except in private. Female team members said that the way to show loyalty was to speak up when they disagreed. They thought that speaking up was a professional responsibility and that it would be immoral to go along with poor ideas. It appears from Shakeshaft's data that women felt the best way to serve their superintendents was to ensure that the best decisions were made by the superintendents for their schools.

The crux of the problem, according to Shakeshaft, is that existing theory and research in educational administration is faulty because it does not account for the experiences of women. She argues that practices based on this research not only are slanted to the male world view but are less effective than would be practices based on theory and research that included the woman's experience. Her solution is to rewrite the literature and to restructure preparation programs. "Only when this is done will we be able to understand human behavior and organizations. Until then, we are writing a history and practice of males in school administration. As scholarship, this is shoddy and deficient. As practice, it is useful to only some practitioners" (Shakeshaft, 1987, p. 208).

Earlier, it was suggested that present efforts to professionalize educational administration may need to be rethought and indeed redirected. As things now stand, increased professionalization in the form of lengthier study, elongated certification requirements, certifying boards, and more advanced degrees may well create a "core technology" for educational administration that is heavily weighted toward management themes. If this remains the emphasis, then professionalization will very likely reinforce rather than reduce androcentrism in educational administration and further divide teaching and school administration into two separate and unequal professions. The solution proposed by the authors is to build a more limited and hierarchically flatter professional administration, one based on shared educational expertness with teachers and limited specialized knowledge in management and organization. The NAESP, NASSP, and NPBEA seem to be moving in this direction by joining with NCATE in developing standards for educational administration that acknowledge the emergence of a new kind of leadership that is more suitable for a professionalized teaching force and that places teaching and learning at the center of the principal's job.

Appendix 5.1
*NCATE Curriculum Guidelines Prepared by the NPBEA for the Educational Leadership Constituent Council**

Area I, Strategic Leadership

The knowledge, skills and attributes to identify contexts, develop with others vision and purpose, utilize information, frame problems, exercise leadership processes to achieve common goals, and act ethically for educational communities.

1. **Professional and Ethical Leadership**
   The institution's program prepares school leaders who demonstrate an understanding of, and the capability to:
   1.1 Facilitate the development and implementation of a shared vision and strategic plan for the school or district that focuses on teaching and learning (*e.g., cultivate group norms, influence institutional culture, and affirm core values*).

**Source:* National Association of Elementary School Principals, Alexandria, VA, on behalf of the Educational Leadership Constituent Council. Reprinted by permission.

1.2 Use motivational theory to create conditions that motivate staff, students and families to achieve the school's vision (*e.g., facilitate collegiality and team-work, arrange significant work, encourage challenging standards, provide autonomy, support innovation, delegate responsibility, develop leadership in others, provide leadership opportunities, recognize and reward effective performance, provide knowledge of results, provide coaching and mentoring, gain resources, serve as a role coaching and mentoring, gain resources, serve as a role model*).

1.3 Frame, analyze, and resolve problems using appropriate problem solving techniques and decision making skills (*e.g., identify problem, seek and analyze problem factors, collect and organize relevant information, identify causes, seek creative solutions, apply ethical standards, determine best solution with others when appropriate*).

1.4 Initiate, manage, and evaluate the change process.

1.5 Identify and critique several theories of leadership and their application to various school environments.

1.6 Act with a reasoned understanding of major historical, philosophical, ethical, social and economic influences affecting education in a democratic society.

1.7 Manifest a professional code of ethics and values.

2. **Information Management and Evaluation**

The institution's program prepares school leaders who demonstrate an understanding of, and the capability to:

2.1 Conduct needs assessment by collecting information on the students; on staff and the school environment; on family and community values, and to develop and conduct research.

2.2 Use qualitative and quantitative data to inform decisions, to plan and assess school programs, to design accountability systems, to plan for school improvement, and to develop and conduct research.

2.3 Engage staff in an ongoing study of current best practices and relevant research and demographic data, and analyze their implications for school improvement.

2.4 Analyze and interpret educational data, issues, and trends for boards, committees, and other groups, outlining possible actions and their implications.

Area II, Instructional Leadership

The knowledge, skills and attributes to design with other appropriate curricula and instructional programs, to develop learner centered school cultures, to assess outcomes, to provide student personnel services, and to plan with faculty professional development activities aimed at improving instruction.

3. **Curriculum, Instruction, Supervision, and the Learning Environment**

The institution's program prepares school leaders who demonstrate an understanding of, and the capability to:

3.1 Create with teachers, parents and students a positive school culture that promotes learning (*e.g., holds high expectations, focuses on accomplishments and recognition, and promotes a supportive climate*).

3.2 Develop collaboratively a learning organization that supports instructional improvement, builds an appropriate curriculum, and incorporates best practice.

3.3 Base curricular decisions on research, applied theory and informed practice, the recommendations of learned societies, and state and federal policies and mandates (*e.g., cognitive development, human development, learning styles, contemporary methodologies, content priorities, special needs legislation on topics such as least restrictive environment, etc.*).

3.4 Design curricula with consideration for philosophical, sociological, and historical foundations, democratic values and the community's values, goals, social needs and changing conditions.

3.5 Align curricular goals and objectives with instructional goals and objectives and desired outcomes when developing scope, sequence, balance, etc.

3.6 Develop curriculum and instruction appropriate for varied teaching and learning styles and specific student needs based on gender, ethnicity, culture, social class and exceptionalities.

3.7 Utilize a variety of supervisory models to improve teaching and learning (*e.g., clinical, developmental, cognitive and peer coaching, as well as applying observation and conferencing skills*).

3.8 Use various staffing patterns, student grouping plans, class scheduling forms, school organizational structures, and facilities design processes, to support various teaching strategies and desired student outcomes.

3.9 Assess student progress using a variety of appropriate techniques.

4. **Professional Development and Human Resources**
   The institution's program prepares school leaders who demonstrate an understanding of, and the capability to:

   4.1 Work with faculty and other stakeholders to identify needs for professional development, to organize, facilitate, and evaluate professional development programs, to integrate district and school priorities, to build faculty as resource, and to ensure that professional development activities focus on improving student outcomes.

   4.2 Apply adult learning strategies to professional development, focussing on authentic problems and tasks, and utilizing mentoring, coaching, conferencing and other techniques to ensure that new knowledge and skills are practiced in the workplace.

   4.3 Apply effective job analysis procedures, supervisory techniques and performance appraisal for instructional and non-instructional staff.

   4.4 Formulate and implement a self-development plan, endorsing the value of career-long growth, and utilizing a variety of resources for continuing professional development.

4.5 Identify and apply appropriate policies, criteria and processes for the recruitment, selection, induction, compensation and separation of personnel, with attention to issues of equity and diversity.

4.6 Negotiate and manage effectively collective bargaining or written agreements.

5. **Student Personnel Services**

The institution's program prepares school leaders who demonstrate an understanding of, and the capability to:

5.1 Apply the principles of student growth and development to the learning environment and the educational program.

5.2 Develop with the counseling and teaching staff a full program of student advisement, counseling, and guidance services.

5.3 Develop and administer policies that provide a safe school environment and promote student health and welfare.

5.4 Address student and family conditions affecting learning by collaborating with community agencies to integrate health, social, and other services for students.

5.5 Plan and manage activity programs to fulfill student developmental, social, cultural, athletic, leadership and scholastic needs; working with staff, students, families, and community.

Area III, Organizational Leadership

The knowledge, skills and attributes to understand and improve the organization, implement operational plans, manage financial resources, and apply decentralized management processes and procedures.

6. **Organizational Management**

The institution's program prepares school leaders who demonstrate an understanding of, and the capability to:

6.1 Establish operational plans and processes to accomplish strategic goals, utilizing practical applications of organizational theories.

6.2 Apply a systems perspective, viewing schools as interactive internal systems operating within external environments.

6.3 Implement appropriate management techniques and group processes to define roles, assign functions, delegate effectively, and to determine accountability for attaining goals.

6.4 Monitor and assess the progress of activities, making adjustments and formulating new action steps as necessary.

7. **Interpersonal Relationships**

The institution's program prepares school leaders who demonstrate an understanding of, and the capability to:

7.1 Use appropriate interpersonal skills (*e.g., exhibiting sensitivity, showing respect and interest, perceiving needs and concerns, showing tact, exhibiting consistency and trustworthiness, etc.*).

7.2 Use appropriate written, verbal and nonverbal communication in a variety of situations.

7.3 Apply appropriate communications strategies (*e.g., identifying audiences, determining messages, selecting transmission mediums, identifying reaction of receivers, soliciting responses, etc.*).

7.4 Promote multicultural awareness, gender sensitivity and racial and ethnic appreciation.

7.5 Apply counseling and maundering skills, and utilize stress management and conflict management techniques.

8. Financial Management and Resource Allocation

The institution's program prepares school leaders who demonstrate an understanding of, and the capability to:

8.1 Identify and analyze the major sources of fiscal and non-fiscal resources for schools and school districts.

8.2 Develop and manage financial and material assets, and capital goods and services, allocating resources according to district or school priorities (*e.g., property, plant, equipment, transportation, and food service.*).

8.3 Develop an efficient budget planning process that is driven by district and school priorities and involves staff and community.

8.4 Perform budget management functions including financial planning, monitoring, cost control, expenditures accounting, and cash flow management.

9. Technology and Information Systems

The institution's program prepares school leaders who demonstrate an understanding of, and the capability to:

9.1 Use technology, telecommunications and information systems to enrich curriculum and instruction (*e.g., CAI systems, CD ROM retrieval systems, online networks, distance learning, interactive video, etc.*).

9.2 Apply and assess current technologies for school management and business procedures.

9.3 Develop and monitor long range plans for school and district technology and information systems, making informed decisions about computer hardware and software, and about staff development, keeping in mind the impact of technologies on student outcomes and school operations.

Area IV, Political and Community Leadership

The knowledge, skills and attributes to act in accordance with legal provisions and statutory requirements, to apply regulatory standards, to develop and apply appropriate policies, to be conscious of ethical implications policy of initiatives and political actions, to relate public policy initiatives to student welfare to understand schools as political systems, to involve citizens and service agencies, and to develop effective staff communications and public relations programs.

10. Community and Media Relations

The institution's program prepares school leaders who demonstrate an understanding of, and the capacity to:

10.1 Analyze community and district power structures, and identify major opinion leaders and their relationships to school goals and programs.

10.2 Articulate the district's or school's vision, mission and priorities to the community and media, and build community support for district or school priorities and programs (*e.g., form collaborative relationships with business, citizen groups, neighborhood associations, social service agencies, parent organizations, advocacy groups, universities, and religious institutions, etc.*).

10.3 Communicate effectively with various cultural, ethnic, racial, and special interest groups in the community.

10.4 Involve family and community in appropriate policy development, program planning, and assessment processes.

10.5 Develop an effective and interactive staff communications plan and public relations program.

10.6 Utilize and respond effectively to electronic and printed news media.

11. Educational Law, Public Policy, and Political Systems

The institution's program prepares school leaders who demonstrate an understanding of, and the capability to:

11.1 Apply knowledge of federal and state constitutional, statutory and regulatory provisions and judicial decisions governing education.

11.2 Apply knowledge of common law and contractual requirements and procedures in an educational setting (*e.g., tort liability, contract administration, formal hearings*).

11.3 Define and relate the general characteristics of internal and external political systems as they apply to school settings.

11.4 Describe the processes by which federal, state, district, and school-site policies are formulated, enacted, implemented and evaluated, and develop strategies for influencing policy development.

11.5 Make decisions based on the moral and ethical implications of policy options and political strategies.

11.6 Analyze the major philosophical tenets of contemporary intellectual movements and analyze their effect on school context (*e.g., critical theory, feminism, poststructuralism, fundamentalism, etc.*).

11.7 Develop appropriate procedures and relationships for working with local governing boards.

Area V, Internship

The internship is defined as the process and product that result from the application in a workplace environment of the strategic, instructional, organizational and contextual leadership Guidelines. When coupled with integrating experiences through related clinics or cohort seminars, the outcome should be a powerful synthesis of knowledge and skills useful to practicing school leaders.

The internship includes a variety of substantial concurrent or capstone experiences in diverse settings planned and guided cooperatively by university and school district personnel for credit hours and conducted in schools and school districts over an extended period of time. The experiences need to provide interns with substantial responsibilities which increase over time in amount and complexity, and which involve direct interaction and involvement with students, staff, parents, and community leaders. Ideally, an internship should include some work with social service organization involved with inter-agency activities affecting schools.

An acceptable internship would be a six-month, full time mentored experience (or the equivalent), preferably involving two or more settings and multiple levels (elementary, secondary, etc.). An optimum internship would be a year-long, full time mentored experience.

Universities and school districts should collaborate to achieve state policies that support these Guidelines for the internship. School district, university and state policies and practices which encourage and facilitate paid internship positions allow interns to engage in a rich variety of mentored leadership activities and decision making responsibilities. These opportunities raise the level of professional preparation and provide evidence of a serious commitment to developing quality leadership for the nation's schools.

12. Internship

The internship provides significant opportunities in the workplace to synthesize and apply the knowledge, and to practice and develop the skills, identified in the eleven Guideline areas. Therefore, the preparation program:

12.1 Requires a variety of substantial in-school/district experiences over an extended period of time in diverse settings, planned cooperatively and supervised by university and school district personnel.

12.2 Establishes relationships with school leaders acting as trained mentors/clinical professors who guide individuals preparing for school leadership in appropriate in-school/district experiences.

12.3 Includes experiences with social service, private, and/or community organizations.

References

American Association of School Administrators. (1993). *Professional standards for superintendents.* Arlington, VA: Author.

Beck, L. G. (1994). *Reclaiming educational administration as a caring profession.* New York: Teachers College Press.

Bell, C., & Chase, S. (1993). The underrepresentation of women in school leadership. In C. Marshall (Ed.), *The new politics of race and gender: The 1992 Yearbook of the Policies of Educational Association.* Washington, DC: Falmer.

Campell, M., & Lam, D. (1993). Gender and public

education: From mirrors to magnifying lenses. In S. K. Biklen & D. Polard (Eds.), *Gender and education* (pp. 204–220). 92nd yearbook of the National Society for the Study of Education, Part 1. Chicago: University of Chicago Press.

Carnegie Forum on Education and the Economy. (1986). *A nation prepared: Teachers for the 21st century* (Report of the Task Force on Teaching as a Profession). New York: Author.

Carver, F. D. (1976). *Administrative-certification and training in Illinois*. Urbana, IL: Department of Administration, Higher and Continuing Education. University of Illinois. Mimeographed document.

Doud, J. (1989). *The K–8 principal in 1988*. Alexandria, VA: National Association of Elementary School Principals.

Dwyer, D. C., Lee, G. V., Barnett, G. B., Filby, N. N., Rowan. B., Albert, B. R., & Kojimoto, C. (1985). *Understanding the principal's contribution to instruction: Seven principals, seven stories* (Vols. 1–8). San Francisco: Far West Laboratory for Educational Research and Development.

Feistritzer, C. E., et al. (1988). *Profile of school administrators in the U.S.* Washington, DC: National Center for Educational Information.

Fischer, F. (1990). *Technocracy and the politics of expertise*. Newbury Park, CA: Sage.

Garfinkel, E. (1988). *Ways men and women in school administration conceptualize the administrative team*. Unpublished Doctoral dissertation, Hofstra University.

Gibboney, R. A. (1987, April 15). Education of administrators: "An American Tragedy." *Education Week*, p. 28.

Glass, T. (1992). *The 1992 study of the American school superintendency*. Arlington, VA: American Association of School Administrators.

Griffiths, D. (Ed.). (1964). *Behavioral science educational administration*. 63rd yearbook. Chicago: National Society for the Study of Education.

Gross, N., & Trask, A. E. (1964). *Staff leadership in the public schools: A sociological inquiry*. New York: John Wiley.

Haller, E. J., & Strike, K. A. (1986). *An introduction to educational administration: Social, legal and ethical perspectives*. New York: Longman.

Hemphill, J. K., Griffiths, D. E., & Fredericksen, N. (1962). *Administrative performance and personal-*

ity. New York: Teachers College, Columbia University.

The Holmes Group. (1986). *Tomorrow's teachers*. East Lansing, MI: Author.

The Holmes Group. (1990). *Tomorrow's schools*. East Lansing, MI: Author.

Kappan editors. (1979). In defense of the external Ed.D. *Phi Delta Kappan, 60*(8), 31–32.

Kellogg Foundation. (1961). *Toward improved school administration: A decade of professional effort to heighten administrative understanding and skills*. Battle Creek, MI: Author.

Lee, V. E., Smith, J. B., & Cioci, M. (1993). Teachers and principals: Gender-related perceptions of leadership and power in secondary schools. *Educational Evaluation and Policy Analysis, 15*(2), 153–180.

Lipsitz, J. (1984). *Successful schools for young adolescents*. New Brunswick. NJ: Transaction Books.

McCleary, L., & Thomson, S. (1979). *The senior high school principalship* (Vol. 3). Reston, VA: National Association of Secondary School Principals.

McDonnell, L. M., & Elmore, R. F. (1987). Getting the job done: Alternative policy instruments. *Educational Evaluation and Policy Analysis, 9*(2), 133–152.

Marshall, K., Patterson, J. A., Rogers, D. L., & Steele, J. R. (1996). Caring as career: An alternative perspective for educational administration. *Educational Administration Quarterly, 32*(2), 271–294.

Meskin, J. D. (1979). Women as principals: Their performance as educational administrators. In D. A. Erickson & T. L. Reller (Eds.), *The principal in metropolitan schools*. Berkeley, CA: McCutcheon.

Moore, H., Jr. (1947). *Studies in school administration*. Washington, DC: American Association of School Administrators.

National Association of Elementary School Principals. (1986). *Proficiencies for principals*. Alexandria, VA: Author.

National Association of Secondary School Principals. (1996). *Breaking ranks: Changing an American institution*. Reston, VA: Author.

National Board for Professional Teaching Standards. (1989). *Toward high and rigorous stan-*

dards for the teaching profession. Detroit, MI: The Board.

National Center for Educational Statistics. (1995). *Digest of Educational Statistics 1995.* U.S. Department of Education, NCES 95-029.

National Commission on Excellence in Education. (1983). *A nation at risk.* Washington, DC: U.S. Government Printing Office.

National Commission on Excellence in Educational Administration. (1987). *Leaders for tomorrow's schools.* Mesa, AZ: Author.

National Conference of Professors of Educational Administration. (1948, August–September). *Educational leaders—Their function and workplace.* A Report of the Second Work Conference, Madison, WI.

National Council for Accreditation of Teacher Education. (1995). NCATE unveils new education administration standards. *NCATE NEWS,* October 2.

National Council of Administrative Women in Education. (1973). *Wanted more women: Where are the women superintendents?* Arlington, VA: Author.

National Policy Board for Educational Administration. (1989). *Improving the preparation of school administrators: An agenda for reform.* Charlottesville, VA: Author.

National Policy Board for Educational Administration. (1990). *The preparation of school administrators. A statement of purpose.* Fairfax. VA: Author.

Noddings, S. N. (1992). *The challenge to care in schools: An alternative approach to education.* New York: Teachers College Press.

Peterson, K. D., & Finn, C. E. (1985, Spring). Principals, superintendents, and the administrator's art. *The Public Interest,* (79), 127–131.

Pharis, W., & Zakariya, S. B. (1979). *The elementary school principalship in 1978.* Arlington, VA: National Association of Elementary School Principals.

Pohland, P. (1992, Spring). Paradigm and prospect: Educational administration and reform. *UCEA Review, 32*(2), 4–14.

Sadker, M., Sadker, D., & Klein, S. (1991). The issue of gender in elementary and secondary education. In G. Grant (Ed.), *Review of research in education* (Vol. 17). Washington, DC: American Educational Research Association.

Sergiovanni, T. J. (1990). *Value-added leadership.* San Diego: Harcourt Brace Jovanovich.

Sergiovanni, T. J. (1991). The dark side of professionalism in educational administration. *Phi Delta Kappan, 72*(7), 521–526.

Sergiovanni, T. J. (1994). *Building community in schools.* San Francisco: Jossey-Bass.

Shakeshaft, C. (1987). *Women in educational administration.* Beverly Hills, CA: Sage.

Shakeshaft, C. (1995). A cup half full: A gender critique of the knowledge base in educational administration. In R. Donmoyer, M. Imber, & J. J. Scheurich (Eds.), *The knowledge base in educational administration multiple perspectives.* Albany: State University of New York Press.

Shakeshaft, C., & Perry, A. (1995). The language of power versus the language of empowerment: Gender differences in administrative communication. In D. Corson (Ed.), *Discourse and power in educational organizations* (pp. 17–29). Cresskill, NJ: Hampton Press.

Texas Education Agency. (1994). *Learner-context school for Texas: A vision of Texas educators.* Austin, TX: Author.

University Council for Educational Administration. (1987, Spring). National Commission report released. *UCEA Review, 28*(3), 1–2.

University Council for Educational Administration. (1993). *Educational administration: The UCEA document base.* University Park, PA: Author.

U. S. Department of Health, Education, and Welfare. (1975). *The condition of education.* Washington, DC: National Center for Education Statistics.

Walton, J. (1969). *Administration and policymaking in education* (rev. ed.). Baltimore: Johns Hopkins University Press.

Wilensky, H. (1964). Professionalization of everyone? *American Journal of Sociology, 70,* 137–158.

Zaleznik, A. (1989). *The managerial mystique: Restoring leadership in business.* New York: Harper and Row.

Zheng, H. P. Y. (1996). *School context, principal characteristics and instructional leadership effectiveness: A statistical analysis.* Paper presented at the annual meeting of the American Educational Research Association, New York City, April 8–12.

$$Chapter \quad 6$$

The Development of Thought in Educational Administration

A general overview of educational administration was provided in Chapters 4 and 5. This overview included definitions of *administration*; a consideration of the critical responsibility areas, processes, and tasks associated with administration; and an analysis of educational administration as a field of professional practice. Special attention was given to the importance of educational leadership roles. Chapter 6 is concerned with the intellectual heritage of educational administration. Administrators and other professionals practice their art from certain perspectives or accepted ways of operating, which are directly related to the development of thought in their respective fields over time. For this reason, professional practice in any field can be better understood by examining its intellectual heritage.

Models of Administrative Practice

In the professions, paradigms expressed as models of practice determine standards, operating procedures, and other characteristics of practice. Models of practice are systematic approximations of reality that come complete with a convincing internal logic—a set of assumptions, postulates, data, and inferences about some phenomena. Sometimes models are formal and explicit, but often models are implicit—and, indeed, are articulated unknowingly by administrators. Models determine what problems are critical for a profession and provide the practitioner with a theoretical framework for understanding and dealing with problems. Models underlying the administration of special education, for example, emphasize remediation of difficulties rather than prevention. Thus, special education administrators are more likely to be concerned with the critical problem of learning disabilities in urban youth than with poor nutrition of pregnant women in urban areas, though the second seems causally related to the first.

Models also suggest which actions or routines are more valid than others and suggest certain standards of proof for determining effectiveness of these methods. An administrator who operates from a human-relations model, for example, might consider interpersonal relationships as the critical administrative priority in a school. This administrator would employ specific techniques, such as participating in decision making, to improve these relationships and would judge his or her effectiveness by positive changes in morale of the staff. An administrator who operates from an accountability model might consider increased performance as the critical concern in this same school. This administrator would employ specific techniques such as management by objectives (MBO) and teaching by objectives (TBO) to improve performance and would judge her or his effectiveness by the number of management objectives achieved or gains in student test scores. The behavior and orientation of each administrator is governed by the model from which he or she is working.

Changes in professional practice are a result of shifts in the models that characterize thinking in the field. In discussing this point, Kuhn (1962) argues that science does not change as a result of piecemeal accumulation of knowledge but by "conceptual revolutions," which result in critical shifts in the intellectual thinking for a particular field—changes in its prevailing models. This chapter examines the development of thought in modern administration, seeking to identify the major models and paradigms that undergird the profession and the shifts that help explain changes in professional practice.

Setting the Stage: Managers of Virtue

It is popular to think of eras as if they have fixed beginnings and endings that coincide with the beginning of the next era. The development of thought in educational administration is more realistically observed as being additive. For example, the moral tone that guided the reformers who sought to create the common school during the period from 1820 to 1880 is alive and well in recent efforts to construct school cultures around themes of shared values and visions; the one-best-way efficiency prescriptions of scientific management during the period from 1890 to 1930 are alive and well in recent efforts to increase school productivity by introducing linear planning and tight alignment of curriculum, teaching and evaluation strategies, and monitoring systems that ensure such strategies are implemented properly. The concern for the social needs of people during the period from 1930 to 1945 and higher-order needs during the time from 1950 to 1980 are alive and well in the present emphasis on building interpersonally competent school climates, on empowering teachers, and on using quality circles and shared decision making.

Today's administrators are giving increased attention to building school cultures and relying on cultural norms as ways to get teachers and students to be better connected to the school and its work. These practices are justified by the literature on nonlinear decision making, loose structure, and nonrational organizational functioning that gained prominence during the politics and decision making eras from 1960 to 1975. In the established sciences, clear-cut "paradigm shifts" often characterize the development of knowledge. A new view emerges to first challenge and then to replace the existing view. By contrast, knowledge development in educational administration tends to accumulate, with different views representing competing claims on policymakers and school administrators. Some views gain prominence and fade; other views then become prominent only to fade themselves. But none seems to go entirely away.

This analysis of the development of thought begins at about 1900, for it was in the twentieth century that educational administration began its trek toward becoming a distinct management profession connected to but still separate from and hierarchically superior to teaching. During the period from 1820 to 1890, a different kind of quest took place—the establishment of the common school in America. The common school was intended to build a nation by socializing, indeed homogenizing, the young to reflect the values of being an American. In Tyack and Hansot's (1982) words:

> *The central challenge for common school crusaders of the mid-nineteenth century was to mobilize the people in support of public education and to construct an educational system. They worked with an overwhelmingly rural nation. State departments of education were small and weak, and the federal government exerted little influence over public schools. Schooling was largely unbureaucratized and unprofessionalized.... Largely Protestant in religion and Anglo-Saxon in ethnic background, they shared a common religious and political conception of the role of public education in shaping a Christian nation.... The school promoters tended to see themselves linked by a common moral earnestness and civic activism. (p. 5)*

The emphasis was quite different from 1890 to the 1950s. According to Tyack and Hansot (1982), this was a period that witnessed a changing of the guard from school administrators as part-time "educational evangelists" who crusaded for the common school to a new breed of professional managers—"administrative progressives." This new breed sought to reshape the school through the use of business efficiency and scientific expertness. Like the crusaders before them, the new breed viewed its trust as sacred—the need to save the schools from uninformed lay participation and willy-nilly politics by separating education from politics. The means to this goal was to create a profession of educational administration based on scientific knowledge. The administrative progressives believed that this scientific knowledge would be respected by laypersons and politicians, thus affording the school administrator greater autonomy in running the affairs of schooling.

As Tyack and Hansot (1982) explain, education leaders of this era

> *were social engineers who sought to bring about a smoothly meshing corporate society.... Their task was not to create but to redesign the public-school system, not to arouse public participation in education but to constrain it, not to campaign*

for a common denominator of education so much as to differentiate it according to the needs of a complex society (as they interpreted these needs). *Most of these leaders made education a lifelong career and were pioneers in its profesionaliza-tion. They wished the state to take an active role in transforming education. (p. 6)*

They note further:

The members of the "educational trust" (as the administrative progressives were sometimes called) embraced the new managerial models developed in business . . . they sought legitimacy through expertise rather than through deference to char-acter or through broad public participation in policymaking . . . they shaped their preferred policies into a standard template of reform which they applied to state after state, district after district, in their school surveys and legislative proposals. They successfully changed the structures of decision-making and sought to turn political issues into matters for administrative decisions, confident that schools could rise "above politics." (p. 7)

The common school crusaders of the nineteenth century saw themselves as con-stituting an "aristocracy of character." By contrast, in the twentieth century, school leaders regarded themselves as professional experts certified by specialized train-ing. They banded together "into exclusively professional associations like the Amer-ican Association of School Administrators (AASA), sponsoring and being sponsored by fellow experts, elaborating legal and bureaucratic rules, and turning to science and business as sources of authority for an emergent profession" (Tyack & Hansot, 1982, p. 6). This quest for professionalism continued throughout the twen-tieth century, reaching a crescendo in recent years with the establishment of the National Policy Board for Educational Administration (NPBEA) and the linking of its efforts with the powerful National Council for the Accreditation of Teacher Edu-cation (NCATE). The underlying theme for determining the nature of this profes-sion changes as various models of educational administration wax and wane.

Earlier common school crusaders such as Horace Mann and Henry Barnard sought to create the common school by enlisting the support of politicians, school people, and lay citizens alike. During this era, schools were considered to be polit-ical enterprises governed by democratic authority. Grass roots participation became the norm. As a result, powerful school boards emerged that often assumed responsibility for hiring and firing teachers and administrators, approv-ing curriculum, and performing other tasks now thought to be the province of professions. Superintendents and other school administrators had to contend with and compete with this political power. In the end, it was the will of the peo-ple that prevailed, not the school person, and the administrative progressives felt that this situation needed to be corrected by professionalizing educational admin-istration.

Some of the leaders of the movement to professionalize educational adminis-tration during this period were Ellwood P. Cubberly, Stanford University; George Strayer, Teachers College, Columbia University; Edward C. Elliott, University of

Wisconsin; Frank Spaulding, Yale University; and Franklin Bobbitt, University of Chicago. Teachers College, Columbia University and Stanford University were particularly influential, preparing the lion's share of professors and superintendents who spread the gospel of efficiency and scientific management and who became charter members of the new profession of educational administration.

The Cubberly story, as told by Tyack and Hansot (1982, pp. 122–128) was particularly revealing. When Cubberly, a physical scientist by training, with no background in elementary and secondary education, was appointed superintendent of schools in San Diego in 1896 he found a school board mired in politics and heavily involved in making decisions that he thought should be the province of the superintendent. He became convinced that school boards should not be political and that school districts should be run by experts—professional administrators who knew their business. This view is still widely shared today by policymakers, school administrators, and citizens. When appointed to the education faculty at Stanford University in 1988, Cubberly welcomed the opportunity to prepare that kind of school administrator. He introduced and taught such courses as "School Administration, School Problems, School Organization, School Statistics, Secondary School, History of Education, Relationship of Ignorance and Crime to Education" (Sears & Henderson, cited in Tyack & Hansot, 1982, p. 124).

Cubberly and other professors of the time relied on the limited literature that existed in educational administration, on their own experiences as school administrators, and, for the most part, on the burgeoning literature in business administration—most notably the works of Frederick Taylor on scientific management and later of other management experts such as Fayol, Gulick, and Urwick. Cubberly, for example, advocated scientific management and bureaucratic conceptions of hierarchy. To him, the superintendent was *the* person to whom and from whom authority, directions, and even inspiration should flow. He was not an advocate of teacher participation in defining school policies, and he felt that schools should give up the idea that all persons were equal (Tyack & Hansot, 1982, p. 128).

Another influential person during this period was George Strayer, a well-known professor at Teachers College, Columbia University and an expert on uniform statistical accounting, school finance formulas, and standardized school building designs. He was prominent in the school survey movement that developed a comprehensive standardized template of how schools should be efficiently organized, staffed, and operated and then measured the extent to which schools and school districts measured up to this one-best-way standard. To Strayer (1914), the survey was designed to provide a record of the "organization, administration, supervision, cost, physical equipment, courses of study, teaching staff, methods of teaching, student body, and results as measured by the achievement of those who are being trained or have been trained therein" (p. 302). Surveys were very popular because their findings provided superintendents with a source of professional authority in the form of "research" to override the democratic authority of board members or the professional authority of teachers who might have alternate visions of what the school should be. After all, what counts more—teacher opinions and board preferences or expert knowledge backed by survey research?

Strayer believed that much of the progress of urban schools during the time from 1905 to 1930 could be attributed to the application of scientific management and to the professional training of school administrators. By progress, he had in mind such advances as:

Development of clear line and staff organization;

Reorganization of traditional uniform elementary and secondary schools into differentiated institutions, including junior high schools, that treated individuals and groups according to abilities and needs;

Creation of special classes for the "backward, delinquent, physically handicapped and the like," vocational tracks, and instruction in subjects like health and physical education;

Professionalization of the occupation of teaching and administration by upgrading standards of education, certification, tenure, specialization of function, and supervision;

Standardization of methods of "public accounting" and enforcement of attendance;

Introduction of "sound business administration" in budgeting, planning and maintenance, and finance. (Strayer, 1930, pp. 376–378, cited in Tyack & Hansot, 1982, p. 153)

Cubberly, Strayer, and other administrative progressives were, in many respects, a small part of a larger movement that sought to professionalize business management, bureaucratize the country's institutions, and transform the United States into a corporate state. For these reasons, one cannot understand the development of thought in educational administration without giving attention to the development of management thought in general. The analysis that follows gives attention to both. It sketches the main strands of thought that have evolved in management in general and how these ideas have affected the ways in which schools have been and are organized, managed, and led.

Major Strands of Thought in Administration

To simplify matters, recent intellectual development in administration will be grouped into four major strands of thought, each of which suggests a fairly distinct model for viewing administration. These models are concerned with *efficiency, the person, politics and decision making,* and *culture.*

The efficiency period began in the early 1900s and remained popular until about 1930. Models of organization and administration that emphasized concern for people were dominant from about 1930 to the mid-1960s and remain popular today in the literature of school administration and among practitioners.

Political and decision-making views span a period from the end of World War II to the present. These views are considered by many to dominate present thinking in educational administration. Models characterized by a concern for efficiency and a concern for the person have not been replaced completely. Both have advocates from within the academic community and from among practicing professionals. Indeed, much of what the models offer remains appropriate and can be incorporated into political and decision-making views. In spite of their present popularity, political and decision-making views, too, will be replaced by others as part of the natural progression of knowledge expansion in the field. An emergent view in educational administration reflects a high concern for culture in its analysis of organizational structure, work design, and organizational behavior. Culture, as is the case with efficiency, person, and politics, is a metaphor used to help one think about organizational life in a specific way.

Academic advocates of one or another model are often ideological and dogmatic about what good practice is in educational administration. Ideas from competing models are viewed negatively. Most experienced administrators, by contrast, assume a more moderate and tolerant posture by looking for the good in all views. They adopt a reflective practice posture within which knowledge from theory and research is not used directly to prescribe practice but indirectly to inform one's intuition and judgment as decisions are made in practice (see, e.g., Schon, 1983; Sergiovanni, 1987). They use knowledge gleaned from available models of administration conceptually rather than instrumentally (Kennedy, 1984). Ideally, models should be used to help school administrators think about professional problems and thus augment subsequent decisions, and not to tell them what to do or blind them to other models. Unfortunately, models of administration sometimes become "mindscapes" for administrators, and when this is the case, their thinking and behavior are programmed in a specific fashion and they become blind to or suspicious of other views. Thus, as the major strands of thought are overviewed here, keep in mind that each has features appropriate to certain aspects of professional practice but not to others. Further, when used exclusively, *none of the views is sufficiently comprehensive or true to be helpful.* The efficiency model, for example, can be helpful in establishing high school scheduling routines or in developing a series of attendance or purchasing-management policies. Applying insights from the same model to problems of teacher motivation, supervision, and evaluation, however, is likely to result in bureaucratic teaching, rigid learning, and subsequently serious staff morale problems. As the strands of thought and inferred models are discussed and compared, keep in mind the costs and benefits of using each in professional practice. This analysis should help one in using the models as alternative possibilities, each appropriate to different aspects of practice. This is the essence of reflective practice in any profession.

An important disclaimer to this discussion is that the overview presented is not exhaustive. The intent is only to provide highlights of the models and to accent the differences among them.

Concern for Efficiency

In many respects, schools today are organized and operated according to certain established principles of good management. A division of labor exists whereby instructional and coordinative tasks are allocated to specific roles. Roles are defined by job descriptions that are clearly linked to some overall conception of what the school is to accomplish. Certain guides, such as span of control and student/teacher ratio, have been accepted to help decide the number of teachers needed and how they should be assigned. Tasks are subdivided and specialists are hired for some functions. Roles are ordered according to rank, with some enjoying more authority and privilege than others. The development of rank helps to ensure that those who are lower in the hierarchy will function in manners consistent with job expectations and goals. Day-to-day decisions are routinized and controlled by establishing and monitoring a system of policies and rules. These, in turn, ensure more reliable behavior on behalf of goals. Proper communication channels are established and objective mechanisms are developed for handling disputes, allocating resources, and evaluating personnel.

Scientific Management and the Efficiency Model

Much of what is taken for granted as good management today can be traced to an era of development in administration referred to as *scientific management*. Frederick Winslow Taylor is credited as the founding father of the scientific-management movement. His impact on organization and management in education is now a matter of record (Callahan, 1962) and will be reviewed only briefly.

In his *Principles of Scientific Management,* published in 1911, Taylor offered four principles that were the foundation for his science of work and organization. The first was to replace intuitive methods of doing the work of the organization with a *scientific method* based on observation and analysis to obtain the best cost-benefit ratio. He felt that for every task, a *one best way* should be determined. The second principle was to *select the best person* for the job scientifically and train this person thoroughly in the tasks and procedures to be followed. The third principle was to "heartily cooperate with the men" to ensure, through *monitoring*, close supervision, and incentive systems, that the work is being done according to established standards and procedures. The fourth principle was to *divide* the work of managers and workers so that managers assume responsibility for planning and preparing work and for supervising. Taylor believed that what workers did needed to be tightly connected to management through systems of monitoring that emphasized data collection on the one hand and close firsthand supervision on the other. Taylor's ideas quickly found their way into the study and practice of educational administration. Franklin Bobbitt, an educator of the period and an advocate of scientific management, stated:

> In any organization, the directive and supervisory members must clearly define the ends toward which the organization strives. They must coordinate the labors of all so as to attain those ends. They must find the best methods of work, and they

must enforce the use of these methods on the part of the workers. They must deter-mine the qualifications necessary for the workers and see that each rises to the standard qualifications, if it is possible; and when impossible, see that he is sepa-rated from the organization. This requires direct or indirect responsibility for the preliminary training of workers before service and for keeping them up to standard qualifications during service. Directors and supervisors must keep the workers supplied with detailed instructions as to the work to be done, the standards to be reached, the methods to be employed, and the materials and appliances to be used. They must place incentives before the worker in order to stimulate desirable effort. Whatever the nature or purpose of the organization, if it is an effective one, these are always the directive and supervisory tasks. (Bobbitt, 1913)

Taylor's theories of management and organization became the means to create a science of education and educational administration themed to efficiency princi-ples—a science that Cubberly believed represented a new professional model for administrators. In Cubberly's words (cited in Callahan, 1962),

The recent attempts to survey and measure school systems and to determine the efficiency of instruction along scientific lines have alike served to develop a scien-tific method for attacking administrative problems which promises to compel us soon to rewrite the whole history of our school administration in terms of these new units and scales of measuring educational progress and determining educa-tional efficiency. All of these developments point unmistakably in the direction of the evolution of a profession of school administration as distinct from the work of teaching on one hand and politics on the other. (p. 217)

For the next three decades, basic concepts and strategies of the efficiency model were applied to the broader question of administration and organizational design by many European and American writers. French theorist Henri Fayol (1949) offered a universal list of good management principles that became very popular. These included division of work, authority, and responsibility; discipline; unit of command; and unity of direction. Gulick and Urwick (1937) offered the principles of unity of command, span of control, and matching of people to the organizational structure. They were advocates of division of work, not only by purpose, but by process, person, and place. Scientific management did not offer a theory of administration and organization as such, but a set of principles and sim-ple injunctions for administrators to follow. Efficiency was to be maximized by defining objectives and outputs clearly, by specializing tasks through division of labor, and—once the *best way* is identified—by introducing a system of controls to ensure uniformity and reliability in workers' tasks and to ensure standardization of product.

The following principles of management offered by Fayol (1949, pp. 20–40) are examples of the efficiency literature of administration in the management of schools—all of which are still used today in various degrees:

1. *Division of work* based on task specialization should be practiced. Jobs should be broken down into small parts and grouped in a fashion that permits individuals to work on only a limited number.
2. *Authority* should be clearly delineated so that responsibilities of each worker are known and their relationships to other workers, up, across, or down the hierarchical chain, are clear.
3. *Discipline* should be established in the sense that superiors (i.e., administrators and teachers) have a right to expect deference and obedience from subordinates.
4. *Unity of command* should be practiced as a mechanism for clearly delineating authority relationships. Fayol believed that an employee should receive direction from and, in return, be accountable to only one superior. (One of the arguments often cited in opposition to team-teaching plans is that the traditional authority structure of the teacher and students becomes confused and students are not sure to whom they "belong.")
5. *Unity of direction*, whereby each objective should be accompanied by a specific plan for achievement of a specific group of people who would be accountable for achieving that objective.
6. *Subordination of individual interest* in favor of those of the organization and of the work group should be encouraged.
7. *Remuneration* should be fair but routinized so that unreasonable overpayments are avoided. The standard salary schedule, for example, is considered better than merit pay.
8. *Centralization* of decision making should be practiced to permit proper coordination, with judicious decentralization accompanied by proper controls when needed.
9. *Scalar chain*, as a mechanism for defining the line of command flow of communication from the highest to lowest rank, should be practiced.
10. Material and social *order* should be the rule to ensure that everything and everyone is in the proper place.
11. *Equity* should be practiced, in the sense that justice should govern administrative action.
12. *Stability* of tenure of personnel is desirable and should be sought.
13. *Initiative* should be encouraged at all levels of the organization.
14. *Esprit*, in the form of harmony and unity of workers, should be encouraged.

Some would argue that the first 10 of Fayol's principles contradict the last 4. Equity, stability, initiative, and esprit are likely to suffer in the absence of more flexibility in management and organization and a greater distribution of authority within the organization.

Efficiency principles persevere today as strong considerations in curriculum development, in selecting educational materials, in developing instructional systems, and in other aspects of educational administration. Scientific-management thinking has weathered ups and downs for three-quarters of a century and today enjoys a resurgence. Fueled by demands for accountability and political conservatism in society, and by advancements in management techniques (such as opera-tion research, systems analysis, and computer systems), earlier scientific management has emerged into a new, more sophisticated form.

In education, this neoscientific or modern scientific management offers such efficiency ideas as performance contracting, behavioral objectives, state and national assessment, cost-benefit analysis, management by objectives (MBO), stra-tegic planning, and management information system (MIS), each prescribed to maximize educational reliability and productivity at decreased cost.

The school-reform movement that began in the early 1980s emphasized man-dates and incentives as policy instruments (McDonnell & Elmore, 1987). This movement reflected a high concern for efficiency in management and embodied many of the principles of scientific management. The tight alignment of measur-able goals with curriculum, curriculum with specific teaching formats, teaching with systems of close supervision and evaluation, and everything with testing is an example. Typically, quality control within this reform movement was viewed as a management problem solvable by designing external control mechanisms such as standardized evaluation systems and testing programs. In most states, the school-reform movement was biased toward identifying the "one best way" to provide schooling.

Even recent reform efforts, such as site-based management, provide schools with the power to decide the means of education yet remain accountable to uni-form standards decided at the state level embody scientific-management charac-teristics. The provided standards wind up determining the means anyway. With this unofficial but real scripting, scientific management endures.

In neoscientific management, however, traditional scientific-management control mechanisms such as face-to-face supervision are replaced by more imper-sonal, technical, or rational control mechanisms. Even when face-to-face supervi-sion cannot be avoided, the control mechanism is so impersonal and so programmed that the faces do not count. This is the case with measurement-ori-ented and teacher assessment systems that script what evaluators must consider and provide the rules that govern this consideration. The evaluation systems themselves function as "decision makers" and call the shots with a minimum of help from people. In a sense, they are both teacher-proof and evaluator-proof. Neoscientific management systems assume that if visible standards of perfor-mance, objectives, or competencies can be identified and measured, then the work of teachers and that of students can be better controlled by holding them account-able to these standards, thus ensuring greater reliability, effectiveness, and effi-ciency in performance.

The issue of motivating workers is handled similarly. In scientific manage-ment, it is assumed that people are primarily motivated by economic and other extrinsic incentives and that they will do that which brings them the greatest extrinsic gain. Workers can be controlled by manipulating these incentives. Appli-cations of scientific-management thinking are perhaps most easily recognized in the organization and instruction of many classrooms. Decisions with respect to class objectives, assignments, activities, and supervision of students are made unilaterally by teachers. Students are evaluated against class objectives, and grades are the primary incentive offered to students. If the curriculum is programmed in sufficient detail, teachers play a minor role in this process—that of following and giving directions—and are themselves supervised and evaluated according to scientific-management principles by administrators. Evaluating teachers by using student test scores or by relying on heavily prescribed and standardized evaluation systems are examples.

In 1916, Cubberly used the metaphors of factory and production to describe schools:

> *Every manufacturing establishment that turns out a standard product or a series of products of any kind maintains a force of efficiency experts to study methods of procedure and to measure and test the output of its works. Such men ultimately bring the manufacturing establishment large returns, by introducing improvements in processes and procedure, and in training the workmen to produce larger and better output. Our schools are, in a sense, factories in which the raw products (children) are to be shaped and fashioned into products to meet the various demands of life. The specifications for manufacturing come from the demands of twentieth-century civilization, and it is the business of the school to build its pupils according to the specifications laid down. This demands good tools, specialized machinery, continuous measurement of production to see if it is according to specifications, the elimination of waste in manufacture, and a large variety in the output. (p. 388)*

At this writing, factory and production metaphors are still very much in control in discussions of schooling. Educators still frequently conceive of students as raw material, the teacher as worker, the principal as supervisor, the curriculum as a processing script, and teaching as the processing itself as students are converted from raw materials to finished products that meet predetermined specifications. Neoscientific thinking in schools remains strong.

Bureaucratic Theories and the Efficiency Model

Bureaucratic thinking refined the norms of rationality and certainty that were characteristic of scientific management. It was assumed that all aspects of the organization—from its objectives, technical requirements, and work flow, to the details of its organizational structure—could be defined and organized into a permanent grand design. All that remained was to find people who could be programmed into this design. According to Weber (1946),

> *The fully developed bureaucratic mechanism compares with other organizations exactly as does the machine with the non-mechanical modes of production . . . precision, speed, unambiguity, continuity, discretion, unity . . . these are raised to the optimum point in a strictly bureaucratic administration. . . . The individual bureaucrat cannot squirm out of the apparatus in which he is harnessed. . . . In a*

great majority of cases, he is only a single cog in an ever moving mechanism which prescribes to him an eventually fixed route of march. (pp. 34–37)

Bureaucracy shares with scientific management the assumptions that people are primarily motivated by economic (or other extrinsic) concerns and work to maximize their economic gain. Economic gain is under control of the organization, however, and the person is to be engineered and controlled by this organization. The individual rationality of scientific management is replaced by organizational rationality as defined by standard operating procedures, formal organization charts, job descriptions, policy manuals, and other organizational routines. This impersonal quality of organizational rationality suggests the metaphor *mechanistic* when one speaks of bureaucratic theories.

Bureaucracy remains a part of the image of most educational organizations, and its advocates work diligently to incorporate its principles of order and certainty. Though the relatively harsh conception of humankind typically associated with this efficiency model may not fully characterize the relationships that generally exist between administrators and teachers, this conception remains ubiquitous as applied to students. Indeed, as one might well predict from bureaucratic thought, the lower a person is in the organizational hierarchy, the more she or he will be seen as fitting the underlying assumptions of human characteristics of the efficiency model.

Bureaucracy in schools endures because of the assurances of order, rationality, accountability, and stability it provides to the public. School administrators are often among its most avid fans. Clear lines of authority and specialization of functions provide a convincing justification for professional management on the one hand and proliferate managerial roles on the other (Parkinson, 1958).

Morgan (1986) sums up the strengths and limitations in practice of the concern-for-efficiency view as follows:

The strengths can be stated very simply. For mechanistic approaches to organization work well only under conditions where machines work well:

(a) when there is a straightforward task to perform;

(b) when the environment is stable enough to ensure that the products produced will be appropriate ones;

(c) when one wishes to produce exactly the same product time and again;

(d) when precision is at a premium; and

(e) when the "human machine" parts are compliant and behave as they have been designed to do. (p. 34)

However, despite these successes, mechanistic approaches to organization often have severe limitations. In particular they:

(a) can create organizational forms that have great difficulty in adapting to changing circumstances;

(b) can result in mindless and unquestioning bureaucracies;

(c) can have unanticipated and undesirable consequences as the interests of those
working in the organization take precedence over the goals the organization
was designed to achieve; and

(d) can have dehumanizing effects upon employees, especially those at the lower
levels of the organizational hierarchy. (p. 35)

Concern for the Person

By the 1930s, an effective counterforce on behalf of the human side of enterprise
began to emerge. This force was later to evolve into a distinct pattern of thought
about administration that is labeled the *person model*. Person views are divided
into two phases, human relations and human resources, with the latter being a
progressive development of the former. The metaphor *organic* is often used to
describe the human-resources version of the person model. The analogy is that of
a biological organism capable of feeling and growing but also capable of ill
health if not properly nurtured. Maintenance and nurturance of the human organization are important concerns of administrators who operate within the person
model. The building blocks to organizational health are individuals and their
needs and groups of individuals. According to this view, an ideal school is one
characterized by highly motivated individuals who are committed to school
objectives from which they derive intrinsic satisfaction. These individuals are
linked together into highly effective work groups. The work groups are characterized by commitment to common school objectives, by group loyalty, and by
mutual support.

Whereas scientific management and bureaucracy emphasize *task* specialization, the human-resources version of the person model emphasizes *person* specialization. Task specialization requires the careful sectioning, dividing, and assigning
of work by those in authority. Person specialization permits individuals to function as experts who enjoy discretionary prerogatives and who are influenced more
by client needs and their own expert abilities than by carefully delineated duties
and tasks.

As early as 1909, Chicago school superintendent Ella Flag Young noted:

> *There has been a tendency toward factory-evolution and factory-management,
> and the teachers, like the children who stand at machines, are told just what to do.
> The teachers, instead of being the great moving force, educating and developing
> the powers of the human mind in such a way that they shall contribute to the
> power and efficiency of this democracy, tend to become mere workers at the tread-
> mill, but they are doing all through this country that which shows that it is diffi-
> cult to crush the human mind and the love of freedom in the hearts and lives of
> people who are qualified to teach school. As a result they are organizing federa-
> tions to get together and discuss those questions which are vital in the life of the
> children and in the life of the teachers—you cannot separate the life of the children
> and the life of the teacher if you know what you are about. (cited in Tyack & Han-
> sot, 1982, p. 181)*

Young was the first woman to become superintendent of a big-city school district and the first woman to become president of the National Education Association. She was a vocal critic of scientific management, a pioneer in advocating democratic planning among teachers and democratic administration for the schools, and a strong voice for women's rights in both teaching and school administration.

Social philosopher Mary Parker Follett was also among the first whose views in opposition to a strictly mechanistic view of organization and administration were heard. Writing in the 1920s, she called for the need to integrate the views of scientific management and efficiency principles of organizational design and functioning with insights from individual psychology and the psychology of work groups. Professional administration, in her view, was to be built on a foundation of science on the one hand and the motive of service on the other (Metcalf & Urwick, 1940). To this end, Follet continued, administration should be built on a trinity of values: artful practice, scientific understanding, and ethical considerations. This "trinity of values" seems remarkably contemporary as one reads today's literature on school leadership. Should any of the three values be unduly emphasized, then the other two are likely to be neglected. In her book *Creative Experience,* Follett (1924) turned her attention to the dynamic nature of administration and the importance of human relationships and a harmonious group climate to this nature.

Follet's and Young's ideas were quite advanced for the time and provided the philosophical base for administrative and organizational theorizing that emphasized concern for the person, particularly as it evolved into the human-resourses view.

Human Relations

The benchmark most frequently mentioned as the beginning of the human-relations movement in administration is the work of the research team that operated from 1922 to 1932 at the Cicero, Illinois, Hawthorne plant of the Western Electric Company. This research team, headed by Elton Mayo and Fritz Roethlisberger, sought to determine the relationship between such physical factors as level of lighting at the workplace, rest periods, and length of the workday on increased performance of workers (Roethlisberger & Dickson, 1939). They found that regardless of whether physical conditions such as lighting, rest periods, and length of the workday were positively or negatively varied, production continued to increase. The researchers finally concluded that changes in physical job conditions did not result in increased production; rather, such increases seemed to result in changed social conditions of the worker. Changes in worker motivation and satisfaction were most often credited with increased production. These, in turn, seemed related to more democratic patterns of supervision used by the researchers and others during the experiments. Relative to existing conditions, workers received unprecedented attention from researchers, were able to socialize easily with other workers, and had some say in deciding working conditions. These conditions, in turn, seemed to have resulted in higher motivation and commitment levels, greater effort at work, and higher production records for people involved in the Hawthorne experiment.

Mayo's (1945) work is of particular importance to the development of this movement. His extensive interview studies at Western Electric revealed that workers subjected to more efficiency-oriented management suffered from alienation and loss of identity. As a result of his work, Mayo offered a set of assumptions to characterize people, which were quite different from those of efficiency management. He suggested that people are primarily motivated by social needs and obtain their basic satisfactions from relationships with others. He maintained that management had robbed work of meaning, and therefore meaning must be provided in the social relationships on the job. On the basis of his interviews, Mayo also concluded that people are more responsive to the social forces of their peer group than to extrinsic incentives and management controls. Finally, Mayo maintained that a person's identity and loyalty to management and organization depended on his or her ability to provide for self-social (interaction and acceptance) needs.

Leadership principles that took into account the social group, satisfaction of workers' social needs, and psychological manipulation of workers through counseling were examples of management to be gleaned from the historic Hawthorne studies.

Human-relations thought is often criticized for overemphasizing human social needs at the expense of needs for accomplishment and responsibility. A person's social needs were often considered separate from other concerns more directly related to the tasks of the organization. It was assumed that as long as a worker was happy and comfortable, he or she would show little interest in the policy decision affecting his or her work.

Human Resources

Human relations began to mature with the work of Kurt Lewin (1951) as he sought to link human behavior more closely with such environmental factors as role expectations and organizational climate. His social-systems view of people in organizations provided a more complete picture of reality. The writings of Abraham Maslow, Douglas McGregor, Chris Argyris, Warren Bennis, and Rensis Likert became the new tenets as human-relations thought matured. These theorists had academic credentials in social psychology or in the new interdisciplinary field at the time—organizational psychology.* Some authors referred to this maturity of human relations as *human resources,* to suggest the change of emphasis from social needs of individuals at work to needs expressed as a desire for more intrinsic satisfaction from increased organizational responsibility and from achievement of organizational goals (Miles, 1965; Sergiovanni & Starratt, 1979).

---

*See, for example, McGregor (1960) and Rensis Likert, *The Human Organization* (New York: McGraw-Hill, 1967). For examples of books in educational administration identified with this era, see Jacob Getzels, James Lipham, and Roald Campbell, *Administration as a Social Process* (New York: Harper and Row, 1968); and Thomas Sergiovanni and Fred D. Carver, *The New School Executive: A Theory of Administration* (New York: Dodd Mead, 1973).

Human-resources theorists agreed with earlier human-relations writers that applications of the efficiency model typically resulted in loss of meaning in work. But this loss was not attributed to neglect of a person's social needs as much as to his or her inability to use talents fully. Certainly, social needs were important, but a person's capacity for growth and challenge were the needs that received the greatest attention from human-resources theorists.

The famous analysis and comparison of Theories X and Y by Douglas McGregor (1960) is a good representation of human-resources thinking. McGregor believed that Theory X and Theory Y managers behaved differently, because they had internalized two very different theories of management. Theory X comprised assumptions and propositions generally associated with efficiency views of administration. Theory Y, on the other hand, had a higher regard for the value and potential of the person. The assumptions and propositons of Theories X and Y follow.*

Theory X

1. *The average human being has an inherent dislike of work and will avoid it if he can.*
2. *Because of this human characteristic of dislike of work, most people must be coerced, controlled, directed, threatened with punishment to get them to put forth adequate effort toward the achievement of organizational objectives.*
3. *The average human being prefers to be directed, wishes to avoid responsibility, has relatively little ambition, wants security above all.*

Theory Y

1. The expenditure of physical and mental effort in work is as natural as play or rest. *The average human being does not inherently dislike work. Depending upon controllable conditions, work may be a source of satisfaction (and will be voluntarily performed) or a source of punishment (and will be avoided if possible).*
2. External control and the threat of punishment are not the only means for bringing about effort toward organizational objectives. Man will exercise self-direction and self-control in the service of objectives to which he is committed.
3. Commitment to objectives is a function of the rewards associated with their achievement. *The most significant of such rewards, e.g., the satisfaction of ego and self-actualization needs, can be direct products of effort directed toward organizational objectives.*
4. The average human being learns, under proper conditions, not only to accept but to seek responsibility. *Avoidance of responsibility, lack of ambition, and emphasis on security are generally consequences of experience, not inherent human characteristics.*

5. The capacity to exercise a relatively high degree of imagination, inge-
   nuity, and creativity in the solution of organizational problems is
   widely, not narrowly, distributed in the population.
6. Under the conditions of modern industrial life, the intellectual poten-
   tialities of the average human being are only partially utilized.
   (McGregor, 1960, pp. 33–34, 47–48)

The nature of interaction between personality and organization became
another key focus of study (Argyris, 1957; Getzels & Guba, 1957). Human-relations
theorists viewed personality and organization as being hopelessly in conflict and
sided with personality. Efficiency theorists shared this view of conflict, but its
advocates sided with organization. Human resources recognized personality and
organization conflict but did view it as inherent. According to this view, the two
were to be integrated, with workers receiving maximum satisfaction and enrichment from achievement at work and, in turn, work reaching new levels of effectiveness because of worker commitment to organizational goals.

Human resources urged that shared decision making, joint planning, common
goals, increased responsibility, and more autonomy be the sorts of power-equalization strategies developed by educational administrators. Motivation was to be
intrinsic because jobs were to be interesting and challenging. Job enrichment was
advocated as a means to build into the jobs of students and teachers increased
opportunities for experiencing achievement, recognition, advancement, opportunities for growth, and increased competence. Human-resources theories reflected
not only an interest in people at work but also a new regard for their potential.
Teachers, for example, were to be considered as professionals, well able to respond
to these progressive, optimizing ideas. In education, such organizational concepts
as team teaching, family grouping, open space, school within a school, open corri-
dor, integrated day, and multiunits are often based on human-resources concepts.
In Table 6.1, assumptions basic to human-relations views and human-resources
views are summarized and compared.

Person views of administration, particularly human-resources views, place a
great deal of emphasis on autonomy, inner direction, and the desire for maximum
self-development at work. As long as these conditions hold for teachers at one
level and for students at another, then the optimizing characteristics of these views
are likely to work. But the desire for universal self-actualization and the centrality
of the work setting in one's life are debatable. In speaking of this issue. Dubin
(1959) notes :

Work, for probably a majority of workers, and even extending into the ranks of
management, may represent an institutional setting that is not the central life
interest of the participants. The consequence of this is that while participating in
work, a general attitude of apathy and indifference prevails. . . . Thus, the indus-
trial worker does not feel imposed upon by the tyranny of organizations, company,
or union. (p. 161)

TABLE 6.1   Comparing Human-Relations and Human-Resources Views

Human-Relations Model	Human-Resources Model
Attitudes toward People	
1. People in our culture, leaders among them, share a common set of needs—to belong, to be liked, to be respected.	1. In addition to sharing common needs for belonging and respect, most people in our culture, teachers among them, desire to contribute effectively and creatively to the accomplishment of worthwhile objectives.
2. Teachers desire individual recognition, but, more importantly, they want to *feel* useful to the school and to their own work group.	2. The majority of teachers are capable of exercising far more initiative, responsibility, and creativity than their present jobs or work circumstances require or allow.
3. They tend to cooperate willingly and comply with school goals if these important needs are fulfilled.	3. These capabilities represent untapped resources, which are presently being wasted.
Kind and Amount of Participation	
1. The administrator's basic task is to make each teacher believe that he or she is a useful and important part of the team.	1. The administrator's basic task is to create an environment in which subordinates can contribute their full range of talents to the accomplishment of school goals. She or he works to uncover the creative resources of subordinates.
2. The administrator is willing to explain her or his decisions and to discuss subordinates' objections to the plans. On routine matters, he or she encourages subordinates in planning and in decision making.	2. The administrator allows and encourages teachers to participate in important as well as routine decisions. In fact, the more important a decision is to the school, the greater the administrator's efforts to tap faculty resources.
3. Within narrow limits, the faculty or individual teachers who make up the faculty should be allowed to exercise self-direction and self-control in carrying out plans.	3. Administrators work continually to expand the areas over which teachers exercise self-direction and self-control as they develop and demonstrate greater insight and ability.
Expectations	
1. Sharing information with teachers and involving them in school decision making will help satisfy their basic needs for belonging and for individual recognition.	1. The overall quality of decision making and performance will improve as administrators and teachers make use of the full range of experience, insight, and creative ability that exist in their schools.
2. Satisfying these needs will improve faculty morale and will reduce resistance to formal authority.	2. Teachers will exercise responsible self-direction and self-control in the accomplishment of worthwhile objectives that they understand and have helped establish.
3. High faculty morale and reduced resistance to formal authority may lead to improved school performance. It will at least reduce friction and make the administrator's job easier.	3. Faculty satisfaction will increase as a by-product of improved performance and the opportunity to contribute creatively to this improvement.

Source: R. E. Miles, "Human Relations or Human Resources?" *Harvard Business Review*, 43(4), 1965, p. 151. Copyright 1965 by the *Harvard Business Review*. Adapted by permission.

Strauss (1963) cautions:

1. Although many individuals find relatively little satisfaction in their work, this may not be as much of a deprivation as the hypothesis would suggest, since many of these same individuals center their lives off the job and find most of their satisfactions in the community and the home. With these individuals, power-equalization may not liberate much energy.

2. Individuals are not motivated solely to obtain autonomy, self-actualization, and so forth. With various degrees of emphasis, individuals also want security and to know what is expected of them. Power-equalization may certainly stir up a good deal of anxiety among those who are not prepared for it, and at least some individuals may be reluctant to assume the responsibility that it throws upon them.

3. Power-equalization techniques are not too meaningful when management needs no more than an "adequate" level of production, as is often the case when work is highly programmed. Under such circumstances the costs entailed by modification in job design and supervisory techniques may be greater than the gains obtained from increased motivation to work. (p. 48)

A further criticism of person views, which applies as well to efficiency theories, is their internal-to-the-organization emphasis. By focusing almost exclusively on individual and group issues, the larger social, political, and legal contexts of educational administration are underemphasized and often ignored. This issue will be explored further in the discussion of the political and decision-making and the cultural models of administration that appear next.

Concern for Politics and Decision Making

Political thinking represents a recent and important development in the literature of educational administration. In many respects, this view of organization and administration represents a major change in thinking—a significant paradigm shift. Four critical emphases distinguish political and decision-making views from those that emphasize efficiency of the person.

1. Whereas each of the other views was primarily concerned with forces, events, and activities internal to the school as an organization, the political and decision-making views are concerned with the dynamic interplay of the organizations with forces in its external environment.

The school, for example, is viewed as an open rather than a closed system and therefore as an integral part of its larger environment, rather than as a bounded entity isolated from its environment. As an organization, the school receives inputs, processes them, and returns outputs to its environment. Since inputs are typically diverse (e.g., youngsters differ in ability) and output demands are generally contradictory (e.g., the school is expected to maintain tight control over youngsters but at the same time teach them self-responsibility and initiative), there is constant interplay between school and environment. The nature of this interplay is political, as issues are resolved, bargains struck, and agreements reached. Internally, the school is comprised of interdependent subunits and groups, each with interests that compete with those of others. Each of these subunits is affected as others are affected, and together they comprise an array of mini-open systems subject to the same laws of political behavior that characterize the school's larger organizational—environmental interplay.

2. Whereas the emphasis in other views is on the administration of policy decisions, the emphasis in political and decision-making views is on policy development.

Political and decision-making views do not consider goals as givens to be administered. Goals are considered to be highly unstable and constantly changing. Therefore, understanding the process of bargaining in the development of goal consensus and understanding the sensitivity of such agreements to external forces are considered important. Further, the notion that educational administrators typically have little control over these forces, and at best play a brokerage role in the development of goal consensus, is central. For these reasons, analysis of goal development and building coalitional strategies for gathering and holding together sufficient support for goals are far more central to political thinking than is mere implementation.

3. Whereas the other views seek to suppress, program, gloss over, or resolve conflict, conflict is considered as both natural and necessary in political and decision-making views.

Conflict resolution is an important concern to theorists and practitioners who work from the person model; indeed, to them, conflict is considered pathological. Since finding and using the "one best way" are characteristics of both rational and mechanistic models, advocates of efficiency also regard conflict as a deviation to be corrected. Contrast these images of conflict with those of Baldridge (1971):

> *Conflict is natural, and is to be expected in a dynamic organization. Conflict is not abnormal, nor is it necessarily a symptom of a breakdown in the organization's community.*
>
> *The organization is fragmented into many power blocs and interest-groups, and it is natural that they will try to influence policy so that their values and goals are given primary consideration.*
>
> *In all organizations small groups of political elites govern most of the major decisions. However, this does not mean that one elite group governs everything; the decisions may be divided up, with different elite groups controlling different decisions.*
>
> *Formal authority, as prescribed by the bureaucratic system, is severely limited by the political pressure and bargaining tactics that groups can exert against author-*

ities. Decisions are not simply bureaucratic orders, but are instead negotiated compromises among competing groups. Officials are not free simply to order decisions; instead they have to jockey between interest groups, hoping to build viable compromises among powerful blocs.

External interest groups have a great deal of influence over the organization, and internal groups do not have the power to make policies in a vacuum. (p. 14)

The emphasis in political and decision-making views is on policy formulation. This emphasis, in turn, requires debate over appropriate goals, values, and strategies. Conflict is considered a natural outgrowth of the process and indeed is seen by advocates of this model as a sign of organizational health, rather than organizational pathology.

4. Whereas each of the other models assumes norms of rationality in decision making, political theories are not based on such norms.

This characteristic is related to each of the other three that distinguish political and decision-making views from person and efficiency models. Since it is assumed that goals are not given but negotiated, and since the interplay within the organization and between the organization and its environment is viewed as based on bargaining, the rational pattern of establishing clear goals—and subsequently programming individual and organizational behavior to maximize these goals—is held suspect by advocates of political and decision-making views. With respect to the organic model, the rational pattern of building a core of common values and commitments among workers is also suspect. In the political and decision-making view, a "satisficing" image of humankind and organization is offered as a substitute for the more traditional rational images. School administrators, for example, do not seek optional solutions to the problem they face but seek solutions that will satisfy a variety of demands. Thus, they are more likely to select not the best reading program for children, but the one that is easier for teachers to implement and costs less.

Rational and Nonrational Perspectives

Political and decision-making views began to receive attention from administrators in the late 1950s as scholars from political science and the decision sciences systematically began to study the problem of organization and administration. As with each of the other models, this group first gained strong acceptance among those interested in business organizations and business administration and later became the dominant strand of thought in educational administration. Herbert Simon's now classic work *Administrative Behavior: A Study of Decision-Making Processes in Administrative Organization,* first published in 1945, is considered by many as the forerunner of this movement. In Simon's (1945) view, the limits of rationality

have been seen to derive from the inability of the human mind to bring to bear upon a single decision all the aspects of value, knowledge, and behavior that would

> be relevant. *The pattern of human choice is often more nearly a stimulus-response pattern than a choice among alternatives. Human rationality operates, then, within the limits of a psychological environment. This environment imposes on the individual as "givens" a selection of factors upon which he must base his decisions. However, the stimuli of decision can themselves be controlled so as to serve broader ends, and a sequence of individual decisions can be integrated into a well-conceived plan. (pp. 108–109)*

Later, in a classic critique of the efficiency models of organization, Herbert Simon and James G. March discussed not only the cognitive and affective limits of individual rationality but also the limits of rationality implicit in the detailed organizational designs characteristic of bureaucratic theories (March & Simon, 1958).

In collaboration with Richard M. Cyert, March laid down the basic tenets of the decision-making view of organizational functioning (Cyert & March, 1963). Organizations, within this view, are composed of various groups and departments holding diverse interests. Decision making is constrained by the inability of people to account for and use all the available information that under optimal conditions would produce a maximum decision; by the need to maintain internal coordination and control and to keep the peace among competing groups; and by a highly uncertain and unstable external environment. Given these conditions, organizations are best viewed as "messy" arenas for shifting multiple-goal coalitions rather than tidy and rational pyramids made up of tightly connected and properly placed building blocks. The job of the administrator is to make sense of this messy situation in an effort to find some basis and enough support for reasonable and supported action to occur.

Conflict is inevitably part of the process of decision making under these conditions. Conflict occurs even where there is a general consensus regarding the organization's overall, albeit vague, goals—for when it comes to articulating goals into operational objectives requiring action, consensus typically disappears. Administrators reckon with conflict by emphasizing "local rationality." When this occurs, attention is given to a problem as defined by a specific interest without concern for other interests. Thus, as Cusick (1983) points out, the problem of maintaining order in high school classrooms and keeping the peace between teachers and students is addressed separately from the problem of academic achievement. His research reveals that principals put pressure on teachers to get along with students and keep them in class, even if it means sacrificing academic goals. He notes, for example, "It was more important to keep them in school, in class, and in order than it was to teach them something and see that they learned it" (Cusick, 1983, p. 39). Standards of rationality are kept simple and focused on the immediate problem at hand. As the problem changes, so does the standard of rationality, and this enables the "quasi-resolution" of conflict (Cyert & March, 1963).

This quasi-resolution is also achieved by adopting *acceptable-level decision rules*. If all goals are to be achieved fully, then conflict among them is heightened. But when one is willing to settle for an acceptable level of achievement, it is possible to pursue several conflicting goals in a satisfactory way. *Sequential attention to goals* is also used to quasi-resolve conflict. Rather than be committed fully to one goal or another (academic achievement or student satisfaction), or to integrating the two goals so that they become one, the school attends first to one, as if it were the only goal, and then to another, as if *it* were the only goal.

In the 1970s, March and his colleagues turned their attention to the analysis of educational organizations. Characterizing educational organizations as "organized anarchies," they identified three distinct, important, and troublesome features of such organizations, which seem to justify the anarchy label.

> *First, their goals are problematic. It is difficult to specify a consistent set of goals. Instead, goals seem to shift over time; they seem to vary from one part of the school to another; they seem to be stated in terms that are hard to translate into action. There is conflict over goals, and the conflict is not resolved easily. Although it is sometimes possible to impute goals to the organization by observing behavior, such imputations appear often to be unstable or to define goals that are not acceptable to all participants in the organization. The decision process seems to reflect more a series of actions by which goals are discovered than a process by which they are acted upon. Speeches on goals express platitudes that are not useful administratively.*
>
> *Second, their technologies are unclear. Although we know how to create an educational institution, to staff it, and to specify an educational program for it, we do not know much about the process by which it works. It does work, at least in some senses. Students seem to change. Moreover, we can duplicate our results. If we recreate the procedures in a new school, they will often have approximately the same outcomes. But we have remarkably little capability for designed change in the system. We do not, in general, know what will happen if we make changes; we do not, in general, know how to adapt the standard system to non-standard students or situations. New occasions require a new set of trial-and-error procedures, either in the school or in an experimental laboratory.*
>
> *Third, participation in the organization is fluid. Participants come and go. Students, teachers, and administrators move in and out. There is even more turnover in other participants or potential participants. Parents, individually and collectively, are erratic in their involvement; community leaders sometimes ignore the schools, sometimes devote considerable time to them; governmental agencies are active, then passive. All of the potential actors in the organization have other concerns that compete with the school for their attention. Thus, whether they participate in the school depends as much on the changing characteristics of their alternatives as it does on the characteristics of the educational organization involved. (Cohen, March, & Olsen, 1972, p. 710)*

This description of schools challenges conceptions implicit in the more traditional theories of administration and organization. March (1962) suggests that organizations should be viewed as political coalitions and administrators as political brokers. As a political coalition, the form, shape, and structure of a school as well as its goals and missions are negotiated. He further notes that within the organization, individuals frequently join together into subcoalitions. Coalition members in schools would include teachers, chairpersons, supervisors, administrators, janitors, students, the school board, the PTA, the teacher's union, the central office, volunteers, interest groups, regulatory agencies, an municipal departments.

Planning and Decision Making as Examples

The concern for politics and decision making suggests that organizational life is not as rational as one might like and that administrative behavior is limited by human characteristics of administrators as persons and by political, financial, and other constraints that define the administrator's work context. In accord with this view, Cohen, March, and Olsen (1972) liken decision making in an organization to a garbage can. Various school problems and solutions are deposited in this can, though typically solutions are only loosely connected to the problem. Given the garbage-can metaphor, March and his associates suggest that a better image of planning and decision making is one assuming that *solutions exist that must be matched to problems.* It is often presumed, for example, that a group of teachers who adopt a teaching program, such as mainstreaming instruction in the arts with the traditional academic program (a solution), do so in response to a problem—such as neglect of the arts in the curriculum. But what may really be the case is that *the problem is invented* to accommodate a "solution" based on the preferences, training, and beliefs of the teacher.

In his important essay "The Science of Muddling Through," Charles Lindblom(1959) makes an important distinction between rational-linear planning and deciding described in theory and the more realistic and practical planning found in administrative practice. Administrators and policymakers, Lindblom maintains, practice disjointed incrementalism by making decisions based on small, incremental successive and limited comparisons of fairly familiar alternatives found close to home. Instead of rationality routing out all the available possibilities, solution search is highly limited. Frequently, the solutions favored do not match the problem at all, and thus the problem is changed to fit the solution. Information is often revised and reinterpreted, solutions are redesigned, and goals are changed in fashions that make each of these components compatible with the other.

Disjointed incrementalism scales problems down to manageable size, limits the amount of information collected, restricts choices, and shortens horizons because all these make the process of decision making more manageable and practical. The net result is a science of decision making that features muddling through. Lindblom's "science of muddling through" fits well with Simon's (1945) assertion that administrators do not search for the best needle in the haystack but accept the first one found that will do the job and with Cohen, March, and Olsen's (1972) metaphor of the garbage can to characterize decision making.

Much remains to be learned about the constructive use of conflict in organizations and about the bargaining role of the school administrator. Recognizing first that conflict can have constructive consequences for schools is in itself an important contribution of the political and decision-making view of schools. Indeed, viewing the school as a political system adds a rich dimension to understanding how schools actually operate. But as enhancing as these glimpses of reality are, serious caveats are in order. Political and decision-making views are largely descriptive, not prescriptive. They attempt to describe and understand what is actually occurring rather than what should be occurring, and these are important undertakings.

School administrators should not assume, however, that because events are as they are, the name of the game is only to learn the rules and play by them. *The rules themselves are at issue and must be evaluated for goodness of fit to the unique values of the school as a particular kind of organization.* In educational enterprises, means and ends are often indistinguishable. Teachers and students alike learn as much from how one organizes and behaves in schools as they do from the official educational program. Management and organization are part of the school's hidden curriculum, and they teach important lessons to students.

Concern for Culture

In recent years, interest in the cultural perspective has mushroomed. Concepts such as school culture, changing the culture of the school, and cultural leadership are now routinely discussed at conferences, in workshops, and in journal articles and books.

Anthropologists speak of culture as webs of meaning organized in terms of symbols and other representations (Geertz, 1973). Symbols are key in understanding cultural meaning. Smircich (1985), for example, suggests that understanding organizational culture requires that one focus on symbols, not culture. "Culture does not exist separately from people in interaction. People hold culture in their heads, but we cannot really know what is in their heads. All we can see or know are representations or symbols" (p. 67). Louis (1980) characterizes a group's culture as follows: "A set of understandings or *meanings shared* by a group of people. The meanings are largely *tacit* among members, are clearly *relevant* to the particular group, and are *distinctive* to the group. Meanings are *passed on* to new group members" (p. 16). Hofstede (1980, p. 13) describes culture as the collective programming of the mind that distinguishes the members of one group from another.

Underlying the cultural perspective is the concern for community and the importance of shared meanings and shared values. The concept of *center* is often considered to be key. Organizational and societal centers represent the locus of values, sentiments, and beliefs that provide the cultural cement for holding together human groups (Shils, 1961, p. 119).

Leadership within the Cultural Perspective
Many studies of successful schools (Lipsitz, 1984; Deal, 1987; Sergiovanni, 1994; Hill, Foster, & Gendler, 1990) suggest that they have central zones composed of values and beliefs that take on sacred characteristics. Indeed, it might be useful to think of them as having an official "religion" that gives meaning and guides appropriate actions. As repositories of values, these central zones are sources of

identity for teachers and students from which their school lives become meaningful. The focus of leadership within the cultural perspective, then, is on developing and nurturing these central-zone patterns so that they provide a normative basis for action within the schools.

Leadership activities associated with the cultural view include articulating school purposes and mission; socializing new members to the school; telling stories and maintaining or reinforcing myths, traditions, and beliefs; explaining "the way things operate around here"; developing and displaying a system of symbols; and rewarding those who reflect the school's culture. Such leadership, according to this view, is designed to bond together students, teachers, and others to the work of the school as believers. The school and its purposes become revered, and in some respects they resemble an ideological system dedicated to a sacred mission. It is believed that as persons become members of this strong and binding culture, they are provided with opportunities for enjoying a special sense of personal importance and significance. Their work and their lives take on a new importance, one characterized by richer meanings, an expanded sense of identity, and a feeling of belonging to something special—all of which are considered to be highly motivating conditions (Peters & Waterman, 1982).

School culture includes values, symbols, beliefs, and shared meanings of parents, students, teachers, and others conceived as a group or community. Culture governs what is of worth for this group and how members should think, feel, and behave. The substance of culture includes a school's customs and traditions; historical accounts and unstated understandings; habits, norms, and expectations; and common meanings and shared assumptions. The more understood, accepted, and cohesive the culture of the school, the better able it is to move in concert toward ideals it holds and objectives it wishes to pursue. It is in this sense, the argument goes, that culture serves as a compass setting to steer people in a common direction, furnishes a set of norms that define what people should accomplish and how, and provides a source of meaning and significance for teachers, students, administrators, and others as they work.

Once shaped and established in the school, this strong culture acts as a powerful socializer of thought and programmer of behavior. But the shaping and establishment of culture does not just happen. It is instead a negotiated product of the shared sentiments of school participants. Often, competing views and competing ideologies exist in schools, and deciding which ones will count requires some struggling. Administrators are in an advantageous position to strongly influence the outcome of this struggle. They are, for example, in control of the communications system of the school and thus can decide what information to share with whom. Further, they control the allocation of resources and are able to reward desirable and sanction undesirable behavior. Bates (1981) further elaborates the principal's influence in shaping school culture: "The culture of a school is therefore the product of conflict and negotiation over definitions of situations. The administrative influence on school language, metaphor, myths and rituals is a major factor in the determination of a culture which is reproduced and the consciousness of teachers and pupils" (p. 43).

Building School Culture

Culture building requires that school leaders give attention to the informal, subtle, and symbolic aspects of school life. It is presumed that teachers, parents, and students need answers to such questions as: What is this school about? What is important here? What do we believe in? Why do we function the way we do? How are we unique? How do I fit into the scheme of things? Answers to questions of this sort provide an orderliness to one's school life that is derived from the sense of purpose and enriched meaning. As Greenfield (1973) states, "What many people seem to want from schools is that schools reflect the values that are central and meaningful in their lives. If this view is correct, schools are cultural artifacts that people struggle to shape in their own image. Only in such forms do they have faith in them; only in such forms can they participate comfortably in them" (p. 570). Greenfield (1984) believes that "the task of leadership is to create the moral order that binds [leaders] and the people around them" (p. 159).

Leadership in culture building is not a new idea but one solidly embedded in the literature of leadership and well known to successful school leaders. In 1957, for example, Selznick wrote:

> *The art of the creative leader is the art of institution building, the reworking of human and technological materials to fashion an organism that embodies new and enduring values. . . . To institutionalize is to* infuse with value *beyond the technical requirements of the task at hand. . . . Whenever individuals become attached to an organization or a way of doing things as persons rather than technicians, the result is a prizing of the device for its own sake. From the standpoint of the committed person, the organization is changed from an expendable tool to a valued source of personal satisfaction. . . . The institutional leader, then, is primarily an expert in the promotion and protection of values. (p. 28)*

Within the cultural perspective, successful leaders emphasize leadership by purpose. Vaill (1984) defines *purposing* as "that continuous stream of actions by an organization's formal leadership which has the effect of inducing clarity, consensus, and commitment regarding the organization's basic purposes" (p. 91). Bennis (1984) defines *purposing* as "a compelling vision of a desired state of affairs . . . which clarifies the current situation and induces commitment to the future" (p. 66). Purposing, according to these researchers, derives its power from the needs of persons at work to have some sense of what is important, some signal of what is of value.

The focus of cultural leadership shares with efficiency, person, and political leadership a highly instrumental bias. In all cases, the emphasis is on how administrators can gain more control over the achievement of school goals and objectives and obtain greater compliance from teachers to ensure that their efforts are sufficiently motivated and coordinated to that end. On behalf of this effort, school administrators within the cultural perspective give less attention to managerial controls, interpersonal psychology, and political negotiating and more attention to understanding, using, and, if necessary, reconstructing school artifacts, perspectives, values, and assumptions. These constitute four levels of organizational culture (Dyer, 1982). The four levels are described by Lundberg (1985) as follows:

1. Artifacts: *These are the tangible aspects of culture shared by members of an organization and include language, stories, myths, rituals, ceremonies, and visible products which are considered to have symbolic value.*

2. Perspectives: *These are the socially shared rules and norms which provide solutions to common problems encountered by organizational members and guidelines which allow members to define and interpret the situations they face and which prescribe the bounds of acceptable behavior.*

3. Values: *These provide the evaluational basis that organizational members use for judging situations, acts, objects and people. Values represent important goals, ideals, standards, as well as taboos of an organization and are often embodied in statements of the organization's philosophy or mission.*

4. Assumptions: *These constitute the tacit beliefs that members hold about themselves and others which govern their relationships and define for them the nature of their connection to the organization of which they are a part. Unlike perspectives and values assumptions are typically not stated and indeed may even be unconscious. (p. 171)*

Can school administrators actually reconstruct the artifacts, perspectives, values, and assumptions of their schools in a fashion that builds the necessary sense of community, shared meaning, and indeed sacred culture to enable highly successful school functioning? Some educational researchers such as Lipsitz (1984), W. Greenfield (1985), and Firestone and Wilson (1985) provide some evidence that suggests they can. Leading researchers in the area of corporate cultures, such as Ouchi (1981), Pascale and Athos (1981), Peters and Waterman (1982), Deal and Kennedy (1982), and Bennis and Nanus (1985), also seem to support this view. But many experts feel that cultural leadership does not create new sacred cultures but rather shapes and legitimizes the culture that emerges within the organization. They would assert that the *lead first* view of cultural leadership attributes too much homogeneity to organizations and views them as having a monolithic and dominant culture. A more accurate view, by their way of thinking, would portray organizations in terms of heterogeneity and lack of consensus and as being composed of overlapping and nested subcultures (Martin, Sitkin, & Boehm, 1985, p. 102). According to this view, "Creating a culture is like surfing. You cannot make a wave. All you can do is wait and watch for the right wave, then ride it for all it's worth" (Martin, Sitkin, & Boehm, 1985, p. 105). Which of these views best describes reality has yet to be resolved.

A nagging question accompanying the cultural view is: *Should* administrators actually reconstruct the artifacts, perspectives, values, and assumptions of their schools in an effort to create strong cultures? Some theorists would argue, if building strong cultures results in administrators increasing their control over the thinking and behavior of teachers and students, then the cultural perspective results in little more than a further refinement of the art and science of manipulation (Bates, 1984). A similar charge of manipulation is leveled by critics at person and efficiency views. For example, is being concerned about work needs of teachers in an effort to "motivate" them little more than a form of manipulation (Foster, 1984)? The question critics raise is whether *any* form of social engineering is appropriate. The issue, however, may be less whether school administrators should seek to influence than whether ethical guidelines can be established to guide such influence (Sergiovanni, 1980.)

During the 1990s, work on the cultural perspective in educational administration took on a new twist. Instead of emphasizing school culture as a manifestation of cultural characteristics in general, the focus changed to understanding schools as a distinct form of social organization that could be understood as a community. According to Sergiovanni (1994), communities are collections of people who are connected together because they share common commitments, ideas, and values. He suggests that schools can be understood as:

1. Learning communities where not only students but all members of the school community are committed to thinking, growing, and inquiring and where learning is an attitude as well as an activity, a way of life as well as a process
2. Collegial communities where members are connected to each other for mutual benefit and to pursue common goals by a sense of felt interdependence and mutual obligation
3. Caring communities where members, motivated by altruistic love, make a total commitment to each other and where the characteristics that define their relationships are moral in character
4. Inclusive communities where economic, religious, cultural, ethnic, family, and other differences are brought together into a mutually respective whole
5. Inquiring communities where principals and teachers commit themselves to a spirit of collective inquiry as they reflect on their practice and search for solutions to the problems they face

Three characteristics are central to gauging the extent to which a school measures up to being a community: the extent to which members share common interpersonal bonds; the extent to which members share an identity with a common place (such as my class, my space, my school); and the extent to which members share a commitment to values, norms, and beliefs. In strong school communities, members share in a community of relationships, a community of place, and a community of mind. Advocates of community argue that as connections in a school strengthen, webs of obligations are created that have moral overtones. The school begins to speak to members in a moral voice, which compels compliance with community purposes and norms (e.g., see Etzioni, 1993).

Educational Administration as an Applied Science

March (1974) has accurately referred to educational administration as being "managerially parasitic," speaking to its tendency to borrow heavily from the insights, theories, and practices associated with the organization and administration of business enterprises. Superior funding and greater demand have brought business organization to the attention of scholars, and most of the literature on organization and administration has been developed with this type of organization in mind. This section discusses some of the differences between management in educational and other public organizations and that in business organizations. These differences suggest that great care must be taken in adapting management practices from other sectors for use in schools.

It is easily recognized that, at one level of analysis, management is management. Although public and private organizations share many features, the differences are significant. The well-known management professor Wallace Sayre has stated that "business and government administration are alike in all unimportant respects" (quoted in Bower, 1977, p. 140). Joseph Bower (1977) of the Harvard Business School notes that "American business is an inappropriate analogy for discussing and evaluating public management. In the public sector, *purpose, organization* and *people* do not have the same meaning and significance that they have in business" (p. 140).

Following are some important differences between schools, as one kind of public organization, and private organizations:

1. Power over money, organization, and personnel rests in the hands of the legislature, school legal code, and local school board rather than in the hands of management.
2. Measures of progress toward goals are difficult to devise. What are the school measures of good citizenship, intellectual enrichment, problem-solving ability, independent thinking, a desire to learn, economic sufficiency, and effective family living, for example? These are contrasted with the readily understood and quantifiable economic objectives of private organizations.
3. Public accounting to which the school is subjected is designed to *control* current expenditures, as contrasted with business accounting, which tends to support future planning, research, and development.
4. Tenure laws and civil-service laws tend to protect educational workers from the control of administrators and supervisors.
5. School purposes and organizational processes designed to achieve these purposes are influenced indirectly by administrators through individuals and groups (a political process), rather than directly by administrators (a management process).
6. Goals and objectives are often unclear and contradictory. The latent custodial functions of schools, for example, contradict the goal-achievement functions.
7. No market exists to determine effectiveness. Expensive special education programs, for example, are maintained for moral, political, and legal reasons,

though if they were subjected to a market economy, general consumer interest would not likely be sufficient to sustain them. By comparison, product lines of firms are thinned out by a market economy.

8. Resources are distributed on the basis of formula and other approximations of *equity* rather than on *merit*. Allocating greater resources to so-called high-producing schools, for example, has historically not been considered appropriate.
9. Administrators work with an array of people whose careers are outside of management control.
10. A tight coupling exists between means and ends, or products and processes. Schooling is a human activity with human ends.
11. Many objectives are pursued with scarce resources, as contrasted with the firm, which allocates more resources to fewer—indeed, more focused—objectives.

Perhaps the most critical difference between the school and most other organizations is the human intensity that characterizes its work. Schools are human organizations in the sense that their products are human and their processes require the socializing of humans. Further, unlike most organizations that rely on machinery and technology, schools are labor intensive. More than 70 percent of the money spent for education, for example, goes to the educational labor force—mostly to the roughly 2 million teachers.

This human intensity in educational organizations makes critically important the role of values in schooling, as Broudy (1965) notes:

The educator, however, deals with nothing but values—human beings who are clusters and constellations of value potentials. Nothing human is really alien to the educational enterprise and there is, therefore, something incongruous about educational administrators evading fundamental value conflicts.... The public will never quite permit the educational administrator the moral latitude that it affords some of its servants. For to statesmen and soldiers men entrust their lives and fortunes, but to the schools they entrust their precarious hold on humanity itself. (p. 52)

For these reasons, many experts find it useful to view educational administration as a distinct applied science. This applied science relies heavily on concepts, insights, and practices from the various disciplines and from the study of organization and administration in general but evaluates these ideas for goodness to fit to the unique value structure of educational organizations. In this process, some ideas are rejected and others accepted. An applied science is concerned with means as well as ends and focuses on quality of process as well as on quality of goal achievement. *Educational administration is also an ethical science concerned with good or better processes, good or better means, and good or better ends, and, as such, is thoroughly immersed in values, preferences, idea, aspirations, and hopes.*

A Reflective-Practice Perspective

Despite the usefulness of the concept of applied science and the importance of ethical considerations, many theorists feel that such a view does not capture the nature of professional practice. Applied science portrays a highly instrumental view of knowledge (Kennedy, 1984) that assumes that professional practice involves the fairly mechanical process of pigeonholing problems and then searching a series of perfected practice treatments for the right ones to apply (Mintzberg, 1979). Schon (1983) says that patterns of professional practice are actually characterized by a great deal of uncertainty, instability, complexity, and variety. Value conflicts and uniquenesses are accepted aspects of educational administration. These characteristics are, according to Schon (1983, p. 14), central to the world of professional practice in all the major professions, including medicine, engineering, management, and education. Schon concludes that "professional knowledge is mismatched to the changing characteristics of the situation of practice" (p. 14). In support of this view, Ralph Tyler maintains that researchers do not have a full understanding of the nature of professional practice in education. He states:

> *Researchers and many academics also misunderstand educational practice. The practice of every profession evolves informally, and professional procedures are not generally derived from systematic design based on research findings. Professional practice has largely developed through trial and error and intuitive efforts. Practitioners, over the years, discover procedures that appear to work and others that fail. The professional practice of teaching, as well as that of law, medicine and theology, is largely a product of the experience of practitioners, particularly those who are more creative, inventive, and observant than the average. (cited in Hosford, 1984, p. 9)*

Science, according to Tyler, "explains phenomena, it does not produce practices" (cited in Hosford, 1984, p. 10).

Professionals rely heavily on informed intuition as they create knowledge in use. Intuition is informed by theoretical knowledge on the one hand and by interacting with the context of practice on the other. When administrators use informed intuition, they are engaging in reflective practice.

Applied science within educational administration seeks to establish a body of "artificial" professional intelligence. Scientific knowledge would be the key aspect of such intelligence. School administrators would only have to diagnose problems they face and draw from this intelligence standard treatments to apply. These treatments would be screened to assure that they meet certain ethical requirements.

By contrast, reflective practice seeks to establish augmented professional intelligence. Here, educational administrators would be key aspects of this intelligence, for it would not stand apart as an abstract body of theoretical knowledge. Augmented professional intelligence serves to inform the intuitions of principals as they practice. As this practice unfolds, practical knowledge is created in use as unique treatments are developed, applied, refined, and shared. Instead of using scientific knowledge instrumentally, as is the case in applied science, this knowledge is used conceptually to inform the administrator's judgment as she or he makes a decision.

The concept of reflective practice is relatively new, and much more thinking needs to be given to its development and use in educational administration.

Educational Administration as a Moral Craft

Blumberg (1989) uses the metaphor *craft* to present a view of the nature of administrative work that can provide the long missing bridge between what is known in the minds and experiences of successful administrators and the practice situations they face. To some, the word *craft* communicates an endeavor that is low level and even pedestrian. Blumberg has in mind, however, the accomplished and prized work of artisans that stands out from the work of amateur hobbyists. This distinction between amateurism and artisanship strengthens the use of the craft metaphor, for though school administrators do not hold the monopoly on exercising management and leadership, their practice should be qualitatively superior to that of others who share these roles.

Blumberg explores the craft metaphor by describing how the mind, heart, and hand of the artisan "potter" working in tandem with the "clay" are brought together to produce something useful. Similarly, the craft of school administration "is the exercise in individual fashion of practical wisdom toward the end of making things in a school or school system 'look like one wants them to look'" (Blumberg, 1989, p. 46). Recognizing that there are certain skills involved in any craft, Blumberg focuses on the know-how that goes beyond just being able to employ these skills. It is this know-how that differentiates the artisan from the more pedestrian amateur—the prized craft product from the run of the mill.

Artisanship is associated with dedication, experience, personal knowledge of the material and mastery of detail, sense of harmony, integration, intimate understanding, and wisdom (Mintzberg, 1987). Artisans, according to Blumberg (1989), develop a special kind of know-how that is characterized as having a refined nose for things, a sense of what constitutes an acceptable result in any particular problematic situation, an understanding of the nature of the materials with which they work, a mastery of the basic technology undergirding the craft, the skill to employ this technology in an efficacious manner, and, most important, knowing what to do and when to do it. School administrators make pragmatic and moral decisions and are able to diagnose and interpret the meaning of what is occurring as they work in any situation.

In sum, reflective school administrators practice as artisans by bringing together deep knowledge of relevant techniques and competent application of tried and true "rules of thumb" with a "nose" for their practice and a penchant for reflecting on this practice as they create something of practical utility. In this effort, craft knowledge represents one source of information and insight that is equal to and sometimes superior to theoretical knowledge; together, craft and theoretical knowledge comprise one's theories of practice. These theories are not designed to *tell* the school administrator but rather to *inform* her or his professional practice. The hallmark of the artisan is the ability to reflect on practice.

Administering schools, as Blumberg suggests, is no ordinary craft, however. It is instead a moral craft, a fate shared with teaching (Tom, 1984) and supervision (Sergiovanni & Starratt, 1993). The reasons for the prominence of the imperative in the work of school administration are as follows (summarized from Sergiovanni, 1995, 309–311):

1. The job of the school administrator is to transform the school from an organization composed of technical functions in pursuit of objective outcomes into an institution. Organizations are little more than technical instruments for achieving objectives. As technical instruments, they celebrate the value of effectiveness and efficiency by being more concerned with "doing things right" than "doing right things." Institutions, on the other hand, are effective and efficient and more. They are responsive, adaptive enterprises that exist not only to get a particular job done but as entities in and of themselves. As Selznick (1957) points out, organizations become institutions when they transcend the technical requirements needed for the task at hand. In his words, "Institutionalization is a process. It is something that happens to an organization over time, reflecting the organization's own distinctive history, people who have been in it, groups it embodies and the vested interests they have created, and the way it has adapted to its environment" (Selznick, 1957, p. 16). He continues, "Organizations become institutions when they are *infused with value,* that is, prized not as tools alone but as sources of direct personal gratification and vehicles of group integrity. This infusion produces a distinct identity for the organization. Where institutionalization is well advanced, distinctive outlooks, habits, and other commitments are unified, coloring all aspects of organizational life and lending it a *social integration* that goes well beyond formal coordination and command" (Selznick, 1957, p. 40). Selznick's conception of institution is similar to the familiar conception of school as a *learning community.* To become either, the school must move beyond concerns for goals and roles to the task of building purposes into its structure and embodying these purposes in everything it does. When this happens, school members are transformed from neutral participants to committed followers. The embodiment of purpose and the development of followership are inescapably moral.

2. The job of the school is to transform its students not only by providing them with knowledge and skills but by building character and instilling virtue. As Cuban (1988) points out, both technical and moral images are present in teaching and administering. "The technical image contains values that prize accumulated knowledge, efficiency, orderliness, productivity, and social usefulness; the moral image, while not disregarding such values, prizes values directed at molding character, shaping attitudes, and producing a virtuous and thoughtful person" (p.

xvii). Technical and moral images of administration cannot be separated in practice. Every technical decision has moral implications. Emphasizing orderliness, for example, might comprise a lesson in diligence for students and might be a reminder to teachers that professional goals cannot be pursued to the extent that bureaucratic values are compromised.

3. Whether concern is for virtue or efficiency, some standard has to be adopted. What is efficient in this circumstance? How will virtue be determined? Determining criteria for effective teaching, deciding on what is a good discipline policy, or coming to grips with promotion criteria standards, for example, all require value judgments. Answers to questions of how and what cannot be resolved objectively as if they were factual assertions but must be treated as normative assertions. Normative assertions are true only because we decide that they are. "We must decide what ought to be the case. We cannot *discover* what ought to be the case by investigating what is the case" (Taylor, 1961, p. 248). Normative assertions are moral statements.

4. Despite commitments to empowerment and shared decision making, relationships between school administrators and others who work in schools are inherently unequal. Though often downplayed and regardless of whether they want it or not, school administrators typically have more power than teachers, students, parents, and others. This power is derived, in part, legally from their hierarchical position, but for the most part is *de facto* by virtue of the greater access to information and people that their position affords them. This access allows them to decide what information will be shared with others, what information will be withheld, and frequently what information will be forgotten. Often teachers and others in the school rely on school administrators to serve as the "coordinating mechanism" that links together what they are doing with what others are doing. In teaching, where much of the work is invisible, the coordinating function is a powerful one. Further, much of the information that principals accumulate is confidential. Information is a source of power and the accumulation of power has moral consequences. Moreover, whenever there is an unequal distribution of power between two people, the relationship becomes a moral one. Whether intended to or not, leadership involves an offer to control. The follower accepts this offer on the assumption that control will not be exploited. The test of moral leadership under these conditions is whether the competence, well-being, and independence of the follower is enhanced as a result of accepting control and whether the school benefits.

5. The context for administration is surprisingly loose, chaotic, and ambiguous. Thus, despite demands and constraints that circumscribe the school administrator's world, *de facto* discretion is built into the job and this discretion has moral implications.

A key point in understanding the moral imperative in school administration is understanding the difference between normative rationality and technical rationality. Normative rationality is based on what we believe and consider to be good. Technical rationality, by contrast, is based on what is effective and efficient. Happily the two are not mutually exclusive. School administrators want both what is good and what is effective for their schools. But when the two are in conflict the moral choice is to prize the former over the latter. Normative rationality provides the basis for moral leadership. Instead of just relying on bureaucratic authority to compel compliance or psychological authority to manipulate compliance, the practice of leadership is based on ideas, purposes, and values.

A nagging question in coming to grips with administration as a moral craft deals with the place of scientific authority in the form of expertness established by educational research. Isn't it enough that research says we ought to do this or that? Of course research is important and the insights gleaned from this kind of knowledge are often invaluable to administrators. But this knowledge cannot represent a source of authority for action that replaces moral authority. As Smith and Blase (1987) explain:

> *A leader in moral terms is one who fully realizes the . . . serious limitations on our ability to make accurate predictions and master the instructional process. Moreover, such a leader must encourage others to fully realize these limitations. Based on this awareness, a moral leader refuses to allow discussions of major pedagogical issues to be dominated by what the research supposedly demonstrates. . . . To do so would be to perpetuate the fiction that we have the kind of knowledge that we do not in fact possess. Rather, disagreements over how and what to teach must be played out in terms of reasoned discourse. The generalizations of educational inquiry can of course be part of these reasons, but they are not epistemologically privileged—they must share the stage with personal experience, a recounting of the experience of others, with philosophical and sociological considerations, and so on. (p. 39)*

This chapter has focused on the intellectual heritage of educational administration. Administrators practice their art from certain perspectives or sets of biases related to the development of thought in educational administration. Efficiency, person, political, and cultural models were used to illustrate and summarize the major strands of thought affecting administrative practice. Though the models exist as objective accumulations of concepts, the ideological and value differences among them add richness and controversy to the field.

Particular attention was given to political and decision-making and to cultural theories, for these represent the most recent conceptions of educational administration. Educational administration was then viewed as an applied science with values and other characteristics unique to the school, as a standard by which concepts from the science of administration and those tried and true from the real world of practice are evaluated for appropriateness. This analysis includes a contrast of differences between administration of public and private organizations. The concept of reflective practice was discussed as a possible alternative to applied science. Reflective practice, it was argued, comprises the basis for understanding school administration as a moral craft—a view remarkably similar to that espoused by Mary Parker Follett in the 1920s. Follett proposed that administration be built on a trinity of values that include artful practice, scientific understanding, and ethical consideration (Metcalf & Urwick, 1940; Follett, 1924).

References

Argyris, C. (1957). *Personality and organization*. New York: Harper and Row.

Baldridge, J. V. (1971). *The analysis of organizational change: A human relations strategy versus a political systems strategy* (R&D memo 75). Stanford: Stanford Center for R&D in Teaching, Stanford University.

Bates, R. (1981). Management and the culture of the school. In R. Bates & Course Team (Eds.), *Management of resources in schools. Study Guide I*. Victoria: Deakin University.

Bates, R. (1984). Toward a critical practice of educational administration. In T. J. Sergiovanai & J. E. Corbally (Eds.), *Leadership and organizational culture* (pp. 260–274). Urbana: University of Illinois Press.

Bennis, W. (1984). Transformation power and leadership. In T. J. Sergiovanni & J. E. Corbally (Eds.), *Leadership and organizational culture* (pp. 64–71). Urbana: University of Illinois Press.

Bennis, W., & Nanus, B. (1985). *Leaders*. New York: Harper and Row.

Blumberg, A. (1989). *School administration as craft*. Boston: Allyn and Bacon.

Bobbitt, F. (1913). The supervision of city schools: Some general principles of management applied to the problems of city school systems. *Twelfth yearbook of the National Society for the Study of Education*. Bloomington, IL: NSSE.

Bower, J. (1977, March–April). Effective public management: It isn't the same as effective business management. *Harvard Business Review,* 131–140.

Broudy, H. S. (1965). Conflict in values. In R. Ohm & W. Monohan (Eds.), *Educational administration: Philosophy in action* (pp. 42–54). Norman: University of Oklahoma, College of Education.

Callahan R. E. (1962). *Education and the cult of efficiency: A study of the social forces that have shaped the administration of the public schools*. Chicago: University of Chicago Press.

Cohen, D. M., March, J. G., & Olsen, J. P. (1972). A garbage can model of organizational choice. *Administrative Science Quarterly, 17*(1).

Cuban, L. (1988). *The managerial imperative in the practice of leadership in schools*. Albany: State University of New York Press.

Cubberly, E. P. (1916). *Public administration*. Boston: Houghton Mifflin.

Cusick, P. A. (1983). *The egalitarian ideal and the American high school*. New York: Longman.

Cyert, R. M., & March, J. G. (1963). *A behavioral theory of the firm*. Englewood Cliffs, NJ: Prentice-Hall.

Deal, T. (1987). The culture of school. In L. T. Scheive & M. B. Schoenheit (Eds.), *Leadership examining the elusive*. 1987 Yearbook of the Association for Supervision and Curriculum Development. Alexandria VA: ASCD.

Deal, T. E., & Kennedy, A. (1982). *Corporate cultures*. Reading, MA: Addison-Wesley.

Dubin, R. (1959). Industrial research and the discipline of sociology. *Proceedings of the 11th Annual Meeting, Industrial Relations Research Association,* Madison, WI (p. 161). (As quoted in Strauss, G. [1963]. Some notes on power equalization. In H. J. Leavitt [Ed.], *The social science of organization* (p. 48). Englewood Cliffs, NJ: Prentice-Hall.)

Dyer, W. G., Jr. (1982). *Patterns and assumptions: The keys to understanding organizatiocal culture*. Office of Naval Research, Technical Report TR-ONR-7. Washington, DC: U.S. Government Printing Office.

Etzioni, A. (1993). *The spirit of community rights, responsibilities, and the communitarian agenda*. New York: Crown.

Fayol, H. (1949). *General and industrial management* (C. Storrs, Trans.). London: Pitman.

Firestone, W. A., & Wilson., B. L. (1985). Using bureaucratic and cultural linkages to improve instruction: The principal's contribution. *Educational Administrator Quarterly, 21*(2), 7–30.

Follett. M. P. (1924). *Creative experience*. New York: Longmans, Green.

Foster, W. P. (1984). Toward a critical theory of educational administration. In T. J. Sergiovanni & J. E. Corbally (Eds.), *Leadership and organizational culture* (pp. 240–259). Urbana: University of Illinois Press.

Geertz, C. (1973). *The interpretation of cultures*. New York: Basic Books.

Getzels, J. W., & Guba, E. (1957, Winter). Social behavior and administrative process. *The School Review,* pp. 413–441.

Greenfield, T. B. (1973). Organizations as social inventions: Rethinking assumptions about change. *Journal of Applied Behavioral Science, 9*(5), 551–574.

Greenfield, T. B. (1984). Leaders and schools: Willfulness and non-natural order in organization. In T. J. Sergiovanni & J. E. Corbally (Eds.), *Leadership and organizational culture* (pp. 142–169). Urbana: University of Illinois Press.

Greenfield, W. (1985). *Instructional leadership: Muddles, puzzles and promises.* The Doyne M. Smith Lecture, University of Georgia, Athens, June 29.

Gulick. L., & Urwick, L. (Eds.). (1937). *Papers on the science of administration.* New York: Institute of Public Administration.

Hill, P. T., Foster, G. E., & Gendler, T. (1990). *High schools with character.* Santa Monica, CA: Rand.

Hofstede, G. (1980). *Cultural consequences.* Beverly Hills: Sage.

Hosford, P. (Ed.). (1984). *Using what we know about teaching.* 1984 Yearbook of the Association for Supervision and Curriculum Development. Alexandria, VA: ASCD.

Kennedy, M. (1984). How evidence alters understanding and decisions. *Educational Evaluation and Policy Analysis 6*(3), 207–226.

Kuhn, T. (1962). *The structure of scientific revolution.* Chicago: University of Chicago Press.

Lewin, K. (1951). *Field theory in Social science.* New York: Harper and Row.

Lindblom, C. E. (1959). The science of muddling through. *Public Administration Review, 19,* 79–88.

Lipsitz, J. (1984). *Successful schools for young adolescents.* New Brunswick, NJ: Transaction.

Louis, M. R. (1980). Organizations as culture-bearing milieux. In L. R. Pondy et al. (Eds.), *Organizational symbolism* (pp. 157–166). Greenwich, CT: JAI Press.

Lundberg, C. C. (1985). On the feasibility of cultural intervention in organizations. In P. Frost et al. (Eds.), *Organizational culture* (pp. 169–185). Beverly Hills: Sage.

March, J. G. (1962). The business firm as a political coalition. *Journal of Politics, 24.*

March, J. G. (1974). Analytical skills and the university training of educacional administrators. *Journal of Educational Administration, 12*(1), 43.

March, J., & Simon, H. (1958). *Organizations.* New York: John Wiley.

Martin, J., Sitkin, S. B., & Boehm, M. (1985). Founders and the elusiveness of a cultural legacy. In P. Frost et al. (Eds.), *Organizational culture* (pp. 99–124). Beverly Hills: Sage.

Mayo, E. (1945). *The social problems of an industrial civilization.* Boston: Harvard Graduate School of Business.

McDonnell, L. M., & Elmore, R. F. (1987). Getting the job done: Alternative policy instruments. *Educational Evaluation and Policy Analysis, 2,* 133–152.

McGregor, D. (1960). *The human side of enterprise.* New York: McGraw-Hill.

Metcalf, H. C., & Urwick, L. (Eds.). (1940). *Dynamic administration: The collected papers of Mary Parker Follett.* New York: Harper.

Miles, R. E. (1965). Human relations or human resources? *Harvard Business Review 43*(4), 148–163.

Mintzberg, H. (1979). *The structuring of organizations.* Englewood Cliffs, NJ: Prentice-Hall.

Mintzberg, H. (1987, July–August). Crafting strategy. *Harvard Business Review,* 66–75.

Morgan, G. (1986). *Images of organization.* Beverly Hills: Sage.

Ouchi, W. (1981). *Theory Z.* Reading, MA: Addison-Wesley.

Parkinson, C. N. (1958). *Parkinson's laws and other studies of administration.* London: Murray.

Pascale, R. T., & Athos, A. G. (1981). *The art of Japanese management.* New York: Simon & Schuster.

Peters, T. J., & Waterman, R. H., Jr. (1982). *In search of excellence.* New York: Harper and Row.

Roethlisberger, F., & Dickson, W. (1939). *Management and the worker.* Cambridge, MA: Harvard University Press.

Schon, D. A. (1983). *The reflective practitioner: How professionals think in action.* New York: Basic Books.

Selznick, P. (1957). *Leadership in administration: A sociological interpretation.* New York: Harper and Row. (California paperback edition, 1984. Berkeley: University of California Press.)

Sergiovanni, T. J. (1980). A social humanities view of educational policy and administration. *Educational Administration Quarterly, 16*(1), 1–20.

Sergiovanni, T. J. (1987). *The principalship: A reflective practice perspective.* Boston: Allyn and Bacon.

Sergiovanni, T. (1994). *Building community in schools.* San Fransisco: Jossey-Bass.

Sergiovanni, T. J. (1995). *The principalship: A reflective practice perspective* (3rd ed.). Boston: Allyn and Bacon.

Sergiovanni, T. J., & Starratt, R. J. (1979). *Supervision: Human perspectives* (2nd ed.). New York: McGraw-Hill.

Sergiovanni, T. J. & Starrat, R.. J. (1993). *Supervision: A redefinition* (5th ed.). New York: McGraw-Hill.

Shiis, E. (1961). Centre and periphery. In *The logic of personal knowledge: Essays presented to Michael Polanyi* (pp. 117–131). London: Rutledge and Kegan Paul.

Simon, H. A. (1945). *Administrative behavior.* New York: Macmillan.

Smircich, L. (1985). Is the concept of culture a paradigm for understanding organizations and ourselves? In P. Frost et al. (Eds.), *Organizational culture* (pp. 55–72). Beverly Hills: Sage.

Smith, J. K. , & Blase, J. (1987). *Educational leadership as a moral concept.* Washington. DC: American Educational Research Association.

Strauss, G. (1963). Some notes on power equaliza-

tion. In H. J. Leavitt (Ed.), *The social science of organization* (p. 48). Englewood Cliffs, NJ: Prentice-Hall.

Strayer, G. (1914). Report of the Committee on Tests and Standards of Efficiency in Schools and School Systems. In *Addresses and proceedings of the National Education Association.* Washington, DC: Bureau of Education.

Strayer, G. (1930). Progress in city school administration during the past twenty-five years. *School and Society, 30,* 375–378.

Taylor, F. W. (1911). *Principles of scientific management.* New York: Harper and Row.

Taylor, P. W. (1961). *Normative discourse.* Englewood Cliffs, NJ: Prentice-Hall.

Tom, A. (1984). *Teaching as a moral craft.* New York: Longman.

Tyack, D., & Hansot, E. (1982). *Managers of virtue: Public school leadership in America, 1820–1980.* New York: Basic Books.

Vaill, P. B. (1984). The purposing of high performing systems. In T. J. Sergiovanni & J. E. Corbally (Eds.), *Leadership and organizational culture* (pp. 85–104). Urbana: University of Illinois Press.

Weber, M. (1946). Bureaucracy. In M. Weber, *Essays in sociology.* H. H. Gerth & C. W. Mills (Eds. and Trans.). London: Oxford University Press. (Reprinted in Litterer, J. [1969]. *Organizations: Structure and behavior.* New York: John Wiley.)

Chapter 7

Theories and the Practice of Educational Administration

Sue Tyler concluded her phone conversation with Harry Bell by promising to get back to Harry no later than next Monday. As Sue hung up the telephone, she jotted that fact down on her already crowded Monday calendar.

Sue paused and thought about the conversation. She had known Harry and Madeline Bell and their children ever since he had assumed the principalship of North High School. The oldest boy, Dale, had been a good athlete in football and tennis and was now a junior at the state university. Colleen, the middle child and only girl, had graduated last year with honors and had won a scholarship to a small private college in a neighboring state. Peter, the last of the York children, was popular and similar to the others in being a good student and citizen. He was a class officer this year and a reporter on the school paper.

Harry had called because he and Madeline had just received Pete's national standardized achievement test scores. Pete had always been a good student and had always done well in classes (solid Bs). There was, however, one exception. Mrs. Boulby, the new history teacher, had given Pete consistently high grades (straight As) and had even visited with the Yorks about Pete seeking a scholarship in history. When the test scores had arrived, Pete's were good, with the exception of social studies. In contrast to the seventieth and eightieth percentiles of most, his social studies scores had been in the low fortieth percentile. Harry wondered if Mrs. Boulby had seriously misread Pete's abilities and achievements.

Sue turned her attention to Mrs. Boulby. She had taught at East High for several years and had sought a transfer to North when the family had bought a new house in the immediate neighborhood. George, East's principal, had given her the highest recommendation. He was a good friend and not one to foist a bad teacher on another school.

Ann stuck her head in the door and reminded Sue of her three o'clock meeting. Sue smiled, knowing that she would have to get back to the Yorks later. She needed to do something; that much was clear.

This chapter examines the problem of relating theory to practice. Beginning in the mid-1950s and throughout much of the 1960s, it was believed that theory should not only inform but should also prescribe practice. But during the last three decades, that assumption has been challenged and some would argue discredited. Why was it popular to believe that theory informed and prescribed practice? What are some of the challengers to that line of reasoning? What is to be learned about educational administration from this debate?

Theory and Practice

The problems that face educational administrators are practical problems. They are problems that require administrators to act. Teachers must be hired, evaluated, supervised, and granted tenure or released. Students must be assigned to classes, provided books, motivated to achieve in classes, provided parking places for their cars or assigned buses for getting to school, and gotten to class on time. Custodians must clean the lunchroom and classrooms. In short, educational administrators are doers.

How do they know what to do? From the earliest on-the-job training and from the beginnings of the teaching of educational administration in universities, two answers dominated. The first was simple: Do what most others have done in this situation. Tradition was a powerful tool for on-the-job training intent on solving the problem of what to do. The second was complex: Develop a strategy that involves defining the problem, generating alternative courses of action, and selecting the best alternative. Those in universities argued that reasoning was a powerful tool for deciding what to do. Most who studied to be educational administrators were exposed to these answers. Many who taught educational administration prior to the 1950s believed that good administrators were grounded on a mix of tradition and rationality.

In the mid-1950s, a new answer was given to that question. A group of universities received funding to develop programs for training educational administrators that were grounded in social science theory. The rationale for this new program directly challenged older beliefs about the training of administrators. First, the newcomers argued that traditional programs in educational administration were based on "war stories" about the ways that practitioners had plied their trade. These war stories had two shortcomings: They were idiosyncratic and they could not be accumulated. The stories were tales of individual deeds; these deeds were driven by the unique characteristics of the actor and of the situation. Equally, the stories could not be gathered, compared, and winnowed into a body of useful information. The stories had no common denominators: The language used to describe, to explain, and to predict the world in which the administrator acted was particular to that actor, time, and place.

In place of the private and the unique, the newcomers argued that social science methods produced empirical generalizations and theories. Starting with single research studies, social scientists such as sociologists and psychologists independently developed sets of research findings. These findings initially created empirical generalizations—commonalities that could be found when several independent research studies were compared. As these studies and empirical generalizations accumulated in journal articles, theories could be developed. These theories linked characteristics of actors and situations in ways that explained what was happening as well as predicted what would happen. Social science theories could provide public and cumulative knowledge about educational institutions and their administration.

During the 1960s and early 1970s, the theory movement, as it came to be known, dominated the research about and training of educational administrators. Using concepts and theories drawn from several social sciences—including sociology, organizational behavior, psychology, political science, economics, and anthropology—researchers studied educational administrators. The theories and findings of these studies guided the curriculum of programs for training new school administrators. Journals such as *Educational Administration Quarterly* and *Administrative Science Quarterly* became part of every student's reading list.

The pattern of the theory movement was clear. Faced by a practical situation, educational administrators should determine what empirical generalizations and theories could be applied. These generalizations and theories provided the tools necessary for describing the situation (What were the key elements or facts?), explaining the situation (What were the invariant relationships?), and predicting what would happen (What will occur because of the key facts and invariant relations?). Lacking such a vocabulary, educational administrators could only fall back on their unique experiences.

What was so wrong with unique experiences? Those in the theory movement worried first about the conservatism inherent in uniqueness. Lacking a common framework for discussing their work, administrators selectively recalled solutions that they believed had worked in the past. Instead of looking to future needs, administrators replicated their past accomplishments; repeating the past limited the future. The newcomers also worried about the lack of standards for judging whether accomplishments were, in fact, accomplishments. What standards could be used to see if what Jones had done in Muddville was better or worse than Smith in Waterstown? Both Jones and Smith could argue that they had done their best. Unless there existed objective standards grounded on research about what could be done, administrators were isolated individuals and educational administration was a practice of loners. Developing a body of knowledge consisting of empirical generalizations and theories provided opportunities for exploring practical options far beyond those suggested by Jones and Smith.

Some engaged with the theory movement took the position that theory should prescribe practice. This "strong" interpretation grounded all the behaviors of educational administrators in social science theories. Most took a "weak" interpretation, which argued that although social science theories were useful, there were unique educational aspects of school administration. Theories drawn from political science or sociology, for instance, could inform but not dictate the practices of educational administrators. Proponents of these positions might quarrel about the scope of theory, but they agreed that educational administrators must attend to the theoretical in the social sciences if educational administration was to improve.

Returning for a moment to the case that opened this chapter, how would those in the theory movement suggest it be handled? Sue Tyler's first move would be to examine the literature of the social sciences and particularly the work in educational research to see what was known about teacher judgments of student achievement. Are there empirical generalizations or theories that inform Sue about this practical problem?

Sue's review of the literature produces a review article by Hoge and Coladarci (1989). As she reads the article, which reviews several empirical studies discussing teacher judgments and standardized test results, she discovers that the authors first note that many believe teacher judgments are filled with bias and error. As the authors examine the nearly 20 studies that met their criteria for inclusion, they find "these studies yielded judgment/criterion correlations ranging from 0.28 to 0.92. The median correlation, 0.66, suggests a moderate to strong correspondence between teacher judgments and student achievement" (p. 303). Teachers, overall, are not so bad in assessing students. However, Hoge and Coladarci do point out that "these data suggest that teachers do, in fact, differ in how accurately they judge their students' achievement" (p. 306).

As Sue reflects, she notes she is dealing with an empirical generalization: Teachers (in general) are reasonably good at assessing student achievement but individual teachers (in particular) differ in how accurate their judgments are.

Armed with this empirical generalization, Sue then reviews the files of other students in Mrs. Boulby's classes to determine if Pete's case is unique or if Mrs. Boulby is one of those teachers who is not very good at assessing student achievement. As she reviews the folders, she discovers that Mrs. Boulby consistently gives students grades that are higher than might be expected, considering their standardized test scores and grades from other teachers in other academic classes.

Sue is able to take two actions. First, she can discuss with the Yorks why Pete's grades and results do not match. Second, she can discuss with Mrs. Boulby ways to sharpen her skills at diagnosing student achievement. Before that visit, Sue will again turn to the research literature to see what empirical generalizations and theories are available. She will be particularly interested in any training programs that are based on empirical research.

The theory movement, in sum, suggested that empirical generalizations and theories that were available could be used by educational administrators to describe, explain, and predict what happened in educational institutions. By understanding the way the world of schools operated, educational administrators could successfully lead these institutions. This leadership was not the result of unique personalities or situations; it was the result of understanding common relationships that could be found and made public. This leadership rested on an accumulating body of theoretical knowledge and empirically grounded practice.

Challengers

By the late 1970s, several challengers objected to this view of the relation of theory and educational practice. Although not an exhaustive list, four challengers provided important insights about theory and the practice of educational administration. Those challengers conceived of educational practice as (1) political, (2) following rules, (3) a craft, and (4) ethical behavior.

Educational Practice as Political

At the height of the theory movement, scholars of educational administration applied many different social science disciplines. One that gained popularity was political science.

Studying educational administrators "as if" they were politicians produced important insights about educational governance and policy. Many of these insights differed from the general argument that theory informed practice.

Instead of finding educational administrators operating as technical specialists in a rational world, researchers found that educational administrators operated in a world in which their judgments were frequently challenged, their authority disputed, and their power limited (Chase, 1995). The political world of the public schools was a world in which marked differences existed over the goals of education, the means to achieve those competing goals, and the costs associated with these means-ends chains.

Even more disconcerting was the sense that there were few empirical generalizations and theories that described invariant relationships in this world. Empirical generalizations and theories that were developed in a particular place and at a certain time were not exportable to a different place at a different time. What was true of a growing community in California might not fit a small village in New Mexico or a dying oil town in Oklahoma.

The advantage gained by studying empirical research was not generalizations of theories but sensitivity to various elements that might exist in the current situation. Generalizations and theories alerted educational administrators to dimensions that might be found; they sensitized practitioners. As good metaphors are provocative, good theories are not guides to action but stimulators of thought.

For example, Iannaccone and Lutz (1970) and Lutz and Iannaccone (1978) developed a model of local politics that suggested that, over time, local school boards and superintendents become insulated from their communities. As closed systems, boards and superintendents tend to ignore changes in the community. If the community changes enough, new board members are elected and the old superintendent is replaced by a new superintendent from outside the district.

Empirical research to show that this theory applies to all communities has produced mixed results. Despite that fact, the theory provides some important suggestions for educational administrators. For superintendents, the theory suggests the dangers of becoming isolated from diverse community groups. Superintendents should attend to the community with an eye to shifts in its makeup. Equally, superintendents should be attentive to school board elections. The campaigns and results may be important omens for shifting community characteristics or sentiments. For principals, the theory suggests succession patterns for superintendents—the current superintendent may well be replaced by an outsider with a new agenda. Principals need to be alert to community shifts that may herald change and that may provide clues to the direction of that change.

In sum, educational administrators often acted "as if" they were educational politicians. They lived in a world of limited resources, multiple and competing wants, and necessary compromises. Empirical studies of this world provided time- and place-specific empirical generalizations and limited theories. The important role of theory was sensitivity and suggestion, not explanation and prediction.

Educational Practice as Following Rules

In contrast to the theory movement, some argued that the gist of educational practice was fulfilling the rules that govern public education. This perspective argues that over the last century, and more particularly over the last four decades, the public schools have become bureaucratized and legalized (Kirp & Jensen, 1986).

The rapid growth of cities and the influx of immigrants in the late 1800s led to the rapid growth of city school systems. At the turn of the century, Progressive reformers argued that these systems had become politically corrupt, educationally derelict, and in need of dramatic changes to ensure their professionalism. By 1920, most larger cities had moved from very large school boards elected by wards to very small school boards elected citywide. This change ensured that board members worried about the entire community rather than the schools of their wards. By 1920, most larger cities required that teachers and administrators have some training in education. A number of institutions of higher education began offering courses in educational administration and normal schools for training teachers were common in most states. By 1920, educators argued that they were developing the one best system for educating the country's children. Copying techniques of scientific management that were popular in industry, the educational system sought to find the best way to teach children, to train teachers to use these best methods, and to supervise teachers to ensure that best practice always existed in the classroom (Callahan, 1962; Tyack, 1974).

The development of one best system created the school bureaucracies. Positions (such as teacher, assistant principal, principal, assistant superintendent for personnel, and superintendent) were specified (position descriptions). Applicants who sought to fill these roles were specifically trained and certified by normal schools and colleges and universities. Procedures were established that detailed what was to be done for clients (students), specified the work of position specialists (teachers), linked the work of specialists through reports (cumulative folders for students), and evaluated the work of specialists (teacher evaluations). Files contained records of clients (students) and of specialists (teachers). Promotions were based on merit (training for new roles). The system, in short, was driven by rules.

The self-perpetuating nature of bureaucracies made challenges to their procedures difficult. Those who sought to change them often found it necessary to turn to the courts. These cases often sought exemptions from the uniformity required by bureaucratic rules. Some sought the right not to salute the flag; others sought the right not to begin class with a prayer; some sought to attend schools that were not segregated by race; others sought to receive schooling to meet their special needs. Moreover, state legislatures passed laws that required the school bureaucracies to fulfill new obligations.

The bureaucratization and legalization has continued. The 1980s witnessed sweeping reforms in which state legislatures mandated that students take standardized tests several times during their school careers, tied student graduation to a successful score on a test, and increased the number of units required for graduation. Legislatures also established committees for the induction of beginning teachers, elaborate evaluation procedures for probationary teachers, frequent evaluations of tenured teachers, and development plans for school administrators. Some of these reforms have been challenged in court cases.

What is the role of the educational administrator? It is a role prescribed and proscribed by the legal context. For example, the principal must evaluate a beginning teacher at least three times during the school year. These evaluations must describe what the teacher actually does in the classroom. The first evaluation must be completed by December 1 and the last by March 15. One of these evaluations must be formally announced, one must be unannounced (informal), and the third can be either. The principal may not discuss these evaluations with other staff members.

The context also includes maintaining the bureaucracy. Paperwork constitutes the lifeblood of the organization; it carries information vital to the organization to the next highest level. Paperwork thus makes possible rational planning and decision making. The organization must know who is leaving, who is succeeding, who is a possible candidate for the next level, and what is happening in a classroom or a school. Paperwork permits the bureaucracy to function.

The context also requires that educational administrators be alert to potential legal issues. Who is likely to go to court to change current standard operating procedures? Do the results of a recent judicial decision affect the district policies or was the judgment limited? What does the school attorney advise about the legality of the form that parents must sign to permit children to go on overnight trips sponsored by the school? What steps must be followed to release an incompetent teacher? These, and many more, possible legal snares or opportunities confront the educational administrator.

Instead of theory or politics, bureaucratic and legal imperatives drive the practice of educational administration. Rather than understanding the nature of an empirical generalization or the suggestiveness of a political model, administrators should understand the increasing rule-boundedness of schools and the role of due process in their actions. Instead of autonomous actors, educational administrators act as agents of the state and are bound by the rules of the state.

Educational Practice as a Craft

In an important book, *School Administration as a Craft: Foundations of Practice* (1989), Blumberg challenges both the conventional wisdom of the theory movement and the recent argument that cooperation between universities and school districts can improve the training of educational administrators. Blumberg argues that these positions are wrongheaded.

Blumberg's case rests on three major premises. First, the ways practicing educational administrators think about problems and link their actions to their world are similar to the ways that craftspersons, such as potters or wood carvers, think about their problems and link their actions to their world. Educational administrators develop a sense of what problems are like and of what solutions are possible in the same way that potters gain a sense of what the clay is like and of how this particular lump of clay might be shaped. This craft knowledge is gained over time as the craftsperson works in the medium and discovers what is possible or impossible with the particular lump of clay, a particular block of wood, or the faculty of a small, suburban elementary school. By reflecting on the medium and its limitations, the craftsperson comes to have a store of practical wisdom. This wisdom is not static but grows over time and can be communicated in part to others who have not worked in the medium; only other craftspersons of the medium can fully grasp the meaning of discussions about working that medium. Potters can talk to others about throwing their pots, but only other potters can fully grasp the complete meaning of these discussions.

Second, the way that professors of educational administration think about problems is the way that scientists studying administration think about and link thoughts to actions. Scientists studying administration seek to find universal and invariant characteristics of organizations that can be expressed as theories. Professors of educational administration opted for theories because the development of theories enhanced their academic respectability on their campuses. Professors of educational administration could now publish, not perish; they could argue that their works were contributing to a body of knowledge that could inform practice. In that sense, they could compete for campus resources (including prestige) with other professional schools such as business, engineering, and nursing.

Third, the pursuit of academic respectability leads to interests on the part of professors that did not aid practicing administrators. The interests of professors fixed on the universal and invariant, whereas the interests of practitioners fixed on the particular and variant. Speaking metaphorically, professors produced theories that suggested the universal and unchanging characteristics of clay. Principals wanted information on the particular and changing characteristics of a particular school.

Blumberg concludes that professors of educational administration should raise questions that link their agendas to those of practitioners. Instead of raising questions about the relationship of scientific theories of administration to the schools, professors need to ask questions that help develop a theory of practice. Blumberg's work suggested a radical change in the training of educational administrators.

What would a theory of practice look like? Blumberg offers some hints. He notes that craftspersons have a vision of their product; the wood carver knows that she will shape a bird from this particular block of wood. But the working out of the vision (the carving of that particular bird) is influenced by the medium (the block has a knot in it that must be dealt with). A theory of practice would examine the ways that craftspersons translate their visions given the problems of that particular piece of the medium. In school terms, how does a principal design and carry out a staff-development program when he has five brand new teachers, three teachers who have just achieved tenure after three years of teaching, and eleven teachers who have more than 20 years of teaching experience? The principal's vision of a staff learning and growing together must be achieved in that particular situation with that particular distribution of teaching experience. Just as potters must deal with bubbles in the clay, principals must deal with a faculty that includes teachers who have both limited and extensive experience.

The role of the professor may be more than recorder of the visions and techniques of practicing administrators. Craftspersons develop standards for comparing how well they and their peers fulfill their visions. They judge some pots better than others, some carving superior and some inferior. Professors who come to understand the way craftspersons think about problems and link these problems to fulfilling a vision through a particular lump of clay may be able to enrich the vision of craftspersons. As constructive critics sensitive to the problems of craftspersons, professors may bring the resources of their study of other craftspersons as well as the resources of the university to bear on the visions and techniques of practitioners. Although professors may not be able to provide universal theories or generalizations, they may well be able to provide middle-range theories that are sensitive to vision and medium and that also expand the sense of craft of the practitioner.

Such a theory of practice means that professors must take seriously the ways that educational administrators do their work; professors must understand the importance of best practice and practical wisdom. A theory of practice must be grounded in the why and how of practice. In turn, educational administrators must take seriously professors who are constructive critics seeking to provide challenging alternatives to current craft knowledge. The university may well provide a setting for the constructive clash of the current best wisdom and its challengers.

Educational Practice as Ethical Behavior

The last few decades have witnessed a renewed interest in ethical behavior of public officials. As numerous public scandals unfolded, many argued that lawyers needed to be trained not only in defending their clients but in legal ethics, that policy analysts needed to know not only cost-benefit analysis but also the ethics of policy debate, and that business leaders needed to know not only how to maximize profits but also how to protect their customers and the environment. These same arguments have been applied to educational administrators.

The works of Hodgkinson (1978) and Strike, Haller, and Soltis (1988) discuss the ethics of school administrators. These authors, and others, argue that many of the important issues surrounding public schools are ethical issues and that educational administrators need to engage in ethical reflection and justification (Strike, Haller, & Soltis, 1988, pp. 2–3). Moreover, there are competing values that may be served in schools.

The practical nature of educational problems requires that administrators act. The problems they face can be seen as a series of practical questions. The first question is: In this situation, should I do X, Y, or Z? The first question provides a sense of the possible alternatives that could be selected. The second question is a series of questions exploring the consequences of doing either X, Y, or Z. What are the consequences of doing X? Of doing Y? Of doing Z? After examining the consequences of each alternative, the administrator asks: Which of the alternatives produces the best solution? The administrator then selects that alternative and acts.

Many of the problems that require administrative action involve issues of fairness and justice. For example, state laws often require that principals evaluate teachers before the granting of tenure. Probationary teachers who are being evaluated expect that these evaluations are conducted consistently, fairly, and in an evenhanded manner. These teachers do not want the principal to be inconsistent or biased. It is not enough that the principal be technically competent; the principal must also be fair.

Proponents of this position suggest that the practical argument of administrators who do consider the ethical dimensions of a problem begins with the question: In this situation, *ought* I to do X, Y, or Z? Once again, the question provides a sense of the possible solutions that exist. The second question remains the same: What are the consequences of doing X? Of doing Y? Of doing Z?

There is a new, and very important, third question. The third question asks: What moral principle or rule would justify doing X? Doing Y? Doing Z? Typically, the moral principles or rules that justify these different lines of action will be in conflict. The administrator must now reflect on these competing moral principles or rules (McLaren, 1989). For example, returning to the example of new teacher evaluation, the ethically aware principal might ask: "I can argue that only one new teacher should be given tenure because of enrollment decline. Of the two new teachers I have, should I argue for granting tenure to Mrs. Floyd, a young mother who needs the job to feed her children and who is an adequate teacher, or to Mr. Stout, an exceptional young teacher from the wealthiest family in town?" A sense of compassion would argue for Mrs. Floyd; a sense of merit for Mr. Stout.

Faced with these conflicting moral principles or rules, administrators may develop a hierarchy of these principles or rules. The principal discussed here might suggest that the major principle guiding teacher evaluations is merit; Mr. Stout as an exceptional teacher ought to be granted tenure. A second option administrators could use is to develop a compromise strategy. The principal might argue for the tenure of Mr. Stout and also get on the phone to principals in other school districts in the immediate area and extol the virtues of Mrs. Floyd. A third option is to find that the competing ethical principles are, in fact, exactly the same. Under such conditions, the principal simply chooses an option and acts. A final option is to try to dissolve the situation by suggesting that the moral principle that must be applied is determined by something other than the administrator's deliberations. The principal might say that state law requires that tenure be granted to the best qualified teacher, regardless of other circumstances.

Arguing from this position, proponents suggest that much of what educational administrators do is ethical behavior. Educational administrators seek to create school environments for students and teachers that are just. Rules that are made for student conduct, for example, do not discriminate by sex or race; teacher evaluations are conducted fairly; and the allocation of resources to academic and extracurricular activities is done in light of some ethical principle.

What Is to Be Learned?

What is to be learned from this debate? What are practicing educational administrators to make of all this noise and spilled ink over theory, politics, rules, craftspersonship, and ethical behavior? At least three important results seem worth noting.

1. *The practice of educational administration is complex.* The debates of the last 50 years show that the practice of educational administration is complex. The multiple and competing perspectives—be they the arguments for experience, theory, politics, legal compliance, craft, or ethical behavior—all describe, explain, and predict something about educational administration. None, however, is powerful enough to grasp the entirety of practice. To grasp such complexity itself requires a complex framework. Those who seek to practice or to understand the practice of educational administration must be reasonably complex. The tools for reasoning about practice must be multiple and must provide many different points of view. The tools for accomplishing the tasks of administering schools must be equally diverse and multifaceted.

2. *These perspectives provide potential resources for improving the study and practice of educational administration.* Since educational administration is complex, these perspectives and others that currently exist or will be developed in the future are useful tools. Each provides some sense of what is happening; each provides some possible insights. One real value in the perspectives is their challenges to other points of view. Those who take the perspective that educational administrators should follow rules, for example, are well served by others who challenge that view. Those who stress the ethical nature of educational administration may well point out instances where ethical principles challenge the current legal mandates. They may point to issues such as the desegregation of schools, the fair treatment of women and the physically challenged, and education of special children that were at one time *not* required by law. Such confrontations allow for the testing of the applicability and limits of the varying perspectives.

3. *Develop a strategy for dealing with complexity.* Practicing administrators need to develop some strategy for dealing with such complexity. One solution, suggested by the ethical perspective, would involve developing a fixed hierarchy of perspectives. For example, an administrator might approach each situation by asking a fixed series of questions:

In this particular situation,
- What are the ethical problems?
- What are the rules?
- What is the best wisdom of practice?
- What theories apply?

An administrator who proposed such a fixed hierarchy should be able to provide reasons for the particular ranking of questions. In this case, the administrator would be expected to suggest that schools are primarily sites for administrators to make ethical decisions.

Another solution might be to study each situation carefully to see if characteristics of the situation help in determining what hierarchy of questions is appropriate. Instead of a fixed hierarchy that applied to every situation, an administrator might seek to create situation-specific hierarchies. There might be hierarchies, for instance, that dealt with very young pupils and other hierarchies that dealt with more mature students.

A third solution might use a mixed strategy. An administrator might adopt a fixed hierarchy that was applied generally but adapt that hierarchy as circumstances differed. For example, an elementary school principal might approach problems from a theory perspective. The principal would be alert, nonetheless, to the particulars of the current situation that might suggest that an ethical or craft perspective would be more useful in this case.

In sum, the debate about the role of theory in the practice of educational administration can enrich both the study and practice of the field. The marked shift in the 1950s away from educational administration as a field dominated by tradition and rationality to one dominated by theoretical frameworks provided a pronounced shift in the language of educational administration. The theory movement spawned studies stressing that theories often were more suggestive than strictly accurate. Moreover, the increasing bureaucracy and legalism of school administration forced all to recognize that administrators were agents of the state. The overreliance on theory as the only source of knowledge about administering schools led to research that suggested school administrators did know something, even if that practical knowledge did not fit theoretical frameworks. The persistence of ethical quandaries in the life of educational administrators provided suggestive evidence for understanding and enriching their ethical behaviors in shaping schools.

References

Blumberg, A. (1989*). School administration as a craft: Foundations of practice.* Boston: Allyn and Bacon.

Callahan, R. E. (1962). *Education and the cult of efficiency.* Chicago: University of Chicago.

Chase, S. E. (1995). *Ambiguous empowerment: The work narratives of women school superintendents.* Amherst: University of Massachusetts.

Hodgkinson, C. (1978). *Towards a philosophy of administration.* New York: St. Martin's Press.

Hoge, R. D., & Coladarci, T. (1989). Teacher-based judgments of academic achievement: A review of the literature. *Review of Educational Research, 59,* 297–313.

Iannaccone, L., & Lutz, F. W. (1970). *Politics, power and policy.* Columbus, OH: Charles E. Merrill.

Kirp, D. L., & Jensen, D. N. (Eds.). (1986). *School days, rule days.* Philadelphia: Falmer.

Lutz, F. W., & Iannaccone, L. (1978). *Public participation in local school districts.* Lexington, MA: Lexington.

McLaren, R. (1989). *Solving moral problems.* Mountain View, CA: Mayfield.

Strike, K. A., Haller, E. J., & Soltis, J. S. (1988). *The ethics of school administration.* New York: Teachers College Press.

Tyack, D. B. (1974). *The one best system.* Cambridge, MA: Harvard University.

Chapter 8

Administrative Work, Roles, and Tasks

What are administrative jobs in schools really like? What roles and tasks actually make up the school administrator's job responsibilities? What are the key responsibility areas to which administrators must attend? What administrative processes are used in executing these responsibilities? What administrative skills are key as these processes unfold? Answers to these questions can help to map various dimensions of the nature of administrative work in education. In this chapter, the focus is on the actual context and nature of administrative work as well as the roles and tasks school administrators actually engage in. The "real world" mapping is a characteristic of the work-activity school discussed next.

The Work-Activity School

Prescriptive lists of competencies and tasks are typically compiled by studying what administrators, particularly successful ones, do, and on the weight of expert judgment and deductions gleaned from theory. This is a deductive approach. Conclusions are inferred from general principles. The principles themselves are based on assumptions or premises. The work flow of deductive research is as follows: Start with assumptions or premises; theorize; extract propositions; state and test hypotheses; analyze results; draw conclusions; reevaluate premises; and redefine theory, thus repeating the process. The work-activity school, by contrast, relies on inductive research. Here, the actual activities of administrators are studied systematically. Diary methods that record actual work of managers and actual distribution of how their time is used, activity sampling whereby through actual observation the researcher records activities of administrators at random intervals, and structured observation whereby administrators are observed over extended periods of time are the techniques typically employed. In work-activity research, conclusions are drawn and theoretical statements are inferred only when they can be supported by empirical evidence.

Work-activity research strives to develop an accurate description of the characteristics and content of administrative work. The descriptions help provide such job-characteristics information as where administrators work, how long they work, what means they use to communicate, how they handle and send mail, and what work patterns exist day to day and week to week. The descriptions also help provide such job-content information as what administrators actually do, what activities do they carry out, and why. Categorizations of job content help one to infer the actual roles that administrators assume. Often these roles are in sharp contrast to the roles administrators should fulfill. Indeed, as the following discussion unfolds, it is worth noting contrasts between the tasks and competencies of administration prescribed by experts and the real world of administrative work revealed here.

The Nature of Managerial Work: Mintzberg

A *role* can be defined as a set of integrated behaviors associated with an identifiable position. Following the thinking of the work-activity school, determining administrative roles requires that one have an accurate picture of the content of administrative work. What an administrator actually does determines his or her real administrative roles. In Mintzberg's (1973) extensive structural-observation study of five executives (one a school superintendent), he sought to describe the content of administrative work. Work-content descriptions were then used to infer a number of critical administrative roles that, Mintzberg suggests, characterize the nature of managerial work.

The managerial activities recorded suggested 10 administrative roles, which could be grouped into three major categories: (1) *interpersonal,* containing figurehead, leader, and liaison roles; (2) *informational,* containing monitor, disseminator, and spokesperson roles; and (3) *decisional,* containing entrepreneur, disturbance-handler, resource-allocator, and negotiator roles. These roles are depicted in Table 8.1 and are examined and discussed within the context of educational administration.

Interpersonal Roles

Interpersonal roles require that the school administrator be involved either directly or indirectly in the activities of others. This set of roles takes a great deal of time. Though demanding, many role activities included here seem only remotely connected to the central job of administering a school. Some of the roles are symbolic, as in the case of *figurehead.* Others are more directly involved in the

TABLE 8.1 A Summary of Administrative Roles and Activities

Role	Description	Identifiable Activities from Study of Chief Executives	Recognition in the Literature*
Interpersonal			
Figurehead	Symbolic head; obliged to perform a number of routine duties of a legal or social nature	Ceremony, status requests, solicitations	Sometimes recognized, but usually only at highest organizational levels
Leader	Responsible for the motivation and activation of subordinates; responsible for staffing, training, and associated duties	Virtually all managerial activities involving subordinates	Most widely recognized of all managerial roles
Liaison	Maintains self-developed network of outside contacts and informers who provide favors and information	Acknowledgments of mail; external board work; other activities involving outsiders	Largely ignored, except for particular empirical studies (Sayles on lower- and middle-level managers, Neustadt on U.S. Presidents, Whyte and Homans on informal leaders)
Informational			
Monitor	Seeks and receives wide variety of special information (much of it current) to develop thorough understanding of organization and environment; emerges as nerve center of internal and external information of the organization	Handling all mail and contacts categorized as concerned primarily with receiving information (e.g., periodical news, observational tours)	Recognized in the work of Sayles, Neustadt, Wrapp, and especially Aguilar
Disseminator	Transmits information received from outsiders or from other subordinates to members of the organization; some information factual, some involving interpretation and integration of diverse value positions of organizational influencers	Forwarding mail into organization for informational purposes, verbal contacts involving information flow to subordinates (e.g., review sessions, instant communication flows)	Unrecognized (except for Papandreou discussion of "peak coordinator" who integrates influencer preferences)

Spokesperson	Transmits information to outsiders on organization's plans, policies, actions, results, etc.; serves as expert on organization's industry	Board meetings; handling mail and contacts involving transmission of information to outsiders	Generally acknowledged as managerial role
Decisional			
Entrepreneur	Searches organization and its environment for opportunities and initiates "improvement projects" to bring about change; supervises design of certain projects as well	Strategy and review sessions involving initiation or design of improvement projects	Implicitly acknowledged but usually not analyzed except for economists (who were concerned largely with the establishment of new organizations) and Sayles, who probes into this role
Disturbance handler	Responsible for corrective action when organization faces important, unexpected disturbances	Strategy and review sessions involving disturbances and crises	Discussed in abstract way by many writers (e.g., management by exception) but analyzed carefully only by Sayles
Resource allocator	Responsible for the allocation of organizational resources of all kinds—in effect the making or approval of all significant organizational decisions	Scheduling; requests for authorization; any activity involving budgeting and the programming of subordinates' work	Little explicit recognition as a role, although implicitly recognized by the many who analyze organizational resource-allocation activities
Negotiator	Responsible for representing the organization at major negotiations	Negotiation	Largely unrecognized (or recognized but claimed to be non-managerial work) except for Sayles

Source: *The Nature of Managerial Work* (pp. 92–93) by Henry Mintzberg, 1973, New York: Harper & Row. Copyright @ 1973 by Henry Mintzberg. Adapted by permission of Harper & Row, Publishers, Inc.

*F. J. Aguilar, *Scanning the Business Environment* (New York: Macmillan, 1967); G. C. Homans, *The Human Group* (New York: Harcourt Brace Jovanovich, 1950); R. E. Neustadt, *Presidential Power: The Politics of Leadership* (New York: John Wiley, 1960); A. G. Panandreou, "Some Basic Problems in the Theory of the Firm" in B. F. Haley (Ed.), *A Survey of Contemporary Economics* (Homewood, IL: Irwin, 1952), pp. 2, 183–219; L. R. Sayles, *Managerial Behavior: Administration in Complex Organizations* (New York: McGraw-Hill, 1964); W. F. Whyte, *Street Corner Gang* (Chicago: University of Chicago Press, 1955); H. E. Wrapp, "Good Managers Don't Make Policy Decisions," *Harvard Business Review,* 45 (1967): 91–99.

work of the school, as in the case of *leader*. Still others are more political in nature, as in the case of *liaison*. But all are critically important to an administrator's success and to the welfare of the school. All are highly visible roles that lend themselves to easy evaluation by students, teachers, parents, other administrators, board members, and various segments of the community.

The most basic and simple administrative role is that of the *figurehead*. This role requires that administrators, because of their formal authority and high status, perform a number of duties most of which on the surface seem to have little direct connection with the information-processing and decision making work of the school. But they are important, as any educational administrator will attest.

Consider the hours that a high school principal spends at basketball and other games, pep rallies, proms, school plays, picnics, honor-society ceremonies, and other events of this sort. Add to this the chores of greeting visitors, leading school tours, attending school/community meetings, hosting social events, and such requirements as being available to parents and other community members whose requests and complaints seem never satisfied unless attended to by the top person. Consider also such responsibilities as the signing of documents, letters, and reports prepared by others on the staff that require the principal's general imprimatur as head of the school, and one begins to sense the flavor of the figurehead role. Though superficiality often characterizes this role, it is carried out with a tone of sincerity befitting the status and dignity the administrator brings to an event. The superintendent receives a call of complaint from a parent about a teacher attentively and sympathetically, only to privately refer the complaint to the principal. The superintendent reads a series of warm and personal statements of commendation for several students at an awards assembly for parents, having only just met the students and reading from a script prepared by the guidance counselor.

Prior to recent interest in the cultural perspective in educational administration, the figurehead role received only slight attention in the literature of administration. It is now considered to be much more important. Still, the *leader* role has received the most attention. As leader, the administrator sets the tone or climate of the school. The focus of this role is on the interpersonal relationships between the leader and those being led. The administrator, for example, uses her or his formal authority to achieve better integration between the needs of teachers and the goals of the school. The administrator does this through such leadership role activities as directing, guiding, developing, motivating, evaluating, correcting, and rewarding subordinates. This role is also manifested in such administrative tasks as recruiting, selecting, training, promoting, and dismissing subordinates.

Unlike the leader role, which focuses on vertical relationships between the administrator and others, the *liaison* role focuses on horizontal relationships. Like the figurehead role, this role has not received the attention it should in the literature of administration. The liaison role involves the web of relationships that the educational administrator maintains with groups and individuals outside the school. As Homans (1950, p. 186) has pointed out, the higher a person's social rank in a group or organization, the more frequently he or she interacts with persons outside the group or organization. Thus, the liaison role is likely to be more visible in administrative activities of the superintendent of schools than in those of the department chairperson or grade-level supervisor.

The network of contacts that are the fruits of liaison activities is cultivated by joining important community organizations, engaging in social activities, and attending conferences. Keeping in touch with important others, building bridges with influential groups, making contact with the right people, and keeping the channels open to all who can have an impact on the school are the benefits sought by the administrator. This external linkage system can be both a source of information and a source of political support.

Informational Roles

Mintzberg (1973) suggests that in exercising informational roles, the administrator can be viewed metaphorically as a nerve center that receives information of various types from an array of sources; processes this information by rejecting, altering, or approving; and disseminates this information to others in the organization. The nerve-center metaphor suggests the central position administrators occupy in receiving and moving information. This influential and advantageous vantage point at the organizational nerve center results from the administrator's unique access to external information (e.g., liaison role) and her or his access to internal information derived from formal authority (e.g., leader role). Three informational roles are identified by Mintzberg to characterize administrative activity associated with this nerve-center position: the *monitor* role, through which the administrator becomes informed about the school and its environment, and the *disseminator* and *spokesperson* roles, through which the administrator transmits information to others inside and outside the organization.

As *monitor*, the administrator seeks information from others and at the same time is bombarded by information from others that helps in understanding what is going on within the school and the school's environment. Information received by the chief executives Mintzberg studied fell into five categories:

1. Information about the progress of *internal operations* and events gleaned from reports, meetings, informal conversations, and observational tours of his or her organization.
2. Information about *external events* concerning parents and other community groups; other schools; political, civic, and governmental agencies; and new developments in education.
3. Information derived from the *analysis of reports* on various issues. Reports come from a variety of solicited and unsolicited sources. Some are internal reports; others are policy memoranda from the state department of education or the federal government; still others arrive in the mail from state universities, professional associations, and seemingly endless other sources.
4. Information gleaned from conferences, formal and informal meetings, and other sources that helps the administrator to better understand significant *ideas and trends* from the environment that touches his or her organization.

5. Information brought to the administrator in the form of, or as a result of, *pressures* and demands from a variety of sources.

Much of the information obtained and processed in the monitoring role is simply transferred into the organization or passed on to others outside the organization.

In the *disseminator* role, the administrator passes into the organization both factual (what is) and value (what ought to be) information. Exactly what information to pass, in what detail, to whom, and how often can pose significant problems for the administrator. Since most of the information he or she has is stored in memory, it generally requires oral dissemination, which can be a time-consuming process. Therefore, in the interest of conserving time, not all of the relevant information gets passed down to subordinates, and this, in turn, affects the nature and quality of the administrator's work.

To ensure that subordinates better meet his or her standards, the administrator can increase the amount and kind of information disseminated, but at the risk of role overload. As Mintzberg characterizes this dilemma, "Hence the manager is damned by his own information system either to a life of overwork or to one of frustration. In the first case, he does too many tasks himself or spends too much time disseminating verbal information; in the second case, he must watch as delegated tasks are performed inadequately, according to his standards, by the uninformed" (1973, p. 75). Though normative views of administration emphasize the maximum flow of information and require that the administrator settle for nothing less than top performance, evidence from the real world suggests that, of necessity, not all the available information is disseminated and administrators do settle for less than best.

In the *spokesperson* role, the administrator transmits information out to the school's environment. The administrator is expected, for example, to speak on behalf of the organization, to lobby for the organization, to serve as a public relations figure, and to represent the organization as an expert. Two groups need to be kept informed: the organization's set of key influencers, as defined by legitimate authority, and the array of publics who by virtue of the political process exert influence on the school. With regard to the first group, for example, department chairpersons are obliged to keep principals informed of department activities, and similarly, school superintendents are obliged to keep school boards informed. The second group to whom the spokesperson role is addressed is vast but typically includes parents, business groups, teacher organizations, state department representatives, suppliers, newspaper reporters, and potential employers of graduating students.

In executing the spokesperson role, the administrator is required to have accurate and up-to-the-minute information about the organization and its environment. Further, the information needs to be disseminated in a dignified and credible manner. The administrator must therefore be an expert on the affairs of the organization and be able to activate this expertise in a commanding and convincing manner. The information roles are summarized and illustrated in Figure 8.1.

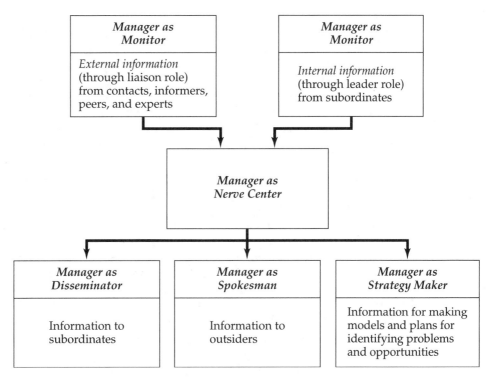

FIGURE 8.1   The Manager as Information-Processing System

Source: The Nature of Managerial Work (p. 72) by Henry Mintzberg, 1973, New York: Harper & Row. Copyright ©1973 by Henry Mintzberg. Adapted by permission of Harper & Row, Publishers, Inc.

Decisional Roles

The third set of administrative activities identified by Mintzberg involves the making of significant decisions. Decisional roles are typically considered to be at the heart of administrative work and to be a natural outlet of the administrator's formal authority and strong access to information. Formal authority and access to information are important sources of power that legitimize the administrator's decision-making prerogatives. On occasions where the former can be successfully challenged, the latter is sufficiently strong to assure these prerogatives. Though the prescriptive literature speaks often of the value of shared or participatory decision making, Mintzberg was impressed with the extent to which the executives he studied were in command of the decision-making process. He notes that they were substantially involved in all significant decisions made by their organizations. He further suggests that, contrary to prescriptive views, which prescribe rational and goal-maximizing decision making, the administrators he studied tended to "satisfice" (Simon, 1957, p. 204). They were inclined to accept courses of action that were "good enough" rather than best. Indeed, decision making might better be viewed as a "science of muddling through" rather than a rational science (Lindblom, 1959).

Mintzberg identified four decisional roles: *entrepreneur, disturbance handler, resource allocator,* and *negotiator.* In the *entrepreneur* role, the administrator initiates and designs programs intended to improve the organization. To this effect, she or he is constantly scanning the organization, being alert to problems. Once problems are identified, a program is begun that may directly involve the administrator further or, more typically, require delegating to others. As this program is implemented, the administrator is constantly called on to authorize and approve activities of subordinates. The administrator maintains supervisory control and retains responsibility for all design decisions associated with the program.

As an entrepreneur, the administrator initiates action of his or her own will but, as a disturbance handler, is forced into situations—some of which may well be beyond her or his control. A teacher strike, cafeteria fight, student insurrection, or false fire alarm might be examples of disturbance crises to which the administrator must respond. But many other instances are less dramatic and require more long-range attention. Handling competition among elementary schools or high school departments for scarce resources, deciding which school will be closed, settling an a reduction-in-force policy, constantly reassigning students in an effort to meet desegregation commitments, and dealing with personality clashes among staff members might be examples.

The *disturbance-handler* role often receives more notice than other administrative roles because of the suddenness with which disturbances tend to emerge, the presumption of high stakes at risk by those involved, emotional overtones, and the general urgency felt to get things resolved. Therefore, though activities associated with other roles may be more important, they take a backseat as the administrator is pressed into the disturbance-handler role.

In any organization, resources such as time, money, materials, equipment, and human talent must be allocated. When an administrator is involved in making decisions about significant organizational resources, he or she is behaving as a *resource allocator.* This role was evidenced in the Mintzberg study in three essential ways—scheduling time, programming work, and authorizing decisions by others. As the administrator schedules time, she or he communicates to others what is important and what is not. Issues of low priority, for example, do not command much of the administrator's time. By programming work, the administrator controls and schedules the time of others. In effect, he or she decides what will be done, by whom, and under what conditions, ensuring that high-priority issues are attended to. Human resources are allocated toward ends considered important. By authorizing action, the administrator maintains control over significant decisions made by subordinates, again ensuring that time and energy are used in a manner considered appropriate. Budget control is, of course, still another facet of the resource-allocating role of administrators. There is no doubt that the administrator is aware of the power implicit in controlling the allocation of organizational resources. Further, she or he shows little hesitation in exercising this power.

The administrator as *negotiator* is the final decisional role identified by Mintzberg. In exercising this role, the administrator represents the group or organization as it negotiates with other units within the organization (one department with another, one school with another), negotiates with identifiable subgroups associated with the organization (the teachers' union), and negotiates with outside agencies (accrediting teams, park district, mayor's office). This role is difficult to delegate because other partners to the negotiation often refuse to settle for substitutes, typically demanding to negotiate with the chief administrator.

Variations in Administrators' Work

The literature in administration suggests that role activities are more similar than different across administrative jobs in different kinds of organizations and across administrative jobs within the same organization. Each of the 10 roles discussed are likely to be present to some degree in virtually all administrative positions. Differences, therefore, would be in emphasis rather than in kind. Though all the roles can be identified in the activities of both elementary and secondary school principals, for example, different combinations of roles will likely be emphasized for each.

Hierarchical level within an organization also seems to influence the combinations of role emphasis one observes. Chairpersons, principals, and superintendents engage in each of the roles but emphasize some more than others, depending on level. The leader role might be dominant for chairpersons; resource allocator for principals; and spokesperson for the superintendent of a given district. Size of school, complexity of educational programs, expectations of teachers and community, and the personal idiosyncrasies of individual administrators can also be expected to influence the emphasis given to activities of each role.

Mintzberg noted in his study that the activities and work conditions of the school superintendent he studied differed somewhat from those of noneducational administrators (1973, pp. 262–264). The superintendent's work, for example, was characterized by greater formality and more scheduled meetings. The meetings often took place in the evening. The superintendent met more frequently than did others with the school board and, particularly, with the parents. He also experienced more formal authority requests and relied more on analysis in the form of written reports. The greater flow of information to and from government agencies was another important difference noted.

Further research is needed to map out the specific role descriptions that typify various educational administrative jobs and settings. We are able, in a very general sense, however, to speak of clusters of role emphasis and of the administrative styles they represent. Mintzberg (1973, p. 127) suggests eight such styles, each of which emphasizes a certain combination of key roles. These are summarized here:*

The Nature of Managerial Work (p. 127) by Henry Mintzberg, 1973, New York: Harper & Row. Copyright © 1973 by Henry Mintzberg. Adapted by permission of Harper & Row, Publishers, Inc.

Administrative Style	*Key Roles*
Contact person	Liaison, figurehead
Political administrator	Spokesperson, negotiator
Entrepreneur	Entrepreneur, negotiator
Insider	Resource-allocator, leader
Real-time administrator	Disturbance handler
Team administrator	Leader
Expert administrator	Monitor, spokesperson
New administrator	Liaison, monitor

The *contact person*, for example, spends a great deal of time outside the organization. The liaison and figurehead roles dominate. Activities that characterize this style are doing favors for others, winning favors in return, building a friendship network of support, giving speeches, and attending a variety of functions. The emphasis is on public relations, and the intent is to build favorable linkages with important individuals and groups outside the organization who are in a position to influence the organization. School/community relations literature and practices reflected the contact-person style popular during the 1950s and 1960s.

The *political administrator* also spends a great deal of time and energy with outside groups and individuals but not for superficial, polite, or ceremonial public relations reasons. This type of administrator, caught in a complex web of controversy, enters the outside arena with the intent to reconcile conflicting forces acting on the school. Key roles here are those of spokesperson and negotiator. Though the contact-person style is popular with administrators in more stable and homogeneous communities (small towns, isolated suburbs), conditions are such in most school environments that administrators are likely to assume the political-administrator style to a greater degree.

The administrator as *entrepreneur* seeks opportunities for change and for introducing programs within the school. Entrepreneur and negotiator roles characterize this style. This style was particularly popular during the 1960s as we experienced a period of expansion and innovation in education, and it still thrives in communities and settings where administrators continue to enjoy strong professional prerogatives. The increased political nature of educational policymaking now being experienced in many school districts, however, makes this style more difficult to articulate.

Insider administrators are primarily concerned with the operation and maintenance of smoothly running schools. Working primarily from resource-allocator and leader roles, they concentrate on overseeing school operations, nurturing and developing internal programs, and supervising the staff. Many elementary and secondary school principals can be characterized as insiders. Sometimes the insider is the second in command, responsible for running the school or district, letting the superintendent or principal tend to outside affairs.

Real-time administrators are insiders of a different sort. They are primarily interested in internal maintenance and focus on day-to-day problems. They are constantly busy with "putting out fires" and seem to have a "finger in every pie."

Disturbance handler is the dominant role. In schools where discipline is a serious problem, school security is tenuous, or other constant crises exist, the administrator may be forced into this style.

The *team administrator* is also oriented to the inside, but her or his interest is in building a highly effective, cohesive work group characterized by high morale and mutual support among teachers. By comparison, other roles are overshadowed by the attention that team administrators give to the leader role. This style suits many principalships, particularly those of smaller schools not characterized by strained labor/management relations where informal organizational designs dominate.

Expert administrators are those who, in addition to assuming administrative responsibility, continue to participate in the specialized work of the school. Special education and art supervisors, teaching principals, and department chairpersons might be examples. Key roles here are monitor and spokesperson.

The last administrative style discussed by Mintzberg is one *new* to the job. Lacking a network of contacts and sufficient information, the new administrator emphasizes liaison and monitor-role activities. "The decisional roles cannot become fully operative until he has more information. When he does, he is likely to stress the entrepreneur role for a time, as he attempts to put his distinct stamp on his organization. Then he may settle down to be one of the other managerial types—contact man, insider or some other type" (1973, p. 129).

Characteristics of Administrative Work

In a study of educational administrators of new educational programs, Sproul (1976) found that words such as *local, verbal, choppy,* and *varied* were used most often to describe the typical administrative workday. The subjects of Sproul's research were administrators of programs considered innovative, such as heading a high school urban career-education program or a regional bilingual education consortium.

Choppiness, for example, was evidenced by the presence of many activities of brief duration. The composite administrator in Sproul's study engaged daily in 56 activities, each averaging about nine minutes in duration, and 65 events, each averaging six minutes. Events were described as periods of time one minute or longer during which administrators used one medium such as a phone, meeting, individual conversation, memo, or letter to work on one purpose. Activities were collections of events devoted to one purpose. This distinction, according to Sproul, was forced by numerous interruptions that characterized the administrator's workday. Conceivably, without interruption, each activity could be completed by one event. Choppiness, then, is reflected in the vast array of events and activities of short duration that characterize the workday. This choppiness is illustrated in the following excerpt from Sproul's field notes:

> *Manager A is sitting at his desk writing a letter of recommendation about one of the students in his program for her college applications (20 min.). Teacher 1 comes*

*in and asks him to have a student project form reprinted because the supply is run-
ning low (1 min.). Teacher 1 leaves and the manager resumes writing the letter of
recommendation (1 min.). Teacher 2 comes in (the manager 3.5 hours earlier had
asked the secretary to tell this teacher to see him) and the manager asks him about
his behavior toward one of his students. (Earlier in the day the manager had
received a call from an angry parent complaining that teacher 2 had mistreated her
child.) After the manager hears Teacher 2's side of the story (he had heard from the
student earlier), he cautions the teacher about "not kidding around too much with
kids who might not understand" (18 min.). The secretary enters with letters that
must be signed right away in order to go out in the afternoon mail (1 min.). After
signing them, the manager continues writing the letter of recommendation
(1 min.). Teacher 3 brings in a list of students chosen to fill out a district-wide
questionnaire about "career awareness." Only half of the listed students, who had
been randomly selected by the district computer from fall enrollment registers,
were still enrolled in the program. The teacher and manager replace the names of
the no-longer-enrolled with the names of "kids who will be around tomorrow," the
day the questionnaire is to be administered (5 min.). Teacher 3 leaves and the manager resumes working on the letter of recommendation (5 min.). (Sproul, 1976, p.
5)*

Consider the following work characteristics identified by Sproul (1976, p. 5).
She notes that on a composite basis:

1. Seventy-five percent of the workday was spent locally in the program office.
2. Seventy-eight percent of the workday was spent in *verbal* interaction, mostly
   in personnel interaction (66 percent) and telephoning (11 percent). In his study
   of an elementary school principal, Wolcott (1973) estimated that 76 percent of
   the workday was spent in verbal interaction.
3. The average number of different topics in a given day to which the administrator attended was 26. Because of this *variety*, each topic received, on the average, only 20 minutes of attention.

Similarly, Mintzberg (1973) finds the work of administrators characterized by
brevity, variety, and fragmentation. He notes that the majority of administrative
activity is of brief duration—often taking only minutes. The variety is not only
great but often without pattern or connectedness and typically is interspersed with
trivia. The administrator, as a result, is required to shift moods and intellectual
frames frequently and quickly. These characteristics suggest a high level of superficiality in the work of administration.

Mintzberg further notes that because of the open-ended nature of the job, the
administrator is compelled to perform a great amount of work at an unrelenting
pace, further contributing to superficiality. Free time is only rarely available, and
job responsibilities seem inescapable. A 1965 study of the secondary school principalship revealed that principals studied spent 50 and often 60 hours a week on job
activities (Hemphill, Richards, & Peterson, 1965). A 1971 study of the superinten-

dency suggests a work week in excess of 60 hours for about one-half of the super-intendents studied (Knezevich, 1971). Evening and weekend work was common to the superintendency.

The administrators in Mintzberg's study demonstrated a preference for live action and for verbal means of handling this action. The current and active elements of the job were preferred over the abstract, technical, and routine. Visiting personally, talking on the telephone, and formal and informal conferences were the common strategies. Because of the propensity for verbal interaction, much of the business of the organization remains unrecorded and stored in the administrator's memory, making delegation and shared decision making difficult. The administrator is overloaded in exclusive knowledge about the organization and in meeting commitments on her or his time as others seek this information. It is difficult to keep on top of events and in control of organizational activities, and seemingly, no mechanism exists to relieve him or her of responsibilities. Faced with the apparent requirement that she or he be involved in almost everything, the recourse is to treat work activities with a distinct superficial flair.

As Laswell (1971) suggests, "The man who keeps on top of his responsibilities is likely to suffer from chronic fatigue and exasperation, and unless he has an exceptional natural constitution, a quick mind, and selective habits of work, he falls further and further behind."

Though educational administrators are likely to find the description of their world of work familiar, this familiarity does not lessen their anxiety over what often seems an impossible dilemma. Understandably, attempts are made to bring order to ones administrative life of apparent confusion, to seek control over one's work activities. This search for order and control is what makes discussions of planning-and-time-management theories and models so appealing to educational administrators.

Time as a Scarce Resource

Time is a scarce resource in the sense that any future allocation of time is diminished by the amount allocated to present activities. Further, since the number of activities that can be simultaneously tended to is limited, time spent on one activity results in neglect of others. But time distribution is a social-psychological concept as well as one in economics. Symbolically, how an administrator uses time is a form of administrative attention with meaning to others in the school. It is assumed that an administrator gives attention to the events and activities he or she values. Spending a great deal of time on interpersonal relationships, developing educational program objectives, building student identity with the school and its programs, or some other area, communicates to teachers and students that this sort of activity is of worth to the administrator and the school. As others learn the value of this activity to the administrator, they are also likely to give it attention. Administrative attention, then, can be considered a form of modeling for others who work in the school. Through administrative attention, the principal contributes to setting the tone or climate of the school and communicates to others the goals and activities that should enjoy high priority.

The three chapters that make up Part III of this book provide an in-depth cultural view of schooling, the superintendency, and the principalship. These chapters provide clues about how school administrators can bring order to their work lives. Mintzberg (1973) believes that one way in which administrators can make sense out of their seemingly chaotic work environment is through the process of self-reflection. In his words *"The manager's effectiveness is significantly influenced by his insights into his own work.* His performance depends on how well he understands and responds to the pressures and dilemmas of the job. Thus managers who can be introspective about their work are likely to be effective at their jobs" (p. 59). In this spirit, Exhibit 8.1 provides a series of self-study questions that Mintzberg believes can help administrators sort out the environment that characterizes their work and can provide them with more solid footing for initiating reasonable administrative action.

The intent of this chapter was to provide readers with a glimpse of the real world and work of administration. Relying on the work of Mintzberg and others

---

EXHIBIT 8.1   Self-Study Questions for Administrators

---

1. Where do I get information and how? Can I make greater use of my contacts to get information? Can other people do some of my scanning for me? In what areas is my knowledge weakest, and how can I get others to provide me with the information I need? Do I have powerful enough mental models of those things within the organization and in its environment that I must understand? How can I develop more effective models?
2. What information do I disseminate in my organization? How important is it that my subordinates get my information? Do I keep too much information to myself because disseminartion of it is time consuming or inconvenient? How can I get more information to others so they can make better decisions?
3. Do I balance information collecting with action taking? Do I tend to act prematurely before enough information is in? Or do I wait so long for "all" the information that opportunities pass me by and I become a bottleneck in my organization?
4. What rate of change am I asking my organization to tolerate? Is this change balanced so that our operations are neither excessively static nor overly disrupted? Have we sufficiently analyzed the impact of this change on the future of our organization?
5. Am I sufficiently well informed to pass judgment on the proposals made by my subordinates? Is it possible to leave final authorization for some of them with subordinates? Do we have problems of coordination because subordinates in fact now make too many of these decisions independently?
6. What is my vision of direction for this organization? Are these "plans" primarily in my own mind in loose form? Should they be made explicit in order to better guide the decisions of others in the organization? Or do I need flexibility to change them at will?
7. Are we experiencing too many disturbances in this organization? Would they be fewer if we slowed down the rate of change? Do disturbances reflect a delayed reaction to problems? Do we experience infrequent disturbance because we are stagnant? How do I deal with disturbances? Can we anticipate some and develop contingency plans for them?

EXHIBIT 8.1 *(Continued)*

8. What kind of a leader am I? How do subordinates react to my managerial style? How well do I understand their work? Am I sufficiently sensitive to their reactions to my actions? Do I find an appropriate balance between encouragement and pressure? Do I stifle their initiative?

9. What kind of external relationships do I maintain and how? Are there certain types of people that I should get to know better? Do I spend too much of my time maintaining these relationships?

10. Is there any system to my scheduling, or am I just reacting to the pressures of the moment? Do I find the appropriate mix of activities, or do I tend to concentrate on one particular function or one type of problem just because I find it interesting? Am I more efficient with particular kinds of work at special times of the day or week and does my schedule reflect this? Can someone else (in addition to my secretary) take responsibility for much of my scheduling and do it more systematically?

11. Do I overwork? What effect does my workload have on my efficiency? Should I force myself to take breaks or to reduce the pace of my activity?

12. Am I too superficial in what I do? Can I really shift moods as quickly and frequently as my work patterns require? Should I attempt to decrease the amount of fragmentation and interruption in my work?

13. Do I orient myself too much toward current, tangible activities? Am I a slave to the action and excitement of my work, so that I am no longer able to concentrate on issues? Do key problems receive the attention they deserve? Should I spend more time reading and probing deeply into certain issues? Could I be more reflective?

14. Do I use the different media appropriately? Do I know how to make the most of written communication? Do I rely excessively on face-to-face communication, thereby putting all but a few of my subordinates at an informational disadvantage? Do I schedule enough of my meetings on a regular basis? Do I spend enough time touring my organization to observe activity firsthand? Am I too detached from the heart of our activities, seeing things only in an abstract way?

15. How do I blend my rights and duties? Do my obligations consume all my time? How can I free myself sufficiently from obligations to ensure that I am taking this organization where I want it to go? How can I turn my obligations to my advantage?

Source: The Nature of Managerial Work by Henry Mintzberg. Copyright © 1973 by Henry Mintzberg. Reprinted by permission of Addison-Wesley Educational Publishers Inc.

of the work-activity school, 10 administrative roles characteristic of most administrative jobs were identified. The roles were grouped into three major categories: interpersonal, informational, and decisional. It was observed that despite the presence of the roles in most jobs, differences could be found based on the emphases each of the roles received. Eight administrative styles were identified, each resulting from a distinct combination of role emphasis. The focus of this chapter is on the "real" rather than the "ideal" the "is" rather than the "ought." This descriptive emphasis, where administrators have to satisfy constraints, is in contrast to the more common prescriptive view of administration, where it is assumed that administrators behave to maximize objectives. Though the balance in the literature is clearly in favor of prescriptive views and the need is great to enrich the descriptive literature, a caveat is in order. Administrators cannot be seduced by the descriptive literature into willy-nilly acceptance of affairs as they are, and behave accordingly. This position would gravely distort the concept of leadership. But neither can administrators ignore the realities of their world. To do so would result in a naive and less effective leadership practice. What is needed is a better balance and integration of both views, and this need suggests a likely future for research-and-development efforts in educational administration.

References

Hemphill, J., Richards. J., & Peterson, R. (1965). *Report of the senior high school principalship.* Washington, DC: National Association of Secondary School Principals.

Homans, G. C. (1950). *The human group.* New York: Harcourt Brace Jovanovich.

Knezevich, S. (Ed.). (1971). *The American school superintendent: An AASA research study.* Washington, DC: American Association of School Administrators Commission on the Preparation of Professional School Administrators.

Laswell, H. D. (1971). *A pre-view of policy sciences.* New York: Elsevier North-Holland.

Lindblom, C. E. (1959). The science of muddling through. *Public Administrator Review, 19*(2), 79–88.

Mintzberg, H. (1973). *The nature of managerial work.* New York: Harper and Row.

Simon, H. A. (1957). *Models of man.* New York: John Wiley.

Sproul, L. S. (1976). *Managerial attention in new educational systems.* Paper prepared for seminar on Organizations as Loosely Coupled Systems, Urbana, IL, Nov. 13–14.

Wolcott, H. J. (1973). *The man in the principal's office.* New York: Holt, Rinehart and Winston.

C h a p t e r **9**

The Everyday Life of Students and Teachers in Schools

This chapter and the next two chapters discuss schools as cultural systems. This chapter begins by providing a brief overview of the concept of culture as it is used to describe and explain schools. It then reviews selected studies about the everyday life of students and teachers and discusses how these studies contributed to efforts to reform schools in the 1980s. The chapter concludes by suggesting some of the questions that arise from viewing these reforms from the cultural perspective.

Chapters 10 and 11 discuss studies of the everyday life of principals and superintendents. It is interesting to note that over the last decade, there have been large numbers of cultural studies of the lives of students and teachers, a few studies of the lives of principals, and almost no studies of the lives of superintendents.

These three chapters also show how the cultural perspective provides insights into the competing values of equity, excellence, efficiency, and choice. How do the everyday lives of students and teachers, principals, and superintendents accomplish or thwart these values? Moreover, the text will suggest how these everyday lives fit different theories of change such as the pyramid, railroad, high-performance, and community theories. Do these studies support one of these theories? Although the cultural studies used provide no definitive answers on some of these problems, they do suggest fruitful lines for research and theorizing.

The Concept of Culture

The concept of *culture* has been defined in many different ways, but these chapters will use the term to "refer to those phenomena which account for patterns of behaving that cannot be *fully* explained by psychobiological concepts" (Kaplan & Manners, 1972, p. 3). Studies that attempt to describe and explain these patterns of behavior that are not psychobiological are often called *qualitative studies*. Such studies are marked by efforts to find patterns of behavior invented by individuals and groups and then taught to others as the ways to behave. These social inventions imbue everyday life with structure and meaning.

An example may clarify the distinction between psychobiological and cultural concepts. In the early 1960s, Stanley Milgram, an experimental psychologist, planned a study to explore the nature of obedience as a psychological characteristic of individuals. Milgram asked an assortment of different people to play the role of teacher in an experiment. He then had a confederate play the role of learner. A directing scientist instructed these teachers to administer shock treatments to the confederates if they were not cooperative learners. Milgram found that many teachers would administer dangerous levels of shock to the learners if the scientist directed them to do so. In reality, the learners were not actually shocked, although they acted as if they were being shocked and in great pain. Milgram concluded from this experiment that many individuals had the psychological characteristic of obedience.

Orne and Holland criticized Milgram's study by pointing out that *in our society*, we do not believe that scientists are mad Dr. Frankensteins. *In our society*, we have learned to expect scientists to be reasonable people who are well educated and who would do no harm either to the learners (who were being shocked) or the teachers (who were administering the shock) (cited in Suter, Lindgren, & Hiebert, 1989, p. 246). When we serve as subjects in a psychological experiment, we bring to that experiment a set of cultural learnings. Had Milgram conducted his experiment in a different society, one that deeply distrusted scientists and that believed they were all mad Dr. Frankensteins, the results would have been considerably different.

For the past 30 years, moreover, psychologists have grown increasingly concerned with artifacts. *Artifacts* are cultural learnings that are often unintended influences that may occur in experimental settings and that may affect responses of subjects and adversely influence experiments. Orne and Holland, in short, suggested that our cultural expectations about behavioral scientists and their treatment of individuals in experiments are an artifact that may have influenced Milgram's teachers. Instead of finding out something about the psychological makeup of individuals, Milgram may have found out something about how members of our society view behavioral scientists.

Qualitative studies that seek to delineate these cultural patterns are often informed by anthropological insights and methods. Anthropology as a discipline fixes attention on the ways that the populations of humankind have produced similarities and differences in the way they live their everyday lives. These patterns of human behavior are shaped by traditions and particular institutional arrangements created by the group. For instance, anthropologists have studied the ways that different groups of people deal with the biological problem of human death. What they discovered is that various groups explain and deal with this event in diverse ways—some sing and dance, others weep and tear their clothing.

Anthropologists can study these inventions of humans from two perspectives. First, they can study the ways a single culture changes over time. What accounts for factors that perpetuate the culture and for factors that change the culture? One of the favorite areas of study is how a group of people deals with the introduction of a new tool. A good question, for example, might be how teachers in a particular school deal with computers in their classrooms. Second, they can study several cultures to find similarities and differences among these cultures. How do different cultures react to the invention of a new tool, for example? A good question might be how American and Japanese teachers deal with computers in their classrooms.

Anthropologists conceive of a culture as a system made up of several subsystems. They are "concerned with the interaction between subsystems or institutions such as the social structural, ideological, and technoeconomic" (Kaplan & Manners, 1972, p. 4). People exist within a culture that is a complex web of tools, social events, and ideas. Their culture and its subsystems explain who they are and who is different from them, how they work and play and things that they should not do, and how they should understand the world and the bizarre nature of other ideas. A female teacher, for example, not only works in a school but also is married and raises a family, has her own individual life, attends church, and is active in a bridge club, a political party, and a physical fitness group. These various subsystems not only compete for the time and energy of the individual but also help her determine positively who she is, where she belongs, and what her world is like. These associations also determine who the individual is *not* like: She is not unemployed, not single, not an atheist, not a chess player, and not overweight.

Anthropologists generally study cultures by living in them. Their studies are done in the setting ("field") and they may live in the setting for an extended period of time. Field observers try to disturb the natural setting as little as possible ("unobtrusive") and use multiple methods—such as observing and transcribing events, conducting interviews, studying documents and other artifacts, and drawing maps—to create a coherent picture of the culture ("triangulation"). The accounts they produce seek insights into the nature of the cultural system and its various subsystems.

In applying this perspective to schools, important questions emerge. Questions might focus attention on similarities and differences in schools in different cultures. For example, what are the similarities and differences in schools in the United States and Japan or in California and Connecticut? Other questions might study similarities and differences within a single culture. For example, what are the similarities and differences in schools in the San Francisco area or in the Hartford area? We might attend to the ways that changes in the culture shape the schools. For example, what impact has the computer had on schools in the United States? Or, as discussed in Chapter 3, how have changes in the conventional cultural wisdom affected the schools? Those who seek to answer such questions will live in the school for an extended period using multiple methods to produce an account.

Student Life in Schools

What is life like in schools for students? Two studies are presented in some detail. These studies highlight two persistent themes that dominate descriptions of the way junior high and high school students live in schools. The first study explores how students behave in classrooms; the second examines student cliques in schools.

Allen (1986) asked how high school students come to understand how they are to behave in classrooms. Do students come to classrooms with some sort of an agenda? Having spent time in classrooms, students may well seek to shape classrooms to what they want. How do the events in classrooms shape the agendas of students? Students may be influenced by factors in the context of classrooms, such as what teachers seek to accomplish, assignments or tasks they are asked to do, and characteristics of other students. Allen was particularly interested in how student agendas and classroom events developed the students' viewpoint (perspective) to "make sense of their classrooms and assign meanings to their behaviors" (p. 438). He believed that previous research had attended to how students reacted to the teacher's agenda for the classroom, not to agendas that students might bring to the room.

To study this problem, Allen followed a typical ninth-grade schedule in a high school in southern California that enrolled 600 students. He focused his attention on 100 students (mostly ninth-graders) and four teachers assigned to five classes. These classes included agriculture, Spanish, health education, and English (two mini-courses). Allen observed classes for approximately 16 weeks, interviewed students, and interviewed teachers.

What Allen found was that students did have a classroom agenda but that this agenda was influenced by the context of the particular classroom. The agenda of students had two major classroom goals: socializing with other students and passing the course. To achieve these goals, students spent time in the first few days of a class figuring out the teacher. Figuring out the teacher meant determining the amount of socialization that would be tolerated and the amount of work that had to be accomplished. Students consciously sought to determine what the rules were for conduct and schoolwork and just how far these rules could be bent or broken.

After this initial period, classroom events became routine. Students sought to achieve the goal of socializing with others by having fun. Having fun included social talking, playing around, and humor. Students also sought to achieve the goal of passing the course by giving the teacher what the teacher wanted. Students worked on assignments and participated in classroom events. They also sought to increase the amount of time they could spend socializing by reducing the amount of work required to pass the course. They challenged the requirements of the teacher or copied the work of others.

Critical events occurred if the teacher's agenda conflicted with the students' agenda. If the teacher's agenda for passing the class was too easy or too hard, students became bored and increased their efforts at socializing with other students. In contrast to routine efforts at having fun, reducing boredom was often defiant or aggressive and sought to change the agenda the teacher was trying to set for the classroom. On the other hand, if the classroom became too noisy from socializing and the teacher began measures to gain control, students adjusted by trying to stay out of trouble by not talking or playing around.

This general agenda of students was affected by the classroom teacher. In agriculture class, for example, in-class academic activities were relatively unimportant and out-of-class activities were critical for passing the course. The teacher also stressed informal relationships with students, increasing opportunities for socializing. In Spanish, however, classroom instruction was structured with high levels of academic expectation, classroom rules were rigidly enforced, and the teacher stressed formal relationships. Most students gave the teacher what the teacher wanted to pass the course and socialized the last few minutes of the class. In health education, classwork was extensive but easy. There were flexible limits on socializing, and the teacher stressed good rapport and cooperation with students. The teacher took a genuine interest in students inside and outside the health ed classroom. For the students, each classroom was a different context that shaped their behaviors as they sought to fulfill their agenda.

Allen (1986) concludes by suggesting "classroom management must not be seen only from a teacher's perspective focused on control and discipline, but also from a student's perspective focused on learning in a sociable environment" (p. 457).

The second study compares teenage cliques in a middle school and a high school in a middle-class suburb. Canaan (1987) is interested in how these cliques may help or hinder teenagers as they develop their own identities. Canaan conducted the research in a middle school with 634 students in sixth to eighth grades and a high school of 1,053 students in grades 9 to 12. The community of Sheepshead is a predominantly upper-middle-class suburb with high per-pupil expenditures.

Canaan (1987) finds that at middle school and high school, there is a three-tiered group-ranking system. The top group in the middle school—the "cool" group—is made up of boys and girls who are "athletically skilled and socially capable" (p. 386) of living by a set of rules. These rules include not admitting to liking school or getting good grades. The middle group of students in the middle school conforms "to the expectations of their teachers and parents and those of the cool group" (p. 386). Members of the middle group may be chided by a "cool" group member for studying too hard or following all the rules adults make. The lower group members are known for socially inappropriate behavior.

In the high school, the highest group is made up of two subgroups—jocks and freaks. Jocks excel in extracurricular athletic activities and dress and act with self-confidence. During the week, they follow coach's orders, but on weekends, they "party" by breaking these orders. Freaks defy adult values in and out of school. Both jocks and freaks are aware of what other members of the highest group are doing. The middle group is made up of various subgroups that are neither as cool as jocks and freaks nor as weird as the low group. Many in the middle group emulate the jocks and freaks. The low group in the high school is made up of several small groups whose "actions do not conform with cool notions of proper social action" (Canaan, 1987, p. 391).

The most visible groups in both schools are the top groups. They serve as model teenagers in both schools, defining what it means to be cool (what the appropriate values of a teenager are) and what the relationship of teenagers to school and adults should be (when and where it is appropriate to accept or reject adult values).

There are differences between the groupings in middle school and high school. For instance, divisions among groups are stronger in middle than high school. Many of the subgroups in high school are not named.

Canaan concludes by suggesting that shared meanings make it possible for groups to differentiate themselves and that comparing groups over middle school and high school illuminates some of the continuities and discontinuities of being a teenager.

What can be made of these two studies? How do they help us understand schools as cultural systems? One important point to notice is that teenagers in U.S. culture have developed their own culture (usually referred to as a subculture) that includes a set of expectations about how to behave as students and how to behave as teenagers. The school provides a setting for this subculture; other settings might include places of employment, parties, athletic events, and dates.

A second point is that the norms of this subculture often do not agree with the norms of adult culture. Teenagers may not agree with their teachers about what should be done in classrooms or with their parents about correct behavior. Teachers confront students with expectations about what it means to be a student and parents confront their children with expectations about what is appropriate behavior. Teachers and parents who contradict the norms of the student subculture encounter difficulties.

A third point is that the teenage subculture is not uniform. It is composed of multiple groupings that follow variously the general norms of the teenage subcultures. Some groups embody these norms while other groups may challenge them or ignore them. Many strive to be cool, but many don't.

As cultural systems, schools are invented by society to initiate the young into that society. The young are not helpless, however. They respond to this adult invention by creating inventions of their own. They learn how to make it in the system and how to use the system to their own ends.

Could these studies be significantly in error? Perhaps both researchers happened on unusual schools and communities. In a survey of teachers in 276 schools in 87 communities, Antes and George (1990) found "completing assignments, attitude toward school, and classroom discipline all increase as problems as students progress through school" (n.p.). Attitude toward school was seen as a serious problem by 21.1 percent of elementary teachers, 39.8 percent of junior high teachers, and 45.6 percent of secondary teachers (Antes & George, 1990). Such surveys suggest that as children spend time in schools in the role of students, they invent their own student subculture—a culture that, at times, may be in serious conflict with the culture the teachers seek to create.

What do these studies suggest about competing values and theories of change? First, student subcultures may accentuate or subvert values and theories held by teachers. Students, for example, may accept and work with teachers who seek excellence. Or they may reject and work against teachers who seek excellence. Moreover, students may accept or resist a pyramid theory of change. Descriptions of schools must therefore include students as powerful agents for shaping what happens in schools. Second, understanding the subculture of students may provide tools for using that subculture to obtain good ends. Understanding how students cope with teachers or how groups shape middle and high schools are pieces of information that can help shape strategies for change. For example, if one tries to change schools using high-performance theory, how are the everyday lives of students to be built into the means of change? In short, in order to provide accurate accounts of what is happening in schools and intelligent advice about how to improve schools, and to attain the values we seek, we must take into account the subculture of students.

Teacher Life in Schools

Research suggests two important dimensions of the life of teachers in schools. First, teaching is a lonely profession. Teachers generally work in the solitude of their own rooms. Recent efforts to improve teaching have challenged this isolation. Second, teachers are involved in a political struggle within their school for valuable resources. Supplies, time with better students, and location are just a few of the issues.

In his pioneering work using interviews and surveys, Lortie (1975) found that teachers were conservative, individualistic, and oriented to immediate issues. Teachers were conservative, in part, because they could look back on 16 years or more of experience in classrooms to determine what they should or should not do in their classrooms. Moreover, teachers had generally enjoyed their school experiences. They were interested in maintaining continuity with their past experiences, not striking out in bold fashion to challenge the ways schools operated. Teachers were individualistic because they were dropped into their classrooms and implicitly told to survive or to leave. What teachers came to realize was that each teacher developed her or his survival tactics. No one could provide universal techniques for classroom success. Living in their classrooms, the primary satisfaction of teaching was what happened in that classroom at this particular moment. The joy of teaching was the reactions of students to the teacher's efforts. A glimmer of insight, a step forward made the teacher's day.

Using qualitative methods, others generally confirmed and added to Lortie's work. Lieberman and Miller (1984), for instance, found that teachers faced a central contradiction in their work. On the one hand, they had to develop their own unique personal affective style while they taught cognitive material that was universal (p. 2). Each teacher seemed to resolve this dilemma in his or her own fashion. Others spoke of the privacy of teaching (McPherson, 1972). The classroom was the kingdom of the teacher.

Others suggest that Lortie's work should be expanded to include the differences between elementary and secondary teachers. In general, elementary schools were smaller, dominated by female teachers, and imbued with an ideology that stressed the development of children. Secondary schools were larger, dominated by subject-matter departments, and stressed the teaching of subject matter to students.

Ball (1987) suggests that schools should be viewed as small political systems where individual teachers, groups of teachers, departments, and administrators are seen negotiating for resources and power. These resources include prime classroom locations, space for storage or computers, particular students, certain classes, supplies, and requirements for students. Often these resources are seen as ways to enhance the prestige and power of an individual or department (math has more computers than business education) or to ease the burden of the work (only the smart kids take physics). Struggles over power include issues of who has the right to make decisions and whether these decisions are enforced or ignored. For instance, it may become part of the political order that while evaluations for non-tenured teachers are important, evaluations for tenured teachers are pro forma or else the teachers of the building will demand that their association file a grievance against the principal.

This micropolitical view of the school stresses that the order of the school is constantly being negotiated and renegotiated. Under these conditions, the relative prestige and power of individuals—be they teachers, department chairs, or administrators—are in a state of flux and may differ from issue to issue.

Reforms and Teachers' Lives

These studies, and others, helped shape the research base for recent reforms that sought to improve teachers. In general, that research base agreed on three major points. First, new teachers came to their classrooms remembering their love of schooling. What they faced when they entered their classrooms was a student population that did not always share this feeling. The first year of teaching forced most new teachers to reexamine their assumptions about teaching and to learn how to deal with a diverse student population. Moreover, many teacher-preparation programs did not adequately prepare new teachers for this reality shock.

Second, the loneliness of the individual classroom teacher had two potentially negative consequences. Teachers were unable to share with each other what they had learned in their classrooms about teaching. Teachers also encountered students who worked diligently to shape teacher expectations about what was to be done in classrooms.

Teachers could not share their goals, methods, successes, and failures with each other. They could not profit from what worked or avoid what failed in classrooms other than their own. The cellular structure of the school meant that information about teaching was restricted to each classroom. The teacher culture lacked a technical language for communicating about teaching.

In contrast, the student subculture had consistent models for cool behavior. This behavior provided clear-cut norms that students could follow as they tended to the tasks of socializing with other students and passing the course. These norms meant that students tried to negotiate with individual teachers to expand socializing and reduce studying activities. While some teachers did not bend, others did. Students could share this information with other students; teachers could not communicate their standards to their peers.

Third, the immediacy of work rewards for teachers gave students even more power in the classroom. If students could reward or punish teachers for what happened, then students had a powerful tool for shaping teacher actions. Cusick (1983) found in one urban high school that teachers faced students who were only marginally interested in the subject matter of the class and who were also deeply interested in possible hostility among racial and ethnic groups. Under these conditions, "teachers had to fall back on . . . good personal relations they had with the students" (p. 52). In fact, in some classes, Cusick found that the subject matter of the class was personal relations between students and teacher.

In general, the reform strategies sought to change these conditions. First, the strategies stressed the induction of new teachers. Second, the strategies sought the development of a common language for teaching. This language was embodied in evaluation schemes. Third, the development of a common language meant that teachers could share their expectations about student achievement and behavior. By sharing expectations, the micropolitics of the schools might be directed to more constructive issues. In short, the reforms sought to build a teacher culture in the schools.

In several states, committees were set up for the induction of new teachers. In Oklahoma, for example, a Residency Year Teacher Committee is formed at the beginning of each school year for each new, noncertified teacher. The committee is made up of a master teacher in that school in the subject area of the new teacher, the school principal, and a representative from an institution of higher education— usually a professor. This committee meets early in the school year with the new teacher and discusses the evaluation form and the format to be followed. In the fall, the master teacher meets frequently with the new teacher and all three members of the committee observe at least two class sessions. The committee meets with the new teacher prior to Christmas and reviews these observations, noting strengths and areas that need improvement. In the spring, the master teacher continues to meet frequently with the new teacher and all three members observe at least one class session. About April 15, the committee formally reconvenes with the new teacher and, after discussing the observations and progress over the year, formally votes on a recommendation for certification. If the majority is for certification, the new teacher may apply to the state department. If the majority votes against certification, the new teacher must repeat the entry-year experience.

This elaborate procedure helps new teachers through many of the problems they normally face. The new teacher finds a colleague in the master teacher; they can share experiences in a nonthreatening way. The new teacher becomes accustomed to observations by the principal and comes to know what the administrative expectations are. The new teacher can share with the professor strengths and weaknesses in preparation programs. These can then be incorporated in teacher-preparation classes.

The keystone of the reform movement was teacher evaluation. Many states adopted a strategy that required teachers to be evaluated using a single model of teaching, often the Madeline Hunter model. The teaching model suggested that good lessons had certain characteristics, that these characteristics could be taught to teachers, and that evaluators could rate how well teachers achieved these characteristics in a lesson. For example, good lessons began with an introduction that included having students recall what had happened in earlier classes, linking what would happen in today's lesson to past and future lessons, and suggesting some specific results for the lesson.

What was necessary for these models to work was the development of a common vocabulary that pointed to similar events in classrooms. If teachers were to begin a lesson with an introduction, teachers had to know what counted as an introduction. Equally, if administrators were to observe and evaluate an introduction, they had to know what one looked like. Or if teachers were to use leading questions as a way to move from one major point in the lesson to the next major point, they had to know what a leading question was and what a major point was. Administrators observing the lesson also had to have an understanding of leading questions and major points if they were to talk intelligently with teachers about the lesson. Without a common vocabulary for describing the lesson, there could be no common ground for evaluation.

During the 1980s, states such as North Carolina, Florida, Georgia, and South Carolina, to name but a few, developed increasingly elaborate evaluation schemes. These schemes initially require that administrators and teachers attend workshops to learn the common language that will be used for evaluating classroom lessons. As these evaluations have proceeded from year to year, further workshops have been offered or mandated that dealt with new problems that developed. For instance, some teachers became interested in working with other teachers to foster teacher improvement in classroom teaching. Some states have provided districts with latitude to develop these mentor teachers. Other states have begun to worry about the issue of interrater reliability—the problem of consistency of rating of teachers across administrators. Would a teacher who was rated superior or inferior at Albert Elementary be rated the same at Brown Elementary? Other states have become interested in the problems of teachers who are nearing the end of their careers. How can their experiences be used to enrich the development of the teacher culture?

Finally, the development of a teacher culture may have important consequences for the micropolitics of the school (Blase, 1988). In a school where teachers cannot talk to each other about important issues, intelligent negotiations are difficult. Teachers assume what other teachers think or how they behave; they often act as if their colleagues are motivated by the lowest of expectations. If teachers can talk to each other about what they want and if they can visit each other's rooms with a common language for describing and explaining events, there are constructive grounds for negotiations. Negotiations will have to take place because wants will exceed resources. Intelligent negotiations, however, will be grounded on more accurate understandings of what is happening, clearer senses of wants, and more reliable estimates of resources. Much of the language of teacher empowerment assumes that the teacher culture includes a common language and intelligent negotiations.

Important areas for these intelligent negotiations may be expectations for student achievement and classroom behavior. If teachers and administrators can develop a common language and understanding about classroom events, they would be armed with tools for dealing with the student subculture. Teachers and administrators would be able as adults to confront the issues of socializing and passing the course among themselves and then with their students. For instance, what is the relationship between passing the course and developing higher-order thinking skills? If teachers and administrators have developed a common understanding of the levels of achievement desired and the nature of higher-order thinking skills, they should be able to discuss these issues intelligently among themselves and with their students. Without this common vocabulary, the micropolitics of the schools involve struggles to gain resources that bestow prestige rather than resources that enhance student outcomes.

Assessing Teacher Reforms

Although it is too soon to assess the impact of these efforts to change the everyday lives of students and teachers, studies using the qualitative approach may permit a clearer understanding of three key issues that may develop.

First, although cultures are contrived or invented, they are often difficult to change. The ways that members of the culture define the world come to be seen as natural and efforts to change these conceptual maps are often seen as aberrant. Thus, teachers may see the teacher culture as one that embodies the virtues of individuality, continuity, and presentation of rewards. They may believe that the good administrator is one who leaves teachers alone and does not intrude in their classrooms, that teacher evaluation is a threat to their jobs and a way of getting more work for less pay, and that the relationship they have with students is one dictated by their own personal style.

The distribution of these sentiments may not be random. It may well be that older teachers who have lived longer in this culture may be the most resistant to change.

Resistance to change may be exacerbated by the attention paid by reforms to issues involved with the induction of new teachers. Current reforms have few concerns for teachers near the end of their careers. Such undivided attention to new teachers may cause teachers with many years of experience to feel slighted in ways that inhibit their participation in reform.

Such speculations suggest why competing values and competing theories of change exist in schools. Teachers at different career stages may well hold different values and theories about schooling. Such effects of different generations of teachers (generations created by chronological age or by date of training) mean that many schools have representatives of all values and all theories. The issue may be one of developing tools for bridging these generations.

Second, cultures are made up of many systems. The life of the teacher involves not only the school as a work site but also life as an individual and as a member of a family (Schein, 1978). Each individual passes through various stages of life—for instance, marriage, child rearing, middle age, and old age. Equally, family issues such as marriage, the decision to have children, educating children, and children leaving home all influence work and individual development. Moreover, the traditional patterns that may have described the 1950s are no longer adequate for examining these stages. The increased longevity of parents, the upsurge in single-parent families, blended families of divorced and remarried parents, and two-professional-career families are all realities of the emerging twenty-first century.

The multiple systems that form the culture of the teacher suggest that efforts to reconstitute a new teacher culture within the schools may conflict with life and family considerations. District policies and individual building administrators will have to help plan careers for teachers that account for individual and family issues if teacher reform is to be successful. Some districts, for example, provide child-care facilities for their teachers. These notions suggest that a part of school reform will require administrators to be involved in career planning.

Third, reforms project an image of rapid change with only good consequences. Changes in culture may take time and may often produce consequences that are unintended. By following efforts to remake the teacher culture over time, those elements of the culture that most resist change and those that change rapidly will become clearer. For instance, do experienced teachers really learn a new vocabulary to describe and explain how they teach or do they simply slap new labels on their old behaviors? Equally, are there unanticipated outcomes as changes are made? Do teachers, for example, adopt reforms that enhance their control of their own classrooms and reject reforms that impede their control? Do beginning teacher committees, for another example, help new teachers learn how to be better teachers or do they unduly restrict the options the new teacher might try?

Of particular interest will be studies of the micropolitics of schools as they undergo reform. Are there significant shifts in the distribution of resources or in the location and use of power? Will teachers come to control their work lives in schools? What will be the role of principals or of community members?

The concept of culture and qualitative methods are powerful tools for examining these and other questions about the everyday life of students and teachers and the efforts to reform this life.

References

Allen, J. D. (1986). Classroom management: Students, perspectives, goals, and strategies. *American Educational Research Journal, 19,* 437–459.

Antes, R. L., & George, R. G. (1990, April). *Teacher perception of students at risk.* Paper presented at American Educational Research Association Annual Meeting.

Ball, S. (1987). *The micropolitics of the school.* New York: Methuen.

Blase, J. J. (1988). The politics of favoritism: A qualitative analysis of the teachers' perspective. *Educational Administration Quarterly, 24,* 152–177.

Canaan, J. (1987). A comparative analysis of American suburban middle class, middle school, and high school teenage cliques. In G. Spindler & L. Spindler (Eds.), *Interpretive ethnography of education: At home and abroad* (pp. 385–406). Hillsdale, NJ: Lawrence Erlbaum.

Cusick, P. A. (1983). *The egalitarian ideal and the American high school.* New York: Longman.

Kaplan, D., & Manners, R. A. (1972). *Culture theory.* Englewood Cliffs, NJ: Prentice-Hall.

Lieberman, A., & Miller, L. (1984). *Teachers, their world, and their work.* Alexandria, VA: Association for Supervision and Curriculum Development.

Lortie, D. C. (1975). *Schoolteacher.* Chicago: University of Chicago.

McPherson, G. (1972). *Small town teacher.* Cambridge, MA: Harvard University.

Suter, W. N., Lindgren, H. C., & Hiebert, S. J. (1989). *Experimentation in psychology.* Boston: Allyn and Bacon.

Chapter 10

The Everyday Life
of the School Principal

Qualitative studies are particularly well suited for developing insights about stable settings and people playing established roles. By spending a good deal of time in an unvarying situation, researchers can find those cultural patterns that persist and that shape everyday activities. Once these persistent patterns have been shown, researchers can then look for change.

In times of turmoil, qualitative studies have difficulty separating the noise from the signal—the transitory from the permanent. This is a time of turmoil for the principalship. There is debate about the role of the principal and many states and school districts are mandating new actions for principals. There is a good chance of confusing noise and signal.

To deal with this changing situation, this chapter begins by reviewing three major qualitative studies of the principalship. These studies suggest some important points about the everyday life of school principals. They suggest something about the nature of the principal. In that sense, they provide a good signal. The chapter concludes by discussing some of the turmoil surrounding the principalship. Much of that turmoil centers on what principals should and should not do. This turmoil provides a sense of the noise surrounding the principalship.

Ed Bell and His School

Published in 1973, Harry Wolcott's *The Man in the Principal's Office* provides a powerful qualitative account of one typical elementary school principal and his school. The account provides insights into Ed Bell as a man, as a principal in a school system, and as the principal of a school.

Ed Bell as an individual seems unremarkable. In fact, Ed seems to have come to education because he could not fulfill his other interests. He does not seem enamored with learning, looks on schooling as a job to be done, and does not seem the least interested in intellectual debates about education and its improvement.

As one of the principals in the system, Ed is aware of and interested in district politics. He knows, for instance, that Tom Nice helped sponsor him for a principalship. He knows that others in the district seek sponsorship and that there are proper ways for these organizational climbers to behave and for their potential sponsors to behave. Ed, and his fellow principals, attend to what may be happening in the system.

As principal of Taft Elementary, Ed seems to have a sense of his task. His attention and actions are aimed at maintaining the school against unusual events and day-to-day disturbances. There are infrequent disasters such as snowstorms, fire drills, and earthquakes. These challenges require the principal, teachers, and students to react but they do not disturb the basic balance of the school. They are clearly unusual events that necessitate unusual responses.

What is more disturbing to the school are the myriad of small mishaps that disturb the school and particularly the continuity of classroom routine. A good school day is a day in which nothing disturbs what happens in the several classrooms of Taft. As Ed sees his job, it is to maintain the school in such a way that continuity is preserved. This may mean that he spends a few moments ushering a stray dog out of the hallway or a good deal of time in the personnel office hiring a replacement teacher. Teachers come and go; rain falls and children track mud in corridors that have just been cleaned; secretaries quit at the last moment; superintendents constantly seem to create new goals for the district; buses do not run on time. These are but a few of the multitude of disturbances to the serenity that Ed seeks to create in Taft.

In many ways, Wolcott's study provides insights into one of the traditional ways an individual can fulfill the role of principal. The role of head teacher or principal teacher appears early in colonial schools. As communities grew, they increasingly needed more than one teacher to educate their young. To ensure that the dictates and requests of the lay citizens' school committee were communicated to all teachers and that needs of the teachers were communicated to the committee, a head teacher was appointed. In most communities, the head teacher was responsible not only for the routine maintenance activities of the school, including ordering supplies and ensuring overall school discipline, but also for providing advice to younger teachers.

In the mid-1800s, the role of principal evolved into one of school-site manager. Increased enrollments in schools and the emergence of the school superintendent as manager of several schools impelled principals toward the posture of running their schools. Exactly how the principal fulfilled this role differed not only from district to district but also within districts. All principals had to deal, first, with routine maintenance activities such as ordering textbooks and supplies, keeping the building and grounds clean and safe, and ensuring through strict disciplinary actions a tranquil setting for teachers and children. Second, principals became involved in helping teachers improve their instructional skills. Some evaluated teachers as required by the dictates of the district or the complaints of parents; others saw instructional improvement as their key role (Cuban, 1986).

By the early 1900s, the role had crystallized in most districts to include both instructional leadership and bureaucratic management of the school. Increasingly, districts and states were requiring that school principals be certified and that this certification be linked to classes taken in colleges or universities.

As the role developed, some teachers aspired to become principals. They completed the requirements for certification and sought opportunities not only to show their administrative abilities but also to be sponsored by principals or other administrators in the district. In some districts, coaching was the first step on the administrative ladder. In other districts, counseling or teaching English was the starting point. What the potential principal had to prove was the ability to get along with peers, to accept the posture of the current administration, and to work effectively with community members. Continuity and stability were seen as virtues; intellectual inquisitiveness and a taste for change were viewed as vices.

In this world, principals seemed to opt for one of three positions. Some stressed their role as instructional leaders. They saw the principalship as the key role for the improvement of classroom teaching. Others sought to be both instructional leaders and effective bureaucrats. These principals sought to fulfill both functions. Still others stressed the administrative and played down the instructional. For these bureaucratic principals, the classroom was the province of the teacher; the principal entered that classroom as few times as possible. Teaching was an individual art form that could not be improved by meddling by the principal. In turn, the hallways were the province of the principal. The principal built the school schedule, set the general standards for decorum and discipline, and, in general, decided the policies of the school—so long as they did not directly conflict with the classroom. The good principal was the good bureaucrat.

Ed Bell illustrates this traditional bureaucratic image of the principalship. His task, as he sees it, is to maintain the school so that teachers can teach. In one sense, his roots are to be found in the colonial period; he is a head teacher who transmits messages of the central administration to his teachers, orders their supplies, and keeps the building neat and safe. It is not his task to worry about the goals of the school or to intrude in classrooms to improve the skills of his teachers. His job is to keep the school afloat in a sea filled with constant, irritating, but minor disruptions. In accepting this image, Ed rejects the role of the principal as an instructional leader who is intent on improving teachers and sharpening the sense of educational purpose of the school. That role is not appealing to Ed Bell. (By the time Wolcott's book is reprinted, Ed's school has been closed because of declining enrollments and Ed has retired.)

Portraits of Good High School Principals

In 1983, Sara Lawrence Lightfoot provided accounts of six high schools—two urban, two suburban, and two private—and their principals. The principals and high schools selected by Lightfoot for study provide a picture of good high schools with good principals. What emerges from Lightfoot's portraits of these schools and their leaders is a sense of diversity in the schools and the principals.

In one of the urban high schools, the new principal works diligently to create a sense of order and discipline. In the other urban school, the principal works to create a sense of responsibility toward others—teachers to students and students to students. While the principal of one of the suburban schools seeks to maintain a status quo that ensures students admittance to outstanding colleges, the principal of the other suburban high school uses a student/faculty governance structure to create a discipline policy. In one of the private schools, the headmaster strives to preserve continuity with the past. In the other private school, the new principal seeks ways to generate faculty involvement in deciding about the school curriculum and testing program. His first move is to create a faculty lounge.

Lightfoot carefully elaborates the diversity of these schools and their principals. For example, St. Paul's School—small, religious, private, privileged—stresses continuity between past and present by holding four morning chapel services and four formal evening meals each week. The Rector, William Oates, holds great power vested in his office but uses that power in a civil and benign manner. In contrast, Dr. Norris Hogans, principal of George Washington Carver High, must constantly fight brushfires to ensure that his inner-city high school remains free of graffiti, that students attend classes, and that order is maintained. Using a walkie-talkie to communicate with others, Hogans imposes order on the scene by his presence.

Why such diversity? Drawing on a theatrical metaphor, the role of principal seems capable of being played or interpreted in several different ways, including instructional leader and bureaucrat. Principals seem to have the latitude to interpret the role as they see fit. At least four explanations have been given to account for this freedom.

First, although schools cover limited territory, the differences across these territories are profound. The boundaries of one school may include a blue-collar neighborhood with several different ethnic and racial groups. The next immediate school may encompass two neighborhoods of upper-middle-class professional families. A third school in the district may straddle a middle-class neighborhood and half of a public housing project. Under conditions of such diversity, it is reasonable for principals to devise unique strategies for resolving the problems dealt to the school by its territory. Principals must play to the audiences that are in attendance.

Second, principals reflect our society's uncertainty about educational means and ends. Disagreements among different individuals and groups are common, even at the level of individual schools. Should the school stress the academic basics or should it stress the development of individual responsibility? Principals have a host of options under these circumstances. Some principals may stress majority rule, others may seek a consensus; some may ignore the claims of the community and follow their own course, others may seek community opinion on all issues; some may follow the course charted by central administration and the school board, others may seek to develop unique programs for their school. Principals play to an audience of critics that cannot agree about what is a good performance. Under such conditions, principals select the critics they attend to. The critics acknowledged by one principal may be ignored by another.

Third, principals are trained at a certain time by colleges and universities and by their districts. The graduate training of a principal reflects those ideas and topics that struck the professors as interesting and helpful at that time. Moreover, the particular individuals who sponsor new principals and who provide them with counsel reflect the interests of the moment. The district, for example, may be deeply involved in efforts to increase citizen participation in school governance. Under these conditions, the district leaders will stress involvement as a key for the successful principal. As principals mature in their roles, they may fix on these notions or they may be forced to change as professors and district leaders shift attention to new topics. How principals play the role depends on who their directors are and who they have understudied.

Fourth, the faculties of schools provide different resources for the school principal. In some schools, the faculty is relatively passive and seems to be asking the principal to provide the direction of the school. In other schools, the faculty is aggressive in asserting its prerogatives to set the tone of the school. The wise principal follows the faculty's lead. In still other schools, the principal and faculty seem to share a common sense of what they are about. Neither the principal nor the faculty seem to lead; the norms of the school are held in common and shared by principals and teachers. Last, some schools are stages where the principal and various groups of teachers with different agendas play. Some teachers want to follow; some want to lead; some want to belong. Principals are a part of a cast of characters that influence the way they play their role.

Hence, each school services a unique neighborhood, contains a unique mix of ends and goals, is led by a principal with unique training, and has a unique faculty. It is small wonder that Lightfoot found six different high schools with six different principals.

Principals as Instructional Leaders

In 1985, David Dwyer and others of the Far West Laboratory for Educational Research and Development published case studies of five elementary principals and two junior high school principals. These principals were studied because they were viewed by many as outstanding instructional leaders. Again, these principals display diversity in how they lead their schools.

For example, Ray Murdock, principal of Jefferson Elementary School, wants his school to be an exemplary model for rural education for the state. Jefferson Elementary, with 410 students, serves an impoverished rural community with a population that is generally lower socioeconomic class and transient. Ray carefully selects his teachers, stresses reading, and strives to build a warm school atmosphere with colorful and bright classrooms. He constantly seeks to generate additional funds for the school through activities such as a carnival.

In contrast, Jonathan Rolf, principal of Larkspur Elementary School, seeks to buffer teachers and students from the demands of zealous parents. Situated in an elite suburban area, parents demand that teachers, programs, and the school perform at above average. Jonathan sees his role as supporting teachers by providing supplies, keeping interruptions to a minimum during the school day, and buffering teachers from parents who often seem unrealistic in their demands for their children.

These accounts suggest many different ways to play the role of principal as instructional leader. They also underscore one important fact about the principalship: The principal must establish some relationship with teachers. Lieberman and Miller (1984) argue that teachers want some sense of order and some sense of how well they are doing their work. These case studies support this line of reasoning.

Teachers want to work in a situation with some sense of order. Ray Murdock builds an order that stresses time for reading, time to provide a pleasant setting for children, and time to generate funds for the school. These givens of Jefferson provide a sense of purpose and continuity. At Larkspur Elementary, Jonathan Rolf provides order by not intruding on the time of teachers. He controls the school day and the access of parents to teachers to provide his faculty with time for dealing with children.

Teachers in these schools can also judge how well they are performing. If teachers at Jefferson are not teaching reading, providing a pleasant atmosphere for students, and participating in the carnival, there is little doubt that Ray will seek their removal from the school. At Jefferson, Jonathan does not want his teachers dealing with parents. Teachers are successful when they maintain an independence of judgment about the capabilities of students.

These seven cases provide a rich source for examining what principals who are seen as instructional leaders do. Although all develop some relationship with their teachers that provides a sense of order and accomplishment, the mix of these relationships differ across the schools.

What Should Principals Do?

There is now much discussion of the role of the principal. In itself, discussion about the role of the principal is not new. In fact, as noted earlier, the role of the principal has been debated on many occasions. The usual debate has involved the question of whether a good principal is a bureaucrat or an instructional leader. As noted in earlier chapters, some proponents of educational reform seek to increase the power of teachers to improve their teaching. This line of reasoning suggests different instructional leadership and bureaucratic roles for principals.

At the core of teacher empowerment is the development of a common language for describing and explaining teaching. The current method for the development of this language is classroom observation. Observations in the classroom are of two types: formative and summative.

Current proponents of teacher empowerment argue that the teachers should dominate the *formative* stage. Efforts to improve teachers—the supervision of instruction—should be made by teachers among themselves. This might involve combinations of two or more teachers in various activities. For example, teachers might pair up and work on a specific part of the lesson or a specific set of instructional skills. Or several teachers might band together and conduct systematic experiments on teaching techniques.

In contrast, the role of the principal should be *summative*—the evaluation of teachers. The principal should judge the worth of the teacher. This judgment would include the decision to grant or deny tenure and the judgment to declare a tenured teacher incompetent.

For such a system to be fair, teachers who are being evaluated should first be supervised. Beginning teachers or tenured teachers with deficiencies should have the opportunity to be supervised by their peers. The aim of such supervision would be improvement.

To make this system work, the teachers and the principal must be in agreement about the evaluation system. The teachers and principal must see and talk about the classroom in the same way. Both parties must share a common vocabulary for describing classroom events and a common evaluation framework for judging the worth of these events. For instance, both teachers and principal must know when they have seen a class summary (description) and that ending a class with a summary is a good teaching strategy (evaluation).

This cooperative effort to improve instruction has results for the current bureaucratic structure of schools. If teachers are to be responsible for teacher improvement, then they should have some say about how resources in the school are distributed. If teachers are to work with other teachers, then they need time to visit before the observation, time to make the observation, and time to discuss the insights gained from the observation. Control of time as a resource means that teachers and principals must agree on how classes are scheduled, how preparation periods are situated in the schedule, and how substitute teachers are hired or how teachers or principals are reassigned to "cover" classes.

The ordering of supplies, the coordination of all school activities such as assemblies or test days, and the adoption of textbooks all seem to be activities in which the cooperation of teachers and principal is critical. The need for these, and other, cooperative activities suggests that the principal and teachers must work together. Some governance structure, such as a school council, needs to develop that permits both parties to decide jointly what should be done in the school.

If schools are to be governed this way, what are some of the characteristics that would be helpful for principals? Four come to mind, considering the qualitative studies reviewed earlier.

1. *Principals need to have a tolerance for ambiguity.* As these and other changes occur, principals need to have a sense of how cultures grow and change over time. That process of change and growth is often untidy. For example, one of the high schools described by Lightfoot (1983) contains a small alternative school program.

As the principal seeks to develop a new governance structure for the high school, the alternative program does not seem to fit. The alternative program is a discordant note in the new emphasis on students and faculty as a self-governing community. The principal tolerates the ambiguity because he sees the problem of what to do about the alternative school as a way of generating important discussions about membership in the school as a community. Growth and change are often messy.

   2. *Principals need to have the ability to listen.* The environment of the principal is others—pupils, teachers, parents, central office administrators, and the community at large. Principals can achieve success for their schools only if others are involved. This involvement requires hearing what others are saying about what changes are occurring and what things they say need to stay the same, how others are dealing with ambiguity and how they have created routines and standard operating procedures, and others' dreams for the future and their fears of the unknown. In the studies of the seven schools, Dwyer and others found that *communication* accounted for the largest proportion of each principal's activities (Dwyer et al., 1985, p. 15).

   3. *Principals need to say "no" infrequently.* Growth for students and teachers, and for the school, involves discounting past experiences for growth opportunities. One of Lightfoot's (1983) principals, for example, grants permission to a teacher to run a second concert although the first concert failed. This principal seems intent on communicating the message to this teacher and other teachers, to the students, and to the school that mistakes are human, that they happen, and that people should learn from them. "No" denies others opportunities to explore and expand the limits of their roles.

   4. *Tolerance for ambiguity, listening, and the infrequent use of "no" suggest a principal who has a sense of what the school is about.* These activities, and others by the principal, suggest coherence of purposes. That coherence is often summarized in simple slogans: "Doing our best for the kids" or "Make it a good day." That coherence is best seen by watching what principals do over time in the multitude of opportunities provided by the school as a setting. The linkage between words and deeds, between what is said about what schools should do and what is actually done, is the test of coherence of purposes. For example, one of the principals in the Dwyer and others study (1985) spent much of her time fulfilling her number-one priority that students leave her school with their reading skills at least at grade level. Understanding this, Dwyer and others were able to see why Orchard Park Elementary School looked the way it did and why the students and teachers behaved as they did. The behaviors of the principal made sense as they provided coherence of purpose for the school. This coherence allowed the principal to deal with ambiguity, listen to others, and say "no" infrequently.

   In sum, the current turmoil about the role of the principal suggests that principals should work with teachers to develop a common language for the description and evaluation of teachers, seek to evaluate teachers fairly, work with teachers to provide resources for the improvement of instruction, and develop a style that accentuates through coherence of purpose the growth of teachers and students.

What Should Principals Not Do?

Are there suggestions in the qualitative literature about things that principals should avoid? Two points come to mind: Avoid the universal and avoid the pro forma.

Is there one best way to play the role of principal? The answer suggested by these studies seems to be no. Two major reasons seems evident from reviewing the works of Wolcott, Lightfoot, and Dwyer and others.

First, individual schools seem to develop as unique cultural systems. The people who make up these systems—teachers, administrators, service personnel, and students—develop a sense of what that school is like. They work hard to build a culture that clarifies the way members of the school treat each other and look at the surrounding world. The six principals described by Lightfoot (1983) all lead schools with unique cultures and characters. Categories such as urban or suburban, for example, provide little help in understanding the similarities and differences among these schools.

Moreover, each of these schools and its unique culture differs in its sensitivity to change and continuity. As the principal of George Washington Carver High School, Dr. Hogans aggressively seeks change; he wishes to impose a new order on the school, its faculty, and its students. As the Rector of St. Paul's School, William Oates seeks continuity; he uses his position of power to ensure that traditions are preserved. The principals described in these accounts all faced problems of maintaining and changing the culture of the school; each faced a different mix of these elements in that particular school.

As unique cultural systems, some principals and schools seem more sensitive to those forces that preserve and challenge them. Some of these principals seemed intent on uncovering the older cultural assumptions of the school, bringing them to the attention of faculty and students, and examining these assumptions with an eye to debate that might change some or all of the examined assumptions. The creation of a faculty lounge by one of Lightfoot's (1983) principals, for example, was a deliberate signal that faculty were expected to talk to each other about the school. In contrast, Ed Bell seemed to avoid opportunities to explore Taft Elementary. He seemed content with maintaining the school as it was against the multitude of minor disruptions.

Second, as cultural systems, schools are intimately linked to their neighborhoods, districts, and states. Each school is embedded in its unique neighborhood. An elementary school in inner-city Chicago does not look or feel like an elementary school in the panhandle of Texas. They are unique institutions because of their environments.

That neighborhood, however, is part of a larger school district. Each school district seems composed of unique neighborhoods and schools. A close inspection of two districts often reveals differences in classification schemes for students, employment practices for teachers, and organizational structure.

One brief example may illustrate this point. Across the United States are schools labeled junior high or middle school. These schools often serve students in grades 7, 8, and 9. A closer look would find that in some districts, these schools serve grades 6, 7, and 8. In other districts, middle schools or junior high schools serve grades 8 and 9. In still other districts, these schools serve grades 5, 6, and 7. What exactly is a junior high or middle school? To complicate the matter even further, middle schools are "supposed" to differ from junior high schools in terms of organization and instruction. Proponents of middle schools often stress team teaching and interdisciplinary studies. Nonetheless, a close inspection of the organizational and instructional patterns reveals that many middle schools lack team teaching and have no interdisciplinary studies, and many junior high schools have team teaching and interdisciplinary studies.

A middle school or a junior high with a certain grade configuration and organizational and instructional pattern exists in a certain district because the people of that district choose to create that structure. It matters little that junior highs or middle schools in the adjoining district have different configurations and patterns.

School districts thus develop patterns over time. These patterns seek to provide continuity as the community changes. Neighborhoods change as children mature and leave home, as incomes change and families leave for better or less costly housing, and as places of employment move to new communities. Blocks that once filled a school bus may now have no young children; neighborhoods where large single-family dwellings were the norm may now be subdivided into many small apartments for immigrants to the community.

These patterns also develop in the sorts of teachers hired and the appointment of administrators. Some districts seek to reduce costs by hiring young, inexperienced teachers. Other districts seek a veteran staff with advanced degrees. Some districts simply take what is available without a conscious personnel plan. Administrators in some districts are insiders who have spent their entire careers in that district; in other districts, outsiders are deliberately sought.

These district patterns are often influenced by state legislation that sets, for example, the conditions for employment of teachers and administrators. The reforms of the 1980s stressed the improvement of teachers; several states adopted different strategies for achieving this end. Some states required teachers and schools to carry out mandated evaluation schemes, whereas other states offered rewards to teachers and schools for developing and implementing their own unique evaluation schemes. What is mandated in Georgia may be rewarded in California.

In sum, it appears that the principalship is a role described and explained best by variation. Each principal develops a unique mix of instructional leadership and bureaucratic competence for a particular setting. The case studies demonstrate differences, not universal formulas. Dwyer (1986) writes, *"There is no single image or simple formula for successful instructional leadership"* (p. 15).

There is a second thing that principals should avoid: the pro forma performance of their role. Halpin (1966) wrote,

> *As we looked at the school in our sample, and as we reflected about other schools in which we had worked, we were struck by the vivid impression that what was*

going on in some schools was for real, while in other schools, the characters on stage seemed to have learned their parts by rote, without really understanding the meaning of their roles. In the first situation the behavior of the teachers and the principal seemed to be genuine, or authentic, and the characters were three-dimensional. In the second situation the behavior of the group members seemed to be thin, two-dimensional, and stereotyped; we were reminded of pâpier-maché characters acting out their roles in a puppet show. (p. 204)

Some 25 years later, Metz (1990) amplified this observation. After studying eight schools in the midwest, Metz noted that these schools had marked differences but also that:

Despite different resources and quite different ideas about the nature and uses of high school education, there was not evidence that any of the communities wanted or expected schools to depart from the basic common script for "The American High School." This support for the common script may seem "natural," but in fact it requires explanation. (p. 77)

Metz suggests the common script serves both technical and symbolic purposes.

Technically, the script is found in places such as the formal curriculum of the district, the architecture of the building, the contracts between teachers and the district, the multitude of state laws, and the assumption that teachers completely control the lives of students. The script is the residue of 100 years of schooling. Schools are no longer being invented; they are now the way they have been for many years. Efforts to change them, to lengthen the school year, for instance, run against the cultural pattern of what schools are like. Every reinvention faces cultural patterns that tell us of the normalcy of our original invention.

Metz (1990) notes that culturally the script serves two purposes. First, the script explains why some children do not succeed. In situations such as poor inner-city minority neighborhoods, the school appears to follow the script. Teachers and administrators do their jobs. Classes meet, some students attend advanced classes, and the language used to describe the school is filled with terms suggesting accountability and improvement. Life in the school, however, did not meet these standards. Metz writes,

The physics teachers taught fundamental measurement skills, and one said that she hoped to complete mechanics with students having a solid grasp of it by the end of the year but might get no further. Teachers at other schools told me they would complete mechanics before Christmas. In senior English, we saw students practising and struggling with the elementary forms and skills of a business letter, even though they would be reading Dante's Inferno *later. (p. 83)*

In short, the script called for English students to read Dante, even though they might lack the skills necessary to gain much from reading Dante. No one, however, could doubt that these students had done what all other students did in high school.

Second, the script suggests that all schools provide equal educational opportunities for all students. The script means that all schools are the same. All physics students have learned how to measure and all English students have read Dante. In that sense, the public can pretend that one school is just as good as another.

In fact, the public knows that schools are not equal. Metz (1990) notes,

> *The public perceives schools to be in practice very unequal. Middle class parents will make considerable sacrifice to locate their children in schools they perceive to be better than others. Communities of parents with the economic and political means to do so will construct schools with special resources for their own children and will keep access to them exclusive. The social class and race of peers is often used by parents as a rough indictor of school quality. (p. 85)*

The script provides the appearance of equality. As it is played out in the everyday life of schools, the script provides the stuff of inequality. For instance, students at Inner-City High, serving a lower-class minority neighborhood, enroll in Algebra I, and students at Suburb High, serving an upper-class neighborhood, enroll in Algebra I. Both groups of students may be required by the state to use the same textbook and by their districts to use the same workbook. The state and school districts are providing equal opportunities for all children. In one school, students may be learning their number facts and well over half of the class may be receiving grades of F. In the other school, students may be mastering simultaneous equations and well over half the class may be receiving grades of B. The script shows that these students are in Algebra I (and so do the transcripts).

Despite the presence of a common script, schools may not be for real. The various actors in the scene may be able to talk and act as if they are authentic, but careful comparison of the everyday life in different schools suggests some are and some are not. Comparing the outcomes of the script on measures such as national standardized achievement tests points out discrepancies between authentic and stereotyped schools.

How can a principal deal with this problem? The notion of leadership provides clues for developing an authentic school by suggesting that the administrator, faculty, and community work together to ensure that the script is acted out in an authentic manner. A part of that acting out may require that the everyday life of teachers and students in some schools center on the development of elaborate directions for fulfilling that script. Those directions may involve the development of a common language for describing and explaining classroom behavior, as noted earlier, and the development of a language for explicitly discussing differences between the actual community setting and the usual setting assumed by the script. By understanding the assumptions the script makes about students and the support provided by their homes, for example, the community may redistribute resources to overcome problems. For instance, if the script assumes that every child comes to school after a good breakfast, the community may decide to provide breakfasts for children who do not get them at home.

In a sense, the principal must achieve the universal (equal educational opportunity provided by the script) using the unique (the particular resources of a specific community). Each principal should seek to develop an authentic school that successfully performs the script for a real school. Such a school strives to provide equality of opportunity by fulfilling the script and authenticity and yet reflects differences among communities. When students finish real school, the script has provided them with the tools necessary to make intelligent decisions about their future. The authenticity of the community has provided them with one vision of how they might live their future lives.

In Peshkin's (1978) account of the small high school in the rural community of Mansfield, for instance, slightly more than half the students want to live the remainder of their lives in that community. The other half wish to leave Mansfield to live in different types of communities. If this high school has provided all the students with real schooling, both stayers and leavers should be successful in their futures. If this high school has not provided all its students with the expectations of real schools, if it has smiled on those who chose to remain in Mansfield and frowned on those who chose to leave, the school has been less than authentic.

This chapter suggests that the everyday life of the principal is made up of individual decisions of how to resolve tensions resulting from different ways of playing the role and different levels of authenticity in the school. Principals must decide the unique mix of bureaucrat and instructional leader; principals must decide whether to be authentic or stereotyped. These decisions have important consequences for the sense of purpose of the school and the way the script of the real school is performed.

References

Cuban, L. (1986). Principaling: Images and roles. *Peabody Journal of Education, 63,* 107–119.

Dwyer, D. C. (1986). Understanding the principal's contribution to instruction. *Peabody Journal of Education, 63,* 3–18.

Dwyer, D. C., Lee, G. V., Barnett, B. G., Filby, N. N., Rowan, B., & Kojimoto, C. (1985). *Understanding the principal's contribution to instruction: Seven principals, seven stories* (Vol. 1–8). San Francisco: Far West Laboratory for Educational Research and Development.

Halpin, A. (1966). *Theory and research in educational administration.* New York: Macmillan.

Lieberman, A., & Miller, L. (1984). *Teachers, their world, and their work.* Alexandria, VA: Association for Supervision and Curriculum Development.

Lightfoot, S. L. (1983). *The good high school: Portraits of character and culture.* New York: Basic Books.

Metz, M. H. (1990). Real school: A universal drama amid disparate experience. In D. E. Mitchell & M. E. Goertz (Eds.), *Education politics of the new century: The twentieth anniversary yearbook of the Politics of Education Association* (pp. 75–91). London: Falmer Press.

Peshkin, A. (1978). *Growing up American.* Chicago: University of Chicago.

Wolcott, H. F. (1973). *The man in the principal's office.* New York: Holt, Rinehart and Winston.

C h a p t e r **11**

The Everyday Life of the School Superintendent

If the everyday life of the teacher centers on students and the everyday life of the principal centers on teachers and students, the everyday life of the superintendent is filled with other adults. Much of what the superintendent does in these meetings with other adults is symbolic; the superintendent represents the schools to the community. This representation may take many forms; it may be the presence of the superintendent at a meeting of community leaders, presenting awards to students at a ceremony staged for the press, attending a committee meeting of the state legislature, or welcoming an accreditation team to the high school.

Only part of the work of superintendents is symbolic. In fact, the work that most superintendents see as most important involves the setting of policy for and the administration of the school district. The most important of these encounters with adults may well be the meetings the superintendent has with the school board. It is in these public meetings that the policies of the school district are decided. The person seen as most responsible for these policies by the public is the superintendent. It is small wonder, then, that superintendents are often viewed as political figures. From the cultural perspective, political roles exist because there are disagreements in the society about cultural patterns. The occupants of these political roles, be they legislators or superintendents, are required to resolve these disagreements (Lewellen, 1983).

In contrast to the other two chapters in this section, there are few qualitative studies of the superintendency. Much of what follows rests on studies that have looked at small segments of the life of superintendents, often relying on interviews to provide insights.

This chapter begins by reviewing the historical development of the superintendent's role and the political purposes built into it. It then focuses on factors that influence the politics played by superintendents, and concludes by suggesting what the future may hold for the superintendency.

Historical Overview of the Superintendency

Created in the mid-1800s, the superintendency exhibited in its very beginnings the political tensions still seen today. On the one hand, the superintendent was to serve as the chief administrative officer of the school district. In this capacity, the superintendent carried out policies for the schools determined by lay citizens serving as school committees or school boards. On the other hand, the superintendent was the chief educational officer of the school district. In this position, the superintendent provided leadership for the professional employees of the district.

These two tasks were often in conflict. For instance, communities frequently wanted to keep educational costs low while professional educators wanted salaries competitive with other professions such as medicine and law. Or communities wanted the curriculum of their schools to stress basic skills and the results of the schools to be certified by standardized achievement tests while professional educators wanted the curriculum to stress higher-order thinking skills and believed that standardized tests provided little understanding of the success of schools. Successfully juggling the demands of these two constituencies required political astuteness and skill.

Even more skill was required if these constituencies displayed internal disagreements. Various groups within the community might disagree, for example, about the disciplining of students, the amount of funding for athletics, or the merits of a particular teacher. Teachers at the elementary school level, for instance, might disagree with teachers at the junior high and senior high school levels about the teaching of history. From its beginning, those who filled the role of superintendent learned to live with conflict.

As the United States became more urban in the years following the War of 1812, more and more communities turned to a chief school officer to run their expanding school systems. Tyack (1974) reports that from 1820 to 1860, the number of cities with population of 5,000 to 10,000 increased from 22 to 136; the number with population of 25,000 to 50,000 increased from 2 to 19; and the number of cities with population of more than 100,000 increased from 1 to 9 (p. 31).

To manage the schools in these developing cities, reformers urged the creation of the office of superintendent. Horace Mann in Massachusetts insisted that larger cities such as Boston hire an individual to administer the entire school system. Such a move, Mann argued, would increase educational standards and decrease the political influence of school committee members. In Boston and nearly all larger cities, school committee members were elected in each ward. This meant that as cities grew, school committee memberships grew. It also meant that members paid close attention to the needs of their wards if they were to be reelected.

Mann and other reformers wanted the superintendent of schools to set standards for the entire school system. Superintendents would create universal bureaucratic formulas for the size of schools, the number of teachers in a school, the size of classes, the number of custodial and secretarial positions, and budgets for school supplies. These standards involved upgrading the qualifications of school teachers and principals.

Committee members, in contrast, sought to gain advantages for the schools of their wards by arguing for the preservation of very small schools, exemptions from rules about teacher preparation, adjustments to the size of classes, the need for many secretaries and custodians, and generous supply budgets for the teachers in their schools. They favored educational qualifications that provided opportunity for interested ward residents.

Reformers often succeeded in creating the office of superintendent but generally failed in efforts to reduce the size of school committees and the power of members. In fact, in many communities, two superintendents were appointed: One dealt with the business matters of the district, the other with school matters.

In the period following the Civil War, cities continued to grow rapidly and their superintendents struggled to build more schools, hire more teachers, and provide more textbooks. In general, schools became more bureaucratic as rules were developed that standardized classrooms by creating grades based on the number of years of school attended, put children of a certain age in a certain grade, required the use of certain textbooks, and dictated the number of pupils in a classroom. School committee members, in turn, pressed for the hiring of Civil War veterans as teachers, wanted those who built the new schools to live in the ward where the school was to be constructed, and demanded that supplies be purchased from ward merchants.

In the 1890s, a great wave of reform swept U.S. life, including the schools. Muckraking journalists pointed to the abuses of the political system and the corrupting influence big business had on politics. Journalists such as Lincoln Steffens charged that robber barons bought and sold politicians at all levels of government, including members of the United States Senate. These journalists sought to expose corruption in all aspects of public life and urged that systems based on merit and professional training replace cronyism and patronage. These professionals would run government in an efficient and effective manner.

In 1893, Joseph M. Rice published *The Public School System of the United States.* This exposé documented the poor educational conditions of several major cities. Schools were often failing to teach children fundamental skills such as spelling. Much of this failure could be traced to the appointment of incompetent teachers. Rice thus provided important information for those seeking to reform governance of the public schools. Many reformers urged a drastic solution: School superintendents should be given complete power to run schools, independent of the opinion of local citizens. This proposal was defeated; school boards retained the power to hire and fire superintendents. But the efforts of the reformers resulted in important changes between 1900 and 1930.

Those districts that had dual superintendents soon replaced them with a single superintendent, the qualifications for the position were increased, and the school committee was reduced in size and its members were now elected at large rather than from wards. In many communities, the school committee was renamed the school board. The superintendent and board moved toward policies that were uniform across the school district. Hiring of personnel, location and construction of new buildings, curriculum and textbooks, and disbursement of funds to schools were decided in light of formulas. These changes reflected the reformers' interest in professionalism and good business practices.

As Callahan (1962) noted, educational reformers, professors, and school superintendents sought to create the one best system in education by the application of the principles of scientific management. Following the pattern of industry, superintendents believed that research would point out the best way to teach, that principals would be foremen who ensured that the work was done in a certain way, and that teachers would be workers who followed the patterns determined by research and accepted supervision by principals. Working in a manner similar to business executives, superintendents and their boards would set uniform rules for the district.

The new superintendents were trained at institutions of higher education. Stanford, Chicago, Michigan, Ohio State, Illinois, and Teachers College, Columbia University professors of educational administration taught the one best way to manage the schools. Teachers College was particularly important because it trained many who became not only superintendents but also professors; it permitted professors to work with school districts to gain information (research) and make recommendations (consulting); and it encouraged professors to write textbooks and make speeches. Teachers College professors were diligent in recruiting bright new students, placing their new graduates, and furthering their careers with timely moves from district to district or to universities.

From our current vista, the acceptance of scientific management and the major changes it produced in the period from 1900 to 1930 ignored three issues that were to emerge as significant problems for superintendents in the 1950s and 1960s. These problems were the role of teachers, students of minority and special needs, and the politicizing of education. (Callahan, 1962, also provides an interesting critique of the failures of scientific management in education.)

Concerning the role of teachers, Peterson (1985) writes, "It was precisely this relationship between a strong, professional superintendency and a professional teaching force that proved to be reform's pedagogically least well defined and politically most contentious position" (p. 166). From the superintendent's perspective, teachers were workers who followed dictates of research about the one best way to teach and who complied with supervision by principals to ensure that no mistakes were made. From the perspective of many teachers, students were workers who learned because teachers as professional managers of their classrooms could determine the best way to teach in that classroom. These perspectives clashed sharply on matters such as the knowledge teachers possessed or the status that should be granted teachers.

Most superintendents saw teachers as workers to be trained and supervised; most teachers saw themselves as professional managers of the classroom. For instance, for superintendents, information about what should be done in classrooms was based on research conducted by research experts, often professors at universities or colleges. For teachers, information about what should be done in classrooms was based on their observations about what was happening in a specific classroom. Outsiders had to understand the dynamics of a particular classroom event, considering antecedent conditions. Moreover, for superintendents, research supplied information that could be used in all classrooms; research provided solutions that fitted every classroom in the system. For teachers, these universal solutions might or might not be helpful; each classroom presented unique problems that had to be dealt with. Years of teaching experience and reflection on that experience provided the basis for judgment.

There were also differences in assessment of status. Most superintendents saw teachers as workers who could easily be replaced; teachers were similar to good assembly-line workers. In contrast, many teachers viewed themselves as professionals with unique knowledge and skills; they were similar to lawyers or doctors. Tied in to this status conflict was the issue of gender. The "important" professional and managerial roles were men's work; teaching children was women's work. In short, many superintendents viewed teaching as a job for women who could be easily replaced; many teachers believed themselves to be trained professionals deserving praise and fair rewards from society.

These perspectives often clashed in districts. In some, such as Chicago, they resulted in the formation of teacher unions. In others, truces developed that often involved perfunctory supervision of teachers and uniform salary schedules that guaranteed some increase in pay regardless of teacher skills. Since the 1960s, more and more school districts have developed formal mechanisms for negotiating contracts between the school district and the teacher association. Many of these conflicts involve differences of perspective about the role of teachers and often involve differences of opinion about the knowledge and status of teachers.

A second problem inherited from scientific management was the issue of students of minority and students with special needs. The proponents of scientific management believed that research would find the one best way to manufacture a product. Such an approach required that raw material be screened so that impurities were not permitted to appear on the assembly line. How could schools deal with the issue of screening students? Two methods developed: One screened students of minorities and one screened students with special needs.

Although roughly three-fourths of the states did not permit racial segregation of students, the southern states used an 1896 Supreme Court ruling to justify the maintenance of racially segregated schools. Beginning in 1935, the National Association for the Advancement of Colored People (NAACP) used the courts to challenge these segregated schools. They argued that race should not be used to determine school attendance. In May 1954, the Supreme Court ruled that separate schools were inherently unequal.

In contrast, school superintendents in the majority of states argued that the schools of their district were color blind. The use of formulas for the assignment of teachers, standard curriculum guides for subjects, and a step salary schedule, for instance, meant that the schools of the district were equal regardless of the racial characteristics of students. School boards and superintendents argued that children, regardless of their racial or ethnic background, were to be treated exactly alike in the system.

What these formulas overlooked in most cases were the special problems of these minority students. Many were children of families that had migrated during World War I from the South to northern cities to work in defense industries. Many of these migrants had limited schooling, were accustomed to the mores of a segregated South, and had spent their lives in small, agrarian communities. Moreover, as they moved to northern cities, they were often forced to live in segregated areas with substandard housing. These migrants had little or no political influence in their new cities.

In the years following World War II, suburbs developed rapidly around many larger cities, and families who could afford to move did—families that were White, middle class, and willing to commute to work. These conditions produced racially and economically segregated school systems in northern states. By 1960, astute observers argued that the differences between slums and suburbs constituted social dynamite.

Educational scientific management also required that children with special needs be separated from the mainstream of the schools. These students were generally denied admission to public schools. It was not until the early 1970s that a coalition of national organizations was able to influence Congress to pass Public Law 94-142. This bill required school districts to provide services to children with special needs. These services allowed these children to enter mainstream classrooms.

In sum, by sorting students into those who could enter the mainstream classrooms and those who could not, scientific management denied opportunities to children with special needs. And by treating all children in mainstream classes as if they were exactly alike, scientific management denied opportunities to children who were disadvantaged in the school environment.

Third, scientific management acted as if education policies were not political. Policy was to be created by technical expertise, not the pulling and hauling that generated political compromise. Policies—such as those that argued that small schools were inefficient and should be consolidated into large schools, that increased training of educators always produced good consequences, and that costs in schools could be cut by increasing class size—were neutral recommendations made on the basis of expert research. Those that opposed such policy recommendations were self-serving.

These debates about U.S. education policy often found the superintendent and the school board wrapping themselves in the flag of value-neutral technical expertise. It was the prerogative of experts, they argued, to define educational problems, frame the alternatives, and decide the best solution without reference to the uninformed or prejudiced opinions of the citizenry.

Nonetheless, citizens did intrude. Supporters of small schools lobbied legislatures to ensure they were not closed; limited rewards for advanced training of educators were often enacted by school boards; and demands by parents and teachers that class size be reduced often cluttered board meetings and contract negotiation sessions.

In the late 1950s, for instance, the launching of *Sputnik I* by the Soviets led to immediate public outcries about the state of math and science teaching in our public schools. The Congress of the United States quickly passed the National Defense Education Act of 1958 (NDEA) to provide funds for curriculum development and teacher training in math and science.

In the 1960s, 1970s, and 1980s, education continued to be politicized (Tyack & Hansot, 1982). The riots in the cities in the mid-1960s, the Vietnam War, student unrest, declining student enrollment, the tax revolt, court cases involving state formulas for school funding, emphasis on student achievement on standardized tests, a spate of reports on the inadequacies of schools, and the increasing number of immigrants—all attest to the politically turbulent nature of education. Superintendents today can no longer present themselves as the neutral experts who ought to make technical decisions about schools. Schools are the people's business.

In sum, the superintendency historically has reflected tensions. Superintendents have sought the power and authority to run schools as value-neutral technical experts. They have existed in a political world in which teachers and the public have challenged this view.

Superintendents and Conflict

In this section, two major questions will be discussed. First, are there factors that influence the amount of conflict that superintendents face? Research by Carlson and by Zeigler and Jennings suggest that career patterns and community makeup influence the amount of conflict. Second, how do superintendents in their everyday lives deal with the realities of educational politics? Studies done by Blumberg and by Bell and Chase provide important clues.

Carlson (1972) identified two distinct careers of superintendents: those who remain in a district for the bulk of their career in education (insiders) and those who move from district to district (outsiders). Superintendents themselves and board members see insiders and outsiders as different types of superintendents.

Insiders seek to maintain a good situation. Both the school board and the insider superintendent are pleased with the relationship between the schools and the community and with the internal operations of the schools. Board members hire as their new superintendent a person who is already in the system, who is a known entity, and who will keep the system running on its present course. Insider superintendents characterize themselves as little interested in proposing or implementing major changes in the system. As long-time members of the system, insiders know the strengths and weaknesses of the staff, understand the characteristics of the community, and know how the system has evolved.

In contrast, *outsiders* are seen by school boards and themselves as forces for change. As board members or community factions become unhappy with what is happening in the schools, they turn to outsiders to bring new ideas and life to the situation. Iannaccone and Lutz (1970) suggest that a pattern develops in many districts that involves the old superintendent and board becoming isolated, a series of contested school board elections, the eventual election of new board members, and subsequent firing of the old superintendent. The newly hired superintendent is an outsider.

Outsiders present themselves as experts capable of producing needed changes in the system. Many outsider superintendents build reputations that suggest they are good at closing schools or at repairing financial messes, for instance. Outsider superintendents are given a mandate by the board to fix up the system. With no ties to the current ways of doing things or to current personnel, outsiders change the operating patterns of the districts (new rules) and move personnel to new positions (new central office personnel and principals). Once the district has made the necessary changes and appears to be operating smoothly, outsider superintendents begin to explore employment opportunities in other districts. Their successor is an insider.

Zeigler and Jennings (1974) found relationships between superintendent turnover and community characteristics and size. In large urban districts, superintendents were surrounded by many different constituencies. Many groups supported the policies of the superintendent while many others opposed these same policies. Conflicts among these groups provided some protection for the superintendent. It was difficult to reach consensus on whether the superintendent should leave or not. In smaller suburban communities, there was a consensus on what the schools should be doing. As long as the superintendent's policies reflected this consensus, the superintendent could stay. In smaller rural communities, superintendents often came and left rapidly. Superintendents in these communities had to reflect the rural values of the community and agree with the community about the role of the school. If the superintendent and community were not a match, the superintendent was quickly released.

In sum, the career patterns of superintendents and the characteristics of the community such as size seem to be related to conflict. Insider superintendents appear to start their terms with little conflict but end their terms with a great deal of conflict. Outsider superintendents start their terms with considerable conflict but leave their terms with little conflict. Larger communities may exhibit more conflict but less superintendent turnover than smaller communities. In smaller communities, the fit between the superintendent and community values is important. A mismatch results in superintendent turnover.

How do superintendents deal with conflict on a daily basis? Blumberg (1985) argues that the modern superintendent lives with conflict. In fact, most of the superintendents interviewed saw conflict as the very nature of the role. Although not all those interviewed enjoyed conflict, most had learned to live with it and expected that conflict would remain the characteristic mode of the superintendency.

Superintendents that Blumberg interviewed faced conflicting groups inside education. Teacher unions or associations, for instance, are a part of the conflicted life of the superintendent. No longer do educational experts stand side by side against public demands. Instead, superintendents worry about the willingness of teachers to strike and whether teachers will honor the negotiated contract. Teacher representatives challenge the expertise of the superintendent on issues such as class size, question the credentials of principals to supervise teachers, and file grievances against the system for purported contract violations. Frequently, teacher associations or unions challenge the district to reduce the number of administrators.

In turn, superintendents demand that teacher unions or associations police their own ranks in ways that remove less-than-competent teachers, strike reasonable compromises about salary increases, honor contract commitments, and upgrade the quality of the teaching staff using systematic supervision programs. As the educational leader of the system, the superintendent is often embroiled in conflict with fellow professionals.

By far the greater source of conflict comes from the community. There are serious debates within the community about the policies that should be adopted and implemented by the school system. The many subpublics that surround the school are concerned about policies that touch on all facets of school life—curriculum, personnel, school-district organization, and financing. For example, many have attacked the school curriculum for teaching "secular humanism" while others have argued that the curriculum should stress the basic skills. Still others want the curriculum to teach the evils of alcohol and drug abuse and the virtues of a moral character. Another group wants the school curriculum to stress higher-order academic skills. Still another group wants the school to stress patriotism. Members of each of these multiple subpublics see their values as more important than the values of other groups. They want the school to teach these values to the children of the community.

How do the superintendents Blumberg interviewed deal with conflicts about curriculum, personnel, school-district organization, and financing? The interviews reveal two general strategies.

The first strategy used by superintendents involves controlling conflict by defining the school's role in narrow terms. The school's task is one of teaching children basic skills and state-mandated courses. Educators must control schools to create a good setting for learning. Anything that goes beyond these basic, and traditionally understood, activities is noneducational and should be avoided. The superintendent and school will accept new, nontraditional activities if and only if the community and board are in complete agreement about the need for the activity and are willing to pay for it. This strategy emphasizes the role of the superintendent as *the* educational expert and suggests that new educational demands are performed by the school system *only if* they have overwhelming public support.

The second strategy involves superintendents in conflict resolution and decision making. Believing that conflict over schools is a normal part of the life of communities, superintendents use conflict-management and resolution skills to help competing groups in the community frame the problem and explore various solu-

tions. This often involves the appointment of committees representing various segments of the community, scheduling public meetings, and seeking advice from
experts on the pertinent issues. Superintendents then use decision-making skills to
reach solutions. They may employ various strategies such as consensus or majority
rule. Using these skills, superintendents help communities resolve educational
problems. In this strategy, superintendents stress the political nature of the role.
They use community involvement to clarify the role that educational expertise
may play in framing and solving the problem. Sometimes educational experts are
given free rein by the community; at other times and on other issues, community
demands are paramount. Superintendents anticipate that the solution developed
in this fashion will become policy and will be administered.

Some of the superintendents interviewed saw themselves as deliberately (and
carefully) provoking community conflict. These superintendents tried at times to
raise controversial or neglected issues for discussion. For instance, the community
might be ignoring the importance of computer literacy. The superintendent might
deliberately create a committee of lay and professional people to examine the district's posture on computer literacy. By careful selection of members, the superintendent ensures that different points of view are present. By careful attention to the
scheduling and agenda of meetings, the superintendent can anticipate that the
committee will make the issue public, receive information, and reach a reasonable
decision about what ought to be done about computer literacy.

Hence, the superintendents that Blumberg interviewed saw conflict as part of
the everyday life of the superintendent. Some sought to reduce conflict by limiting
the role of the school; others used community conflict to decide what the schools
should be doing.

Bell and Chase (Bell & Chase, 1989; Bell, 1988; Chase & Bell, 1990) approach the
problem of conflict from a different angle. They begin by noting that superintendents are overwhelmingly White males (96 percent) and that school boards are
dominated by White males (66 percent). They also note that the superintendency
is a political position: It requires juggling the demands of competing groups.

Bell and Chase then ask: How do the few women who hold the superintendency deal with issues of conflict in light of what the male-dominated literature
says about dealing with conflict? In seeking to answer this question, Bell and
Chase face the general problem of conflict and the superintendency: How do
superintendents (both men and women) deal with conflict? They also face the
unique problem of women superintendents: Do women superintendents deal with
conflict differently from men superintendents? Bell and Chase thus can describe
methods of conflict resolution that are used by men and women (all superintendents) and methods that are gender specific (men could use them but women
could not or women could use them but men could not). Such a perspective allows
insights into problems of conflict in general as well as problems of conflict based
on societal views of gender.

In a series of interviews with women superintendents and their boards, Bell
and Chase found several important themes:

1. Similar to their male counterparts, women superintendents must assert their authority in the school organization and with the school board. Yet as women, they felt that they faced added pressures to show that they were competent to carry out the tasks of the superintendency since the superintendency is typically "man's work."

2. In contrast to typical male superintendents, women superintendents sought to reduce the distance between themselves and other educational professionals. One asked that she not be addressed as "Doctor," another organized a health program, and a third held a cookout where she was the chef. Bell and Chase suggest that these women superintendents employ a style that resembles the relationship of a teacher and colleague rather than a bureaucratic plant manager. These women superintendents sought to listen to staffs and teachers and to use their suggestions.

3. Many of these women superintendents suggested that traditional social roles of women—giving, mothering, homemaking—influenced their leadership style. They focused their attention on teaching and learning and on the welfare of their employees and students. In contrast, many of the rules passed by male-dominated state legislatures require superintendents to stress distancing, demanding, and impersonality.

4. Board members who hired women superintendents often faced the issue of whether a woman would be as strong a leader as a man. This issue is more easily resolved if the woman candidate has shown that she is a capable superintendent in another district. This performance can be shown to the community as evidence that she can perform and that she has overcome the hurdles faced by women.

5. Women superintendents are often hired in districts that are in crisis. These districts have a history of turmoil highlighted by frequent superintendent turnover and have been shunned by White male superintendents as undesirable, although African American and Hispanic male superintendents are often considered by such crisis districts.

6. Women superintendents work with a board and community that are accustomed to male superintendents. While these women must assert authority, the cultural expectations of women contradict just such behavior. How differences between role-required behavior and cultural expectations were resolved differed from community to community.

As Bell and Chase continue their research, these themes will be explored further and others developed. To date, their work suggests common themes for all superintendents such as negotiating their relationship to the school board and special themes for women superintendents such as higher priority on instructional issues.

This section, in sum, suggests that conflict is a part of the superintendency. The amount of conflict is influenced by the career patterns of superintendents and the types of communities they serve. Superintendents develop strategies for dealing with conflict; women superintendents also confront conflict whose source is cultural expectations.

The Future of the Superintendency

Historically, educational reformers emphasized the role of the superintendent. Superintendents were seen as leaders who brought a sense of overall purpose to educational personnel and who helped the community generate the resources necessary to accomplish this purpose. In contrast, today's reformers have emphasized the roles of teachers and principals. Superintendents have rarely been mentioned as the keys to reform. In part, this view suggests that the proper role of the superintendent is to fulfill state mandates that dictate teacher improvement and to follow the rules and regulations of the state funding formula.

What is troubling is that few accounts of the everyday life of the superintendent are available either to certify the older image of the superintendency or to suggest whether the role of the superintendent has changed. It is safe to say that the role of the superintendent has been understudied (Crowson, 1987). Little is known about how superintendents see the role changing in the future or if, in fact, they see it changing at all.

Given these conditions, what reasonable speculations can be made about the superintendency? Three come quickly to mind. First, states will continue to set standards for school districts and to provide a greater percentage of funds for local districts. This movement toward centralization at the state level suggests that superintendents will have less discretion in setting goals and generating resources at the district level. State control will press superintendents to behave in a bureaucratic manner.

Second, as teacher supervision and evaluation schemes improve over time, teachers and principals will develop school-based governance structures. These structures will demand that schools no longer be controlled by districtwide policies. Teachers and principals, for instance, may ask to be given bloc grants of money by the central office to be spent as they see fit. Some districts currently have these site-based management schemes, but they will flourish at the turn of the century. They require that superintendents learn a new set of skills in dealing with the delegation of authority and responsibility to local school personnel and a new vocabulary for dealing with the usual policymaking role of the school board.

Third, the next decade will see more and more women and minority superintendents. Enrollments of women and minorities in graduate programs in educational administration are increasing rapidly. This supply of talent is available; more and more school boards will wish to hire women and minorities.

In sum, as the twenty-first century dawns, those who hold superintendencies will more and more often be women and minorities, will have to deal with increased state control, and will develop local policies that expand site-based management of the district's schools. These shifts appear to reaffirm the politicized nature of the modern superintendency.

References

Bell, C. S. (1988). Organizational influences on women's experience in the superintendency. *Peabody Journal of Education, 65,* 31–59.

Bell, C. S., & Chase, S. E. (1989). *Women as educational leaders: Resistance and conformity.* Paper presented at the 1989 American Education Research Association Annual Meeting, San Francisco.

Blumberg, A. (1985). *The school superintendent.* New York: Teachers College.

Callahan, R. F. (1962). *Education and the cult of efficiency.* Chicago: University of Chicago.

Carlson, R. O. (1972). *School superintendents.* Columbus, OH: Charles E. Merrill.

Chase, S. E., & Bell, C. S. (1990). Ideology, discourse, and gender: How gatekeepers talk about women school superintendents. *Social Problems, 37,* 163–177.

Crowson, R. L. (1987). The local school district superintendency: A puzzling administrative role. *Educational Administration Quarterly, 23,* 49–63.

Iannaccone, L., & Lutz, F. W. (1970). *Politics, power, and policy.* Columbus, OH: Charles E. Merrill.

Lewellen, T. C. (1983). *Political anthropology.* South Hadley, MA: Bergin and Garvey.

Peterson, P. E. (1985). *The politics of school reform 1870–1940.* Chicago: University of Chicago.

Rice, J. M. (1893). *The public school system of the United States.* New York: Century.

Tyack, D. B. (1974). *The one best system.* Cambridge, MA: Harvard University.

Tyack, D. B., & Hansot, E. (1982). *Managers of virtue.* New York: Basic Books.

Zeigler, L., & Jennings, M. K. (1974). *Governing American schools.* North Scituate, MA: Duxbury.

Chapter 12

The School as a
Political Organization

Thirty years ago, it would have been heresy to characterize the school as a political organization; today, it raises few eyebrows. For one thing, schools have changed in ways that make it more difficult to maintain the fiction that education is nonpolitical. A dramatic surge of education legislation at both the state and federal levels, controversial court cases, and more contested school board elections are just a few of the ways the political nature of schools is brought to our attention.

Equally important, our view of what is political has broadened. Take, for example, the following three scenarios. Each describes an issue in the realm of education that will be resolved according to certain political processes.

The Milwaukee school board voted five to three to create one elementary and one middle school designed to meet the needs of African American males. The superintendent justified the "radical" solution as necessary in a system where African American males have the highest dropout and course-failure rates in the city. A member of the NAACP Legal Defense and Educational Fund in Washington, DC, labeled the plan illegal because it discriminates on the basis of race and gender. Doris Stacy, an 18-year veteran of the school board, said she voted against the plan because, although she agrees with the goal, segregating students is "a very dangerous idea." (*Education Week*, October 10, 1990)

A delegation of classroom teachers has scheduled a meeting with their middle school principal concerning difficulties they are having with the school's new "inclusion" program. Last year, a task force led by special education teachers recommended a mainstreaming program in which all but the most profoundly handicapped children have been placed in regular classrooms. Special educators in the district are enthusiastic about the new program, and parents of the children with disabilities have mixed, but generally support-ive, reactions. But some regular classroom teachers say the students with disabilities make their jobs more difficult and take time away from other stu-dents in their classes.

Cordia Booth, an African American science teacher in the Denver public schools, and 45 supporters are trying to persuade the Denver school board to let her set up a new school under the Colorado charter-school law. Colorado, like 18 other states, had passed legislation to encourage the development of alternative "charter" schools by waiving most existing state regulations. Booth and her supporters envisioned a "no frills" Thurgood Marshall Middle School with rigorous curriculum, strict discipline, class sizes under 20, and no princi-pal, counselors, librarians, or security guards. The Denver board had rebuffed Booth on several earlier occasions despite an order from the Colorado state board of education to reverse its decision. Tonight, the board denied her request once again, citing concern about cost to district taxpayers. One mem-ber told Booth, "I have a problem with you taking public dollars to experi-ment." (*Education Week*, October 4, 1995)

Each of these situations finds people in disagreement about what should be done in some area of educational policy. When such disagreement becomes sub-stantial and public, we call it a political *issue*. Issues are the starting point in our analysis of the political process. Without them, there would be no need for politics. One measure of the worth of a political system is how successfully it deals with issues that arise. As each of the three cases clearly shows, some kind of resolution is needed.

So when the school is referred to as a political organization, the authors do not necessarily mean that it is a focal point for partisan politics, with Democrats and Republicans squabbling over educational matters. Nor do the authors mean it in quite the same sense as the disgruntled citizen who complains that "it's just all pol-itics!" Schools are political in the sense that they, along with most other organiza-tions, confront and respond to essentially political questions. What objectives should be emphasized? How will scarce resources, such as money or teaching tal-ent, be allocated among various programs? And, in the memorable phrase of Harold Lasswell, "Who gets what, when, how?" (Lasswell, 1958).

The Four Values Revisited

As suggested in Chapter 1, in education policy, the "what" Lasswell referred to has often been thought of as falling along four value dimensions. Marshall, Mitchell, and Wirt (1989) sum up the literature on this point as follows:

> *The fundamental and sometimes competing values for education policy are equity, [excellence], efficiency (Garms et al., 1978), and choice. Policymakers constantly*

face dilemmas when they must choose among these values. Thus, a vote for stan-
dardizing the curriculum materials may increase efficiency and [excellence], but
the bilingual student's opportunity to choose and have equity of access to the cur-
riculum is compromised. (p. 12)

Which side of an issue you support may depend on your own hierarchy of values. For some, the most important thing to strive for in education is *equity*. They seek out issues and take positions that promise to extend greater educational opportunity to those who might not otherwise have a fair chance to succeed in a predominantly White, English-language, school system. Historically, the targets for equity-based programs have included youngsters whose first language is not English, those from cultural or ethnic minorities, and those who have physical or mental conditions that may put them at a disadvantage in our educational system. Equity was the primary concern in the struggle for desegregated schools that gave African American children access to the same schools Whites attend. Equity was also the major value driving campaigns for programs like Head Start, bilingual education, and girls' sports. State school-aid formulas that give more money to poorer school districts are yet another example of a policy based on the idea that all children should have an equal opportunity in the educational arena.

Other people place greater emphasis on the value of *efficiency*. Whatever schools do, they want it done at the least possible cost. They will question whether teachers have to be paid as much as the current salary schedule provides, wonder whether the district needs all those assistant superintendents, and point out that money could be saved by closing a school building or phasing out the special program for high-ability children. Many professional educators, including most teachers, are so thoroughly convinced of the importance of what they are doing that cost does not matter much to them. But good education is expensive, and there is no shortage of citizens bent on making the best possible use of every tax dollar.

Choice about what kind of education you or your children obtain and where you get it, is a value that has received much attention in recent years. Educational proposals by recent Republican administrations included tuition tax credits that would make it cheaper for parents to choose to send their children to private schools if they wished and voucher plans that might provide a choice between different kinds of public and private schools. Even within a single school, the value of choice supports efforts to provide students the opportunity to select courses and construct academic programs suited to their own needs, interests, and abilities.

Most pervasive in recent years, however, has been the value of *excellence*. Many of the changes in schools during the 1980s and 1990s have been made in the name of excellence or quality. Although educational quality can be defined broadly enough to include many other values, in practice, it is usually associated with the call for higher pupil achievement, better teachers, and more rigorous academic standards. Many of the state educational-reform movements were triggered by a concern about the quality of public school systems. Stiffer high school graduation requirements, grade-level tests used as a criterion for promotion, tests of teacher competency, and higher salaries designed to attract and retain quality teachers are all part of the attempt to assure quality educational programs.

These are not the only values that enter into educational policymaking, but they are the four justifications for policies most frequently heard. Most of us prize each of these to some degree and, in fact, most policy issues involve more than one of them. Nevertheless, the position you take on issues will probably be shaped by your own sense of which values are most important. Moreover, the values you will defend most vigorously will depend on the role you play in the educational policy process as well as your own personal value hierarchy.

Reconciling Interests: The Problem of Collective Choice

If everyone agreed on what outcomes are desirable from schooling, making educational policy would be a lot simpler. Disagreement over what constitutes an appropriate education, however, is natural within any complex society. We have been socialized to value different things. Even more obviously, we hold different positions and play different roles within our society, which may lead us to take different positions on educational questions. Gallup Polls of the U.S. public, for instance, found that:

- Nonwhites were more likely than Whites to favor providing free public education, school lunches, and other benefits to children of immigrants who are in the United States illegally (1995).
- Parents of children in private schools were more likely than public-school parents to favor proposals for the government to pay all or part of the tuition of students who choose nonpublic schools (1994).
- Women were more likely than men to favor the teaching of "character education" in public schools (1994).
- Young adults were more likely than older adults to favor contracting with profit-making corporations to operate public schools (1994).
- Protestants were more likely than Catholics or Jews to favor prayers at graduation ceremonies.
- Citizens with household incomes of over $40,000 were more inclined than their less affluent neighbors to raise taxes if necessary to raise educational standards (1988).
- College-educated citizens were more likely than citizens who have not been to college to favor increasing the number of courses required for high school graduation (1987).
- Parents of children in public school were more likely than citizens with no children in public school to support a school tax increase (1984).*

None of that is very surprising. These and most other differences of opinion between segments of the public are readily understandable. Somehow they have to be reconciled, however, if we are to get on with the business of educating children.

*Results of Gallup Poll surveys of beliefs about education have appeared in the *Phi Delta Kappan* annually since 1969.

The most difficult challenge in the area of government and politics is to find the best way to arrive at *collective decisions* in the face of differences. Individual decisions are difficult enough, as anyone who has vacillated between two new automobiles or two careers knows very well. With collective decisions, however, there is the additional complication that various individuals in the collectivity will prefer different outcomes and propose different ways of achieving them. In the case of schools, some students care very little about having a strong girls' athletic program, whereas others care very much. Some parents want almost exclusive emphasis on the three Rs, whereas others favor expanding art education, and still others believe it is the computer literacy program that needs more teachers and more equipment. Many teachers are concerned about obtaining smaller class sizes; the local chapter of the taxpayers' association may propose larger classes. Although almost everyone believes that some kind of an organizational effort is required to educate children, not everyone has the same view of what constitutes an *appropriate* education or what kind of system will bring it about.

In short, educating youngsters for productive lives in the twenty-first century requires organization, and organizations require governance. Governance includes such things as setting some priorities among all the possible objectives of the organization, allocating resources to meet these objectives, and coordinating the activities of members of the organization to accomplish the objectives more effectively.

Individuals or groups who want different outcomes from a social process are said to have different *interests.* For many years, the myth was sustained that everyone wanted the same thing from the educational system and that there are thus no separate interests in this area. Today, it is clearer that the interests of academically talented students, the academically disadvantaged, parents, teachers, taxpayers, employers, professional administrators, and nonacademic staff may not coincide.

In the world of education, interests are defined as policy preferences that are shared. Individuals who agree which policies they prefer may be said to have the same interest in a certain issue area such as education. The important thing, whether we are dealing with shared attitudes or shared preferences about policy, is that no policymaker, administrator, or social scientist can unilaterally decide what is in another individual's interest. Only that individual can determine what policies he or she prefers.

There are a number of natural interest groups in education that make their own distinctive demands on the school system. Much of the attention of policymakers—all the way from principals, superintendents, and school-board members to state and federal officials—is devoted to reconciling the competing demands of these interests. Where the difference of opinion arises because of different beliefs about what will happen if a certain policy alternative is adopted, convincing evidence about what is most likely to happen should help.

Supporters of Texas's "no pass–no play" law requiring students to have satisfactory grades in all subjects before they would be allowed to participate in interscholastic activities argued that the requirement would make students work harder and learn more in school. Opponents doubted that the rule would inspire greater academic effort and worried that it might, in fact, encourage marginal students to drop out of school. These are empirical questions that, in principle, can be tested. Much of policy research in education attempts to provide better knowledge about the probable consequences of certain policy changes.

Just as often, however, the disagreement is over questions of value. In 1990, the state textbook advisory committee in North Carolina recommended against state adoption of *Impressions,* an elementary reading series of classic children's literature and folktales published by Holt, Rinehart and Winston. Parents and conservative religious groups had attacked the selections as overwhelmingly "morbid," violent, and laced with references to the occult. The issues director of People for the American Way defended them as "real literature that might expose them to potentially controversial topics in contrast to the pabulum of 'See Spot run'" (*Education Week,* October 10, 1990, p. 13).

There is no simple way for any school administrator to decide who is right and who is wrong on questions of this type. Resolutions that leave all parties reasonably satisfied (or at least not at each other's throats) may be the best we can hope for. The process of finding, presenting, and justifying such resolutions characterizes the political process. The goal is not so much to come up with the "right" answers by some ideological standard, as it is to come up with policies that keep all of the people affected as satisfied as possible.

This view of the political process emphasizes the importance of bringing legitimate differences of opinion about policy into the open and attempting to resolve them within the political system. Conflict between groups representing different interests is viewed as perfectly natural and healthy for the society, as long as it is resolved in accordance with established democratic procedures. The basic ground rules by which the game is played become very important, however. All parties and interests must be able to assume reasonably fair play in the political process, including the expectations that the results of elections will be accepted, that all potentially affected interests will be heard, that policy or legislation enacted by legislative bodies will be put into effect, and that the rights of minorities will not be abused. It is important that citizens know and are committed to these democratic norms so that no political faction can violate them and survive politically. As a society, we spend substantial time and resources socializing younger citizens into consensual democratic norms.

Although there is no magic formula for finding such resolutions, we can all think of ways that would strike us as arbitrary, unjust, or just plain foolish for arriving at collective decisions. On the other hand, there are methods of reconciling differences that are widely viewed as legitimate in our culture. Four time-honored ways are listed here:

1. *Consensual Decision Making.* Given time and the requisite skills of persuasion, some members of the collectivity may simply be able to convince others that their goals, or ways of reaching them, are preferable. The aim, in this case, is consensus of all those involved on the best choice. Even when consensus is not achieved, persuasion plays an important part in shaping the coalitions that may decide the outcome of political battles.

2. *Institutional Authority.* Consensus, however, is not always possible. Institutions—a supreme court or a state department of education, for example—are granted the authority to make some decisions for the collectivity. Superintendents have the authority to resolve some issues on their own. Institutional leaders are usually chosen by election or appointment for such positions of authority.

3. *Majority Rule.* On the theory that no one person is wise enough or evenhanded enough to make choices for the collectivity, votes may be taken to obtain a more representative expression of individual interests. This is the form of collective decision making used by most legislative bodies.

4. *Bargaining.* Parties may simply negotiate their differences until a resolution is found that is acceptable to everyone. Not all disagreements are negotiable, because bargaining assumes that a possible resolution exists that leaves all parties better off than they would have been if no agreement had been reached. The most notable example of bargaining in education today is the formal process of collective bargaining used by teachers' organizations and school boards in many districts to settle the terms of employment for teachers.

As already noted, none of these means of reaching a collective decision is without its problems. Most decisions of educational governance (as well as other areas of governance) are made by one or another—and often a mixture—of these four processes.

A Closer Look at Policy

Organizations control the actions of individuals within them by making and enforcing policy. A *policy* is any authoritative communication about how individuals in certain positions should behave under specified conditions. Thus, the principal who issues a memorandum saying that "no teacher should leave the building before 3:45 P.M. on school days" has fashioned a policy—so has the superintendent who directs principals not to suspend pupils for more than three days without board approval, and the state legislature that enacts a law requiring students to pass a competency test before high school graduation.

An older notion reserved the term *policy* for statements of major goals or far-reaching programs. According to this view, school boards, state legislatures, and Congress established policy, whereas school administrators simply carried out their wishes. Careful observation of the policy process, however, indicates that that distinction is largely imaginary. Teachers, principals, and superintendents all make policy in certain important areas. Even in implementing policy made by others, these key actors are often in a position to change the policy dramatically.

It is hard to imagine any complex organization operating effectively without some policies in force. All organizations, including schools, face certain recurring problems. All that is needed, it would seem, is for members of the organization to sit down and consider dispassionately how best to deal with a familiar problem when it occurs again; they will surely be able to think up a way of handling the problem that will serve the ends of the organization better than if every employee were left to her or his own devices. Furthermore, it will usually be to the advantage of the organization if that problem is dealt with in the same way each time it recurs. Aside from promoting effectiveness and consistency, policies protect those who follow them. Put yourself in the position of an English teacher who conscientiously assigns books only from a list approved by a districtwide committee. Any complaints from parents about a book on that list can be neatly parried by pointing a finger at the committee that approved the book. Woe to the teacher who strays beyond the approved list, however, when irate parents descend on the principal.

German sociologist Max Weber saw bureaucracy as a sort of ideal type of organization and placed a great deal of importance on written policies and regulations (Gerth & Mills, 1958, Chapter 8). In an age when personal favoritism was far more prevalent than today, making an organization into a sort of impersonal machine seemed like a good idea. At least it would reward according to merit rather than according to who a person is or who a person knows. Weber was not as sensitive as we are today to some of the more vexing aspects of modern bureaucratic organizations, but he had a point: Organizations, like people, should strive to be as rational as possible. First, get the objectives clearly in mind, then calmly determine what policies will be most likely to achieve them. This was surely something that a few reasonable people, working together, could accomplish. Or was it?

Today, we are aware of so many more complexities in the process of making policy that we are no longer sure. Some, like Charles Lindblom, argue that policymaking seldom proceeds in a very rational manner. Lindblom painted a picture of an organization which, instead of finding optimal solutions to problems, staggered uncertainly toward marginally better ways of handling them. He called it the method of "successive approximations" (Braybrooke & Lindblom, 1970, pp. 123–124).

Gone was the notion of wise men sitting around solving recurring problems for all time. Replacing it was a notion of fallible human beings, limited in their ability to see very far ahead, unable to examine all conceivable alternatives, settling for the first suggestion that promised to yield better results than the present policy. Lindblom and others who saw the same kind of limitations on rational policymaking became known as *incrementalists*, and Lindblom (1959) dubbed his view the process of "muddling through" (pp. 79–88).

Muddle or no muddle, policies are the main way people try to get organizations to do their bidding. They are not the only reason schools change, but they are the intentional part of change. Now that we have some idea of what policies are and why we make them, we are ready for the big question: How do policies change? All the elements discussed next are usually present, often behind the scenes.*

---

*See Jones (1977) for an excellent introductory discussion of the concept of policy and policy stages. Thomas (1975, pp. 172–217) applies his own formulation of policy stages to federal decision making.

Dissatisfaction with Existing Policy

Someone, somewhere, expresses dissatisfaction with the way things are currently being done. If that dissatisfaction is strong enough and general enough, a policy issue will have been created. The ability to create an issue and get the matter on the policy agenda is a basic weapon in any interest group's political arsenal. Most issues do not just happen. Political interests use valuable resources to develop them. The formation of policy agendas is now recognized as one of the most important parts of the policy process (Kingdon, 1984).

Policy Formulation

An alternative way of doing things will have to be proposed at some point. Often more than one alternative is proposed. As the various interests try to enlist others in support of their preferred alternatives, coalitions will form and compromises may be struck. Persuasion, bargaining, and political power all come into play at this point as each interest develops strategies and employs its resources in an effort to gain an outcome as close to its own position as possible.

Policy Enactment

The person or body vested with authority in the matter at hand now decides which alternative to adopt. Depending on the issue, authority may lie with the Congress, the president, the U.S. secretary of education, a governor, a state legislature, a chief state school officer, a district superintendent of schools, a local school board, a principal, a teacher, or some combination of these. Even that list is far from complete. The authority may, of course, decide to stick with the old policy rather than enact a new one.

Policy Implementation

Now things really get interesting. In most cases, someone will be designated to disseminate the new policy and to check to see whether it is being obeyed. Should he or she find that it is not being obeyed, that individual may be empowered to enforce it by applying sanctions.

Ultimately, though, policies are changed to change the behavior of people. It would be a lot easier to enforce some policies if people did not have so much invested in their old ways of behaving. Even if people are in full agreement with the change, it may be hard for them to break old habits or learn new ones. The best time to think about possible impediments to compliance is early, when the policy is being formulated.

A long-standing question about implementation is the extent to which it should be spelled out in the policy. Individuals charged with putting a policy into effect often complain about overprescriptive language that leaves them little room to tailor the implementation to local conditions. They would rather have policymakers sketch out the grand design and leave the details to them. Policymakers, on the other hand, recognizing how easy it is to subvert some policies at the implementation stage, may be blatantly prescriptive if they suspect that those charged with implementing the policy are less than enthusiastic about it. State legislators, for example, may want to leave very little discretion to local school boards or superintendents regarding how statewide high school graduation requirements are to be interpreted and implemented.

It is all too easy to design and enact sweeping new policy only to encounter some unanticipated obstacle to its successful implementation. The most frequent advice from those who study implementation is to think carefully about how the policy will be put into effect even before the policy is enacted. This may mean considering the variety of sites in which the policy will be implemented and attempting to foresee what will need to be done to bring about the desired results. It will also mean asking what is likely to impede implementation at any of those sites and how impediments can be overcome. Some policies fail simply because they cannot be implemented. Others, once implemented, spawn unanticipated consequences that occasionally delight everyone but more often send policymakers into emergency session to reconsider what once seemed a good idea.

Policy Evaluation

The deluxe treatment calls for trained policy evaluators to come in at this point and find out what the policy change has accomplished and how people feel about it. More often it will just be people somewhere in the school system saying, "This sure beats the way we used to do it!" or "I knew this wouldn't work!" If the latter sentiment becomes prevalent, the whole business begins again.

Several generalizations become apparent as we contemplate these five elements. First, there is a lot more to the process than simply sitting back and making wise decisions. Generations of students of policy have been preoccupied with the behavior of authorizing bodies—why legislatures vote the way they do or why a governor vetoes a bill, for example. By looking more closely at the policy process, we see that other kinds of behavior may be just as important The ability to register dissatisfaction effectively with present policy so authorities will recognize it as an issue and move it onto their agenda is an extremely important aspect of the process (Cobb & Elder, 1972). Some individuals and groups are very skilled at this, but others have difficulty even getting their discontents publicly acknowledged. Similarly, the creative act of inventing new policy alternatives or developing ingenious compromises that satisfy all interests is a crucial part of the process. Finally, we need to know more about the two kinds of behavior that characterize the implementation process: compliance, and administration, which aims to assure compliance. If few comply with the new policy, it has not accomplished very much.

Depending on the resources and skills they possess, different individuals and groups will participate in the process in quite different ways. Some groups specialize in creating issues by mobilizing opposition to existing policies. Other groups and individuals have the resources to create new proposals, draft legislation, or hammer out compromises. Others may be adroit administrators able to get everyone quickly into line with a new policy.

There is one problem with any portrayal of the various stages of the policy process. The list gives a misleading appearance of orderliness. In the real world, a lot of influence behavior and even deliberation by the authoritative decision body may already have occurred when someone suddenly proposes a brand-new alternative that changes things drastically. That new proposal may, in turn, be effectively vetoed by a powerful interest group whose leaders urge their members not to comply if the new proposal becomes policy. And so the process goes, careening wildly from proposal, to reaction, to coalition building, to more proposals. It is useful to suggest the variety of activities that go into the policy process, but the preceding five elements do not serve as a very accurate guide to the sequence of events. Furthermore, the process is never-ending. As soon as any new policy comes into being, people affected by it will start evaluating. When dissatisfaction surfaces, a new issue has been forged and the process begins again.

Influence, Power, and Authority Patterns

At the heart of politics is the idea that some individuals or factions will prevail over others by obtaining policies closer to their own preferences. The mysteries of influence, power, and authority have intrigued scholars for centuries. We are still far short of a satisfactory understanding of how these processes work, and some of our problems can be traced simply to a lack of uniformity in the way we use the terms. The authors of this book will confine themselves to the three most used terms—*influence, power,* and *authority*—but you should be aware that the distinctions made are not the only ones possible.

Let us start with the simplest case: two individuals, X and Y. Say that X has exercised *influence* over Y whenever Y's behavior is different from what it would have been without the presence of X. That kind of definition is broad enough to cover everything from passing the salt at X's request to handing over all your money at the point of X's gun.

There are, however, two special cases of influence that are especially helpful in analyzing political processes. The first of these is *power*, which is usually defined as a kind of influence in which sanctions are employed. More precisely, a power relationship exists when X influences Y by setting up a contingency in which better things will happen to Y if Y follows X's wishes. Bribery, blackmail, and armed robbery are all clear cases of the exercise of power, but there are also many legitimate ways to exercise power in most organizations. A superintendent's intimation that principals who help most in pruning the district budget will be first in line for future promotions is one example. Another is the threat of a strike by the local teachers' organization in their efforts to obtain a higher salary schedule.

Power, then, does not reside in an individual or group, but is a relational concept. If Y wants nothing that X can offer and is not threatened by anything X can do, there is no way X can exercise power over Y. It is also worth noting that X's threats or promises will be effective only to the extent that they are believed or judged credible by Y. Thus, one necessary step on X's way to power is to establish credibility as one who carries out promises and threats. Finally, most exercise of power requires the control, and frequently the expenditure, of resources. This is most obvious in the case of bribery, but almost any exercise of power entails what Harsanyi (1962) calls "opportunity costs" to the person exercising power (pp. 67–80).

A *political resource* is anything useful in influencing other individuals or groups. An individual who successfully resists offers of money may yield to promises of increased status or prestige. One skill of many "political" individuals is their ability to sense the vulnerabilities of other political actors and select the right kind of resource to exert power. Some interest groups enjoy an abundance of political resources that may be used in the exercise of power, whereas others suffer from a distinct shortage of resources. The unequal distribution of political resources in all societies is one of the hard facts of political life (Dahl, 1976, pp. 56–57).

So far, discussion has focused on the simple case of *interpersonal* power, or power relationships between people. The relevance of this to school systems is not difficult to see. Teachers exercise power over students, on each other, and against their administrators. By the same token, school administrators, board members, custodians, and pillars of the community may attempt to influence each other through the use of political resources. Not all power in organizations, however, is interpersonal.

The extension of the concept of power—and, more generally, influence—to organizations that make extensive use of policies to control the behavior of individuals is straightforward. If a policy is effective in controlling the behavior of someone in the organization, it follows that anyone who influences the substance or implementation of that policy will have exercised influence, albeit indirectly, over the behavior of others. If we can identify the people who have impact on the shape of policy and the way it is enforced, we can be confident that we have found the "influentials" in the organization.

The other special case of influence is *authority*. In this case, Y complies with the demands of X, not because of threats, promises, or even gentle persuasion, but because Y recognizes the legitimate right of X to make those demands. Now, Y may grant X that right for any of several reasons, but the reason of most interest to organization theorists is the *position* X holds in the organization. If we are school principals, there are certain things we do just because the person who wants us to do them happens to be superintendent.

In considering authority relationships, we speak of subordinates and superordinates. In a sense, the subordinate suspends critical judgment as to the merit of the superordinate's request. It is even possible that the subordinate will comply with an order that she or he does not agree with. Formal authority relationships are an important part of any organization, including schools, but there may also be informal authority patterns—such as the tradition in some schools that younger, less experienced teachers should defer to the wishes of older, more experienced hands in such things as the classroom assignments of students or the curriculum design.

There is a subtle, murky relationship between authority and power. An authority figure, such as a police officer, relies to the extent possible on authority rather than a gun; but there is usually the specter of power backing up authority. The advantage of using authority, rather than power, is that it costs little or nothing. But authority requires a period of socialization during which subordinates learn and internalize the desired authority patterns. Most adults can remember such childhood lessons about the authority of their parents or the police officer at the corner. Boot camp in the military is as much an attempt to instill appropriate reactions to authority as it is a physical-training and skill-development exercise. Officers want the lines of authority well ingrained, to avoid having to rely on persuasion, or even power, in a crisis situation. Similarly, students, teachers, administrators, board members, bureaucrats, and legislators are all part of the intricate authority patterns that exist in public education. Each goes through a socializing experience, learning what he or she has a right to expect from each of the others.

Community Power Structure

One of the issues that has engaged political analysts for many years is how to describe the structure of influence relationships in the U.S. system. Two broad camps have spent years defending their points of view and attacking the other. The first of these views, labeled *power elite* theory, postulates a single ruling elite that makes, or at least significantly colors, most of the major collective choices faced by the society. Stated in fullest form by C. Wright Mills, the captains of industry, government, and the military make the major, highest-level decisions for the society, based on a more or less common set of values and ample opportunity for interaction among themselves (Mills, 1956). Mills did not contend that middle-level decisions (which probably include most education policy) are made by the power elite, but he did argue that even these decisions may be constrained and shaped by the grand lines charted by the ruling elite.

Floyd Hunter, a sociologist who developed a "reputational" approach to the study of power, supported elitist theory from yet another angle. In a seminal community-power study of Atlanta, Georgia, Hunter found that a business-oriented group of top policymakers determined the general direction of community affairs (Hunter, 1963, p. 111). Although there is no necessary implication of a conspiracy, it is clear from his description that these men had a common outlook on the world and the opportunity to interact in deciding the affairs of the city.

At about the same time, the political scientist Robert Dahl was studying the power structure of New Haven, Connecticut (Dahl, 1961). Dahl broke down the governance of New Haven into "issue areas" (e.g., political nominations, urban redevelopment, and public education), then observed the activities of individuals in each of these areas to try to ascertain who was exercising influence. His conclusion was that the power structure of New Haven was *pluralist*, with competing elites arising in each issue area. Furthermore, he found little overlap in the composition of these elites from one issue area to the next. It was a conclusion that obviously did not square with Hunter's, and a great deal of energy has gone into trying to settle the dispute between the two versions of community-power structure.

The issue has never been resolved, but out of it came a heightened appreciation that Who exercises power? is not the only important question to be asked about governmental systems. In recent years, there has been a steady shift to the equally important question of Who *benefits* from public policy programs? It would, after all, matter very little who is responsible for setting education policy in either New Haven or Atlanta, except that the kinds of programs that result benefit some interests more than others.

The analogue of the community-power controversy in education is the dispute over who exercises power in local school districts. Is there a single, identifiable community elite that influences education policy in most communities by informal and sometimes covert means? Is the education profession itself a sort of power elite in school matters, imposing its own values on the community (Zeigler & Jennings, 1974, p. 6)? Elected school boards would be little more than symbolic bodies in this case, usually rubber stamping the initiatives of the superintendent of schools. Or, as the pluralists would have it, Is the realm of education simply another issue area that spawns its own competing interests, each trying to get its own preferences established as policy?

As with communities, it is entirely possible that some districts operate one way and others the other way. Yet, the last four decades have witnessed the emergence of a large number of organized interests in education, each making demands on the system. Certainly at the federal and state levels, and to an increasing extent at the local level, there is conflict and competition among these interests in pressing their claims. Any analysis of educational policy that ignores the existence and activity of these interests misses a great deal of the process of educational governance. The rest of this chapter will examine several of the more important of these interests.

The Interests of Students and Parents

The most likely place to begin one's search for major interests in education would seem to be with the highest-stake players in the game—students and their parents. Although not all students want precisely the same range of outcomes from their education, in some respects they do have a collective interest in the educational process. A preponderance of students everywhere, for example, might rally to the cry of less arbitrary treatment, more understanding and competent teaching, fewer invasions of privacy, better employability upon graduation, or more freedom of expression.

Unfortunately for students, they are a classic example of an almost powerless interest. They enjoy few of the political resources that traditionally influence policy. Money, status, experience with the political process, contacts, organizational skills—all are in short supply among students' groups. Furthermore, students are often in a vulnerable position when it comes to pressing for change in the status quo. Grades, promotion, and letters of recommendation have all been used at one time or another in retaliation against student activists who work too strenuously to change educational policy.

Even if powerless as individuals, can students at least exercise influence through their student governments? In most cases, probably not. However useful student governments have been in teaching leadership skills and democratic norms (and even that can be debated), they have done little to change school policy. Student-council sponsors and school administrators typically listen politely to students' proposals, tolerate the innocuous, and veto the potentially harmful, knowing full well that they, not the students, will be held accountable for the outcome. Spontaneous student groups that occasionally arise at the secondary and higher-education level are plagued with rapid turnover in leadership, which renders the development of expertise and continuity difficult. The time available to most students simply does not permit them to understand many policy issues in-depth or to follow those issues through to their resolution.

The one variety of power that has sometimes been used effectively by students is the power to disrupt. The classroom of uncooperative adolescents trying to "break in" a demanding neophyte teacher, and the large student protest groups on campus in the late 1960s and early 1970s are examples of the principle that the ability to make one's discontents known is the first step toward changing policy. Sometimes just creating an issue is enough to get the ball rolling a certain way. Still, protest alone is a crude tool with which to try to shape educational policy to one's liking on a day-to-day basis.

One of the historic functions of the judicial system in the United States is to protect individuals and classes of individuals who have little power to defend their own interests. Not many years ago, students were routinely sent home from many schools if their hair was too long or their jeans did not have a belt. Student-authored stories in the school newspaper might be censored by school officials. Suspension from school was sometimes meted out arbitrarily and without recourse to appeal.

In the 1960s and 1970s, the courts increasingly turned their attention to the rights of students. Landmark cases, many engineered by the American Civil Liberties Union (ACLU), affirmed students' rights to dress as they like, print what they want in student newspapers, and express themselves as they please on public issues as long as the educational process was not substantially disrupted. The right to due process of law was strengthened in matters of search and seizure and in disciplinary proceedings. A more careful examination of some of these constitutional questions appears in Chapter 16.

Parents, also, might be expected to represent their children's interests in educational matters, and to some extent they do. Lay control of education is still an important norm in the United States, and professionals ignore the proprietary attitude of parents at their own peril. The private telephone call from parent to school administrator about some problem experienced by a son or daughter frequently gets results. That is one of the aspects of our educational system that leaves Europeans shaking their heads. Still, parents have difficulty organizing effectively to bring collective pressure to bear on school policymakers. They are not a very cohesive group when it comes to education policy. Once in a while, an issue will come along that will galvanize a group of parents into action. It may be books branded as obscene, atheistic, or un-American that stirs them, or perhaps closing a school building, implementing busing to achieve racial balance, instituting a new sex-education program, banning (or permitting) corporal punishment, or closing down the athletic program. But more usually, parents find themselves in disagreement about what the proper course of action should be, uncertain of how to make their feelings known, or simply too far removed from the central issues to worry much about having an impact on policy.

In 1988, a bold school governance experiment in Chicago gave parents the authority to elect 6 of the 11 members of the Local School Council from their own ranks. The state law establishing the reform was struck down in 1990 by the Illinois Supreme Court, however, because the law discriminated against nonparents, violating the "one person, one vote" standard of the U.S. Constitution.

The most noteworthy attempt to organize parents in the United States has been by the National Congress of Parents and Teachers. Most elementary and secondary schools today have a local unit of this organization or perhaps a parent-teacher organization unaffiliated with the national PTA. The majority of local units are content to assume a supportive posture with respect to educational policy, steering safely clear of most controversial issues. They may, of course, endorse school-tax increase referenda when called on or finance new warm-ups for the track team or a set of encyclopedias for the school library, while extolling the virtues of public education in general—and the local schools in particular—at every opportunity. That is an important role, but not one that lends the PTA or its leaders great influence in determining the course of educational events within a community.

At the state and federal levels, a subtle shift of role occurs. State PTA organizations command respect in most state capitals. As the legislature and the governor grapple over education legislation, including the all-important funding of school-aid formulas, PTA lobbyists may be much in evidence. In Washington, the PTA is also usually to be found on the side of higher appropriations for education and may take strong positions on controversial legislation such as their stand against tuition-tax-credit proposals in the early 1980s. The national office also orchestrates campaigns on student-welfare issues designed to appeal to most parents and alienate few. Crusades against child pornography and the entertainment industry's exploitation of sex and violence in records and TV programming have been launched in recent years.

Teachers and Their Organizations

Although teachers take pride in being able to fathom the best interests of children and their parents, it is evident that teachers' own interests are not always identical to those of other interest groups. In her essay on democratic theory and the role of teachers, Amy Guttman (1989) argues,

> *Democracy demands that citizens be authorized collectively to influence the purposes of schooling, but it also demands that they not be authorized to control the content of classroom teaching so as to repress reasonable challenges to dominant political and parental perspectives. Teachers who served simply to perpetuate the beliefs held by dominant majorities or minorities would be agents of political repression. (p. 186)*

Teachers want enough independence to be able to withstand the challenges of students, parents, and other citizens when matters of principle are at stake. They also want higher salaries, safe schools, better working conditions, job security, and more influence in matters that affect their professional lives, such as hiring other teachers and selecting textbooks.

Nowhere has the power structure of education changed more rapidly than with respect to the role teachers play in the development of policy. For well over a century, teachers in this country have been organizing to further the cause of education and, in the process, to advance their own interests in the realm of school politics. In the last four decades, the movement has gathered steam rapidly. Some would argue that their organizations are destined to become the dominant force in education policy, if they are not already.

Although students and their parents are at a disadvantage in attempting to shape the nature of their schools, teachers probably enjoy more organizational advantages than any other interest group. Most of the traditional political resources (e.g., numbers, experience, affluence, status, inside information, and political skill) are available to teachers. By virtue of the fact that they spend most of their working lives in schools, teachers also have an incentive to shape education policy which may be missing in interests further removed from the scene. In order to gain a better picture of how teachers have exploited these strengths through their organizations, here is a brief look at the two large teacher organizations in the United States.

The National Education Association and the American Federation of Teachers

By far the oldest (founded in 1857) as well as the largest (with more than 2 million members) of teacher organizations, the National Education Association (NEA) has a long and venerable past. Advertising their organization as a professional association rather than a union, its leaders worked in the early years for their vision of a highly professional educational system, with teacher-welfare issues playing a relatively minor role. Administrators as well as teachers were welcomed into the fold. For years, in fact, NEA leadership positions were dominated by school administrators and university professors, who enjoyed more visibility and the luxury of being able to attend professional meetings.

In the late 1800s and early 1900s, the NEA was the closest thing this country had to a maker of national education policy. Even as late as the 1950s, the pronouncements of the NEA and the U.S. Office of Education were almost indistinguishable.

Yet there was a conservative cast to NEA activity in its first hundred years. Its membership was largest in southern and rural parts of the country. A long-term alliance with the American Legion reinforced its staid character. Eschewing the strike and most other militant tactics as "unprofessional," NEA affiliates attempted to persuade school boards with reason and facts provided by the state and national organizations. The concept of teachers bargaining collectively with the local school board smacked too much of unionism.

The American Federation of Teachers (AFT), on the other hand, made no apologies about being a union. From its earliest days in Chicago, it was clearly identified with the American labor movement. It did not, however, sanction the use of strikes in school matters. Its growth was slow through the 1920s and 1930s. One turning point came when, in 1944, an AFT local in Cicero, Illinois, signed a collective-bargaining agreement with the board of education; another in 1947, when the Buffalo Teachers Federation struck for higher salaries despite their parent organization's no-strike policy. Although the AFT maintained its official ban on strikes for a time, it became clear that striking locals could expect sympathetic treatment from the national union.

The AFT traded on its union connection with the AFL-CIO, especially in the large metropolitan districts, where teachers were less likely to be squeamish about labor affiliation and labor tactics. Competition between the upstart AFT and the NEA developed in several states and culminated in a showdown in the New York City schools. By 1960, the AFT had launched a major organizing drive in New York, focused on its largest local—the United Federation of Teachers (UFT)—in New York City. A bitter strike in that year had done much to create an atmosphere of militancy and to catapult Albert Shanker into the forefront of the teacher movement. A scheduled vote the following year on which teacher organization should represent New York teachers at the bargaining table was instrumental in shaping the teacher movement for years to come.

To understand why that was so, and much that has happened since then, we need to know a little about the nature of the competition for membership between the AFT and the NEA. The advent of collective bargaining had changed the rules of that game so that it was no longer just a matter of trying to interest as many teachers as possible in the monthly journal and the high-sounding objectives of the organization. For collective bargaining to work, some bargaining agent has to be designated to bargain for all the teachers. No self-respecting school board is going to want to bargain simultaneously with two or three organizations, arriving at separate agreements with each. Any district that was considering collective bargaining, then, would have to have an election to determine the sole bargaining agent for teachers. Both the NEA and AFT had local organizations in New York schools, but it was the nature of collective bargaining that precipitated the showdown.

The NEA had recognized the challenge. Although their membership figures were still several times greater than those of the AFT, the metropolitan battlegrounds ahead would be more difficult for the NEA. Furthermore, there was a shift of mood among U.S. teachers toward bolder, more militant tactics, which might make the AFT attractive to many. Within a relatively short period, the NEA revised its long-standing policies against collective bargaining and teacher strikes and gently expelled school administrators—now suspect with the turn toward adversary processes like collective bargaining—from the fold. Yet despite a major effort in New York, the NEA lost. AFT victories in other large cities swelled their membership to almost 500,000. Over the years, the two groups have become closer in their positions on major issues and tactics, leading to serious discussions of merger.

Three changes in the power structure of education have been brought about by the growing teacher movement. First, a larger proportion of teachers are politically knowledgeable and politically active today than a generation ago. More are members of one or the other of the major organizations, and these organizations have played a part in the politicization of the teaching profession. Teachers today are more likely to see their interests as somewhat distinct from those of taxpayers, administrators, board members, parents, or even students. Their organization and political awareness has made teachers a force to be reckoned with at every political level.

Second, the nature of collective bargaining, which rapidly supplanted older board-controlled methods of arriving at teacher salaries and working conditions, has fundamentally changed the way in which resources used for education are allocated. Professional administrators and elected board members used to have a monopoly on that process. Today, in many districts, every item on the proposed budget for next year will have to be justified to representatives from the teachers' bargaining agent sitting across the table before a contract between teachers and the district will be forthcoming. The strike, of course, remains the ultimate threat used by teachers in this process. But one should not underestimate the effect of having the teachers' case argued by negotiators who know as much about the district's financial situation as the business manager and who may know even more about trends in surrounding districts, the state, or the nation. Those are powerful resources that have channeled an increased share of the educational dollar into the pockets of teachers and have provided them more job security, better working conditions, or more favorable teaching climates.

Third, since the establishment of collective bargaining in many districts, there has been a subtle shift in authority relationships within school districts and in the way schools are viewed by people on the outside. Teachers no longer project the image of good-hearted samaritans who, despite low salaries and miserable working conditions, teach just for the love of children. They are unlikely to accept direction from school administrators as uncritically as they once did. They may draw the line more quickly than before, the line beyond which they will not go in the performance of their duties. They are skeptical of the efficacy of teacher training provided by colleges and universities and are eager to have a hand in developing their own training programs.

These are perfectly natural reflexes in the process of becoming a stronger profession. The changes, however, may have contributed to a more recent shift in public attitudes toward schools. With teachers bargaining hard and looking out for themselves, the public seems less inclined to give its once almost automatic approval to school-tax increases. The days when almost anything done in the name of education would be looked upon favorably by the public are clearly over.

Minority Interests

There was a time when Americans bragged that the United States was a collection of minorities. Today, there is little point in denying that an English-speaking, Anglo-Saxon, Protestant majority dominates the culture of U.S. schools. The language of instruction in most cases is the majority language; the history that is taught emphasizes the development of western civilization; the school calendar is built primarily around the religious holidays of the Christian majority. The difficulty for the minority child in adjusting to the sometimes alien culture of the school, along with the economic, social, and academic disadvantage of many minority students, has made the representation of their interests in educational policy matters a critical concern. African Americans, Latinos, Native Americans, Southeast Asians, Chinese, Japanese, Jews, atheists, and the Amish have all felt the heavy hand of the majority at one time or another.

The largest single minority issue in the postwar period has been the racial desegregation of schools. The historic role of the National Association for the Advancement of Colored People (NAACP) in the U.S. Supreme Court case that led to the 1954 *Brown* v. *the Board of Education of Topeka* decision is well documented. Other groups, including the Urban League, the Southern Christian Leadership Conference (SCLC), and Jessie Jackson's Rainbow Coalition, have articulated the interests of African American school children. The American Indian Movement (AIM) has attacked the Bureau of Indian Affairs, which directs much of the federal effort in Native American education, and tribal councils have pushed for changes in both public and government schools in which Native American children are enrolled. Latino interests have been instrumental in obtaining substantial federal aid for bilingual programs in districts with heavy Hispanic populations. On the religious front, there are also organizations with interests in education, including the National Catholic Education Association, that have attempted to modify the relationship between public and private education.

The importance of minority concerns in U.S. education is destined to grow in the coming decades. Demographic trends already underway ensure that ethnic minority students, many with limited proficiency in English, will make up a higher proportion of most classrooms. Each of these children will bring his or her own cultural heritage to school. Each has an obvious interest in having that heritage treated with respect by teachers, administrators, and other students. The old notion of a melting pot in which every student from an ethnic, linguistic, or religious minority was expected to become like other students has given way to a more exciting concept of multicultural education in which distinctiveness is not only tolerated, but appreciated.

Business Interests

The role of business in the most recent education reform movement has highlighted the legitimate interests of the business community in the system of public schools. Most businesses depend heavily on being able to hire employees who have mastered at least basic skills in school. Some, of course, also require highly trained engineers or accountants. Although critics of the U.S. system have argued that the top priority of business is a bountiful supply of uneducated workers who can be hired for low wages, it seems clear that the larger concern of most business leaders is that there will not be a sufficient supply of employees with the self-reliance, work ethic, and literacy and numeracy skills to work effectively in the workplace of the future. Part of this concern stems from the fact that the society is transforming itself from one in which most workers were industrial employees to one in which most will be engaged in service occupations or information processing. An industrial system that once capitalized on cheap labor and plentiful natural resources to produce huge steam engines will need more highly educated workers to produce the Web-browsers and gene-altering drugs demanded by international markets in the years ahead.

At the national and state levels, the Chamber of Commerce expresses keen interest in projections of work-force size, the labor market, and technical and vocational educational programs in the schools. Quite independent of this, many business leaders have expressed their interest in reforming the public schools in recent years and committed their corporations to the task. One manifestation has been the development of school-business partnerships of various kinds throughout the country.

At the community level, the business interests connect with schools in a somewhat different way. Rotary International, Kiwanis, the Lions Club, and other business-oriented service groups take a proprietary interest in the development and prosperity of the community; schools are one obvious element in their ability to sell the community to new residents, businesses, or industry. Their ideas about how those schools might be improved are usually available to school administrators, who may have been invited to join one or another of the clubs. Taxpayer associations, on the other hand, are in evidence in most states and large cities and may actively oppose increases in education funding.

Other Education Interests

Historians of education have frequently stressed the influence of two less obvious kinds of institutions on education policy. The Ford Foundation, the Rockefeller Foundation, and the Carnegie Corporation are only the most familiar examples from an array of charitable foundations spawned by large private corporations. Their policy of giving money away for educational programs and research provides the parent corporation both a tax shelter and excellent public relations, but their impact on U.S. education has also been significant. Over the years, most have developed an organizational independence of their parent industries that makes it difficult to say whose interests they serve, on balance. Many of their more notable initiatives (e.g., the Carnegie Corporation's sponsorship of an influential study by James B. Conant, which precipitated a national wave of school-district consolidations, or the Ford Foundation's advocacy of community-action programs to break the cycle of poverty, which led to Project Head Start) have been reformist in character.

The accrediting association has also had a decided effect on U.S. schools. These private professional organizations came into being largely to assure universities and prospective employers of the quality of the high schools and colleges that their applicants had attended. On-site inspections by accrediting associations have encouraged many schools to bring their staffs, course offerings, or procedures into line with the standards required for accreditation. Those standards were usually arrived at by professionals, and the charge is frequently made that accrediting associations have reinforced the already tight grip of professional educators over the direction of public education, at the expense of public influence (Spring, 1978, pp. 198–201).

More extensive treatment of specific interest groups at the state and federal levels is reserved for Chapters 14 and 15. It is interesting to mention here, however, that there are over 200 education groups maintaining lobbyists in Washington, DC. The United States has been called a nation of groups, and the educational establishment is doing its part to perpetuate that image. Guidance counselors, English teachers, publishing firms, universities, school superintendents, educational researchers, teacher educators, and even an organization of chief state school officers have advocates on the spot looking out for their interests. It is a system that encourages noisy, sometimes rancorous, debates on most educational issues. It is also a system that attempts to minimize the chance that the claims of any significant interest in U.S. education will go unheard.

The Role of the Public

Schools are ultimately responsible to the citizens they serve, and those citizens play an important role in guiding school policy. This is not to say that most citizens have detailed knowledge of educational issues or more than casual interest in how they are resolved. From friends, radio, television, newspapers, or their own children, information about schools drifts in—fragmentary, biased, and sometimes wrong. From these bits and pieces impressions form: "Enrollments are down," "SAT scores are up," "Discipline is a big problem," "There is too much fat in the budget," "Teachers are underpaid," and so on. When a school issue heats up or an election approaches, the impressions people have formed about schools influence the way they will react.

One reason that school leaders need to pay attention to public opinion is that public schools ultimately depend on citizens for financial support. If broad segments of the public were to become disenchanted with the performance of schools, the very structure of public education would be threatened. One gauge of the level of confidence people place in public schools has been the Gallup Poll question asking respondents how they would "grade" their own public schools—A, B, C, D, or FAIL. Table 12.1 shows that the proportion of people who rated schools either A or B dropped off in the mid-1970s and picked up again after *A Nation at Risk* (1983) called attention to the need for education reform.

TABLE 12.1   **National Ratings of Public Schools by Local Residents**

	1974	1977	1980	1983	1986	1989	1992	1995
A or B rating	48%	37%	35%	31%	41%	43%	40%	41%
C, D, or Fail rating	32	44	47	52	44	48	50	54
Don't know/no answer	20	19	18	17	15	9	10	5
	100%	100%	100%	100%	100%	100%	100%	100%

Question: Students are often given the grades A, B, C, D, and FAIL to denote the quality of their work. Suppose the *public* schools themselves, in this community, were graded in the same way. What grade would you give the public schools here —A, B, C, D, or FAIL?

Source: George H. Gallup, "The 21st Annual Gallup Poll of the Public's Attitudes toward the Public Schools," *Phi Delta Kappan* (September 1989), p. 198, and Stanley M. Elam and Lowel C. Rose, "The 27th Annual Phi Delta Kappa/Gallup Poll of the Public's Attitudes toward the Public Schools," *Phi Delta Kappan* (September 1995), p. 42.

When compared with other U.S. institutions, public schools have historically inspired less public confidence than churches, the military, and banks, but they come out ahead of Congress, big business, and organized labor in the confidence polls. It is worth noting, however, that public confidence in all public institutions appears to be affected by historical events. A Watergate scandal or an economic repression may dampen public confidence across a variety of institutions.

Public opinion enters into school governance most obviously when citizens vote on a proposed tax increase, on a plan to consolidate their district with a neighboring one, or on some other issue put to a referendum. Citizens also vote for local school-board members, and board elections may change district priorities sharply, as will be seen in the next chapter. But even between referenda and board elections, public opinion limits what elected officials and school administrators can do. Proposals that stray too far from what most citizens consider sound education may be rejected by school officials anxious to avoid arousing a slumbering public.

Summary

In any complex policy system, there are always issues about the best course of action to be followed. Various interests will have different policy preferences on these issues. Their differences must be reconciled through a collective decision arrived at politically. School systems are not exempt from this process, and thus, in this broad sense, they are political organizations.

Processes for reaching collective decisions include persuasion, authority, voting, and bargaining. Most issue resolutions, in fact, involve a mixture of these processes. The policy that eventuates will authoritatively prescribe the behavior of certain actors in the system. Thus, policy is a means by which authorities may attempt to control the behavior of other actors. A policy may serve to make the organization operate more effectively or with greater consistency or to protect individuals who faithfully follow its prescription.

Policies usually change only after dissatisfaction is expressed in some quarter. Once the issue is on the agenda, alternatives will be proposed and weighed amidst influence attempts aimed at gathering support for preferred alternatives and defeating others. Authoritative enactment of one alternative will result in a new policy. Two important aspects of the policy-change process remain, however. Will the target individuals comply with the prescribed behavioral change? If not, who will enforce the new policy and how? Only after a new policy has been implemented will substantive changes in the operation of the organization take place.

Interests in the educational process include those of students, parents, teachers, taxpayers, and minorities, among others. Political resources useful for increasing the adoption of preferred policy alternatives are unequally distributed among these interests. The most apparent recent change in the power structure of education has been the effective organization of teachers bargaining collectively with authorities at the local, state, and national levels.

References

Braybrooke, D., & Lindblom, C. E. (1970). *A strategy of decision: Policy evaluation as a social process.* New York: Free Press.

Cobb, R. W., & Elder, C. D. (1972). *Participation in American politics: Dynamics of agenda-building.* Boston: Allyn and Bacon.

Dahl, R. A. (1961). *Who governs: Democracy and power in an American city.* New Haven, CT: Yale University Press.

Dahl, R. A. (1976). *Modern political analysis* (3rd ed.). Englewood Cliffs, NJ: Prentice-Hall.

Education Week. (October 10, 1990), pp. 1, 12–13.

Education Week. (October 4, 1995), pp. 23–29.

Garms, W., Guthrie, J., & Pierce, L. (1978). *School finance: The economics and politics of education.* Englewood Cliffs, NJ: Prentice-Hall.

Gerth, H. H., & Mills, C. W. (1958). *From Max Weber: Essays in sociology.* New York: Oxford University Press.

Guttman, A. (1989). *Democratic theory and the role of teachers in democratic education.* In J. Hannaway & R. Crowson (Eds.), *The politics of reforming school administration.* New York: Falmer Press.

Harsanyi, J. C. (1962). Measurement of social power, opportunity costs, and the theory of two-person bargaining games. *Behavioral Science, 7,* 67–80.

Hunter, F. (1963). *Community power structure: A study of decision makers.* Garden City, NY: Anchor Books.

Jones, C. O. (1977). *An introduction to the study of public policy* (2nd ed.). North Scituate, MA: Duxbury Press.

Kingdon, J. W. (1984). *Agendas, alternatives, and public policies.* Boston: Little, Brown.

Lasswell, H. D. (1958). *Politics: Who gets what, when, how.* Cleveland: Meridian Books.

Lindblom, C. E. (1959). The science of muddling through. *Public Administration Review, 19,* 79–88.

Marshall, C., Mitchell, D., & Wirt, F. (1989). *Culture and education policy in the American states.* New York: Falmer Press.

Mills, C. W. (1956). *The power elite.* New York: Oxford University Press.

Spring, J. (1978). *American education: An introduction to social and political aspects.* New York: Longman.

Thomas, N. C. (1975). *Education in national politics.* New York: David McKay.

Truman, D. B. (1951). *The governmental process: Political interests and public opinion.* New York: Knopf.

Zeigler, L. H., & Jennings, M. K., with Peak, G. W. (1974). *Governing American schools: Political interaction in local school districts.* North Scituate, MA: Duxbury Press.

Chapter 13

Policymaking in the Local School District

Some teachers tend to view educational policy as too distant and too abstract to make much difference in their classrooms. Isn't it, after all, the special relationship between students and teacher that is at the heart of the educational enterprise? How can long debates in state legislatures or school-board meetings, or decisions handed down from the superintendent's office affect that relationship very much? Let the politicians govern and administrators administer; the essence of education will be little changed.

A moment's reflection on the crucial nexus of student and teacher in the classroom leads one to question that assessment. What happens in that classroom may be largely a function of who has been chosen as teacher. Who, out of all those who might want to, will be allowed to teach in that classroom? What kind of person will be charged with the educational development of those children? What qualifications will he or she have? What kind of experience? What professional training? And, of all those who meet the criteria, who will find the salary schedule and working conditions attractive enough to take the job? Answers to these kinds of questions are shaped by the state and local policy process, and there can be little doubt that those policies fundamentally affect the nature of the educational process.

We must also remind ourselves that a teacher does not have complete control of what will be taught once she or he has been hired. Curriculum guides provided by the state, district, or school can influence what is taught and may even dictate the texts and other instructional materials to be used. Even in the absence of such guides, subtle pressures may be brought to bear on the elementary teacher to emphasize math this year, as opposed to social studies. Schoolwide or district-wide testing programs may obligate the teacher to "cover" certain subject areas. Nor do teachers at the secondary level have complete control over what they teach.

The assistant superintendent for instruction may rule that calculus cannot be taught next year because too few students have indicated an interest in it. Reassignment of teachers from primary to secondary teaching specialties is not unheard of. Teachers of Spanish may find themselves teaching English when district needs so dictate.

How the teacher goes about the job will also depend on previously made policy decisions. What kinds of resources will be made available? Will the textbook ordered three years ago by a predecessor have to be used again simply because it has been budgeted for a five-year life span? What is available in the way of microscopes or analytic balances for the science laboratory? Is there a school library, and if so, can teachers order whatever supplementary materials are deemed necessary? Will prompting from administrators or other teachers encourage a phonics approach to reading, the use of manipulatives in mathematics, or a "constructivist" approach in science? How much preparation time is provided for the development of those creative teaching ideas that one gets from time to time but just does not have time to put into practice?

There is also a myriad of contextual and organizational factors that may dramatically affect the interactions of teachers and pupils. Is the classroom we have been visualizing 1 of 90 in a suburban high school of 3,000 students or 1 of 4 in a small rural school? Are there 18 students in the class or 38? Are only the most academically talented students found in this class, or is a cross-section of the student body represented? If it is a secondary school, will class periods be 35, 50, or 80 minutes? Will a split lunch schedule mean that the class has to be interrupted in the middle to send students off to the cafeteria? Will school buses whisk some children away to homes in distant corners of the community immediately after the last class period, depriving them of an opportunity to try out for the track team or go over least common multiples one more time with the math teacher? What procedures and support will be available to our teacher when the inevitable occurs and some student is insubordinate or creates a disruption in the classroom?

Each of these questions can be answered only if one knows something about the educational policymaking system within the local district. Despite the encroachment of state and federal regulations and programs, there is still remarkable latitude for the local district to provide its own answers to questions of this type. The objectives emphasized and the manner in which available resources are allocated to meet these objectives significantly shape the classroom relationship between teacher and student. This chapter will look at the way these objectives are transformed into policy within the political system of the local school district.

The Locus of Authority at the Local Level

Providing a general map of the formal structure of authority in making educational policy is not difficult. Despite numerous exceptions across the 50 states and the local school districts within them, a general pattern prevails. A state grants certain legal authority to a board of education, usually elected, to provide a public school system in that area. The school board hires a superintendent of schools to manage the day-to-day affairs of the district. Building principals and teachers are also hired, with the authority to exercise some discretion with respect to policy at their levels.

For present purposes, it will be helpful to think of educational policy at five different levels. At the *classroom level*, teachers set their own policy across a surprising range of topics. Within fairly broad limits, most teachers can establish their own grading policy and classroom-discipline policy, select their own materials, and structure learning activities in the way they believe will be most effective. The discretion of the U.S. teacher on questions of this kind is in sharp contrast to the French system, for example, where many more questions of classroom operation are addressed in directives emanating from the Ministry of Education.

Just above the classroom level is the *building level* of policy. Principals of U.S. schools enjoy their own authority to create policy in certain realms. Policies promulgated from the principal's office typically concern some of the most fundamental educational questions, such as course offerings, student assignment to classes, school discipline and promotion policy, and how the students' time in school will be scheduled.

At the *district level*, the school board, along with the superintendent and his or her assistants, will determine policies meant to apply to all schools in the district. Principals, as well as teachers and students, may be constrained by district policy. A plan to bus students to combat racial segregation would involve more than one school and would usually be crafted at the district level. Similarly, decisions to require three years of high school science for graduation or to reduce the teaching force in response to a districtwide budget deficit would, in most instances, be made at the district level.

Important policy, then, is made at the classroom, school-building, and district levels, and it is the manner in which those policies evolve that this chapter addresses. Discussion of the federal and state levels will be presented in the next two chapters. There is, however, one point that will already be apparent. Issues arise not only over the substantive questions of educational policy but also over the procedural question of which level is the appropriate level for the resolution of any given policy issue. Heavy-handed principals stir the ire of teachers who are convinced that they can resolve many issues better at the classroom level. Some of the best principals fight for more and more independence from the district office to fashion policy in their school as they think best. Superintendents lapse into high dudgeon when the state legislature mandates a program that restricts their own options. And the top education officials at the state level often join with district superintendents and board members in decrying the attempts of their federal counterparts to mold U.S. schools in accordance with national priorities.

Proponents of local control argue that most educational policy questions should be decided at the lowest possible level. Only then can decisions take account of all of the idiosyncratic features of the particular locale in question. Proponents of more centralized approaches to policy point out that when the interests of people beyond the confines of the local unit are significantly affected, a collective decision at a higher level is in order. Only a higher-level decision can acknowledge the interests of all parties involved. In an increasingly mobile and interdependent society, matters of literacy, teacher certification, sex education, driver training, graduation requirements, special education, and equity are concerns that frequently transcend district boundaries.

Policymakers at the Local Level

Teachers do not spring to mind when one starts listing policymakers in education. We forget just how much policy is made, sometimes on the spot, by teachers in a classroom. Yet many of the problems that inexperienced teachers have stem from their not having their own classroom policy worked out to apply to the scores of problems that confront them each day in the classroom. By the same token, students spend much of their spare time discussing, testing, and complaining about each teacher's way of handling recurring situations in the classroom. Is homework assigned regularly? Collected? How much talking is permitted in class? What about gum chewing? Are pop quizzes to be expected? Will tardy students be reported to the office? Can missed work be made up? Will too much (or too little) exuberance in class result in a detention? These are not inconsequential questions in the education of youngsters, and, in most cases, the teacher is granted undisputed authority to run the classroom as she or he wants, within rather broad limits. In larger schools, where coordination is deemed important, grade-level chairpersons (elementary) or subject-matter department chairpersons (secondary) may supervise the determination of some intermediate-level policy questions such as the selection of textbooks or the adoption of a common approach to a subject across classes.

That part of the teacher's role that includes policymaking is important in one other sense. In U.S. education, principals are recruited from the ranks of teachers, superintendents from the ranks of principals, and many (but not all) state and federal authorities from the ranks of superintendents. Although the career administrator may have a slightly different view of the enterprise from each new vantage point, earlier experiences as policymaker at a lower level lend some perspective.

Even as teachers exercise authority within the classroom, their influence over educational policy outside the classroom has been expanding. In their professional role, teachers now assert themselves on a host of educational questions that used to be the private preserve of administrators and board members. Take, for example, the practice in many districts of involving teachers in personnel decisions about the appointment or retention of teachers and administrators.* That is a major responsibility that can quickly reshape a school. Teachers a few decades back would have had little part in these decisions. Furthermore, the influence of teachers, through their professional organizations, on salary schedules, class size,

*For an informed view of this and other areas in which the influence of teachers has been expanding, see Donley (1976).

school calendars, and reduction-in-force clauses, has markedly changed the tenor of district policymaking. (The advent of collective bargaining is discussed later in this chapter.)

One of the themes to emerge in the "second wave" of the most recent school reform has been the call for further empowerment of teachers. Some have envisioned virtually all building-level policy being made by committees of teachers in collaboration with each other and their building administrators. The touted benefits of teacher empowerment include teachers who, by virtue of their engagement with key issues of the day, perform better in the classroom, display more support for their colleagues and their school, and are more committed to teaching as a profession. It is also likely that an active policy role for teachers would make the teaching profession a more attractive alternative for those contemplating a career in teaching.

If one is to believe a frequent finding in school-effectiveness research, the building principal may hold the most crucial single position in the educational enterprise. Although it is often difficult to ascertain the effects that a superintendent, or even teachers, have on the system, study after study has indicated that this or that program succeeds in schools where it has the active and enthusiastic support of a competent principal and fails in schools where that support is lacking (Chesler, Schmuck, & Lippitt, 1975, pp. 321–327). Not only are the principal's substantive decisions apt to make a difference, but the style of the principal sets the tone for the entire school. Those who look with disdain on the contributions of administrators (and many teachers do) would do well to contemplate the overwhelming evidence that principals make a difference.

Despite the ability of the principal to shape such consequential matters as the array of course offerings or the extent of parent involvement in the school, principals have lost ground as authorities in recent years. While teachers have been demanding more say in how the building should be run, directives from the district office, the state capital, and Washington, DC, have multiplied.

Atop the local school administrative hierarchy sits the district superintendent of schools. It is a position that demands all the administrative skill and political wisdom one can muster. The successful superintendent is expected to detect potential trouble areas before they become major problems. Bold, innovative districtwide programs will usually come about only at his or her initiative. Disagreement among building principals must be resolved, and mountains of paperwork spawned by state and federal agencies must be tended to. Annual budgets will have to be prepared, defended, and deftly steered through the board. The superintendent is at once not only that board's agent and expert but also the leader of the professional staff and the most visible single official in the district.

In many matters, a memorandum from the superintendent is sufficient to establish district policy. On broader questions requiring board approval, the superintendent may still have a hand in virtually every stage of the policy process from identifying the problem and getting it on the agenda, to proposing alternatives, lining up support, and seeing that the new policy is communicated and enforced. When support for the educational program is high, the superintendent will thrive; when support crumbles, the superintendent is usually the first to pay the price.

To most foreign observers, however, the most remarkable feature of U.S. education is the local board of education. This unique institution shoulders the ultimate legal responsibility for the education of children in the district. Perhaps most important, political accountability rests with the board members. In most districts, they are elected for two- or three-year terms in nonpartisan, at-large, elections. The size of boards and the electoral arrangements vary considerably throughout the nation, but a seven-member board with two or three members elected each year is the modal case. It will meet once, twice, or perhaps several times a month, depending on the size of the district, the wishes of the superintendent, and the press of political issues.

Much of what the board does is specified by state law, but there is enormous discretion as to how active its members wish to be and on which issues. The approval of a budget and the appointment of new teachers are powers usually delegated to the board by state law. But the board also has the formal authority to bring about changes in district policy in virtually any area of the educational program.

As in all collective-decision systems featuring shared responsibility, there is considerable potential for tension between superintendents and boards. Extreme cases can be found, to be sure, in which a board simply does the bidding of the superintendent or the superintendent follows the lead of the board on every major matter. But their roles are different, and in many cases, beneath the air of cordiality, there is an edginess about prerogatives.

One might assume that the board tends to dominate the superintendent whenever their judgments about appropriate courses of action diverge. It is true that superintendents seldom win 30-year-service pins by openly confronting the elected officials who appointed them and have the power to dismiss them. Still, there are some good cards in the superintendent's hand as well. First, as a full-time professional constantly meeting with other school administrators, teachers, students, and parents, the superintendent will become aware of most problems before board members do. Second, the superintendent can draw on the resources of her or his administrative and professional staff to propose alternatives to a policy that is not working. Board members frequently have neither the time nor the expertise to work out an alternative proposal in detail. Also, in arguing for his or her proposal, the superintendent will have the benefit of much more detailed information about the day-to-day operation of the schools. Fourth, although the board members may speak with the authority that accrues to elected officials, the superintendent wears the mantle of expert. On certain kinds of questions, the superintendent's pronouncements are not likely to be challenged by anyone in the room. Finally, should the board be anything but unanimous in its opposition to the superintendent, its larger numbers may turn into a liability. An adroit superintendent can marshal the evidence in the most advantageous way possible to support his or her position, without much fear of direct contradiction from subordinates. But any board member, in attempting to present a case for or against the proposal, may find her or his position neutralized by the board member who speaks next.

The superintendent's leverage works best when things are going smoothly. A major issue that drags on, the rise of widespread public dissatisfaction, and the loss of board confidence all may find the board quickly becoming the dominant force. Furthermore, as will be seen later in this chapter, some have argued that even in quiet times the board may be far more influential than it appears. To better understand what makes a board tick, it will be necessary to look more closely at the political side of U.S. school boards.

School-Board Politics

One indication of the special place education has enjoyed in the political history of the United States is that, in the vast majority of districts, a separate governmental structure, largely insulated from the rough-and-tumble partisan politics of municipal government, has been erected. The school board has symbolized the importance of lay control, but it has also served to reinforce the local, nonpartisan nature of educational policy.

Just how representative is the typical school board of the electorate it represents? Although females and minorities are much more in evidence on school boards now than 40 years ago, board members are still disproportionately White males. They are also more likely than the typical citizen to have a college degree and high income. Some 60 percent of board members hold a professional or managerial job and 60 percent have children in the public schools (see Table 13.1).

It is a long and perhaps unwarranted inferential leap to suggest that because school board members come disproportionately from the more advantaged segments of society, they do not adequately represent the interests of the disadvantaged in educational matters. When asked to indicate their top concerns, however, school board members came up with a list strikingly different from the one citizens provided when asked to name the biggest problems facing public schools. The most frequently mentioned concern of board members was financial matters, followed by worries about increasing enrollment, curriculum, and at-risk students. The two top concerns of the general public were drug abuse and lack of discipline, followed by fighting/violence/gangs. It is not surprising that serving on a school board sensitizes members to the importance of providing adequate financial support, but the experience may also reassure many of them about such things as school discipline (see Table 13.2).

Even where board members and their constituents agree on what the major problems are, there is no guarantee that they will agree about how to handle them. Zeigler and Jennings found moderately high agreement between board members and their constituents on such items as whether prayers should be used in schools, whether there is too much or too little federal control over local education, and whether teachers should have a stronger voice in educational policy. On the other hand, board members' views about the appropriateness of the federal role in school integration or the right of teachers to strike bore little relationship to the views of their constituents. Across the country as a whole, board members were

TABLE 13.1   Demographic Comparison between School-Board Members and the General Public

Characteristics	General Adult Public (1996)	School-Board Members (1996)
Sex		
Males	47%	59%
Females	53	40
Race		
White	84	94
Nonwhite	13	4
Other	3	2
Education		
College or advanced degree	22	68*
Income		
$40,000 or over	37	85
Occupation		
Professional or managerial	32	60*
Family		
Children in school	32	60*

Source: School-board data are reprinted, with permission, from *The American School Board Journal* (January 1997), p. 29. Copyright 1997 The National School Boards Association. All rights reserved. Data for the general public are reprinted, with permission, from the *Phi Delta Kappan* (September 1996), p. 59.

*1989 data.

somewhat more opposed to prayers in public schools, to giving teachers the right to strike, to giving teachers a stronger voice, to federal control over local education, and to state control over local education than was the national sample of constituents. They were, however, more favorably disposed to the federal government's taking the lead in school integration (Zeigler & Jennings, 1974, p. 137). More recently, Tarazi, Curcio, and Fortune (1997) found that although 54 percent of the school-board members they surveyed considered themselves "religious conservatives," and 65 percent considered themselves "political conservatives," only one-third of them support voucher plans or public-school prayer.

These findings support a mixed interpretation of the representativeness of U.S. school boards. Board members nationwide do not accurately reflect the social, educational, racial, economic, and demographic characteristics of the public, and their general sense of which problems are most pressing appears to be quite different from that of the public. Within any given district, however, board members are likely to reflect community sentiment regarding whether general societal problems (e.g., racial problems in the schools) deserve a place on the policymaking

TABLE 13.2 Top Ten Concerns/Biggest Problems Facing Local Schools: School-Board Members Compared with Sample of Adult Citizens*

School Board Members		Adult Citizens	
Concerns	*Totals*	*Biggest Problems*	*Totals*
School finance/Budget	28%	Drug abuse	16%
Increasing enrollment	12	Lack of discipline	15
Curriculum development	10	Fighting/Violence/Gangs	14
At-risk kids	8	Lack of financial support	13
Facilities	7	Overcrowded schools	8
Technology	5	Pupil's lack of interest	5
State mandates	5	Family structure/Problems	4
Parent involvement	4	Crime/Vandalism	3
Management issues	2	Poor curriculum/Low standards	3
Collective bargaining	2	Difficulty getting good teachers	3

Source: Adult citizen data are printed, with permission, from *Phi Delta Kappan* (September 1996), p. 49. School-board data are printed, with permission, from *The American School Board Journal* (January 1997), p. 29. Copyright 1997 The National School Boards Association. All rights reserved.

*Respondents to the *American School Board Journal* / Virginia Tech survey were asked to indicate their concerns about their schools, whereas respondents to the Gallup Poll were asked to name the biggest problems facing their public schools. Responses listed were those receiving the most mentions. All percentages are rounded to the nearest whole number.

agenda. Community concerns are not as apt to be reflected by board members in their assessment of more distinctly educational problem areas. On school-policy preference questions, there is little evidence that board members systematically depart from the views of the general public, except for a discernible tendency to guard their own decision-making prerogatives jealously against encroachment from teachers on the one hand and state and federal agencies on the other. Correlations between the views of board members and their constituents range from almost no relationship on some issues to moderately high relationship on others. The worst that can be said is that on some issues, it would be difficult to predict the position a board would take simply by knowing the preferences of constituents in that district (Ziegler & Jennings, 1974, p. 137).

The manner in which candidates are recruited and elected to school boards varies over time and place. To illustrate this, here are two fictitious cases that typify quite different selection systems, even though the formal rules are the same.

Model 1: Noblesse Oblige and the Politics of Consensus

Ted Sumner hung up the telephone and turned to face his puzzled wife.

"That was Charlie Martinez. You won't believe what he wants me to do now. Seems as though there is going to be an opening on the school board. Old Jerry Rice has decided to give up his seat. Of course, he hasn't announced it yet, but as president of the board, Charlie wanted me to consider running. Said if it was handled right there shouldn't be much opposition."

"You told him no, I hope. You were complaining just the other day about how you haven't had much time with the family since Joe left the firm. You don't need this on top of everything else."

"How do you say no to Charlie? Besides, it's sort of expected around town that I'd take my turn when the time came. I've heard several people mention it."

Ted didn't tell Charlie no, but he didn't say yes for a while either. In the next week or two, several other members of the school board urged him to take the plunge. It would amount to only a couple of nights a month, and Frankton needed people with his judgment on the board. Finally, as the filing deadline approached and no other candidate appeared, Ted agreed to run.

As an unopposed candidate, Ted created few waves. He spent a grand total of 95 dollars to have some campaign buttons made up. There were the obligatory rounds of service clubs and several neighborhood tea gatherings to air his viewpoints on the schools. At these affairs Ted invariably settled for a few platitudes about how Frankton needed the best schools possible and how he would do everything he could to see that those schools were run efficiently and fairly. He also wanted everyone to know that as their representative on the board, he would listen to them. At that point, he usually threw the meeting open to questions and spent the rest of the evening listening. Whenever someone tried to pin him down on an issue, he would simply plead that he didn't have all the facts yet but that they could be sure that he would weigh all sides of the question before deciding.

Ted was widely known throughout the community, and most people respected him. His bearing inspired trust. Though no one, including Ted himself, knew exactly where he stood on teachers' demands for higher salaries and lower class size, the state's new charter school legislation, or the superintendent's plan to phase out a special program for gifted youngsters, most voters agreed that he would approach these and other questions responsibly, honestly—even wisely.

On the day of the election, only 28 percent of the eligible voters in the district went to the polls. As in most low-turnout elections, the established, well-off voters were most likely to trudge to the polls. There was little incentive for new residents, the unemployed, minorities, or other voting groups, who might have been forces for change in Frankton's schools, to come out to vote in an uncontested election. Most of those who did vote dutifully marked their ballots for Ted Sumner and went home feeling rather noble about having fulfilled their civic duty and contributed to the future well-being of Frankton's schools.

Congratulations poured in—from other members of the school board, from the local Parent-Teacher Association president, from the teachers' organization, and from the superintendent. Ted was feeling a little noble himself. The superintendent suggested that they have lunch so that Ted could be briefed on some of the current business before the board. This would make it easier for him to plunge right in at the regularly scheduled meeting next month. Ted agreed and spent two hours over a club sandwich listening to a rundown of the district's prospects and problems as seen by the superintendent.

Over the next year, Ted faithfully made each of the sparsely attended biweekly sessions on Tuesday nights. On the Friday before each meeting, he received a packet of information from the district office, including the agenda for the upcoming meeting. He would always spend part of his weekend going over the material and deciding what his reaction would be to items that would be considered. School-district matters became a part of his conversations with associates and the subject of occasional telephone calls from friends at night. But, for the most part, Ted had decided that the district was being capably managed. He argued rather strongly for a tougher position in bargaining with the teachers' organization that spring and wound up on the board's negotiation team. He found little occasion, however, to go into any school, other than for award banquets or other ceremonial events.

When his wife raised questions about his plans for the future, Ted was evasive. In truth, the job was not much more of a strain than he had expected. It didn't hurt his practice any to be identified as a community leader. But sooner or later, perhaps after one more term of office, it would be someone else's turn.

Model 2: Issue-Oriented Candidates and Competitive Elections

Sarah Sandberg could hardly believe it! The evening paper said that the board of education was considering cutting back the science program at the high school that her son Tim went to. Sarah remembered perfectly well that the superintendent had assured parents that despite the deficit in district finances, the basic curriculum would not be weakened. George Sandberg was unhappy too, but he ventured that there were no doubt good reasons for dropping a few of those advanced courses that enrolled so few students. Sarah found a better sounding board for her indignation with a call to Jane Stewart, longtime friend, former president of the League of Women Voters, and presently serving on the PTA board with Sarah. "It's just a crime," she gasped, "to start cutting the science curriculum just when they ought to be strengthening it. You know they'll be trying to lay off teachers next—that's the only way they can save any real money. Seems like they would fire some of those assistant superintendents before they start dropping courses our kids need to get into a good college."

"Well, Sarah," Jane half-teased, "sooner or later we're going to have to elect some people with common sense to that board. You'd make a perfect candidate."

It was George's condescending smile that made Sarah's decision final. She would challenge "those smug bastards" next fall. In the meantime, she started attending every board meeting, noting who voted which way, studying every issue right along with the board members. More and more often she spoke out from the floor, especially whenever the curriculum came up.

By the time she declared her candidacy in September, administrators, board members, and a few teachers knew who she was and where she stood on a number of issues. Two other newcomers, similarly upset about the financial management of the district, had also emerged to challenge the three incumbents up for reelection. Since the election was "at large," the three candidates receiving the largest number of votes would win seats. Sarah knew that most of the advantages would normally lie with the incumbents in such a race. But strong resentment was brewing in the community about the way district finances had been handled and the possibility of another tax increase. Challengers who didn't have high name recognition among voters, or the experience of the incumbents to point to, would have to rely on that major issue and the general feeling that it was time for a change in Edgewood School District. It would take an active campaign to get Sarah and her message before the voters.

Sarah made many telephone calls to potential supporters and spent mornings poring over district budgets, advisory-committee reports, and state and national statistics. More than once in the weeks to come, her research would pay off in telling exchanges with opponents. She gave the impression of being not only earnest, but knowledgeable about schools. More of her personal savings account than George thought wise went into her candidacy. Television and newspapers are not very suitable advertising media for suburban campaigns, so a volunteer Committee to Elect Sarah Sandberg was formed to distribute handbills door to door with a personal touch. Large advertisements were placed in an area shopping guide distributed at supermarkets.

Everywhere Sarah spoke—at PTA meetings, at the League of Women Voters, on a panel TV show—she lashed out at "rubber-stamp board members who don't do their homework and don't find out what the public wants." Then she would make her pitch for improving the curriculum and organizing strong advisory councils of students, teachers, parents, and other citizens for each school building. Much to the consternation of district administrators, she visited first-grade classes, high school English classes, and special education classes. When not observing classes, she was peppering the district business manager with questions about the state school-aid formula. Board members not up for reelection were somewhat patronizing. Several favorable letters to the editor appeared. The only area daily newspaper endorsed her, along with a host of candidates in other districts. Many citizens were at first bemused but soon started listening. Still, Sarah was not at all sure, by election eve, whether she would be first or last in the balloting. She and her small coterie of supporters celebrated as the turnout edged toward 40 percent and it became clear that she would run second to the other leading challenger. Between them they had narrowly ousted two of the three incumbents running for reelection.

Sarah's term on the school board marked a turning point for Edgewood School District. For the first time in memory, the superintendent was grilled about the details of almost everything he presented. Proposals for new programs or action started coming from the board, with requests for the administration to look into the feasibility of the idea and report back at the next board meeting. A well-orchestrated show of support for stiffer graduation requirements scuttled the tentative plans for eliminating the advanced placement program in math and physics. Then came the administration's quiet decision not to renew the contract of an untenured geometry teacher who had publicly declared that he was gay. Sarah sprang to the young man's defense and rallied at least two and maybe three other board members to her side. She argued that there was absolutely no evidence that the man's sexual orientation had affected his teaching in any way. The press picked up the issue about what had happened in the board's executive sessions. Shortly after the American Civil Liberties Union started making inquiries, the superintendent renewed the contract.

Later the same year, the superintendent of Edgewood School District announced that he had accepted a position as deputy commissioner of education in a neighboring state. Sarah saw to it that several of her supporters were named to the search committee for a new superintendent. "Sooner or later," she said, "we're going to have to get someone with some common sense in that job."

Three Versions of the Policy Process

It is one thing to paint, in rather broad strokes, the manner in which local school policy is made but quite another thing to consider that process in terms of democratic theory. At least three major interpretations are possible. As indicated in the previous chapter, there is enough variety from one district to the next that it is doubtful that any single interpretation will do for all. But let us consider the three possibilities in turn.

The most romantic and the most popular version is that school policymaking at the district level is the last bastion of grass roots democracy. In this interpretation, citizens control their schools by electing like-minded, responsive board members who chart the future of the district by enacting policy for the superintendent and the administrative staff to implement. Board members who lose sight of citizen priorities are voted out of office. Any major problem with the schools is quickly and accurately communicated to board members, who then bring about the necessary changes. Citizens have ready access to the policy machinery and are able to keep close tabs on what is happening in the schools through their elected representatives. One presumed by-product of this classical democracy is a feeling of close identification with the school as an institution. This identification may be translated into support during times of need, such as tax-increase referenda.

The classical democracy interpretation is one carefully fostered by civics textbooks and school-board associations. It does have its weak points, however. Evidence to date indicates that, in general, public knowledge of and interest in education policy is far lower than one might expect. For most citizens, reports of six-car pileups on the local interstate, results of the NFL play-offs, and what the president is doing about crime in the streets will be read, whereas the page-4 article about last night's school-board meeting goes unnoticed. It is not that the public is incapable of becoming aroused over educational issues on occasion, but the notion that very many citizens will monitor, much less react to, the week-to-week vicissitudes of public schools is, to say the least, naïve.

A second interpretation focuses on the alleged domination of school policymaking by superintendents as the salient feature. Given the inability of elected, lay board members to control the routine operation of the district effectively, proponents of this view see a professional, managerial class—headed by superintendents—that has imposed its values on public schools. Although professional educators are not all from the same mold, they have had extensive and, to some extent, common socializing experiences. The vast majority have taught school, earned teaching and administrative credentials in teacher colleges, read many of the same books and journals, attended the same professional meetings, and committed their work lives to education. These kinds of experiences fairly effectively weed out people who believe too much money is spent on educating children. They tend to produce administrators who believe that all children—even those with severe physical, mental, emotional, economic, or social disadvantages—should have an opportunity to develop to their fullest potential.

Those advancing the professional-dominance interpretation of local policymaking argue that professional socializing experiences have also produced a cadre of educators who feel that they are so firmly in possession of truth that what parents, students, and other citizens want does not matter very much. Years of arguing about the "right" answer to many problems have left professionals less sensitive than they might be to preferences of groups and individuals in the community. A more "political" system, these critics believe, is called for, in which discontents would be aired openly, issues joined and argued out, and professional dogma challenged by representatives emerging from competitive, issue-oriented, elections.

More recently, a third interpretation of the policy process has emerged that falls somewhere between the classical democracy and the professional-domination versions, while rejecting both. According to this view, although citizens do not keep very careful tabs on their schools, they do elect board members who roughly reflect their most deeply held values. In a sense, these board members become the public's agents to make sure things do not get too far out of hand. Though the board does not have the effective means to challenge or control the superintendent every step of the way, if things get bad enough, the board does have one ace up its sleeve—its power to dismiss the superintendent. Public apathy and "rubber-stamp" boards may, then, simply be symptomatic of districts where things are proceeding well and everyone is relatively satisfied. Districts in turmoil, on the other hand, are those where the professional leaders have strayed beyond the limits imposed by the values of board members and the public.

For those who find that process a cumbersome, inefficient way to proceed, there is some solace. Boyd (1976) has reminded us of the old "law of anticipated reactions" and applied it to educational policymaking (pp. 556–558). Since superintendents know that despite their tactical advantages over the board in day-to-day affairs, they must ultimately keep that board satisfied or lose their jobs, they will attempt to anticipate the reactions of board members to initiatives they are considering. Looking ahead, a superintendent may discern quite a range of actions that the board of education would support and confine his or her leadership to these programs. There may also be a number of things that a superintendent would like to do but that are simply rejected as unfeasible given the present makeup of the board. What we wind up with, then, is a mechanism by which the board can control, or at least limit, the behavior of the superintendent without lifting a finger. It is a very difficult mechanism to document, because it takes place without overt actions. Intuitively, however, it seems plausible that board members, by merely communicating their values to the superintendent, may encourage that superintendent to give greater attention to their agenda or head off adventures that might ultimately force the board to take matters into its own hands.

Collective Bargaining

The most pervasive changes in the local educational power structure have been brought about by the now prevalent practice of negotiating formally with an organization, designated as the bargaining agent for teachers, over the provisions of a contract that will set forth the terms of their service in the coming academic year. From the standpoint of policymaking, this means that decisions—concerning a salary schedule and a host of other questions as well—once made exclusively by the board of education and the superintendent are now made in a bargaining mode. From the standpoint of power relationships, collective bargaining has strengthened the hand of teachers at the expense of board and administration.

The financial aspects of collective bargaining will be dealt with more extensively in Chapter 18. For now, however, this section will examine the effects of negotiation on local policymaking. A prime concern of each of the major teacher organizations nationally has been to obtain bargaining rights for teachers. National collective bargaining legislation that would clarify the position and status of teachers in collective negotiation was a priority item of professional groups for years, but Congress has preferred to leave it to the states. Most states now have a collective bargaining law for public employees, and the vast majority of teachers have now organized and bargain effectively with district authorities.

There is little mystery about how teachers have enhanced their own power vis-à-vis district authorities. Recall that the exercise of power requires the ability to make a credible promise or threat. Once teachers established that they were willing and able to withhold their services if the board did not negotiate in good faith, the scales began to tip. Board members might claim that teachers' demands were unreasonable, but the prospect of turning children away because of a teacher strike was sobering. Where strikes did occur, parents proved perfectly capable of holding teachers, administrators, and the school board all responsible. Pressure quickly mounted on board members to get the thing settled and get the children back in school, where they belonged. Attempts to replace striking teachers were sometimes of dubious legality and more often simply not feasible.

The deck is not stacked entirely in favor of teachers in a strike situation, however. Successful work stoppages require substantial solidarity among teachers. If large numbers of teachers do not belong to the organization, or cross picket lines, the effectiveness of the strike is reduced accordingly. In most cases, teachers will not be paid for the time they are on strike and, although strike funds may help, the salary foregone in a long strike has lowered the resolution of many teachers to hold out for a more favorable settlement. Furthermore, if a strike ends without a favorable settlement for teachers, the effectiveness of a strike threat in future years is likely to be reduced.

Site-Based Management

One of the potentially far-reaching reforms of the late 1980s and early 1990s, at least in organizational terms, was the movement toward site-based (i.e., school-based) management. In most proposals, a local school council would be given some policymaking authority over the school budget, curriculum, and personnel issues. In Chicago, that authority even includes the power to review the performance of the school principal and remove the incumbent. In some other districts, school councils have been formed but are given little real authority by which to exercise influence on the important policy issues facing the schools.

Proponents of site-based management argue that more authority at the school site will break the logjam of bureaucracy that they think keeps schools from being as effective as they might be. In large urban school districts, the school board and central office can be far removed from the hundreds of schools in the district. In the typical centralized district, requests from teachers or principals may be ruled on by a deputy superintendent or central office staff member with little knowledge of the particular circumstances in that school. Critics of these highly bureaucratized systems see little hope of bringing about significant innovations in an organizational environment characterized by "top-down" management with little opportunity for input from below.

Site-based management may mean nothing more than giving more authority to building principals in a traditional hierarchical structure. Recent proposals, however, have usually called for a school council of professional educators and lay citizens. By this device, site-based management connects with the political demand for more choice in the educational system. Advocates of school councils lash out at the "monopolistic" educational system which, because the bureaucracy imposes uniformity on all schools in the district, affords very little choice to parents or school children. The remedy, according to these advocates, is to give school councils sufficient discretion to develop the kind of schools they want. Then schools will be more imaginative and more diverse.

The next step of the argument brings the issue back to choice. If schools are not all alike, then parents should be permitted to choose where their children go to school. Aside from giving parents the opportunity to put their children in schools that better serve their individual needs and interests, the resulting competition between schools should serve as an incentive to teachers and administrators to make their school more attractive to pupils and their parents.

Whether or not site-based management will bring about the dramatic improvement in schools predicted by its advocates, it is clear it has the potential to alter authority relationships dramatically in the local school district. Depending on the composition of a school council and the powers granted to it, the principal, teachers, and the superintendent may all find their roles significantly changed from the traditional pattern that emerged in the twentieth century.

Referenda

One of the legacies of the political-reform movements of the first half of the twentieth century that had a special impact on education is the referendum. As big-city political machines and state legislatures made headlines with various kinds of corrupt practices, many states turned to three varieties of "direct democracy"—the initiative, the referendum, and the recall—as ways of keeping their elected representatives in line. Of the three, initiative and recall were destined to be used only infrequently, but the referendum, by which voters reserved the right to vote directly on certain kinds of substantive questions, became an important part of the way in which many school districts were financed.

As separate taxing units, most school boards may set tax rates for their districts within the maximum set by state law. But to provide flexibility in districts where the maximum rate will not generate sufficient revenue, districts may be allowed to submit to the voters of the district a proposal to increase taxes beyond the maximum. A simple majority of those voting is usually required to approve the issue. Similarly, proposals to sell bonds as a means of financing a new building or meeting other major expenditures may require, by state law, the endorsement of the voters. Partly because of the nature of school finance, referenda and bond elections have been more common in education than in any other field of government.

The most interesting thing about referenda, other than that they constitute a rare vestige of direct democracy in the U.S. system, is that they frequently become something more than straightforward decisions about tax rates. They may be viewed by many voters as an opportunity to hold the board and the superintendent more or less accountable for the district's fortunes.

Voters' calculations in deciding whether to support a tax increase include their assessment of whether the schools need the additional funds, their views on whether the new funds will be used wisely, and their opinion about how much the tax increase will hurt them individually. The reputation of district administrators for sound fiscal management clearly increases the chances of passing a tax increase. High unemployment or recession hurts those chances (Coombs & Bell, 1985).

Hundreds of studies have been done on various aspects of school referenda. Although few have systematically examined more than a single district's experience, we now have at least tentative answers to three interesting questions: Who votes in them and why? What kind of voter is most likely to support increasing taxes for educational purposes? And what factors, in general, contribute to passage of a proposed tax increase or bond sale? Let us look at what researchers have found with respect to each of these questions.

In referenda, as in school-board elections, it is not a cross-section of the eligible voters who actually go to the polls. Higher-status voters—the better educated, higher income, middle-aged—have historically been more likely to vote in all elections, and the effect is even more pronounced in nonpartisan, low-information local elections than in presidential elections. The two explanations most often advanced for this phenomenon revolve around the concepts of civic duty and political efficacy. Many higher-status citizens apparently have been more thoroughly indoctrinated in the importance of voting. They tend to view voting as a civic duty irrespective of the outcome of any particular election.

It may also be that higher-status individuals have a better-developed (some might even say overdeveloped) sense of their own ability to affect things by voting. Political scientists have dubbed this a person's "subjective sense of political efficacy" and find that it is higher in people who are economically and socially advantaged (Verba & Nie, 1972, p. 19). It is a plausible guess that those who believe that their votes matter in shaping the future of the local schools will be more likely to get to the polls than other individuals who believe that their votes probably will not make any difference.

The answer to the second question—Why do individuals vote for or against tax-increase proposals?—is not quite the same. Here, one finds that younger citizens with school-age children, coming from either the skilled-labor or white-collar ranks, are most likely to support school-tax increases. There is some evidence that those recently arrived in the community are also more likely to vote yes. On the other hand, young adults without children, parents of youngsters in private schools, the elderly, professionals, and long-time community residents are more likely to oppose the increased financial burden (Wirt & Kirst, 1972, pp. 101–104).

Once again, two kinds of explanations have been advanced by voting scholars for why people vote the way they do in nonpartisan elections such as referenda. The first of these emphasizes what Banfield and Wilson (1963) called a sense of "public regardingness" (pp. 234–240). Although some citizens are primarily motivated, even in public affairs, by privatistic "What's in it for me?" concerns, others appear to be largely motivated by their perception of the public interest. Thus, even the elderly, wealthy property owner without children might support school referenda just because she or he believes that education is a great opportunity for everyone and that society would be much better off if efforts in that domain were increased.

There is, however, another side to voting choice, as other scholars have been quick to point out. For many, it may boil down to a calculation of whether the voter's own interests will be served. Following this line of reasoning, people with children who would benefit more directly should, on balance, be supportive, whereas those who are least able to bear the brunt of the tax increase (including renters, since tax increases are usually passed on to the tenant) should lead the opposition. Furthermore, the larger the tax increase, the more people should be inclined to vote against it. Even the economic climate at the time of the referendum may be a factor, persuading some voters to vote against another assault on their pocketbooks during times of inflationary pressure, unemployment, or recession.

Many observers have been struck by the manner in which referenda quickly become symbolic opportunities for the voter to express displeasure with almost any aspect of public, or even private, affairs. In the normal course of events, citizens have little opportunity to vent their indignation about budget deficits, the increasing cost of health care, government bailouts, or a recession that threatens their own jobs. A school referendum coming along at the wrong time may be a tempting opportunity for a citizen to let "them" know that he or she cannot be pushed any further. To put it another way, a citizen has to have a high regard for education and its consequences to vote against his or her other apparent financial interests by supporting a tax increase.

Theory about why people vote and which way they vote should be a help in listing the factors that augur well for a successful referendum. Most generally, the chances for success of a referendum are higher when turnout is small. Small turnout indicates that voters with a high sense of citizen duty and "public regardingness" are about the only ones to make it to the polls. Higher turnout is often symptomatic of dissatisfaction. One or more major issues may have captured public attention and activated the privatistic interests of voters who would otherwise not have voted. As one would expect, there also appears to be an empirical relationship between the size of the increase sought, the general economic climate, and even the time of year (administrators understandably try to avoid scheduling referenda in the period just after citizens have paid last year's real estate taxes) (Wirt & Kirst, 1972, pp. 104–108).

The successful management of a tax-increase referendum will be a feather in the career cap of the district superintendent. Teachers, the PTA, many parents, and administrators in other districts will all applaud his or her political wizardry in extracting more revenue from the public for such a good cause. Yet more than one superintendent has noted an awkwardness about the process. From the research just discussed, it seems clear that prospects for passage will be better if the whole thing is kept rather quiet: Avoid mobilizing the opposition; ignore them if they do mobilize; play down any issues that emerge; and reassure one and all that the local schools are the best schools possible and that they just need a little more money to keep them that way.

Political scientists such as Zeigler and Jennings complain that school governance is not political enough, that some issues are never raised, that the public is not as interested or as well informed as it should be, and that the public exerts little guidance—even through elected board members—over the professionals running the district (Zeigler & Jennings, 1974). It is difficult to argue with suggestions that local school policymaking should be more open, better publicized, and even more conflictual if the public is to maintain its long-standing tradition of lay control in an era of strong professionalism. When dealing with referenda, however, school administrators have usually favored attempts to develop consensus rather than engage in noisier battles that might serve to stimulate competing claims from various interests within the district—claims that would then have to be reconciled.

Summary

Although authority has shifted in recent years toward the state and national levels of educational policymaking, local school districts retain sufficient discretion to shape educational programs dramatically. By looking at three local levels of policymaking—the classroom, the school building, and the district—one finds a surprising range of important educational decisions being made at each level.

District policy is the outgrowth of community interests as interpreted and adjudicated by the superintendent and a board of education. The relationship between superintendent and board may take many forms, but their different role definitions create a climate often characterized by underlying tension. Superintendents typically have the advantage in managing the day-to-day operations of the district, but boards may still play a major role in charting the future of the district, directly through their power of appointment and dismissal and indirectly through the probability that the superintendent will attempt to anticipate board reactions to administrative proposals and to tailor major initiatives to reflect dominant values and interests represented on the board.

A challenge to the authority of the superintendent and board has come from teachers, in the form of collective bargaining. Although ultimate authority to approve a contract with teachers may remain with the board, one effect of collective bargaining is to involve teachers much more intimately in an array of policy issues once left largely to the board.

Referenda for approval of tax increases and other educational purposes provide interesting insights into the nature and distribution of public support for education. While that support appears to be relatively solid today, compared with other social and political institutions, there are many who fear that erosion of support, stemming from demographic and social changes in the years ahead, will change the public school system in fundamental ways.

References

Banfield, E. C., & Wilson, J. Q. (1963). *City politics.* Cambridge, MA: Harvard University Press.

Boyd, W. L. (1976, May). The public, the professionals, and educational policy making: Who governs? *Teachers College Record, 77.*

Chesler, M., Schmuck, R. A., & Lippitt, R. (1975). In J. V. Baldridge & T. Deal (Eds.), *Managing change in educational organizations: Sociological perspectives, strategies, and case studies* (pp. 321–327). Berkeley: McCutchan.

Coombs, F. S., & Bell, C. S. (1985). *Who believes the schools need more money?* Paper presented at the American Education Finance Association meetings, Phoenix, AZ.

Donley, M. O., Jr. (1976). *Power to the teacher: How America's educators became militant.* Bloomington: Indiana University Press.

Elam, S. M., Rose, L. C., & Gallup, A. M. (1996, September). The 28th annual Phi Delta Kappa/ Gallup poll of the public's attitudes toward the public schools. *Phi Delta Kappan, 41–59.*

Tarazi, G. J., Curcio, J. L., & Fortune, J. C. (1997, January). Where you stand: Do school board members' religious and political beliefs affect their board decisions? *The American School Board Journal, 26–29.*

Verba, S., & Nie, N. H. (1972). *Participation in America: Political democracy and social equality.* New York: Harper and Row.

Wirt, F. M., & Kirst, M. W. (1972). *The political web of American schools.* Boston: Little, Brown.

Zeigler, L. H., & Jennings, M. K., with Peak, W. G. (1974). *Governing American schools.* North Scituate, MA: Duxbury Press.

Chapter *14*

The Influence of the Federal Government

Should you come across a retired school administrator whose career started before, say, 1960, you are probably in for a lecture about the "good old days." It was, in many ways, a simpler world for most administrators—a world that seldom required bargaining with powerful teacher organizations or responding to civil suits. The federal government had a limited agenda in education and affected the day-to-day life of school administrators very little. Warnings about the dire consequences of "federal control of education" were enough to fend off most congressional adventures into the realm of public schools.

What contrasts would a retired school administrator find today if he or she wandered into the district offices of a modern prototypical school district? Spread out on a conference table is a large map of the district, with residential housing patterns delineated and school enrollments pinpointed by race. The district desegregation plan, drawn up three years earlier, is being revised, and the report to the state office, showing compliance with state and federal guidelines, is due next week. Those guidelines—an amalgam of policy set by the state board of education, courts, and various federal agencies—serve as a standard for determining whether the district is in compliance and, if not, what it needs to do to remedy the situation. Changes in those guidelines, as well as shifting residential patterns and decline in school enrollment, have made each review a major undertaking.

Meanwhile, the business manager is completing the Title I count of children in the district who meet the criteria of "economically disadvantaged." Even minor errors in interpreting the convoluted rules and regulations applying to this report may mean the loss of thousands of dollars in federal aid to the district.

An assistant superintendent is on the phone with one of the elementary principals. The father of a third-grade girl with Down syndrome wants his daughter placed in a private program at school-district expense. At the girl's "staffing,"

269

everyone except the father agreed that the special education program she is already in is the appropriate placement. The principal wants the central office to check PL 94-142, the Civil Rights Act, Section 504 of the Rehabilitation Act, the Individuals with Disabilities Education Act, and the regulations set up to administer each of these laws one more time to make certain the district has done everything it should to comply with federal law. Next door, a clerk is preparing the district's application for reimbursement by the federal school-breakfast-and-lunch program.

Today, it is no longer enough for the school administrator to know what citizens in the local district want and to try to bring that about. A welter of state and federal laws, court decisions, rules and regulations, guidelines, and deadlines have changed both the local administrator's job and the locus of authority within the educational-policy system. Although many vital decisions are still made at the district, building, and classroom levels, intervention by state and federal government in educational matters is no longer limited to superficial or noncontroversial matters. Indeed, one can make a strong argument to the effect that the most important policy *changes* in education since World War II have been introduced by federal or state authorities.

The Early History of Federal Involvement

No reference to education is made in the U.S. Constitution. Under the Tenth Amendment, which says that powers not delegated to the federal government will be reserved to the states, the founding fathers left primary responsibility for this important governmental function to the states. Had they opted instead for including education as a responsibility of the federal government, U.S. schools might have developed as a national system similar to those found today in many European countries.

Even before the Constitutional Convention, the colonies had taken some responsibility for developing a system of schools. As early as 1647, the legislature of colonial Massachusetts required its communities to provide schooling from public tax money. As the young republic forged into the nineteenth century, two principles that are more or less taken for granted today took root. The first principle claimed that education was a public good and should be provided at public expense to common folk as well as the aristocracy. It was resisted by some of the wealthy, who sensed that sharing their monopoly on education would also mean sharing power, and by individualists who argued that one person should not have to pay for the education of another person's child.

The second principle that emerged was that not only should the public benefit from free education but it should also control it. Lay control of public schools became a distinguishing feature of the country's system as it grew. The notion that schools should be held accountable by local citizens led to elected school boards, as well as elected county and state superintendents. It was not that trained professionals had nothing to contribute. Indeed, they came to be seen as indispensable. But the U.S.

public developed a strong proprietary feeling about its schools. Seldom paying detailed attention to school matters, the public still reserves the right to decide when its schools have gone too far astray and how to put them back on track.

The fact that responsibility for education was not expressly delegated to the federal government by the U.S. Constitution did not mean that Congress would avoid all educational issues. The general-welfare clause of Article 1 provided ample warrant for the federal government to enact and implement a great deal of educational policy. Even as delegates to the Constitutional Convention debated the form of the new republic, Congress passed the Northwest Ordinance of 1787, which set aside the sixteenth section of every township in the new territories for public schools. The rationale was simply that the "religion, morality, and knowledge" provided by schooling were "necessary to good government and the happiness of mankind."

Federal initiatives in the educational realm were infrequent throughout the nineteenth century, however. In 1862, the Morrill Land Grant Act gave federal land to the states to be used for colleges specializing in agriculture and engineering. The "land grant" colleges that resulted remain a central feature of the country's system of higher education today. In 1867, Congress established the U.S. Office of Education, the forerunner of today's U.S. Department of Education, and placed the U.S. Commissioner of Education at its head. The first half of the twentieth century saw the Smith-Hughes Act (1917) provide aid for industrial, agricultural, and home-economics programs in vocational education.

The Federal Role after World War II

A dramatic increase in federal involvement in education came in the years following World War II. In the most significant piece of federal education legislation to that date, Congress passed the Servicemen's Readjustment Act (popularly known as the GI Bill) in 1944, providing more than $15 billion worth of free college education to more than 8 million returning veterans. The legislation was inspired largely by the threat of wide-scale unemployment, but it gave thousands of young men an opportunity to attend college and it established a strong precedent for federal intervention in educational matters. In 1946, the National School Lunch and Milk Programs helped reduce food surpluses and maintain prices, while providing nutritious meals for needy schoolchildren. Financial assistance for school districts that found their enrollments swelled and their property-tax bases diminished by military bases or other federal institutions came through the Federal Impacted Areas Aid Program of 1950.

For those who still had doubts about the extent of federal interest in elementary and secondary education, the U.S. Supreme Court's 1954 decision in *Brown* v. *Board of Education of Topeka* set them straight. That decision declared schools that were racially segregated by law to be unconstitutional. Although the full force of that decision was not to be felt for another 15 years, it left no doubt about the willingness of the courts to apply federal law to school affairs.

The National Defense Education Act (NDEA)

On October 4, 1957, the world awoke to learn that a Soviet satellite was orbiting the earth. For many Americans, the U.S.S.R.'s success with *Sputnik I* raised questions about the state of U.S. military preparedness. The shock of being beaten to space slowly gave way to a wave of public concern about the state of science, mathematics, and engineering education in the United States. Congress passed the National Defense Education Act (NDEA) the following year.

The new legislation provided loans to undergraduates, fellowships to graduate students, and funding for many college programs aimed at improving the training of U.S. teachers. Curriculum projects were funded immediately in mathematics, physics, chemistry, and foreign languages, soon to be followed by others in language arts and social studies. The "new math" appeared with a flourish, and other subject areas followed suit, each revising its niche in the elementary and secondary curriculum to reflect more faithfully the current state of their disciplines.

It was Washington's most intimate brush with curriculum. Most federal officials were sensitive to fears that federal involvement could lead to a standardized set of courses and texts, each with a stamp of approval from the U.S. Office of Education. More than one project was funded in each area of the curriculum, and developers still had to rely on private publishing houses for dissemination of their materials. Nevertheless, a Harvard anthropology curriculum project named "Man, a Course of Study" (MACOS) drew fire from the political right for its alleged cultural relativism.

The results were heartening if measured by America's subsequent success in space, but the longer-range impact of this era of curriculum development is still debated. Textbooks and lesson plans today give less attention to the structure of academic disciplines and discovery learning—two hallmarks of 1960s curriculum.

The Elementary and Secondary Education Act of 1965 (ESEA)

By 1965, the stage was set for a quite different federal initiative. With the assassination of President John F. Kennedy in 1963 and the succession of Lyndon B. Johnson to the presidency, Congress and the White House launched an attack on poverty and racism with one of the most sweeping legislative programs in the history of the country. The Civil Rights Act of 1964, which authorized withholding federal funds from segregated schools, and the Economic Opportunity Act of 1964, which fostered programs such as Operation Head Start, Follow Through, and Upward Bound, were joined by the Elementary and Secondary Education Act of 1965.

The Elementary and Secondary Education Act (ESEA) constituted a major effort to improve the educational opportunities of low-income and educationally disadvantaged pupils. The United States had been among the first nations to achieve virtually universal education for all children through age 16. Still, it was painfully evident that youngsters from educationally disadvantaged backgrounds displayed much lower academic achievement, on average, than children from educationally advantaged backgrounds. Furthermore, the gap appeared to widen, rather than close, at higher grade levels. By far the largest portion of the funds appropriated for ESEA went to Title I, a set of programs providing financial assistance to local school districts that served areas with heavy concentrations of children from low-income families. Local education authorities made application for funding to the U.S. Office of Education after counting the number of low-income children residing in their districts who were eligible for Title I assistance. Federal funds obtained were to be used to supplement educational programs already offered and could not replace existing funding from local or state sources.

Over the years, Title I has pumped up to $7 billion a year into some of the nation's most financially strapped school districts, including most of the urban districts in the country. Its remedial programs have spawned a political constituency that strives to protect its funding in periods of intense federal budget cutting.

Other titles of ESEA funded such things as school libraries and supplementary educational centers. In the 1972 amendments to ESEA, Title IX was added, addressing questions of sex equity in schools. The most immediate impact of Title IX was felt in girls' athletics and physical-education courses, but the law was aimed at all structures or practices that discriminate against females in admissions, course offerings, employment, or financial aid. Courses such as auto mechanics or home economics would now have to be offered to everyone, irrespective of gender.

The Education for All Handicapped Children Act (Public Law 94-142)

In 1974, Congress passed the Education for All Handicapped Children Act, a bold declaration of the rights of children with disabilities to a free, adequate education in the "least restrictive environment." The special education lobby had strongly endorsed the concept of mainstreaming, which would place youngsters with disabilities in regular classrooms and programs to the fullest extent feasible. The other revolutionary aspect of PL 94-142 was the requirement that an individualized educational program (IEP) be prepared by a team of professionals (teacher, principal, counselor, social worker) and the child's parent or parents.

Improving America's Schools Act of 1994 (IASA)

In 1994, Congress passed the Improving America's Schools Act (IASA), which consisted primarily of reform-oriented amendments to ESEA, the General Education Provision Act, and other existing legislation. The underlying themes of the new act were high standards for all students, flexible programs that would serve to stimulate initiatives by local districts, and the encouragement of partnerships between schools and community agencies, corporations, academic institutions, or parent groups. Title I remained the centerpiece of the federal government's compensatory efforts, but was amended in 1995 to focus on "extended time-for-learning" programs (e.g., after school, summer school) rather than the traditional practice of pulling students out of their regular classrooms for individual help. The same legislation encouraged schoolwide projects in schools serving large numbers of disadvantaged children.

Individuals with Disabilities Education Act of 1995 (IDEA)

The first substantial revisions to PL 94-142 were enacted in 1995 in the Individuals with Disabilities Education Act (IDEA). These amendments continued to stress meeting the individual needs of the nation's 5.4 million children with disabilities in the least restrictive environment and including them in the general curriculum to the maximum extent appropriate, but many of the changes were aimed at providing better teaching and learning within that context.

Categorical Aid for Economic and Social Problems

By now, you have probably noticed that federal dollars were hardly ever appropriated simply to help out a school's existing programs. General aid of that kind comes largely from local and state sources. Historically, the federal government has initiated specific educational programs to try to solve society's noneducational problems: unemployed veterans, a shortage of engineers, threats to national defense, a racially segregated society, malnutrition, poverty, gender inequities, and so on. Most federal aid has been targeted for these and other specific programs through "categorical" grants. Categorical aid, such as Title I, can be used only for clearly defined objectives. Local school districts must adhere to program guidelines and be able to demonstrate that the funds were used for the intended purpose.

There is a sharp divergence of opinion about how effective federal categorical programs in education have been. Those who support them argue that many of the needed changes in schools—upgraded curricula, school desegregation, compensatory programs for the educationally disadvantaged, bilingual programs for pupils of limited English proficiency, and individualized programs for special education students, to name but a few—were stimulated by federal categorical programs. Detractors of categorical programs counter that the money would be better spent if policymakers closer to the local district had more discretion in how it is used. Almost everyone agrees that the mountains of paperwork created by federal categorical programs must somehow be reduced.

Exit Equity, Enter Excellence

The federal education programs of the late 1960s and early 1970s, with few exceptions, were attempts to expand equality of educational opportunity. African Americans, Latinos, Native Americans, the poor, the disabled, women, immigrants—all were the beneficiaries of legislation written to remove at least some of the existing barriers. Full access to schooling was part of the equity movement, but the movement also included compensatory programs designed to help overcome cultural, social, economic, or physical impediments to learning.

Starting in the late 1970s, the federal preoccupation with equity began to give way to concerns about the quality of U.S. schools. The "excellence movement," as some have dubbed it, was fed by news stories about declining Scholastic Aptitude

Test (SAT) and American College Test (ACT) scores registered by college-bound high school seniors and a widespread perception that school discipline was not the way it was in the good old days. Public confidence in the country's schools was waning. By 1981, the situation was ripe for a new conservative, budget-conscious administration to deemphasize equity programs and call for states and local districts to improve schools for all children.

Presidential Politics and School Reform

Ronald Reagan's campaign for the presidency in 1980 left no doubt of how he felt about the U.S. Department of Education that President Jimmy Carter had created. He placed its elimination high on his list of presidential priorities, once elected. The fact that the National Education Association (NEA) had lobbied for it, together with his own ideological commitment to provide state and local education leaders more latitude in policy matters, had persuaded Reagan that this would be a good place to start trimming the Washington bureaucracy. It became clear in the first year of Reagan's administration, however, that there was little support in Congress for abolishing the young department. Secretary of Education Terrel H. Bell quickly turned his attention to other items on the Reagan education agenda.

What the new administration's team wanted was nothing less than a basic transformation of the federal role in education. If there had to be a Department of Education, it would serve as a beacon for good educational practice rather than a growing source of funding for all public schools. Research on school improvement would show the way; state and local education agencies would make more of the key decisions and cough up more of the money.

There was a substantive agenda as well. In the name of family choice, bills allowing tuition tax credits of up to $500 for families who send their children to private schools received the administration's blessing in Congress. Congress resisted, many members fearing that tuition tax credits might erode vital support for public schools. Others were concerned about possible constitutional challenges based on the separation of church and state or were simply unwilling to add billions of dollars in lost revenue to an already critical federal deficit.

One of Reagan's most frequent campaign promises was to get prayer back into the public schools. By the second year of his presidency, pressure for action was mounting from representatives of the political right, such as Moral Majority. In May 1982, he forwarded to Congress a proposed constitutional amendment that would allow voluntary group prayer in public schools. It read:

> *Nothing in this Constitution shall be construed to prohibit individual or group prayer in the public schools or in other public institutions. No person shall be required by the United States or by any State to participate in prayer.*

Since 1962, the U.S. Supreme Court decision in *Engle* v. *Vitale* had prohibited officially composed school prayers. According to public-opinion polls, however, 8 of 10 Americans favored permitting voluntary prayers in public schools (Gallup, 1983). The House of Representatives approved the proposed amendment, but in the Senate the administration could not muster the required two-thirds vote necessary to send it to the states for ratification.

A Nation at Risk

As discussed in Chapter 1, the most far-reaching educational initiative of the early Reagan years was the publication, in April 1983, of a report by the National Commission on Excellence in Education (NCEE) entitled *A Nation at Risk: The Imperative for Education Reform.* Secretary Bell had appointed the 18-member commission, made up primarily of educators, to assess the quality of education at all levels in both public and private schools. Their report warned that "the educational foundations of our society are presently being eroded by a rising tide of mediocrity that threatens our very future as a nation and a people." The immediate threat posed by this erosion of educational quality, according to the report, was to our "once unchallenged preeminence in commerce, industry, science, and technological innovation" by foreign competitors in international markets as our nation moves from an industrial-based to an information-based economy (National Commission on Excellence in Education, 1983, p. 5).

Recommendations of the commission included a call for strengthening state and local high school graduation requirements to include four years of English, three years of mathematics, three years of science, three years of social studies, one-half year of computer science, and, for college-bound students, two years of foreign language. Colleges and universities were to raise their admission requirements accordingly. In order to devote more time to the new basics, a longer school day, a lengthened school year, or more effective use of the existing school day was proposed. The teaching profession was to be strengthened by tightening standards in teacher-preparation programs, increasing teaching salaries, rewarding superior teachers and improving or terminating poor ones after peer evaluations, and establishing career ladders.

The response to this document may have been unprecedented for a government report. The president hailed it, national television gave it detailed coverage, and the print press scrutinized it. Its authors soon found their sense of urgency and some of their recommendations echoed in reports from the Education Commission of the States, the National Science Board, the Twentieth Century Fund Task Force on Federal Elementary and Secondary Education Policy, and thoughtful books by three of the nation's respected educators—John I. Goodlad (1984), Ernest L. Boyer (1983), and Theodore R. Sizer (1984).

The impact of the "excellence" movement triggered by *A Nation at Risk* and its progeny was not primarily at the federal level. Most of the reforms called for were matters for state or local policymakers. The real measure of the report's influence was the number of state legislatures enacting significant educational-reform programs in the years following. As the scope of the national reform became clear, the Reagan administration could claim to have provided federal leadership for school improvement while leaving the implementation of the changes to lower levels of government.

In November 1989, President George Bush convened an education summit in Charlottesville, Virginia, with the nation's governors in attendance. The primary accomplishment was adoption of a set of national education goals to be reached by the year 2000.

- *All children in America will start school ready to learn.*
- *The high school graduation rate will have increased to at least 90 percent.*
- *American students will leave grades four, eight, and twelve having demonstrated competency over challenging subject matter including English, mathematics, science, history, and geography; and every school in America will ensure that all students learn to use their minds well, so they may be prepared for responsible citizenship, further learning, and productive employment in our Nation's modern economy.*
- *U.S. students will be first in the world in science and mathematics achievement.*
- *Every adult American will be literate and will possess the knowledge and skills necessary to compete in a global economy and exercise the rights and responsibilities of citizenship.*
- *Every school in America will be free of drugs and violence and will offer a disciplined environment conducive to learning.* (Goals 2000, *1994*)

The promised change in the federal role was on schedule.

In reviewing federal education policy in the 1980s, Clark and Astuto (1990) remind readers that despite President George Bush's campaign as an education president, federal education programs continued to be characterized by low priority, few initiatives, and declining fiscal support. For one thing, the economic, ideological, and public opinion contexts within which federal policy is fashioned create constraints that make movement away from the status quo highly improbable; for another, President Bush's personal convictions were perfectly consonant with this lower federal profile established during the Reagan years.

One of the governors who had played a leadership role at Charlottesville was William Jefferson Clinton. When the Arkansas Democrat was elected president in 1992, he wasted no time in reaffirming his commitment to national educational standards. George Bush's "America 2000" program became "Goals 2000" under Clinton, adding foreign languages, civics and government, economics, and the arts to the subjects in which achievement would be monitored. The list of goals was expanded to include better preparation of teachers and increased parental involvement. Financial incentives were offered to states and local education agencies (LEAs) that developed their own plans for meeting these goals.

Many professional educators find irony, and sometimes dismay, in the alternating cycles of political neglect and reform one experiences over the course of a career. Long-standing educational problems and familiar solutions reappear every so often, disguised in the latest terminology.

The tides of reform may change the educational seascape but they, in turn, are products of larger forces. Profound social and demographic changes have occurred in U.S. society, and others are just around the corner. Urban education clearly poses a major challenge for the future of the nation's society. Today, 30 percent of children in large cities live in poverty, and in some cities, the figure is over 60 percent. Minority students make up 75 percent of the enrollment in the largest city schools but these large urban districts spend $900 per child less each year than other districts (Bracey, 1993). Some 47 percent of the African American and 56 percent of the Hispanic adults in these cities are functionally illiterate or marginal readers. Almost one-third of the children of these Hispanic adults are dropping out of high school before graduation. Meanwhile, African American youngsters growing up in Washington, DC, have a fifty/fifty chance of finishing high school and, for those who don't finish, only a fifty/fifty chance of finding employment. The "inexorable cycle of failure" for the urban poor includes health problems, school failure, and adult illiteracy, leading to limited employment opportunities, unstable family relations, dependence on public aid, and in some cases incarceration (Clark & Astuto, 1990).

The Federal Education Establishment Today

Despite the welter of education programs emanating from Washington, one can question whether the United States has ever had a federal policy in education. Certainly there is no single center of planning and coordination within the nation's capital. The $26 billion appropriated (fiscal year 1997) for discretionary programs in the Department of Education is less than half the total federal expenditure for education. About 300 education programs are scattered across dozens of agencies. For example, overseas schools for the children of U.S. military personal are run by the Department of Defense, the Bureau of Indian Affairs in the Interior Department assumes much of the responsibility for the education of Native Americans, the $2 billion Head Start Program for disadvantaged preschool children resides in the Department of Health and Human Services, and the Department of Justice plays a role in the enforcement of the civil rights provisions of several laws affecting public schools. Nevertheless, there is a recognizable set of agencies, committees, and interest groups that, when the pieces are put together, constitutes an education establishment that is involved with many mainline policy issues in Washington. Here is a brief look at a few of the pieces of that puzzle.

The U.S. Department of Education (ED)

When President Jimmy Carter made his campaign pledge to establish a new Department of Education, he doubtless intended to fashion a coherent organizational structure out of the inchoate bureaucratic tangle. Early drafts, in fact, did call for collecting most federal education programs under the same roof. By the time the fledgling department squeaked into existence on a narrow vote in the House of Representatives, however, most other departments still had a firm grip on programs that had been slated for transfer. In fact, the final list of programs under ED was not very different from the roster found in the old U.S. Office of Education.

The department was controversial from the start. The NEA was the most powerful advocate for a cabinet-level secretary of education and had supported Carter's candidacy following his commitment to the reorganization. They argued that only with such a department would education wield sufficient clout in status-conscious Washington to compete successfully for its share of the budget pie. Others, even within the education community, were not so sure. The American Federation of Teachers (AFT) opposed the creation of the new department on the grounds that moving from a protected position in one of the largest federal departments (HEW) to a more exposed position as its own small department might well make education more vulnerable than ever.

The Department of Education's 5,000 employees make it by far the smallest federal department in terms of personnel. The money it spends each year, however, ranks it above the departments of Commerce, Energy, Interior, Justice, and State but far behind such bureaucratic behemoths as the Department of Defense or the Department of Health and Human Services.

The high priesthood of the Department of Education is composed of the secretary of education, a deputy secretary, and an under secretary. A set of assistant secretaries supervise certain agency programs such as elementary and secondary education, postsecondary education, vocational and adult education, special education and rehabilitation services, and educational research and improvement.

Agencies sheltered under the organizational umbrella of the department include the Fund for the Improvement of Postsecondary Education, the Institute of Museum Services, the Office of Libraries and Learning Technologies, the Office of Dissemination and Professional Improvement, and the National Center for Educational Statistics. Secretary William Bennett announced in 1985 the incorporation within the Department of Education of the major research, development, and dissemination functions that had been performed by the National Institute of Education since its establishment as a semiautonomous organization in 1972. One of the last acts of Secretary of Education Lauro Cavazos was to establish a new Center for Choice in Education within the Office of Education Research and Improvement (OERI) of the Department of Education. His successor, Lamar Alexander, pledged upon his appointment in 1991 to continue the federal effort in school improvement, move energetically toward systems of choice, and launch a program designed to invent new kinds of schools. Richard Riley, former governor of South Carolina, was appointed Secretary of Education in 1993 and focused on school improvement through closer cooperation with the states.

The Department of Education and its many offices have primary responsibility for implementing and administering educational programs passed by the Congress. That charge includes the development of detailed rules and regulations that spell out the way the law will be applied. An administrative agency is required by law to provide ample notice in the *Federal Register* of proposed new rules and must extend an opportunity to interested groups and individuals to introduce evidence at hearings. Such hearings have, on occasion, persuaded ED to withdraw or modify proposed rules. The storm of protest greeting new bilingual education rules drawn up after the U.S. Supreme Court decision in *Lau* v. *Nichols* (1974) brought administration of that program to a virtual standstill in the ensuing months.

The work of executive agencies is not confined to implementation, however. The Department of Education plays an active role in initiating legislation and in nudging their bills through the Congress. Furthermore, congressional staff will usually consult officials in ED about education-related bills not originating in ED. The doctrine of separation of powers has not ruled out close, if wary, working relationships between employees of the executive branch and the Congress.

Congress and Its Committees

Congress, of course, plays a central role in the passage of all education legislation. The House and the Senate rely heavily on their committees for careful consideration of pending legislation. The Economic and Educational Opportunities Committee of the House of Representatives reviews many, but not all, education bills passing through that house. On the Senate side, the Education, Arts, and Humanities subcommittee of the Labor and Human Resources Committee is the place where many education bills receive their first legislative scrutiny.

Members of Congress request committee assignments in areas that hold special interest for them (or their constituents). The leadership of each party then makes its own decisions on committee assignments. Two important advantages go to the majority party. First, that party will be awarded a majority on each committee and subcommittee roughly proportional to its majority in that chamber. Second, the chair of each committee will be a member of the majority party.

Most members of Congress covet assignments on powerful and prestigious committees, and few are more powerful than the appropriations committees. The House Appropriations Committee is also broken down into subcommittees with the Labor, Health and Human Services, and Education Subcommittee handling most education appropriations. Similarly, the Senate Appropriation Committee sends its education bills to their own Labor, Health and Human Services, and Education Subcommittee.

Authorization of a particular piece of legislation normally involves scheduled hearings at which proponents and opponents of the bill testify before the subcommittee considering it. This process may be followed by a "markup" session, at which committee members and their staff go through the bill line by line, deleting passages or penciling in changes suggested by one interest group or another.

Usually, a favorable report out of the subcommittee and committee will be required to move the bill to the floor for debate and vote by the entire house. Similar bills passed by the two houses of Congress frequently contain somewhat different provisions, language, or authorized expenditures. When this happens, the discrepancies must be reconciled by a joint conference committee with members appointed from both houses. The reconciled version will be resubmitted to both houses. A majority vote in both the House and the Senate then sends the bill to the

White House for the president's signature before it becomes law. Should the president veto the bill, a two-thirds vote in both houses is necessary to override the veto and make it law. A "line item veto," already available to 44 governors and coveted by all recent presidents, was granted to President Clinton at the start of his second term. This provision permits the president to sign a bill into law but veto specific items or programs that the White House finds objectionable. If the new law survives constitutional challenges, it will significantly enhance the power of the president to shape legislation, including laws affecting public schools.

There is an important distinction in Congress, however, between the authorization of a program and the appropriation of money to pay for that program. It is entirely possible for a program to be authorized by Congress but not funded in separately considered appropriations bills. More often, the appropriations committees of the House and the Senate simply trim the amounts authorized to bring them into some correspondence with the overall federal budget.

All members of Congress, and especially members of the House of Representatives, develop special areas of expertise, depending on their own backgrounds, their constituencies, and their committee assignments. Other members may then look to them for guidance on especially complex or obscure legislation in their areas of expertise. Such specialization extends to congressional staff as well, especially staff assigned to committees. Top congressional staffers, predominantly able, hard-working young people, often match their counterparts in the executive branch in their understanding of educational issues and command of legislative detail.

On many education bills there is not a clearly defined Democratic or Republican position. A representative's vote is as likely to be influenced by the nature of her or his constituency as by party. A senator from a state with a large Latino population will be hard pressed to oppose better funding for bilingual programs. Representatives from districts with large universities will tend to support more liberal guaranteed-student-loan programs.

Congress seldom makes a law without input from the executive agency involved. By the same token, once a law is on the books, Congress exercises legislative oversight of the way the program is administered. The oversight function includes the authority to conduct congressional investigations on public problems or issues. Oversight of educational programs has been provided more often by the General Accounting Office (GAO), an arm of Congress. The oversight capabilities of GAO were expanded in 1974, with the establishment within it of an Office of Program Analysis, which routinely reviews and evaluates existing educational programs.

The White House and the Office of Management and Budget (OMB)

Presidents have never given the kind of attention to education they give to tax legislation, welfare reform, health care policy, or international trade. Nevertheless, there has been a marked increase in presidential statements on education during press conferences or on the campaign trail. George Bush understood the symbolic value of being seen as a president interested in raising educational standards across the nation. Bill Clinton continued that theme and mixed in more personal issues, including school prayer, school uniforms, and proposed tax breaks for students pursuing postsecondary education.

On some issues, such as vouchers or school lunches, it is possible to ascertain a Republican and a Democratic position. On many major issues, however, including school-to-work programs, Head Start, and special education, coalitions have formed that cut across party lines.

Education funding is, of course, affected by the federal budget process itself, which now entails year-round negotiation between the White House, the OMB, executive agencies (including ED), and the congressional budget committees. The OMB employs program officers, each responsible for reviewing categories of programs, to ascertain where cuts may be made or where more money is needed in the next fiscal year's budget. In recent years, the influence of OMB program officers in determining the funding level of educational programs has been growing.

The Federal Courts

Over the years, the federal courts have probably influenced U.S. education more than either the executive or legislative branch. Landmark U.S. Supreme Court decisions about religious instruction, aid to religious schools, school prayer, racial desegregation, students' freedom of expression, suspension, corporal punishment, bilingual education, schoolboard censorship of library books, state school-aid formulas, and provision of education for immigrant children have played a major role in shaping the way schools are organized and operate. We will return to the role of the courts in Chapter 16.

Education Interest Groups in Washington

There is a formidable array of educational interest groups in Washington. First among them in terms of political resources is the NEA, closely followed by the AFT. Recently, both of these organizations have been flexing their political muscle during presidential and congressional election campaigns as well as through extensive year-round lobbying efforts. The National School Boards Association is another group able to make bureaucratic and congressional heads turn, in part because of its organizational depth at the state and district levels throughout the country. The Council for Exceptional Children and the Children's Defense Fund are illustrative of interest groups that do battle over a narrower range of issues.

Increasingly, governmental units at lower levels—state offices of education, universities, and even major metropolitan school districts—have permanent lobbyists in Washington to keep watch over their interests as the policy process unfolds. Many professional associations, such as the National Association for Elementary School Principals, the American Vocational Association, and the National Association for Bilingual Education, lobby effectively for the interests of their membership. Finally, powerful groups representing more general interests—

labor, minorities, churches, business—enter the fray on selected educational issues.

In one way, the collection of education interests is not quite so disparate as it might appear. Most share a desire to strengthen the nation's public schools. Furthermore, much of the sound and fury in each congressional session is not over which educational programs should be authorized, but over how much money should be provided. Education is still only a 1.5 percent slice of the federal budget pie, and most education interests would like to see the president, OMB, and Congress be more generous in the size of the piece they cut for education next year. And so it is that many of the national education organizations band together in a loosely knit consortium, formed to promote the cause of public schools and to work for more adequate funding.

Summary

In 1995–1996, the federal government provided just 7 percent of the tax revenues going to public elementary and secondary education. This represents a drop from a high point of 9 percent in 1980–1981 (Plisko & Stern, 1985, p. 7). Although the federal portion of school funding is relatively small, many school districts, especially those in southern states and in the large urban centers of the North, rely on federal funds for a larger share of their budget than that would indicate.

Since federal aid has usually been targeted for specific programs, those programs suffer when federal funding is cut. Over $7 billion of the federal money goes to the Title I program for the educationally disadvantaged. Aside from Title I, the 1997 fiscal year budget slates 3.6 million low-income college students for Pell Grant aid ($6.4 billion), while special education ($4 billion) and vocational education basic grants ($1 billion) are the only other programs that top $1 billion.

The Reagan and Bush administrations worked to transform the federal education role from protector of the interests of the poor, the disabled, children with limited proficiency in English, women, and ethnic minorities, to a leadership role that would exhort states and local districts to employ sound educational practice for all children. Although unable to persuade Congress to eliminate either the U.S. Department of Education or the largest categorical programs, the Reagan and Bush years saw the equity-driven programs of the 1970s yielding centerstage to programs and rhetoric aimed at improving the academic achievement of America's youths. The task force that produced *A Nation at Risk* triggered unprecedented changes at the state level, as will be seen in the next chapter. Nor did the election of a Democratic president in 1993 and Richard W. Riley's appointment as Secretary of Education fundamentally alter the course of the reform. Clinton was already committed to much of the reform agenda, including efforts to improve all schools, and captured that issue in his campaign for reelection in 1996. But as former governors, both Clinton and Riley understood that not much would happen without the active engagement of the states.

References

Boyer, E. (1983). *High school: A report on secondary education in America*. New York: Harper and Row.

Bracey, G. W. (1993, October). The third Bracey report on the condition of public education. *Phi Delta Kappan, 75,* pp. 104–117.

Clark, D. L., & Astuto, T. A. (1990). The disjunction of federal educational policy and national educational needs in the 1990s. In D. E. Mitchell & M. E. Goertz (Eds.), *Education politics for the new century: The twentieth anniversary yearbook of the Politics of Education Association* (pp. 11–25). London: Falmer Press.

Gallup, G. (1983, 8 September). The 15th annual Gallup poll of the public's attitudes toward the public schools. *Phi Delta Kappan, 65,* pp. 33–47.

Goals 2000: Educate America Fact Sheet. (1994). Washington, DC: U.S. Department of Education.

Goodlad, J. I. (1984). *A place called school.* New York: McGraw-Hill.

Grant, W. V., & Lind, C. G. (1978). *Digest of education statistics 1977–78.* National Center for Education Statistics. Washington, DC: U.S. Government Printing Office.

National Commission on Excellence in Education. (1983, April). *A nation at risk: The imperative for educational reform.* Washington, DC: Author.

Plisko, V. W., & Stern, J. D. (Eds.). (1985). *The condition of education.* National Center for Education Statistics. Washington, DC: U.S. Government Printing Office.

Sizer, T. (1984). *Horace's compromise.* Boston: Houghton Mifflin.

Chapter 15

The New State Role in Education

As discussed in the last chapter, the states have primary constitutional responsibility for the provision of education. Historically, this has meant the enactment and enforcement of legislation that specifies who must go to school, sets the requirements for certification of teachers, establishes minimum standards for high school graduation, and assures that school buildings are safe. Great latitude was left to the local districts to determine the programs and curricula that made most sense in their locales.

In the early 1970s, states were drawn into a much broader array of issues affecting public schools. Although *Serrano* v. *Priest* ultimately fell short of requiring states other than California to make school finance more equitable, the lesson was not lost on other state leaders. School-aid formulas that provided more general state aid for poorer local education agencies (LEAs) were adopted in state after state. The press and corporate leaders, responding to revelations about declining Scholastic Aptitude Test (SAT) and American College Test (ACT) scores, created strong pressure for greater state accountability for what happens in the schools. In many states, the first response was in the form of minimum competency tests intended to ensure that no student escaped public schools without basic competencies necessary to function in a more complex society.

As the excellence movement gathered steam in the 1980s, states turned their attention to graduation requirements, curricular standards, pupil assessment, teacher qualifications, and incentives for attracting and retaining good teachers, including career ladders, merit pay, improved base pay, and teacher competency testing. By 1984, 35 states had beefed up their high school graduation requirements, 21 states had made revisions of curricula or textbooks, and longer school days or school years had been enacted in 21 states (Kirst, 1984, p. 189).

The first wave of state education reforms was devoted to raising standards and achieving more accountability among teachers, administrators, and schools. More rigorous high school graduation and college entrance requirements, an end to automatic grade promotions, more selective recruitment of teachers, and development of tests to keep tabs on how well pupils, teachers, and schools were doing received most of the attention. These reforms had the virtue of being quick and relatively inexpensive. But would they work? The assessment data over the next few years proved spotty, at best. Slowly, the realization set in that meaningful school reform would involve basic changes in classroom teaching strategies. The cost of restructuring schools to encourage and prepare teachers to adopt essentially new roles would not be accomplished so quickly and would be much more costly.

An interesting aspect of the state reforms of the 1980s was that in almost every case, they were initiated by governors, the legislatures, or business groups (Kirst, 1984, p. 191). The mainstays of the education lobby—teachers' associations, school-board associations, and the various organizations of school administrators—reacted to the initiatives but did not propose them. The national reports of 1983 and the media attention they inspired provided simple and sometimes simplistic solutions to the difficult problems facing public schools. States departed from their characteristic incrementalist mode of policy development and rushed sweeping reform packages into law (McDonnell & Fuhrman, 1985, pp. 50–57).

Who Makes State Education Policy?

Part of the recent assertiveness of the states in educational affairs can be attributed to some dramatic changes in the nature of state governments. Since 1962, court-ordered reapportionment of state legislatures has guaranteed equal representation to citizens in urban areas while bringing new, younger, better-educated legislators into state government. Party competition returned to many areas that had previously been safe, one-party districts, and legislators became more responsive to their constituencies. The image of stodgy, antiquated legislatures meeting once every two years, bent on keeping things the way they were, slowly gave way. More streamlined bodies sporting less-cumbersome committee structures, better-qualified staffs, and annual sessions began to emerge. Part-time amateur legislators were slowly replaced by well-paid professional politicians who devote most of their attention to questions of public policy.

A high-quality staff is indispensable when the modern state legislator confronts the hundreds of education bills that cross her or his desk in a typical legislative session. These bills may have been drafted by legislators responding to constituent pressure, by the governor's staff, by staff in the state education agency, or by any of the numerous education interest groups. Many of them will receive close scrutiny by policy analysts working for the governor, a budget director, the state school board, the chief state school officer, and the education committee that will first consider the bill. The level of state school aid for the next academic year will usually emerge as one of the major items on the legislative calendar, but changes in high school graduation requirements, teacher certification laws, new guidelines for the assessment of pupil progress, or a charter school bill may take center stage during any given session.

The Governor

The hand of the governor in molding education policy has also been strengthened in recent times. Changes in state constitutions and giving more governors a four-year term of office and the opportunity to serve more than one consecutive term have contributed to the enhancement of gubernatorial power. The governor's major opportunity to influence education policy, however, lies in his or her power of appointment and, even more importantly, in the area of fiscal authority. In most states, the governor has primary responsibility for preparation of the state budget. That provides substantial opportunity for input into decisions about which new educational programs will be funded and at what level old programs will be supported. In every state, the legislature has the authority to override the governor's budget recommendations, but the item-veto and reduction-veto powers granted the chief executive in some state constitutions, and the governor's political clout, make wholesale legislative restructuring of the budget very difficult indeed.

In recent years, governors have been taking stronger stands on substantive educational issues. The opposition of southern governors to desegregation in the early 1960s and, more recently, the positions of chief executives in Florida and Georgia on minimum-competency graduation requirements set the stage for assertive leadership by many governors during the educational-reform movement of the 1980s. There was political capital in being associated with the drive toward educational excellence, and governors throughout the country became champions of longer school years, merit-pay plans for teachers, math and science academies, stiffer graduation requirements, and higher standards for teacher certification. Half of the governors made education their top priority in state-of-the-state addresses in 1984 (McDonnell & Fuhrman, 1985, p. 47). In 1985, Republican governor of Tennessee, Lamar Alexander, blending the themes of better schools and better jobs, made career ladders for teachers the centerpiece of his educational-reform package. Governor Bill Clinton spearheaded educational reform in Arkansas the same year.

The State Education Agency (SEA)

The state agency delegated responsibility for educational affairs goes by many names, but the generic term is State Education Agency (SEA). In most states, it is a growing bureaucracy headed by a chief state school officer (CSSO) and a state school board.

SEAs perform at least three important functions. First, the agency is invariably delegated responsibility for administering and regulating many aspects of schooling under state and federal law. Teacher certification, approval of private schools, stipulation of the number of days that schools must be in session, accreditation of teacher education programs, and enforcement of school building codes are just a few of the regulatory tasks undertaken.

Most SEAs also perform a service or "technical assistance" function for local districts through its staff of professional educators. In recent years, most of this technical assistance has been provided through state or federal categorical programs. Consultants might be available to help regular classroom teachers learn how to work more effectively with special education students in their classes or to help LEAs provide better compensatory programs for educationally disadvantaged children.

Federal officials realized early on that if the federal programs of the 1960s and 1970s were to be effectively implemented, SEAs would have to be strengthened to do the job. Much of the growth of SEAs is attributable to federal reliance on them to provide these services. With the advent of the excellence movement, however, SEAs have beefed up their consulting staffs in the traditional academic subjects— science, math, English, social studies, and foreign languages—as well. Large school districts may be able to provide consulting services to teachers from their own staffs, but small or isolated districts often profit from state assistance in these areas.

Finally, SEAs are increasingly the source of new legislative proposals. The requisite records, expertise, and political savvy are more likely to be found here than in any other single agency. Drafts of desired legislation may be ordered up by the state school board, by the CSSO, or by another administrator in the SEA. But the SEA is also a likely place for the state teacher associations, the PTA, or interested legislators to come for advice, support, and skilled assistance when seeking changes in education law. Thus, state education agencies are beginning to play a role at the beginning as well as the end of the policy process.

The State Board of Education

The state school board—elected in 11 states, but appointed by the governor in the others—gives special status to education within the structure of state government. It represents, in fact, an extension to the state level of the principle of lay control of education. It also reflects a distrust by reformers of political party leaders in educational matters.

Few state school boards have developed sufficient muscle to hold their own in the rough-and-tumble world of state politics, however. In periods of intense policy activity, the legislature moves to center stage. Special commissions may be established by the governor or legislative leaders to point the way toward needed reform.

State school-board members get frustrated when their presumed expertise and authority is bypassed, but some believe their day is coming. As their staffs and resources grow, they may find that they have both the clout and the discretion to affect state education policy materially in a different way. Legislative policy is typically painted in broad strokes. It often falls to the state school board to write the rules and regulations that influence how the policy will be carried out. Beyond this, many state boards appear to be developing a capacity to influence, if not to dictate, the fate of policy proposals from interest groups or from other sectors of state government. They also serve to legitimate proposals of the CSSO and, on occasion, to shift the focus beyond the short-term preoccupations of the current legislative session. Although most policymaking at the state level places little premium on long-range planning, a state board of education can look at the broad sweep of educational issues in an attempt to establish some longer-range goals and programs. Whether these programs will be honored in the press of legislative infighting and gubernatorial budget cutting is always open to question. But if state educational policy is to receive any direction beyond year-to-year decisions on specific issues, it is the state school board and the bureaucracy headed by the CSSO that will have to provide it.

The Chief State School Officer (CSSO)

Historically, the CSSO (variously referred to as the state superintendent of schools, state superintendent of education, state superintendent of public instruction, or commissioner of education) was elected; now, the state board of education appoints the chief in over half of the states. Though CSSOs are heads of the states' education establishments, their actual influence on education policy varies widely from state to state. Most CSSOs have contented themselves with performing the maintenance functions of their office—keeping the machinery operating smoothly. Several have charted bolder courses of educational growth or reform. The incumbent of this position, whether elected or appointed, is likely to be a career educator with experience in elementary, secondary, or higher education.

In a very real sense, the CSSO provides the link between lay policy direction from the state board of education, the legislature, and the governor's office, on the one hand, and the thousands of professional educators throughout the state on the other. Loss of confidence from either of these sectors may make satisfactory resolution of educational issues difficult.

The chief state school officer has yet another constituency. In many states, the most fundamental change in the policy process has resulted from the growth of bureaucracies within the executive branch. The state office of education has typically been in the forefront of this development, usually staffed by a blend of career government workers and professional educators. The sense of mission and effectiveness of personnel in this complex organization blossoms under professional leadership, but may wither under a neglectful or politically troubled CSSO.

State Courts

Few are unaware of the role that federal courts have come to play in the educational-policy process, but the extent to which state courts have also entered the fray is often overlooked. Most states have felt the influence of their courts in educational matters. Interpretation of law with respect to state school-funding formulas, collective bargaining, teacher tenure, district reorganization, teacher liability, and tax rates has become a significant part of the docket in many state courts. State supreme courts in California, New Jersey, and Texas delivered important decisions bearing on the constitutionality of their school finance systems. The most sweeping state supreme court decision, however, came out of Kentucky, where the court ordered state officials essentially to revamp their entire educational system.

Landmark court cases, even at the state level, do not just happen; carrying them through the judicial system to completion is apt to be an expensive and exhausting process. Consequently, many interest groups actively seek out the "best" case for a desired court test from their point of view and provide much of the needed legal aid. Even the supposedly neutral judicial process is not immune to the influence of political interests.

There is an indirect, as well as a direct, effect from the rapid rise of litigation in the states. A decision on whether striking teachers can be dismissed under the state's collective-bargaining law will establish a precedent in other similar cases that follow. That court decision may also stimulate new legislation and will probably affect the regulatory activity of the state bureaucracy. Furthermore, the state school board, the CSSO, or even the legislature will try to anticipate the court's position on the constitutionality or legality of any policy they are considering. The resulting interaction of courts and other state agencies in resolving some of the most controversial issues is just one more instance of the expanded role that state government has assumed in determining educational policy.

The Emergence of a New State Role

Because of their constitutional authority in the realm of education and their financial resources, the states have long played a central role in U.S. education. In broad terms, they have been one of the primary sources of revenue for schools, enacted policy on some of the most important issues, monitored district compliance with both state and federal policy, and provided assistance to local districts that did not have the expertise or infrastructure to cope with the intricate curricular, personnel, and financial problems confronting a modern school system.

Mitchell, Marshall, and Wirt (1985) catalogued the functions of state governments in the educational realm into the following seven domains:

1. School finance: *controlling how education funds are distributed and how human and fiscal resources are allocated to the schools;*
2. School personnel training and certification: *controlling the conditions for getting or keeping various jobs in the school system;*
3. Student testing and assessment: *fixing the timing and consequences of testing, including subjects covered and the distribution of test data;*
4. School program definition: *controlling program planning and accreditation or otherwise specifying what schools must teach and how long they must teach it;*

5. School organization and governance: *the assignment of authority and responsibility to various groups and individuals;*
6. Curriculum materials: *controlling the development and/or selection of textbooks and other instructional materials;*
7. School buildings and facilities: *determination of architecture, placement, and maintenance for buildings and other school facilities.*

In the six states they studied, they found that individual policymakers tended to specialize in these domains and that decisions in one domain were made with little attention to the other domains. They also found that policy debates in any area tended to focus on a relatively small number of competing approaches to the development of policy in that area (Mitchell, Marshall, & Wirt, 1985, pp. 13–14).

Until recently, most states were content with performing these conventional functions. In recent years, however, some researchers have detected a basic change in the way state leaders view their responsibility to education. Many governors and legislative leaders are now resolved to hold local districts accountable for more than their use of state funds and the safety of schoolchildren. Increasingly, local superintendents and school boards are being held accountable for the academic performance of children in their schools. Academic achievement data are now collected in many states and often serve as the standard by which school performance is judged. Schools that fail to meet state standards may be required to participate in a state-sponsored school improvement program. South Carolina and New Jersey each have provisions that allow them to take over the governance of districts that fail to meet state standards. Arkansas forces districts that cannot meet accreditation standards to dissolve and merge with a neighboring district (Cohen, 1990, p. 280).

Proponents of this new state role reason that although state governments cannot improve schools unilaterally, they can be much more active in setting standards and holding local districts to them. Michael Cohen (1990), director of education programs at the National Governors' Association, has argued that the states "must significantly strengthen their efforts to set educational goals and assess school performance, provide rewards and sanctions linked to performance, and stimulate local diversity and experimentation" (p. 285). If states continue to move from a nurturing, largely permissive role to one of watchdog and taskmaster, the relationship between states and local school districts will be fundamentally altered.

Interest Groups at the State Level

Many organized interest groups have the potential to affect educational policy at the state level. Foremost among these in most states are the state teacher associations. State affiliates of the National Education Association (NEA) have enjoyed great influence in many states, and the affiliates of the American Federation of Teachers (AFT), often bolstered by the state affiliate of the parent AFL-CIO, are also making their presence felt in many state capitals. The state association of school boards may be a natural ally of the teacher organizations on some issues and an antagonist on others. Associations of school administrators, parent associations, and advocates of special education bring their influence to bear on legislators and other state officials on selected issues. In some cases, these professional groups will command the resources necessary to staff an office and will lobby for their preferred positions on issues that affect their clientele.

Lobbyists are one of the more maligned groups in U.S. politics. The vision of strong-arm tactics and backroom deals is pervasive but overdrawn. Among other things, lobbyists function as information sources, providing data and possible arguments to officials within the policymaking system. Such information, even if it only spells out the reasons for the position of the group, may sometimes enlighten a beleaguered official and inform the ensuing debate. Legislators grow to rely on the best lobbyists as fountains of accurate, if selective, facts and persuasive debating points.

There is, of course, the specter of political power just below the surface. If political promises and threats are usually implicit, they may still be accurately perceived and influential. One important way that interest groups with substantial financial resources gain the attentive ear of a legislator or governor is by contributing to his or her electoral campaigns. Some major interests make it a practice to contribute to all candidates who have a chance of being elected to an influential position, regardless of their party affiliation or political philosophy. This seemingly contradictory action is taken to ensure access to key authorities regardless of who wins the election. Even groups that have little ability to deliver votes directly may endear themselves as regular contributors to a key legislator's campaign.

There are also noneducation-interest groups that exert substantial influence on the resolution of educational questions at the state level. Labor unions, chambers of commerce, groups representing particular minorities, civil rights groups such as the ACLU, and state taxpayers' associations may all campaign actively for or against an education bill that affects their members or the ideals they represent.

Often there will be an attempt among the various education interest groups (frequently in concert with the SEA) to work out their differences and present a united front to the legislature, the budget office, and the governor. This pattern, which Iannaccone (1967) has called the "monolithic" pattern, has most of the educational expertise in the state lined up on one side. It is most effective in budgetary matters where the quest for more education dollars induces the interests to bury their differences and emphasize their common need. When that approach breaks down, the education associations may find themselves in open conflict with each other, forcing the legislators to take sides in their internecine struggle. A variant of this pattern finds the state organizations so fragmented that they constitute little effective influence on the policymaking machinery. In states that display this pattern, local school administrators may fill the void by exercising influence directly on legislators from their home districts.

Although the traditional education-interest groups remain major players in the ongoing debates over education policy, the particular nature of the excellence reform has modified their roles significantly. The drumbeat of press releases from political and business leaders implying that public schools in the United States had gone soft put groups representing teachers, administrators, and school boards in an essentially reactive mode. Sensing the popularity of the reforms and anticipating increases in state and federal aid, most of the "educational establishment" supported the broad objectives of the reform while quietly opposing specific bills deemed detrimental to the interests of teachers or to local control (McDonnell & Pascal, 1988).

Another subtle but perceptible shift has occurred over recent years in at least a few states. Education has seemingly begun to lose its special favored position in the allocation of the budgetary pie. The rapid increase in cost per pupil (even after adjusting for inflation) between 1960 and 1990 and the increasing share of total education costs shouldered by state governments have resulted in a more searching analysis of every education line in the budget. Declining school enrollments in the late 1970s and early 1980s were seen by many governors and legislators as an indication that the time had come to rein in fiscal growth in the educational realm. Whereas the relatively smaller amounts requested two decades ago were often approved more or less automatically, the competition with other policy sectors—most notably corrections, public assistance, public health, and environmental concerns—is toe to toe and no holds barred today.

Federal, State, and Local Relations

If one looks at the percentage of expenditures for elementary and secondary public education provided by local, state, and federal sources, a clear trend is visible. After the boom years of the 1960s, federal contributions grew only slightly and unevenly, then dropped. The major shift came in the increasing burden assumed by state governments and the decreasing share contributed by local districts. By 1985, state governments were outspending local units in their support of public schools for the first time in history (see Table 15.1).

In the 1980s, strong public and political sentiment existed in many states to limit both taxation and expenditures. Tax-limitation legislation may take the form of limiting either local property-tax revenue or state taxation. In California, the public supported Proposition 13, an amendment to the state constitution that rolled back and limited the growth of property taxes. It is now quite clear that the ultimate effect of that measure was to shift the primary financial burden from the local level to the state. Along with the state's increased financial responsibility came more state attention to the details of local educational governance. It is ironic that an anathema for the amendment's conservative sponsors, the rapid centralization of school policy in California, turned out to be an important side effect of Proposition 13.

As state revenues began to swell again in the mid-1980s, this pressure to limit taxes declined, but citizens in many local districts were still reluctant to vote for increases in the local property tax. With the advent of state reforms, the shift from

TABLE 15.1   **Estimated Expenditures of Public Elementary and Secondary Schools by Source of Funds**

	1969–70	1977–78	1985–86	1993–94 (est.)
Federal	8.2%	9.4%	6.7%	7.0%
State	38.6	44.9	49.3	45.2
Local	52.9	45.6	43.8	45.1
All other	.3	.1	.3	2.7
	100.0%	100.0%	100.0%	100.0%

Source: W. Vance Grant and C. George Lind, *Digest of Education Statistics, 1977–78,* National Center for Education Statistics (Washington, DC: U.S. Government Printing Office, 1978), p. 21; Valena White Plisko and Joyce D. Stern, *The Condition of Education, 1985 edition,* National Center for Education Statistics (Washington, DC: U.S. Government Printing Office, 1985), p. 36; Thomas D. Snyder, *Digest of Education Statistics, 1989,* National Center for Education Statistics (Washington, DC: U.S. Government Printing Office, 1989), p. 32; and Internet (1996), http://gopher.ed.gov/NCES/pubs/96303 html table2.

local to state revenue sources accelerated. The trend toward greater financial responsibility for public education by the states slowed in the late 1980s, and at last count, local districts were once again matching states as a source of education dollars.

Although much of the state share is provided in the form of general state aid, there is also an increasing tendency for state governments to mandate programs and standards that had previously been left to the discretion of local districts. Resentment of this perceived encroachment by the state runs high in many district offices throughout the country, but the sense of loss is seldom strong enough to prompt district administrators to spurn the financial aid accompanying the mandates. A similar situation exists with respect to the federal government and the local district. Even today, federal aid makes up a relatively small portion of the total budget of most school districts. It is a large enough part, however, that few superintendents can afford to seriously contemplate rejecting federal aid for which their district may be eligible. Nor can school administrators take lightly the ultimate threat of the federal government to cut off federal funds to any district that does not abide by federal guidelines.

The form in which aid from Washington should be made available has been a divisive issue since the beginning of the federal largess. As mentioned in Chapter 14, those with specific objectives in mind argue for *categorical* grants tailored to specific programs, leaving relatively little discretion to the recipient (i.e., the state or local district) about how the money is to be used. Those who are concerned primarily with strengthening the role of state and local governments at the expense of the federal bureaucracy favor *general revenue sharing,* under which funds will be distributed by formula to states or localities, with relatively few restrictions on how the money is to be spent. Between the two extremes lies the block-grant concept, wherein funds are distributed by formula for use in certain broad functional areas. Under a block grant, similar programs will be grouped into the same block. The state or local unit has more flexibility than with a categorical grant but more restrictions than under general revenue sharing.

In general, Democrats in Washington have opted for categorical grants as the most efficient way to achieve the social purposes they seek. Republicans, on the other hand, have tended to support general revenue sharing and, more recently, block grants, both out of skepticism about the equalizing objectives of many Democratic-sponsored programs and from an ideological conviction that discretion in these matters is better placed at the state and local levels. In principle, state officials could be expected to prefer general revenue sharing or block grants, which leave them more latitude to shape programs as they wish. In practice, they have found that shifts from categorical to block grants are often accompanied by funding cuts.

Some grants in aid are made by federal agencies directly to local school districts. Increasingly, however, federal education agencies have realized their own real limitations in implementing and enforcing complex policy in school districts throughout the land. Given insufficient personnel and inadequate administrative channels to do the job themselves, they have turned to state education agencies to administer many federal programs. Much of the growth of state offices of education has been due to this additional responsibility. Thus, from the vantage point of the local school administrators, the state has become even more powerful, because it is often administering federal policies as well as its own.

The Centralization-Decentralization Issue

Today, almost no one argues that more federal involvement and control are needed in education. To the contrary, there is strong sentiment for putting the authority back in the hands of local board members and administrators. "Devolution" is more than an appealing slogan. Yet one is hard pressed to find examples of recent vintage where either a state or the federal government has relaxed its grip on an area of educational policy and turned it back to the local districts to do what they will with it. Why is it apparently so easy to centralize education policymaking and so difficult to decentralize?

First, U.S. society is becoming more interrelated with each passing decade. In the case of education, what and how youngsters are taught in their local community today will affect people far beyond their local community tomorrow. Geographical mobility and an interlocking economic system tie the nation together and make every community dependent in hundreds of ways on the rest of the state or nation. Ignorance, disease, and crime no longer respect school-district or even state boundaries. In other words, issues that were once largely local issues now transcend the community and are likely to be viewed as state or national issues.

Add to that fact the observation that, in state and national political forums, minority interests that would have great difficulty carrying the day in their local communities have an opportunity to pool their efforts and affect policy in ways not available to them at home. This aggregation of minority interests has been most noticeable at the federal level, where education policy throughout the 1960s and 1970s was directed at expanding the educational opportunity of African Americans, Latinos, women, the disabled, the poor, and other historically disadvantaged groups.

Finally, there is a sort of political accountability that makes federal and state officials reluctant to turn over tax funds generated at their level, with no strings attached, to local school districts. Few governors, state legislators, or CSSOs would wish to be held accountable for the manner in which each district might spend its state aid if there were no restrictions at all. Without guidelines and regulations to avoid at least the worst abuses, any future political opponent would have only to point with indignation toward one or two flagrant examples of districts that accepted state aid but turned away students with disabilities, maintained all-Black schools, or purchased "un-American" textbooks with the money. There is a well-conditioned response among most career politicians to cover their backsides whenever funds are appropriated.

Some forces appear to be running in the other direction, toward decentralization. Instead of hoped-for economies of size that would make centralized administration more efficient, an excessively rigid bureaucratic system has resulted. A constant stream of paperwork tries the patience of state and local officials alike. Special reasons why their particular school, district, or state should be exempted from this or that ruling are ignored.

All this, along with the knowledge that important decisions are being made far from the classroom where they will have their effect, may progressively alienate teachers and administrators who see little opportunity to influence their own schools for the better. If that feeling grows, the vitality, experimentation, and flexibility that have become trademarks of U.S. schools may be in jeopardy.

At first blush, it would seem that a strong national reform such as the excellence movement would have a centralizing effect on education. The reports, after all, had articulated a fairly explicit national agenda based on several common themes. As Fuhrman (1989) points out:

> *Some of the policies suggested by the reports became so popular as to be virtually universal. For example, 45 states modified requirements for high school graduation, predominantly by increasing the total number and adding to specific requirements. Over three-fourths of the states increased math and science requirements, for example. Between 1980 and 1986, 46 states required one or the other, or both, types of teacher assessment (Darling-Hammond & Berry, 1988). New student testing programs were also very common. Thirty-one new state testing programs began in the 1980s; and, between 1988 and 1990, 11 new programs will start. Only two states have no state-level testing program or provision (CCSSO, 1988).*

Despite these similarities across states, Fuhrman reports that a closer look at six states reveals that the progress of reform in each of the six states is affected by important differences in their political cultures. States accustomed to "big legislative fixes" crafted large reform packages, whereas states that typically favor incremental approaches proceeded incrementally. Political factors such as the balance of power between the state and local districts influenced strategic decisions about whether to create reform policies that rely on mandates or incentives. Finally, the political context appeared to affect the implementation of reform legislation. Some states found policymakers continually fine-tuning reforms, whereas in others, local districts locked horns with the state over the implementation of policies that they deemed ill advised (Fuhrman, 1989). The point is worth remembering. Even in a nationally inspired reform, the political cultures of individual states shape policies and their implementation in important ways. All 50 states, then, each with its own political historic, demography, economy, and mix of interest groups, arrive at remarkably diverse school policies. Although this untidy spectacle frustrates advocates who are certain their preferred policy is best for everyone, the existence of 50 different laboratories trying out a range of alternative policies in different settings adds much to the vitality of U.S. education.

Summary

There is little doubt about where legal responsibility for education lies. Because the U.S. Constitution contains no reference to education, authority in this domain is reserved to the states and the people, under the Tenth Amendment. The issue is only slightly obscured by the fact that historically the states have passed along discretion for many kinds of policy to the local school districts they established.

The most dramatic shift of the last few decades has found states assuming a larger share of the fiscal burden of education and, at the same time, flexing their policymaking muscle in areas once left to the local districts. There are several reasons for these shifts, but the two most important are the increased capability of state governments and the drive for statewide school improvement. Active advocacy by interest groups representing minorities and disadvantaged groups, and legislatures and educators dedicated to the principle of equal educational opportunity, have also contributed to this change.

Despite strong sentiment for local control of education and frustration with bureaucratic elements of state and federal intervention, the trend toward higher-level intervention in a wide array of policy areas is well established. Nor does there appear to be a viable formula for reversing the trend. The reasons underlying this gradual shift in the authority structure start with a more and more geographically mobile society. The case for local control would be stronger if products of a community's schools never left the community. However, in a nation where youngsters from Tuscaloosa may wind up in Birmingham, Chicago, or Sacramento, the quest for general assurance about the variety and quality of education available in all communities is strong.

References

Cohen, M. (1990). Key issues confronting state poli-cymakers. In R. F. Elmore (Ed.), *Restructuring schools: The next generation of educational reform.* San Francisco: Jossey-Bass.

Council of Chief State School Officers. (1988). *Accountability reporting in the states: Report of a survey: 1987.* Washington, DC: Council of Chief State School Officers.

Darling-Hammond, L., & Berry, B. (1988). *The evo-lution of teacher policy.* Santa Monica, CA: Rand Corporation.

Fuhrman, S. H. (1989). State politics and education reform. In J. Hannaway & R. Crowson (Eds.), *The politics of reforming school administration* (pp. 61–75). New York: Falmer.

Iannaccone, L. (1967). *Politics in education.* New York: Center for Applied Research in Educa-tion.

Kirst, M. W. (1984). The changing balance in state and local power to control education. *Phi Delta Kappan* (November), pp. 189–191.

McDonnell, L. M., & Fuhrman, S. (1985). The politi-cal context of school reform. In V. D. Mueller & M. P. McKeown (Eds.), *The fiscal, legal, and political aspects of state reform of elementary and secondary education.* Cambridge, MA: Ball-inger.

McDonnell, L. M., & Pascal, A. (1988). *Teacher unions and educational reform.* Santa Monica, CA: Rand Corporation.

Mitchell, D. E., Marshall, C., & Wirt, F. M. (1985). Building a taxonomy of state education poli-cies. *Peabody Journal of Education, 62*(4), 7–47.

Chapter 16

Public Schools and the Law

Understanding the Legal System

Public-school districts are creatures of state legislatures, and local boards of education govern according to the authority granted them by state law. During the 1960s and 1970s, an activist U.S. Supreme Court, taking an expansive view of the Constitution, interpreted many matters as constitutional, thereby articulating rights and protections that had not previously existed. These constitutional rights placed limitations on the authority of state legislators, school boards, and school administrators. During the 1980s, the level of federal involvement declined because of decreased federal financial support and a less judicially active Supreme Court. During that same decade, state legislatures increased their oversight control of local school boards through a number of educational reforms. This reform legislation tended to increase the authority and power of the state office of education at the expense of the autonomy and discretion of local school-district administrators.

Understanding Power Relationships

The relationship between the state legislature and local school districts is bounded by the statutory authority granted to the districts by the legislature and limited by state and federal constitutions. With a variety of participants acting in public-school systems—school boards, district and building administrators, teachers, support staff, parents, and students—some confusion exists about who has how much authority, how far it extends, and over whom it can be exercised. Not only is it necessary to understand the power relationships among the actors in public schools, it is also important to understand how the legal system conveys responsi-

Special thanks are given to Arthur Lehr and Theresa Robbins who assisted in the research and writing of Chapters 16 and 17. Their knowledge of law, insights about public education, editorial acumen, and collaborative spirit have contributed immensely to these two chapters.

bility. Consider, for example, how the issue of student residency has been understood and acted upon.

Legislatures and courts have a significant amount of power over an individual school and an individual school administrator in the issue of residency. All states, usually as a matter of constitutional guarantee, promise a free public education. Operationally, this is translated to mean that students have access to the public school district in which they reside. This raises some important questions: What is the statutory standard provided for determining the district of residence? How much latitude is the school district allowed in developing and enforcing a residency policy? When a controversy concerning the district's policy is brought to the courts by parents who believe their child is a district resident and is being denied that status or by a district that does not accept a student as a resident, the courts assume power and responsibility for determining if the district's policy is consistent with the residency statute and with the state and federal constitutions. Thus, authority and responsibility is shifted from the legislature to the school district to the courts. The district assumes the final responsibility, for it will be required to revise its residency policy within constitutional guidelines and within the most recent court interpretation of the residency statute.

Sources of School Law

School-law decisions come out of a variety of legal principles, including contracts, torts, administrative law, and constitutional law, each of which involves a different mode of analysis. Although the terms *school law* and *education law* are used as though they describe a body of knowledge separate from the law in general and although the context of education is a distinctive theme in school law, the analysis employed cuts across a wide range of legal specialties. When confronted with a school-law issue, the initial consideration is to know the source of the legal principle involved in order to decide what type of analysis to apply.

A particular issue may involve several types of inquiry. For example, the issue of school residency forces a school administrator into a constitutional due process inquiry. The residency issue is rooted in due process because all children are required by state compulsory education laws to attend school. This requirement places a responsibility on public-school systems to provide a free education for students who reside within the school district. When a school district denies a student access to education due to a claim of nonresidency, the school must provide that student with a chance to prove residency. If the school district does not afford the student this opportunity, the school can be sued for denying the student's right to due process. The student's due process protections are found in the Fourteenth Amendment—"No state shall deprive any person of life, liberty or property without due process of law"—and the ability to attend school is a property interest from which the student cannot be deprived without opportunity to prove residency.

Residency analysis does not end with due process, for it is an issue that is intertwined with many current social problems. In *Plyer* v. *Doe* (1982), the Supreme Court considered the constitutionality of a state statute that barred children of illegal aliens from attending public schools, removing a whole class of students from the guarantee of a free public education upon which the residency test is based. The Texas statute was held unconstitutional as a violation of the equal protection clause. In an earlier equal protection case, *Brown* v. *Board of Education* (1954), the Supreme Court ruled that residency determinations cannot be made for the purpose of racially segregating students. With concerns about homeless children, Congress passed the Homeless Children and Youth Act in 1994 and stated its policy to be:

> *In any State that has a compulsory residency requirement as a component of the State's compulsory attendance laws, or other laws, regulations, or policies that may act as a barrier to the enrollment, attendance or success in school of homeless children and youth, the State will review and undertake steps to revise such laws . . . to ensure that homeless children and youth are afforded the same free, appropriate education as provided to other children and youth. (§ 114341(2))*

Clearly, the issue of residency is intertwined with many other issues and involves several types of inquiry in its analysis.

Lawyers are trained to analyze fact situations according to particular legal specializations, but educators are not. Contracts, torts, administrative law, statutory law, and constitutional law are areas of legal specialization. Historically, educational administrators have been able to stay abreast of statutory requirements by mastering the school code. With the explosion of constitutional cases in the past 35 years, however, knowledge of the school code alone is insufficient. A fundamental principle of the U.S. constitutional system is that statutes, regulations, and policies are valid so long as they are constitutional. School-board policies are enforceable so long as they are constitutional and authorized by state law. Judges hold potential power over legislatures and school boards, therefore, because they have authority to interpret regulations, statutes, and constitutions.

Judicial Actions and Legal Standards

Whereas a statute is general and attempts to deal with all future circumstances, a judicial decision by necessity deals with interpreting a statute, contract, regulation, or constitution in the context of a particular dispute. School law has developed to a large extent from the expanded interpretation of the U.S. Constitution as applied by federal judges to public schools. Statutes and judicial decisions are ordinarily treated as law, and both influence the conduct of educational administrators. Judges, however, apply the judicial standard that pertains to a particular set of facts and the resulting interpretation is valid only for that set of facts.

Judicial Precedent

Judges are conscious of the precedential nature of their decisions, but the applicability of a decision is often limited by the particular facts involved in a case. The tricky part of determining the importance of a court decision is in deciding how broadly the standard and result reached in one decision can be generalized so as to be applicable to other fact situations. Consequently, administrators cannot define a general standard of conduct for schools in a particular area until several cases in that area, examining slightly different fact situations, have been decided. Identification of a legal standard requires a careful reading of judicial opinions within the proper jurisdiction. Though a state may have a clearly written residency statute, for example, administrators must remember that the law is a combination of a statute and the judicial opinions interpreting that statute.

Many states give a significant amount of power to individual districts to create their own residency policies within the confines of judicial interpretations of the statute. Thus, a school administrator must work with the school board to create a residency policy that will deal with concerns unique to the district and that is legal in the sense that it meets statutory and judicial requirements. Although some districts may prefer to have a liberal standard, offering easy access to the district by as many students as possible so as to increase state aid, other, wealthier districts may choose a more restrictive standard that is difficult for students to satisfy. Property-wealthy districts that receive little, if any, state aid have no financial incentive to enroll more students. In a district located in the midst of a group of similar suburban districts, wherein students may not typically prefer one district over another, an administrator may choose to adopt a policy such as that presented in Exhibit 16.1.

Suppose that the year after this policy in Exhibit 16.1 is formally adopted, a administrator is notified of a potential residency problem with a sophomore student who has openly stated that she moved in with a married, older sister living in the district for the purpose of attending a district school because the drama department is better than the one in her old school. Because there is a legitimate doubt

EXHIBIT 16.1   Sample Residency Policy

Residency of Students

To attend school in this district without a tuition charge, a student shall have a bona fide residence within the boundaries of the district, and such residence shall not be maintained for the purpose of enabling the student to attend school in the district. In case of doubt, an administrator may require proof of residence and proof that motivation for residing in the district is not for the purpose of attending the school.

A student whose family moves out of the district during the school year shall be permitted to attend school for the remainder of the year without payment of tuition. Transportation shall be the responsibility of the parent or guardian or the new district of residence. If a student's family plans to move into the district after the beginning of school and can provide verification that such a move is imminent, the student will be allowed to start school at the beginning of the school year.

about whether the student should be considered a district resident, the administrator requires the student to provide proof of her residence and of her motivation for that residence. Suppose that the student and her parents tell the administrator that although the quality of the school district was one reason for the residency change, the primary motive was the fact that residing with the student's older sister reduced her commute to ballet classes by an hour and a half each day. Because the student attended ballet classes five days a week, this constitutes a significant hardship for the student. She therefore moved in with her sister. Suppose the administrator verifies the parents' claim about the student's ballet classes. What should the administrator do? Is this student in violation of the residency policy if she has more than one purpose for her move into the district?

In determining whether the student is in violation of the residency policy, the administrator must first look at the state statute. The statute in this case, however, is not very helpful, for it merely states that "school districts shall charge tuition to nonresident students" and that "school districts shall create residency policies for determining a residency of students." The administrator must next look at the most recent state supreme court opinion interpreting the residency statute and at school policies written under that statute. Suppose the most recent decision in the state is *Turner* v. *Board of Education* (1973), which states that "while generally the residence of the parent will be considered the residence of the minor child, a minor child may, however, for school purposes have a different residence from his parents." The court further held that where a child dwells with relatives in a school district solely for the purpose of attending a public school in the district, the student will not be considered a resident of the district. From this case, the administrator now knows that if proof can be found to show that the child is living apart from her parents solely for the purpose of attending the district school, the student can be denied enrollment.

The administrator in this situation may not believe that the student's sole reason for moving was to attend school in the district. The basic question, however, is not answered, as part of the reason for the student's move was to attend school in the district. How can an administrator determine the true purpose where a dual purpose may exist? To answer the question, the administrator may look to decisions of other courts within the state that interpret and expand upon the *Turner* decision, or may consult the district's legal counsel. A relevant case is *Herscher* v. *Kankakee* (1981), which holds that only one home may be the residence of a child for school-district purposes. Another relevant case is *Kraut* v. *Rachford* (1977), which explains that there is a presumption that the residence of a student is the residence of the parents or primary parent. This presumption is rebuttable where evidence is presented that shows that the child was living with someone, other than the parents, who had assumed parental responsibility. *Kraut* also reaffirms previous case law that states that moving in with someone other than parents for the primary purpose of attending school will not overcome the presumption. *Connelly* v. *Gibbs* (1983) reveals that a student who moves in with an older sibling although all other siblings remain living with the parents is evidence of sole reason intent. To determine the true residence, the court and the school administrator should attempt to discover where discipline and guidance of the child occurs, which parent is financially contributing most to the child, and who has the most day-to-day supervision and discipline of the child.

Although an administrator may feel somewhat overwhelmed by these judicial declarations, none of which expressly address the issue in question, the cases do offer a strong sense of the state court trends in dealing with residency. If the married sister in this example is financially responsible for the student and is in charge of the student's discipline, this seems to be sufficient evidence to rebut the presumption that the student's residence is the same as the parents' residence. The fact that one of the child's purposes in being in the district to attend school makes this case a close one. Because the district's residency policy does not contain sole purpose language, the administrator could properly deny enrollment to this student because one of her admitted purposes for moving into the district is to attend a district school. Where the facts of a case are not identical to the facts in a precedential case in the same jurisdiction, a residency denial is open to attack in the courts. The administrator's best bet is to make an informed decision that appears to be consistent with the reasoning of state courts.

In relating their own school situations to general expectations established by statute and by judicial action, administrators will need to become familiar with legal reasoning, which relies on precedent and analogy, to enable them to determine logically their own courses of action (Bull & McCarthy, 1995, p. 616). A clear analysis of their own situation in the legal context is a fundamental step for administrators in understanding their own sphere of authority and responsibility.

Administrative Responsibility

Knowledge of how the law works will help administrators to determine what actions are reasonable and just in most school situations. Educators, not courts or legislatures, are responsible for such determinations (Bull & McCarthy, 1995, p. 620). Knowledge of the legal system provides a means of understanding a variety of circumstances where conflict may occur. The relationship between parties in the school setting is bounded by legal sources—statutory, regulatory, constitutional, contractual, and tortious—and these relationships must be understood because they have implications for potential liability as well as for defining the scope of administrative authority and responsibility.

Many educational practitioners view the law as an external force that dictates what they can and cannot do, a prescription that places limits on professional autonomy rather than a framework for expressing public values and decisions (Bull & McCarthy, 1995, p. 615). They may, therefore, assume that school authorities have discretion to act according to their own preferences so long as they do not violate the "rules of the game." Another view of the law, one more problematical but widely held, is that the law becomes a metaphor for how an administrator behaves. The law sets up a series of standards, establishing a variety of rules, and it is the responsibility of the administrator to convey these rules to the district or school. ③ A more practical view would be to regard knowledge of the law as relevant to administrative decisions and actions because it provides insights that will improve the quality of decision making and performance.

Knowledge of the law provides administrators with a broad perspective. At one level, it offers an understanding of the parameters of administrative discretion. It is important, from this point of view, to understand the subtleties of legal authority and liability. At another level, the law provides a set of aspirations with which it is important for administrators to wrestle. Many of these aspirations are embedded in constitutional principles, such as due process, equal protection, and free speech. The way in which these principles are translated into legal standards raises important educational issues for administrators. In any case, it is important to understand that legal standards do not necessarily define best educational practice.

Constitutional standards will define minimal levels of constitutionally acceptable conduct, but the extent to which a district wants to go beyond this minimum is a matter of choice that must be determined by educational goals. Consider, for example, a fundamental constitutional safeguard that will be described in more detail in the next chapter: due process. Although the due process clause of the Constitution's Fourteenth Amendment does not require that the same level of procedural protection given to persons under the criminal law (i.e., Miranda rights or the right to legal counsel), school officials must respect the due process rights of students when disciplining them. In *Goss* v. *Lopez* (1976), the Supreme Court held that in student suspension cases, the due process clause requires that the student receive oral notice of the charges against him or her. Although oral notice may be all that the due process clause requires, school administrators may want to consider whether mere oral notice meets their educational due process objective.

A more laborious but arguably educationally effective policy may be to contact the student and the student's parents orally and in writing to assure that notice was actually provided and understandable. This policy would serve the educational goal of maintaining maximum parental involvement in the school and in student discipline. Legal knowledge is important in understanding how to work within the system to accomplish desired educational objectives, but it is not a substitute for an educational philosophy.

State and Federal Judicial Structures and Jurisdictions

A fundamental principle of the federalist system is the dual authority enjoyed by states and the federal government. At different historical periods, the states and the federal government differ in their activism toward public schools. Currently, state legislatures and state courts, particularly in the interpretation of state constitutions, are more active on public-school issues than their federal counterparts. Because the source of a decision has bearing on its authority and significance, it is important to understand the structure of state and federal court systems.

The State Three-Tiered Judicial System

Most states have a three-tiered judicial system that includes a court of general jurisdiction, a court of general review, and a court of last resort (see Figure 16.1). Small states may not have the intermediate court of review. The name given to each of these levels differs considerably from state to state and can be a source of some confusion. The court of general jurisdiction may be called a district court or circuit court. It is usually organized on a county basis, and the judge or magistrate is not required to render a written opinion. Decisions at this level are not published and generally have little precedential value, although they are watched with considerable interest to see what new developments are occurring. The party who loses at this level can appeal to the second level, the appellate court. Finally, the courts of last resort can choose to accept cases on appeal. This process of selective appeal, known as *certiorari*, protects the highest court from minor or routine cases that could result in case overload. State courts enjoy jurisdiction over disputes involving state legislation, the state constitution, and the U.S. Constitution. The highest state court has the final word in interpreting the meaning of state laws or state constitution.

The Federal Three-Tiered Judicial System

In the federal three-tiered court system, district courts, circuit courts of appeal, and the Supreme Court are the most important courts at each level for educational decisions (see Figure 16.2). Federal district courts have general jurisdictional requirements that must be satisfied in order to use that forum.

Appeals from the district courts are made to the circuit courts of appeal. Figure 16.3 provides the boundaries for the 13 circuit courts of appeal. At the final level of review, the U.S. Supreme Court enjoys selective review. At least four of the Supreme Court justices must agree to hear a case before it will be briefed (stated in a concise summary), argued, and decided by the Court. The criteria the justices generally use in selecting cases for review include the case's potential for develop-

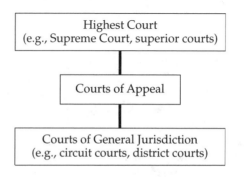

**FIGURE 16.1   Typical Three-Tiered
State Judicial Structure**

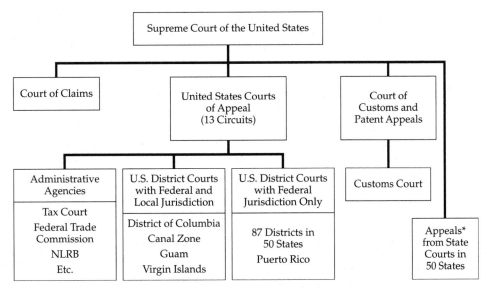

FIGURE 16.2   Three Jurisdictional Levels in the Federal Court System

*Appeals from state courts can be taken by the U.S. Supreme Court only if they involve matters of federal constitutional, statutory, or regulatory law.

Source: "The United States Courts," House Document 180, 88th Congress, 1st Session.

FIGURE 16.3   The Thirteen Federal Judicial Circuits
(See U.S.C.A. § 41)

Source: Reprinted with permission from West's Federal Reporter, Third Series, Vol. 89, Copyright 1996 by West Publishing Company. All rights reserved.

ing a more precise interpretation of the law and the case's potential for resolving conflicts between different circuit courts of appeal.

Although consistency under the law is an objective of the legal system, it is not always realized. The issue of school prayer at graduation ceremonies, for example, is still unsettled in the federal appellate courts. The U.S. Supreme Court, in 1992, held that it is unconstitutional for a school to invite and include a member of the clergy to offer prayers at a graduation ceremony (*Lee* v. *Weisman*, 1992; see Exhibit 16.2). The Fifth Circuit subsequently held that where students initiated the invitation and inclusion of the clergy member, the Constitution is not violated (*Jones* v. *Clear Creek Independent School District*, 1992). Contrary to the Fifth Circuit, the Ninth Circuit interpreted *Lee* v. *Weisman* to deem even student-initiated convocation prayer as unconstitutional (*Harris* v. *Joint School District No. 241*, 1994). The

---

EXHIBIT 16.2   *Lee* v. *Weisman*, 505 U.S. 577, 112 S. Ct. 2649 (1992)

Cases are often cited in support of a proposition, and the citation communicates how the case can be easily located in its entirety. Cases are collected according to reporter systems, each of which has its own title and abbreviation. The number in front of the reporter identification is the volume; the number following the reporter is the page number where the decision can be found. Therefore, the Supreme Court decision in *Lee* v. *Weisman*, 505 U.S. 577, 112 S. Ct. 2649 (1992), can be found on page 577 of Volume 505 of the *United States Reporter*. A decision may appear in a variety of reporters. Supreme Court opinions, because of their importance, are published in more reporters than any other decisions. The official reporter for the Supreme Court, the *United States Reporter*, is listed first in citation. The second citation is for the *Supreme Court Reporter*, often cited because it is published more quickly after a decision than the official reporter. Very recent opinions will not yet be cited in any reporter due to delays in publishing. These recent opinions can be found, however, in either Lexis or Westlaw, two computerized legal research companies that provide online opinions within 24 hours of a released decision. The Lexis cite to *Lee* v. *Weisman* is 1992 LEXIS 4364. The Westlaw cite to arguments on this decision is 1991 WL 636285. Computerized research can provide access to much more information than the mere published opinion (i.e., briefs and argument transcripts). Federal district court decisions are collected in the Federal Supplement Series, abbreviated F. Supp., and the circuit courts of appeal opinions are collected in the Federal Reporter Second and Third Series, abbreviated F.2d and F.3d. The *Lee* v. *Weisman* district court decision is reported at 728 F. Supp. 68 (D.R.I. 1990), and the appellate courts decision is reported at 908 F.2d 1090 (1 Cir. 1990). State court decisions are not collected for courts of general jurisdiction (the lowest level), but state appellate courts are collected either under the official state title (e.g. the *Illinois Reporter* or the *California Reporter*) or under a regional reporter. West Publishing Company publishes state opinions by regions. For example, the *Atlantic Reporter*, Second Series, abbreviated A.2d, reports cases from Connecticut, Delaware, Maine, Maryland, New Hampshire, New Jersey, Pennsylvania, Rhode Island, and Vermont. There are seven regional reporters—Atlantic, Northeastern, Northwestern, Pacific, Southeastern, Southern, and Southwestern—that report all 50 states. West Publishing Company also collects cases in reporters according to the subject area of the law upon which the decision is focused. Since 1982, West has been collecting education cases reported in various regional and federal reporters in a single source entitled West's *Education Law Reporter*. The *Lee* v. *Weisman* Supreme Court decision is reported in the *Educational Law Reporter* at 75 Ed. L.R. 43 (1992).

Supreme Court granted certiorari for *Harris* and ultimately vacated the decision on procedural grounds, never reaching the merits of student initiation of prayer or resolving the contradicting approaches of the appellate courts.

Federal courts enjoy jurisdiction over disputes involving federal legislation and the U.S. Constitution. It is possible for federal constitutional questions to move from state courts to federal courts. Beyond this, the systems try to protect the jurisdictional autonomy implicit in the federal system.

Litigation and Preventive Law

A court's decision may have an impact much broader than its jurisdiction. Technically, a court's decision is binding authority only within its own jurisdiction. The Supreme Court is, of course, binding authority for the United States. When school issues are litigated, school administrators must take a keen interest in the decision. Unless they feel strongly about the matter in question, administrators tend to follow a course of action consistent with the court's decision. If, however, an administrator feels that the decision reached is inappropriate because of improper application of a judicial standard, that administrator and his or her colleagues may wait to have the disputed practice challenged further.

The Cost of Litigation

Because litigation is costly, it cannot be undertaken lightly. Courts do not provide advisory opinions. There must be a real dispute between parties for a court to hear arguments and render an opinion. Because litigation is a costly process, people typically try to avoid it whenever possible, leaving many significant legal questions unanswered. Even though legal questions may not be answered by the courts, an administrator should not feel frozen within the legal system, unable to make an informed decision concerning whatever issue he or she is currently facing. The school administrator has a variety of options for acquiring the understanding needed to make an informed decision. He or she can peruse the law, reading cases, statutes, and attorney general or state education advisory opinions to determine the contours of the legal issue in question. Although many administrators are willing and academically able to conduct this search, most do not have the time or the resources to do so on their own. The administrator in that situation may turn to the school attorney. The key to a district that avoids legal problems is an administrator who knows when to resort to the school attorney, knows what questions to ask that attorney, and, most importantly, has enough legal background to evaluate the worth of the information that the attorney provides.

A school attorney will be able to answer an administrator's legal questions only to the extent that the law in the area in question is settled. Legal standards are not always clear and most develop over time. It is important, therefore, to remember that a school attorney can only furnish currently available information. An attorney can also provide advice based on a thorough rendition of the facts in question. If the attorney does not have access to all of the facts, he or she may not be able to provide accurate advice. When information is received from a school attorney, the attorney should explain the facts upon which the proffered opinion is based to be sure that they are pertinent to the case.

The advice of a school attorney should be carefully evaluated on the basis of an administrator's own knowledge of the legal system and on the basis of the administrator's own educational objectives. An administrator should ask as many questions as are necessary for understanding the reasoning behind the attorney's advice, including questions about the strength of the judicial precedent, the effective date of statutes, and the extent to which the facts of the case in question match those of the case upon which the attorney may be relying. A lot of information is likely to be included in an attorney's advice, and it is important to understand each component to properly evaluate the significance of that advice in making school or district decisions.

Preventive Law

School administrators are typically faced with a great many decisions that require a legal perspective. To regard school law as a prescription for proper behavior or as a set of boundaries within which any behavior is acceptable is to treat law as static and unresponsive to the ongoing changes in the society it is designed to regulate. Because the law undergoes frequent changes through new legislation and judicial action, administrators must understand and keep track of its current status. This understanding will enable administrators to anticipate situations that might cause legal vulnerability. Knowing how the law works should lead administrators to take actions that are reasonable and just and that avoid placing their schools in situations that unnecessarily invite conflict and litigation. It is educators, not courts or legislatures, who must determine what actions are reasonable and just in most school situations (Bull & McCarthy, 1995, pp. 619–620). School administrators are primarily responsible for providing the best means available for student achievement. An understanding of the legal context within which schools operate is essential to making that best means possible.

Harold Hawkins's 1986 monograph on preventive law describes five strategies to minimize litigation:

> *Strategy 1: Increase communication on a regular basis among teachers, administrators and parents.*
>
> *Strategy 2: Improve understanding of educational law.*
>
> *Strategy 3: Strengthen consistency in the implementation of policies and procedures.*
>
> *Strategy 4: Engage in periodic internal review of school district policy.*
>
> *Strategy 5: Develop a system for external preventive legal audit. (pp. 34–42)*

Basically, these strategies call for regular review of school district policies in light of current legal standards and systematic communication among teachers, administrators, and parents. This communication connects the policies with the educational philosophy of the district.

Summary

Schools are governed under authority granted by state law within the limitations of constitutional rights and protections; therefore, the relationship between the state legislature and local school districts is bounded by the statutory authority granted to districts by the legislature within state and federal constitutional limitations.To properly analyze and act on a school-law issue, administrators must understand the source of the legal principle involved, and because the source of a judicial decision has bearing on its authority and significance, administrators must understand the structure of the state and federal court systems. Knowledge of how the law works will help administrators to determine what actions are reasonable and just in most school situations; however, as judges interpret statutes, contracts, regulations, or constitutions and apply judicial standards that pertain only to the context of a particular dispute, the resulting decision is valid only for that set of facts. Administrators must therefore understand the extent of contextual as well as statutory and constitutional limitations.

Understanding how the law affects community schools should help administrators to avoid placing their schools in situations that unnecessarily invite conflict and litigation. As an administrator's decisions affect many aspects of his or her school's operation, including student welfare, learning climate, and school reputation, each administrator must understand and anticipate the legal consequences that may result from his or her actions. As an alternative to costly litigation, administrators can seek advisory opinions of the state attorney general or the legal staff of the state department of education, or they may apply for legal advice from the school district's legal counsel, although courts do not find such advisory opinions binding in any way. Decisions made by school administrators in the course of their workday can have far-reaching legal consequences. They must understand those consequences, know when to consult with district legal counsel, and know enough about legal procedures to evaluate the advice they receive from such counsel.

Administrators should become familiar with legal reasoning to enable them to determine their own courses of action rather than to attempt to define a general standard of conduct for schools in a particular area before several cases in that area have been decided and judicial precedent has been determined. In making decisions, school administrators must remember that their power is restrained by the authority vested in the school board by state and federal governments, by the courts, and by the communities that their schools serve. Their authority is tempered by a direct responsibility to those entities.

References

Brown v. *Board of Education*, 347 U.S. 483 (1954).

Bull, B. L., & McCarthy, M. M. (1995). Reflections on the knowledge base in law and ethics for educational leaders. *Educational Administration Quarterly, 31*(4), 613–631.

Connelly v. *Gibbs*, 445 N.E.2d 477 (Ill. App. 1 Dist. 1983).

Goss v. *Lopez*, 419 U.S. 565 (1976).

Harris v. *Joint School District No. 241*, 41 F.3d 447 (9th Cir. 1994).

Hawkins, H. L. (1986). Preventive law: Strategies for avoidance of litigation in public schools. *UCEA Monograph Series.* Tempe, AZ: University Council for Educational Administration.

Herscher v. *Kankakee*, 422 N.E.2d 273 (Ill. App. 3 Dist. 1981).

Homeless Children and Youth Act of 1995, 42 U.S.C.A. § 114341(2) (West 1995).

Jones v. *Clear Creek Independent School District*, 977 F.2d 963 (5th Cir. 1992).

Kraut v. *Rachford*, 366 N.E.2d 497 (Ill. App. Dist. 1977).

Lee v. *Weisman*, 505 U.S. 577, 112 S. Ct. 2649 (1992).

Plyer v. *Doe*, 457 U.S. 202 (1982).

Turner v. *Board of Education*, 294 N.E.2d 264 (1973).

Chapter *17*

Legal Considerations in Public-School Administration

Legal Sources and Specializations

The content of education law draws from a wide variety of legal sources concerned with K–12 education. These sources range across the core legal areas of property, contracts, torts, administrative law, constitutional law, and statutory interpretation. Administrators must understand the areas of the law in which educational issues or problems are grounded. When a board of education decides to sell a school building, for example, it is easy to understand why the superintendent would want a lawyer who is expert in property to execute the sale. Various areas of legal specialization draw on different principles and different precedents.

Knowledge of substantive law is important for administrators because it provides a framework for understanding the authority and limitations that frame the professional responsibilities of administrators and teachers. This chapter provides a brief introduction to several substantive areas of law. Because public education is primarily a matter of state responsibility in the nation's federal system, the first part of this chapter will explore three important areas of state law: delegation of authority to local districts and state boards of education, torts (negligence), and contracts. Federal and state constitutions provide significant limitations on the authority of public education officials. The second part will examine three examples of this federal Constitutional limitation of authority: Fourteenth Amendment due process, First Amendment free speech, and First Amendment separation of church and state. A third part will consider legal standards of liability, and a fourth part will explore a developing area of concern in schools: student-to-student sexual harassment.

The decisions made and the actions taken by school administrators that may dramatically affect the lives of so many people should be assisted by an understanding of the legal system. Administrative decisions and actions are generally routine and often dictated by tradition. Effective schools, however, are not static places. In these dynamic times, administrators need to be able to change or develop policies that can shape the educational environment. To make such policies, administrators need not only have some vision of desired objectives, but also must understand the constraints and opportunities that the legal system provides. This knowledge can be helpful in conceptualizing policies that support and align with educational objectives. An important challenge for educational administrators is to actively utilize the considerable power and authority they enjoy. School administrators work in a legal context where they must comply with statutory and constitutional requirements, but they also have considerable authority to write policies and shape practices that affect the teachers and students in their schools or districts.

This introduction to substantive law is intended not as a statement of the black letter law that needs to be memorized and applied in schools. Rather, it is the relationship between these legal standards and educational policymaking that will be explored. These legal standards provide a framework, but considerable latitude exists in how educational philosophy is translated into practice.

State Legal Considerations

State legislatures have plenary power in education and in establishment of educational policy, and this power is limited only by the federal Constitution and the states' own constitutions. This plenary power allows a state legislature to delegate authority, normally to state administrative agencies or local boards of education in the area of education, and to alter or revise its delegation. Except in Hawaii, which operates only one statewide school district, the states have delegated major authority to local school districts for the provision of public education. The operation of these schools is enough of a routine that there is seldom a question of authority or power. But when a school district faces a new type of problem and wants to develop a policy about the problem that goes beyond anything that has been done before, there can be a question about whether authority exists for such action. Or when a school district takes a certain action that upsets a certain district's constituency, this constituency may consider legal challenges to the proposed district action, and one of the most common challenges will be to the district's authority to undertake such action.

The existence of appropriate power or authority can be critical in determining what actions a particular board or state agency can make. The following sections consider several important themes that run through this area of the law and provide a few examples of litigation in which these themes have been used. Issues of authority will be increasingly important as school administrators move away from bureaucratic and traditional norms of administrative behavior and move toward activist, aggressive administrative styles responsive to the needs of students.

Legislative Delegation of Authority

The rule applying to a state legislature's authority to delegate is much easier to say than it is to predict the court's application of it in specific circumstances. The rule is that the legislature may delegate by statute administrative powers to administrative agencies in the executive branch of government but may not delegate legislative powers. The rationale for this distinction between legislative and administrative delegation is drawn from the constitutional distinction between legislative and executive powers. The transfer of legislative authority to administrative agencies would dilute legislative autonomy and threaten the basic principle of separation of power so central to the constitutional system in the United States. In addition, this would tend to put the decision maker out of reach of the electorate, the important political check that exists in the country's democratic system. As matters become more complicated, it is impossible for the legislature to administer vast and varied administrative agencies that are ultimately under its authority. Therefore, courts, in distinguishing delegable administrative power from nondelegable lawmaking power, search the enabling statutes for reasonably precise guidelines that might describe the policy objectives of the legislature or guide administrator discretion in implementing the legislative goal. The general legal theory is that the delegation is valid so long as the statutory guidelines limit the discretion of the administrators and do not allow for administrative judgment to be substituted for that of the elected legislators.

The application of this rule is much more difficult to predict. Particular cases include passages that describe some of the elements that go into the balance. For example, consider the following:

> The line separating that which is purely regulation, and that which is purely legislation, is necessarily indistinct, and becomes more so as in the line separating such authority is approached. Therefore, courts . . . will resolve the doubt in favor of the validity of the [delegating] act rather than holding it invalid . . . which is especially true when the [administrative] act is essential and necessary for carrying out the broad purpose and intent of the Legislature. (Dicken v. Kentucky State Board of Education, 1947)

As this suggests, it will be important to identify the subject matter of the legislation, the specificity of guidelines surrounding the legislation, and the extent to which other interests, either individual interests that may be protected by the Constitution or group interests that may be dealt with in other legislation, are present.

Even when powers are appropriately delegated, it can be difficult to know how those powers will extend. Consequently, courts are often called on to determine whether the administrative body has acted beyond its legally delegated authority. It is easy to read the statute and determine what has been expressly authorized to the administrative agency. But since many statutes also provide broad discretionary power, which may be necessary for the proper and efficient management of public education, the courts will recognize implied power to act in certain ways that may be necessary to accomplish the desired legislative policy during changing times and conditions. If, however, the desired authority goes beyond the intent of the statute, it moves past being an implied power to being a nondelegated activity and becomes illegal.

A North Carolina case involved a challenge about the appropriate authority of a school district to initiate an extended day-care program to better satisfy the different home needs of many of its latchkey students. The case provides a good example of what the court found important in deciding whether such action was authorized. The school district initiated an extended-day program that, for a fee that supported the program, provided activities after school for children who might not have parents at home at the end of the normal school day. The only costs to the school district were fuel and lighting costs associated with use of the building. A coalition of day-care-center operators challenged the authority of the school district to initiate such a program. The North Carolina Court of Appeals in *Kiddie Korner Day Schools* v. *Charlotte-Mecklenburg Board of Education* (1981) held that the school district had the authority under state statute to operate such a program for latchkey children. Additionally, the court upheld the authority of the school district to expend money for heating and lighting the building for the benefit of these extended-day pupils because this was a public benefit. The program provided academic improvement for many of these students. Because the school board had the authority to absorb the fuel and electricity costs of the program, since it was for a public purpose, to improve the educational achievements of latchkey children, the court rejected the contention that the expenditure must be approved by the voters in a referendum.

A Nebraska statute allowed high school districts that were receiving high school students (from districts that did not have a high school) to reduce the high school tuition charges set by the State Department of Education to any amount decided by the receiving district so long as it was not less than the per-pupil cost in the district. This statute was challenged as being unconstitutional. The Nebraska Supreme Court in *Ewing* v. *Board of Equalization* (1988) held that the statute, in general, was constitutional in that the legislature could, in certain situations, delegate taxing authority to a school district. The particular provision that gave very broad discretion in its taxing authority, however, was declared unconstitutional precisely because it did not have the necessary "reasonable limitations and standards." This amounted to an unconstitutional delegation of legislative authority.

Redelegation: Appropriate Administrative Delegation of Authority

The law is clear that an administrative agency may not redelegate those discretionary powers conferred upon it to another body or a subordinate employee. In the public-school context, this standard is most significant in limiting the actions to which a district employee can legally bind the district in a situation where the board of education has taken no official action. Some cases distinguish between the ministerial actions of employees, which are purely mechanical and therefore legitimate, from those that are discretionary and therefore not proper. Two cases from different states demonstrate how widely divergent results from this redelegation doctrine can be reached, depending on the specifics of the statute and the inclinations of the particular state courts.

In *Community Projects for Students* v. *Wilder* (1982), the North Carolina court of appeals held that a supplier of merchandise to school for sale by students could not sue the district for the value of unsold and unreturned merchandise when the school board had not entered into the contract. The court articulated who had the authority to make contracts: "Under the system of public education in this state, local school boards alone have the duty or authority to enter into or authorize purchases of supplies and equipment for the respective local school systems." The action of the high school principal could not obligate the school board. In addition, the law recognizes that public officials are deemed to have notice of the limited nature and extent of the authority of principals or other school officials to bind the board of education. Consequently, an argument that the principal had apparent authority to bind the board of education to the contract was rejected.

In the second case, a student in the junior class of a Louisiana high school decided to rent a sound system and have a disk jockey play records for the junior-senior prom, rather than employ the more traditional band. A disk jockey was selected and a contract signed by one of the two class sponsors after discussing the matter with the building principal. When the principal later discovered that it was a sound system rather than a band, something he apparently had not understood at the time of the signing, he tried to break the contract because he did not think it appropriate for the prom. In an action for damages for breach of contract, a Louisiana appeals court held that the school district was liable for the amount specified in the liquidated-damages clause stated in the contract (*Herbert* v. *Livingston Parish School Board*, 1983). The court held that the principal had implied authority to represent the school board and that this authority was properly delegated to the faculty sponsor who actually signed the contract. Because the principal was properly exercising his authority as principal, the school board was a party to the contract and could be held liable for its breach. In addition, there was no personal liability on the principal, even though he was the one who broke the contract, because he was acting on the implied authority given him by the school board. There is no Louisiana statute limiting the authority of the district to be bound by contract only upon certification approval and signature by the board, as exists in other states.

The delegation doctrine can also be important in hiring and firing decisions. A South Dakota district, for example, had an unexpected resignation in late August. The position was announced, and a candidate visited the district and interviewed for the position. The candidate was told he would have a two-week trial period, as the board was not scheduled to meet before then. The candidate refused the position on a trial basis, so the contract was prepared, and he accepted by signing the contract. Before the contract was signed by any board members, the new teacher had trouble with his class, and the district refused to approve the contract and terminated him after nine days of teaching. The South Dakota Supreme Court held that no contract existed because the contract had not been signed by the appropriate district representatives as required by law. "A teacher shall be employed only upon written contract signed by the teacher and by the president of the school board and business manager of the school district" (*Minor* v. *Sally Buttes School District 58-2*, 1984). The court did award compensation for moving expenses and housing costs that were incurred because of detrimental reliance on the teaching position. Contracts can be formed only according to the specific standards stated in law.

Shared Authority with Another Administrative Agency

Occasionally, a conflict will arise when one administrative agency is seeking to take action that impinges on the authority of another administrative agency. In this highly regulated world during a period of rapidly changing circumstances, this conflict over turf is not unusual. Normally, courts resolve these disputes by identifying the particular activity and determining which administrative agency has the more central responsibility. As one example, consider the attempt of an Ohio school district to develop its own electrical contract.

An Ohio board of education voted to purchase electricity from a different company than the one supplying the rest of the municipality. The municipality challenged the authority of the school district to make such a purchase. The Ohio Supreme Court, in *Village of Lucas* v. *Lucas Local School District* (1982), interpreted the state constitution to grant exclusive authority for the contracting of public-utility services to municipalities. Consequently, although there is no explicit limit on the school district's power to purchase electricity, the court held that the grant of authority to the municipality means that school districts are prohibited from contracting for public-utility services absent the express consent of the municipality. To do otherwise would limit the ability of the municipality to obtain the best utility rates for its residents.

In Illinois, a dispute arose over the authority of a county health department to make sanitary and health inspections of public school cafeterias. The school district argued that this authority to inspect the schools resided exclusively in the regional superintendent of schools. The appellate court, analyzing the appropriate statutes, determined that the regional superintendent was not given exclusive authority.

Because the county health departments were given general authority for sanitary and health inspections while the regional superintendents were given general building inspection authority, the court concluded that the county health department had the authority to inspect school cafeterias (*County of Macon* v. *Board of Education*, 1987).

Statutory Authority Granted to State Boards of Education

State boards of education are important sources of authority. These state boards differ on where they draw their legitimacy: About half are created by statute and half by state constitution (Valente, 1980). Even when created by state constitutional authority, the state board of education is still subject to the commands of the legislature. Consequently, state boards of education derive authority from state statutes and have authority to do only that which is expressly or implicitly delegated to them.

As state boards attempt to carry out their perceived responsibilities, disagreements can arise about whether the state board actually does enjoy such power. Often, such disagreements occur between a state board and a local school district.

The Illinois Supreme Court in 1982 had to decide whether the Illinois State Board of Education had the authority to promulgate and enforce rules designed to prevent racial segregation. In 1971, the Illinois legislature had passed a statute that provided, in part:

> *As soon as practicable, and from time to time thereafter, the [local] board shall change or revise existing [attendance centers] or create new [attendance centers] in a manner which will take into consideration the prevention of segregation and the elimination of separation of children in public schools because of color, race or nationality. (Ill. Rev. Stat. 1977, Ch. 122, 10-21.3)*

Pursuant to this statute, the state board developed rules to eliminate and prevent racial segregation in schools, and these rules were officially adopted by the board in 1976. The most difficult requirement of these rules was that each attendance center in a district not vary by more than 15 percentage points from the minority racial composition of the pupils in all attendance centers. This, in effect, defined nonconformance as a 15 percent plus or minus quota from the districtwide composition of minorities. The state board also identified compliance standards, and noncompliance would lead to nonrecognition and possible loss of state funding. Two school districts could not meet the 15 percent quota in individual attendance centers without instituting busing of students outside neighborhood schools. Refusing to do this, and in fear of losing state aid for noncompliance, the districts challenged the authority of the state board to promulgate such rules.

The state board argued that it enjoyed statutory authority to promulgate such rules because of general language in the Illinois School Code. The Illinois Supreme Court rejected this claim.

> *Nowhere in [the statute] is the board granted expressed authority to determine standards for racial desegregation. And the fact that the board may set standards for the "Operation, maintenance, administration and supervision" of schools does not imply the authority now sought. If we were to hold otherwise, it would be dif-*

ficult to conceive of any regulation which could not be justified under [this stat-ute]. (Aurora East Public School District *v.* Cronin, 1982)

The court also noted that a different statutory section provided a procedure the board could use in combating segregation. The 1971 statute did not provide any standard or guidelines governing the board's discretion to enforce the statute. Looking at another section of the school code, the Illinois Supreme Court was persuaded that the local school district had the authority to decide how to comply with the 1971 statute. The rules of the state board in this area were unenforceable.

Legislative Attempts to Reduce Administrative Burdens

Many state legislatures are passing laws that allow waivers of specified mandates and allow schools the opportunity to propose alternative organizations that may exempt them from many laws and regulations that apply to public schools. This is apparently in response to criticism about the high degree of legislative control that states exert on public schools and the inertia created by this administrative burden and in hope of providing a more daring, entrepreneurial spirit toward the operation of public schools. Illinois, for example, passed legislation that provides a mechanism for school boards to obtain waivers from a wide range of legal mandates or administrative regulations (Hosea, Colwell, & Thurston, 1996). Many states have charter school legislation that provides a mechanism for chartering a school that can be exempt from specified laws and regulations. The scope of exemptions differs widely from state to state. For example, charter school legislation in Minnesota, California, Georgia, Wisconsin, and Arizona allows amnesty from most state education requirements and district rules, while most other states allow waivers of rules and regulations as part of the charter approval process. (For a short, thoughtful introduction to the topic of deregulation and school improvement, see "Ten Lessons," 1992.)

Torts (Negligence)

Tort is a general term used to define any of several independent civil causes of action based on noncontractual legal responsibilities that individuals have to avoid harming or injuring another's person, property, or reputation. Torts are actually separate, independent causes of action that define a particular level of conduct that the law recognizes individuals owe one another. Torts range from the common areas of negligence, defamation (libel and slander), and assault and battery to the more esoteric ones of privacy, false imprisonment, and intentional infliction of emotional distress. Because school districts and administrators might be defendants in a tort action—most likely a negligence action—it is important to understand torts in general and the tort of negligence in particular. Knowledge of negligence liability can also help an administrator take precautions to minimize dangerous situations.

Knowledge of the legal subtleties of negligence can also help an administrator understand the nuances between the particular facts and the legal standard. The administrator consequently may talk to teachers and students in a way that is sensitive to their circumstances and not solely driven by hard and fast rules that may not be totally accurate.

Negligence: The Prima Facie Case

For an injured party to secure monetary damages from another party for allegedly negligent action, the injured party will need to plead and prove, at minimum, four elements (Prosser, 1984). The exact elements necessary for carrying the plaintiff's burden in the prima facie case will vary from state to state. Some states, for example, require the plaintiff to plead an absence of contributory negligence, whereas other states do not. Schools and their employers are not responsible as insurers for any and all injuries that occur. For liability to be present, it must be shown that the school has a particular responsibility to the injured person, that the behavior fell short of that required, that this breach was the proximate cause of the injury, that there were real injuries, and that the plaintiff was not responsible for causing the injury. Consider the elements, the prima facie case, in more detail:

1. *Duty of care.* There is a duty of care that the law recognizes one person owes to another. It requires a certain standard of conduct for the protection of others against unreasonable risks. One has a legal duty to act as an ordinary, prudent, reasonable person in the circumstances. A child is expected to conform to the standard of conduct of a child of like age, education, intelligence, and experience. The duty can be specified by statute or as a matter of common law. Usually in the school context, it is not hard to show that the school (and its teachers) have a duty to protect the health and safety of the students while they are in the custody of the school.

2. *A breach of the duty.* This amounts to a failure of one party to conform to the standard required toward another. This can occur from either an action or an omission. The breach of the duty of due care in a specific case is a question of fact. Making a showing of this breach involves both showing what actually happened and showing how the defendant acted unreasonably. Alleging failure to supervise, for example, is alleging that the teacher failed to take the appropriate action.

3. *Causation.* There must be reasonably close causal connection between the alleged misconduct and the resulting injury. This requires both a cause-in-fact relationship between the behavior and the injury and that the behavior and injury be sufficiently close in time and foreseeability.

4. *Actual damages.* The plaintiff must show an actual loss or real damages. Nominal damages, to indicate a technical right, or the threat of future harm, not yet realized, are insufficient injury on which to bring a negligence action. The amount of damages awarded depends on the particular circumstances of the person injured and what amount of money it will take to make that person whole.

5. *Foreseeability and the reasonable-person standard.* Two other components of the prima facie case, foreseeability and the reasonable-person standard, are basic to understanding its operation. Foreseeability, which is either subsumed under the duty-of-care element or the proximate-cause element, means that the defendant could or should have seen the potentially dangerous consequences of the action when it was taken. This does not mean that the defendant subjectively or person-ally actually foresaw the potential danger. Rather, the defendant is presumed to be a reasonable person and the jury then is given instructions, like the following, to determine foreseeability: "Would you, as a reasonable person, standing in the place of Y defendant at X time, have foreseen the occurrence of Z injury?" Notice that under this instruction, the jury enjoys the luxury of hindsight when determin-ing foreseeability—something that often leads to sharper vision than the defen-dant actually may have had.

The application of these legal standards depends on the particular set of facts involved. The jury usually plays the central role as fact finder for all the elements of the prima facie case. Still, the judge controls, as a matter of law, which cases involve factual allegations sufficient to go to the jury.

Affirmative Defenses

Affirmative defenses provide a bar, either total or partial, to recovery even if all of the elements of the prima facie case are proved.

Assumption of Risk
Assumption of risk is one affirmative defense, and the concept behind it is that the injured plaintiff, through either actual knowledge or extreme recklessness, knew that the action engaged in would lead to injury and that this knowledge should bar recovery where the injury does in fact occur. A district court in Virginia articulated the test for assumption of risk in the following way:

> *The defense of assumption of risk focuses on the injured person's subjective state of mind, asking whether the plaintiff fully understood the nature and extent of known danger and voluntarily exposed himself to it.* (Freeman *v.* Case Corpo-ration, *1996)*

Contributory Negligence
The general rationale for contributory negligence as an affirmative defense is that where the injured plaintiff's conduct was unreasonable or negligent in its own right, given the circumstances, and led in some way to the resulting injury, the injured plaintiff ought not to be rewarded for an injury at least partially the result of his or her actions. An injured plaintiff found contributorily negligent, therefore, would receive no damage compensation. Many states have replaced the idea of

contributory negligence with that of comparative negligence. The general concept behind contributory negligence is an all-or-nothing determination. In a pure comparative-negligence state, the plaintiff may be found 5 percent or 45 percent or 95 percent negligent by the jury, for example, whereas in a contributory-negligence state, the jury must choose either 0 percent or 100 percent negligence.

Consider two different cases in which these legal principles are involved. A 13-year-old special education student was hit in the eye by a chalkboard clip thrown by another student. This incident occurred at a time when the classroom teacher was on her lunch break, and the class was being supervised by a teacher's aide who was simultaneously responsible for supervising a second-grade class on recess. Thus, the aid left each group unattended while checking on the other group for which she was responsible. The district, the teacher, and the teacher's aide were sued for the injuries sustained by the plaintiff. In weighing the claim, the court had to articulate a standard for the teacher's and the teacher's aide's duty of due care:

> *A teacher's mere act of leaving children unsupervised will not be sufficient to establish [a violation in the duty of due care]. . . . Rather, a plaintiff must show that the teacher or school was aware or should have known that the absence of supervision posed a high probability of serious harm or an unreasonable risk of harm. . . . A plaintiff's general allegation that a teacher or school should have known that harm would occur without adult supervision is insufficient to satisfy this standard.* (Jackson *v.* Chicago Board of Education, *1989)*

Based on this, and an insufficient number of previous serious incidents to have put the teacher on notice about safety concerns in the classroom, the Illinois Court of Appeals affirmed the lower court's directed verdict dismissing the claim against the teacher and the district.

In the second case, a 14-year-old student in an agriculture class where instruction in welding was being given was badly injured by a power saw. The saw had been stored in the back of the classroom and was used by the student during the class period without authority and at a time when the instructor was absent from the room. The Louisiana appellate court affirmed the trial court in holding the school board liable for having breached its duty to protect the health and safety of its students by allowing such a dangerous instrument to be stored in the back of a classroom in a condition in which it could be so easily used. The school district raised both defenses of assumption of risk and contributory negligence. The court dismissed the assumption-of-risk defense because the injured student had never used a power saw before or been instructed in its use. Even though the district had told students not to use this equipment, the court held that the act of the student in switching on the saw did not amount to contributory negligence because this behavior was foreseeable. The saw should not have been stored in the back of the classroom in an area so accessible to students. The teacher was negligent for not properly supervising the classroom, and the school board assumed his liability under the respondeat superior doctrine, which holds the employer responsible for acts of an employee. The trial court award of $70,000 against the school board was sustained (*Lawrence* v. *Grant Paris School Board*, 1982).

Contracts

The school district is granted authority by the state legislature to enter into contracts to provide educational services. In most states, the process of collective bargaining between the district and its various employee groups is carefully controlled by statutes and administrative regulations. There are detailed requirements about who is covered in the collective bargaining process, the scope of the negotiations, what is appropriate for each side of the negotiations process to do as part of the negotiations, and the availability of various options when impasse is reached in the bargaining process. Administrators who have any personnel responsibilities need to be aware of applicable public bargaining requirements.

School districts also form contracts with other parties to provide a variety of goods and services. Milk contracts, textbook contracts, and additions to existing buildings all require the formation of a contract. Agreements are made and disagreements resolved according to the general law of contracts. Some school districts are exploring more broadly the services that they can purchase through contractual agreements. Contracting for transportation services has been common for decades. Recently, there has been more attention given to contracting custodial services and food services from private vendors. Hill (1994, 1996) argues that districts ought to become much more active in contracting for the delivery of teaching services from private vendors as well. The wisdom of contracting for these instructional services through private vendors is widely debated. There is a climate that is more hospitable toward contracting.

Limitations of Authority by the Federal Constitution

Supreme Court decisions have shaped substantive law in a number of constitutional areas affecting schools. Three areas of considerable significance to school administrators are Fourteenth Amendment due process, First Amendment free speech, and First Amendment separation of church and state. A major component for administrators in understanding the involvement of schools in the legal process is awareness of the limitations on authority that may be imposed by Supreme Court decisions.

Fourteenth Amendment Due Process

Due process is a fundamental part of jurisprudence in the United States. Applicable only to the federal government in the Fifth Amendment of the original Bill of Rights, due process was expanded in the post–Civil War Fourteenth Amendment to protect individuals from the power of the states. "No state shall deny any person of life, liberty or property." This simple statement has important implications for the way public school administrators perform their jobs. Courts make a distinction between substantive due process and procedural due process.

Substantive Due Process

Substantive due process refers to a core set of fundamental personal rights that every person enjoys, and for which a person cannot be denied by federal or state government unless there is a compelling state interest. Such substantive due process rights include the right to procreate, to marry, and to refuse medical treatment. In *Ingraham* v. *Wright* (1977), the Supreme Court refused to apply the Eighth Amendment's prohibition against cruel and unusual punishment to corporal punishment in schools. The Court did leave open the question, though, whether severe forms of corporal punishment might amount to a deprivation of substantive due process. Subsequent lower court decisions have examined this question and hold that students do enjoy a substantive liberty interest in not being exposed to excessive corporal punishment. The Fourth Circuit Court in *Hall* v. *Tawney* (1980) concluded that the "right to ultimate bodily security—the most fundamental aspect of personal privacy—is unmistakably established in our constitutional decisions as an attribute of the ordered liberty that is the concern of substantive due process.... We simply do not see how we can fail also to recognize it in public school children under the disciplinary control of public school teachers" (p. 613). (Also see *P. B.* v. *Koch* [1966] for case citations in circuit court of appeals decisions from the Third, Sixth, Eighth, Ninth, and Tenth Circuit Courts of Appeals affirming this substantive due process right.)

Procedural Due Process

Procedural due process focuses on the procedural safeguards that need to accompany certain sanctions being considered by public officials. The determinations of what procedures, if any, are constitutionally required involves a two-step analysis. The first question, coming directly from the operative Fourteenth Amendment clause, is: Has there been a deprivation of a liberty or property interest? The meaning given to the critical terms *liberty* and *property* differ for various claimants. A property interest exists where a person has some objective claim to a job or source of money. Property interests include benefits granted by the state. Compulsory education statutes, for example, confer a benefit to students to attend public schools. Removal of a student from public school, whether because of application of a residency policy or suspension or expulsion for violation of disciplinary rules, involves a property interest.

For teachers, the primary sources of property derive from contract and tenure status, which is simply a continuous contractual status provided by state law. Consequently, a teacher cannot be dismissed from a contractual status (during the course of a contract term, for nontenured teachers; nonrenewal, for tenured teachers) without accompanying procedural safeguards.

A liberty interest for employees exists when one's reputation or honor in the community is damaged or when one's opportunity to obtain equivalent employment is foreclosed. These potentially significant avenues to due process have been all but closed by a number of court decisions. For example, nonrenewal of nontenured teachers for incompetency has been held not to involve a liberty interest, regardless of how other people in the community or other potential employers might view it.

If no deprivation of a liberty or property interest exists, then the inquiry ends and no procedural safeguards need be provided. Yet if a liberty or property deprivation is found, the Court asks a second question: Given this deprivation, what level of procedural safeguards must be minimally provided to protect the threatened interests?

No mechanical formula exists for determining appropriate procedural safeguards. The court is guided by a general conception that due process is equated with fairness and that the level of procedures provided should be commensurate with the severity of the deprivation to protect the various interests involved. Justice Frankfurter described this notion of due process as fairness. "It is not a technical conception with a fixed content unrelated to time, place and circumstances . . . due process is not a mechanical instrument. It is not a yardstick. It is a delicate process of adjustment" (*Joint Anti-Fascist Refugee Committee* v. *McGrath*, 1951).

The procedures provided to the defendant charged with breaking the criminal law are used as a benchmark when less serious matters are involved. The criminal defendant is entitled to the following procedures:

1. Written notice of the alleged violation and adequate time to prepare a defense
2. Right to be represented by counsel
3. Right to hearing by impartial tribunal
4. Right to compel witnesses to attend and testify
5. Right to confront and cross-examine adverse witnesses as well as to present own friendly witnesses
6. Right to having a record of the proceedings be kept
7. Right to a decision based on the information presented during the hearing

Courts have systematically rejected attempts to require procedural due-process safeguards for students or faculty members equal to those provided in a criminal trial (see *Linwood* v. *Board of Education*, 1972). Nonetheless, these procedures stand as the benchmark for determining what level of safeguards is necessary for the particular deprivation. The level of procedural safeguards required will vary according to the seriousness of the inappropriate behavior and the severity of the applicable sanction (Bittle, 1986; Bruin, 1989; Phay, 1982). Consider how this analysis has been employed for students and faculty members.

Where a short-term suspension is involved for student misconduct, the Supreme Court provides clear guidance about the minimal procedural safeguards constitutionally required. The leading Supreme Court decision in this area, *Goss* v. *Lopez* (1976), involves a short-term suspension. During a period of widespread student unrest, approximately 80 students were suspended for up to 10 days from the Columbus, Ohio, public schools. These suspensions were made pursuant to an

Ohio law that empowered a public school principal to suspend (up to 10 days) or to expel a pupil for misconduct. Under the Ohio law, parents had to be notified of the suspension or expulsion within 24 hours and had to be given reasons for the action. In the case of an expulsion, the student and parents were entitled to a hearing before the board of education, but suspended students were entitled to no such hearing. Nine of the suspended Columbus, Ohio, students challenged the constitutionality of this statute as violating the Fourteenth Amendment due-process clause because they were suspended without a hearing. They sought invalidation of this statute and the removal of all reference to each suspension from their records.

Justice White, writing the majority opinion for the Supreme Court, undertook a two-step analysis in declaring the Ohio statute unconstitutional. First, he determined that removal of a student from school for a period of up to 10 days was a property deprivation. These suspensions "could seriously damage the students' standing with their fellow pupils and their teachers as well as interfere with later opportunities for higher education and employment."

Having identified a property deprivation, Justice White then had to decide the minimal level of procedures constitutionally required to accompany the suspension. Although suspensions are not as damaging as expulsions—which require a written notice and opportunity for a formal hearing before the board of education—suspensions must be accompanied by a lower-level notice and hearing.

> *Students facing temporary suspension have interests qualifying for protection of the Due Process Clause, and due process requires, in connection with a suspension of ten days or less, that the student be given oral or written notice of the charges against him and, if he denies them, an explanation of the evidence the authorities have and an opportunity to present his side of the story. The clause requires at least three rudimentary precautions against unfair or mistaken findings of misconduct and arbitrary exclusion from school.* (Goss v. Lopez, 1976)

Minimal procedural safeguards require that oral notice and oral hearing be provided in a student suspension, but the two can be given simultaneously. The administrator can tell the student what she or he is charged with, and then ask if the student has anything to say about the charge. If there is no information given to doubt the veracity of the charge, the student can be suspended on the spot. Where a question is raised about the validity of the charge, the administrator needs to seek more information. This notice and hearing should be provided prior to the suspension but can be put off until after the suspension where the continued presence of the student jeopardizes the health or safety of other students or threatens to disrupt the academic process. In such circumstances, the necessary notice and hearing should follow as soon as possible after the suspension.

Although there is no Supreme Court decision analogous to *Goss* v. *Lopez* involving a student expulsion, there are a number of lower federal court decisions. The administrator will need to be aware of the relevant precedent in his or her area. The level of procedural safeguards generally required in these student expulsion cases includes written notice of the alleged student misconduct, a right of the student to appear before the board of education (or its authorized representative) and tell his or her story, and a right that the punishment decision made by the board of education be based on the information provided in the record. Beyond this, there is disagreement among judicial districts about the nature of the factual presentation of evidence. For example, some courts require that all adverse testimony made against the accused come from the actual witnesses to the incident (see *Tibbs* v. *Board of Education*, 1971), whereas other courts allow school administrators to provide the testimony of other witnesses as they know it (see *Boykins* v. *Fairfield Board of Education*, 1974). Because technical rules of evidence are not necessary, hearsay evidence like this may be allowed, but it is then difficult to allow the defendant-student to engage in meaningful cross-examination. Courts also differ on the extent to which the defendants will be allowed to develop their cases, ranging from full right of cross-examination and presenting one's own witnesses, to merely allowing one's own witnesses to testify and make a statement.

There is disagreement over whether the defendant has a right to be represented in the hearing—by counsel or by someone else, possibly a friendly teacher. Some jurisdictions have upheld the banning of these representatives to avoid adversariness (see *Madera* v. *Board of Education*, 1967), whereas other courts will allow counsel to be present to help present a better case (see *Givens* v. *Poe*, 1972).

The concept of notice requires that the charges be sufficiently specific that the student will know precisely what conduct is deemed undesirable. As an example, one district court decision found the expulsion notice defective for using such general language as "your son . . . continues to conduct himself in an irresponsible and disruptive manner" and "he has been deliberately defiant of reasonable requests by teachers" without providing more specific information about approximate dates and sufficient detail to identify the student's inappropriate behavior (*Keller* v. *Fochs*, 1974).

The procedural safeguards for employees are similar. Where a tenured teacher is being threatened with dismissal, the teacher can expect to receive written notice of the dismissal charges specifying reasons for dismissal, an impartial hearing, the right to be represented by counsel, the right to present testimony, and that the decision be based on the evidence presented in the hearing. The teacher can be dismissed without pay prior to the hearing, but if the teacher wins, reinstatement with back pay to the time of dismissal is the usual remedy. A significant aspect of due process is the way it acts to shift the burden of proof. When an employee has a protected liberty or property interest, the employer-school district has the responsibility for pleading and proving the incompetence, immorality, or whatever other cause might exist for dismissal. Yet, if no such protected interest exists, the teacher may be dismissed at the end of the existing contractual term, and the teacher has the burden of showing that the dismissal was based on protected constitutional grounds.

In *Cleveland Board of Education* v. *Loudermill* (1985), the Supreme Court held that two public employees who were covered under Ohio civil service laws enjoyed constitutional due-process rights. These rights include a pretermination hearing, although the Ohio statute had provided for only a full posttermination hearing. State law can create the property interest but does not determine what the minimal constitutional procedures are. The Court held that due process requires that a civil service public employee is entitled to oral or written notice of the charges against him or her, an explanation of the employer's evidence, and an opportunity to present her or his side of the story prior to dismissal.

The two-step analysis provides the constitutional framework for understanding what minimal procedures are constitutionally required. The administrator will also need to stay abreast of procedural safeguards required by state law, contractual agreements, and district policy.

Purposes of Procedural Safeguards

It is important for prospective administrators to understand the purpose and value for providing procedural safeguards. Although procedural safeguards may appear onerous and seem to impede the efficient handling of cases, they do provide an important mechanism for administrators to engage in fact finding. Much of an administrator's time is spent managing conflict. This conflict often involves violations of state law or school-district policy. The administrator needs to gather information, listen to people, ask questions, and then apply this information to the applicable standard. Clear understanding of the facts is essential to applying an appropriate sanction; and due process is a significant way to engage in fact finding.

The skills of listening and asking questions that are broadly connected to understanding the facts of a dispute involve making subtle judgments about how to apply due process. The type of hearing and investigation appropriate to a particular case could differ drastically depending on the underlying problem. A typical student discipline case, for example, would likely involve interrogation of the student by a principal or dean. Yet, in a case where a parent raises a concern that a school janitor has molested an elementary school child, information needs to be obtained from the student. It is likely, in such an instance, that someone other than the principal may be better able to get the child to talk about the accusations. Conversations need to be held with the child and with the parent, and some of them, perhaps, will need to occur separately to be most effective. Where a minor is involved, the district needs to be concerned about conducting such an interview without parental permission. Someone also needs to speak to the janitor, and this will need to be conducted according to the terms of the contract. The principal has a duty to protect the health and safety of the students in the school and, minimally, a duty to handle the investigation of the janitor according to specific standards. This is the kind of case where legal advice is important from the beginning, clear commitment to fact finding is essential, and access to persons with special skills, such as nurses and counselors who may be able to talk with involved parties in a way that a principal may not be able to do, is needed. Basically, due process involves a commitment to administrative fact finding while respecting privacy interests that parties to the dispute enjoy.

Harris (1996), an urban high school dean in northern California, provides a short rumination about student discipline in a racially, ethnically diverse high school. He describes a disciplinary report filed by a teacher, upset about the attitude of a Hispanic student who had been disruptive outside the teacher's classroom. The report indicated that the student said to the teacher, "something to the effect that he was going to get me." The teacher later said publicly, "I want to get this kid" (p. 18). During the suspension hearing—attended by the police officer assigned to the school, the building union representative, and the student's mother, who spoke only Spanish—the teacher was admonished by the police officer for leveling a hard, confrontational stare at the student. The student was suspended for two days for the disruptive activity in the hallway, but the dean refused to file a police report because he could find no evidence of a direct threat against anyone. The next day, the teacher filed a formal police report dated to the previous week at the time of the incident. The dean resisted acting on this police referral, and the assistant principal convened a meeting to discuss the appropriateness of the referral. As Harris describes it:

> The assistant principal advised me to write up the disciplinary report, but I insisted that the teacher go before the committee to back up his charges. This was agreed upon, but of course the situation continued to escalate once the union was involved. Around the school, the issue took on the somewhat warped proportions of a deep and angry division between two camps: those who wanted the teacher protected and the student removed, and those who felt that the teacher had behaved unprofessionally and had victimized the student. The entire discipline policy of the school became a point of contention. Arguments ensued, teachers argued with teachers, rumors flew wildly about, and the student's family hired a lawyer. The administrative machinery has pushed on, and we are currently awaiting the outcome of the district's disciplinary hearing. (p. 18)

This example describes a highly polarized system in which fears for safety, differences in power relations, and the way language can be used can be turned into a major legal production. This case also shows the limits and the need for effective due process. As in the larger society, discipline is a major concern in schools. Harris (1996), trying to make sense out of this experience worries about getting beyond threats to a more nurturing, caring climate in a school. He explains:

> When I deal with threats and the sequence of events that precede them, I think of this. How easily we could have avoided the threats, in so many cases, if we had simply met the challenges of the day with an attitude of nurturing instead of punishment, of firm guidance instead of cutting castigation. I am still groping for answers to these issues, and they are slow in coming. I know this, however: the answer does not lie in police reports, nor in some unfounded idea of "appropriate consequences." Calling a kid a jerk won't do anything except send the kid away, angry and hurt. Suspension only removes a student from your influence and guidance. But I begin to see the shape of the answers, and they have to do with

respect and truth and the intangible dynamics of the relationship between adult and child. Some might call these intangibles love and understanding and compassion. I just might agree with them. (p. 19)

Understanding the minimal standards of constitutional due process is only the tip of the iceberg associated with managing school discipline and mediating conflict. In addition to practicing the listening and questioning skills associated with due process, administrators responsible for student discipline will also need to become acquainted with police officials in the community and have clear understanding of how they will work with the police. This involves setting the boundaries of school and police authority as well as knowing the areas of cooperation. School administrators will also want to explore the literature and programs available on conflict resolution and peer mediation. Many schools are introducing peer mediation and conflict resolution training that can be used to deal with conflict that has spilled over from the discipline system and other forums that students experience outside of the school (Johnson & Johnson, 1995; Bush & Folder, 1994; Girard & Koch, 1996).

First Amendment: Student Freedom of Expression

When a school administrator sets out to create or to modify a school policy that affects the speech rights of students, that administrator's most obvious constitutional restraint is found in the First Amendment, which provides that "Congress shall make no law...abridging the freedom of speech." Although the First Amendment speaks of congressional action, it is applied to state actors through the Fourteenth Amendment. Public schools, as creatures of state funding, are state actors and are subject to the free speech constraints of the First Amendment.

The first case that an administrator must address when writing a policy affecting speech rights of students is *Tinker* v. *Des Moines Independent Community School District* (1969), a Supreme Court case holding that students have constitutionally protected freedom of expression in the public school system. In *Tinker*, students and parents publicized their objections to the conflict in Vietnam by planning to wear black arm bands to school during the Christmas holiday season. In anticipation of this plan, the principals of the Des Moines schools adopted a policy stating that any student who refused to remove the arm band would be suspended until the student returned to school without the arm band. The policy was applied to three Tinker children who refused to remove their arm bands and were suspended from school. The Tinker family filed suit in federal district court, seeking an injunction ordering the school not to suspend the students.

The case reached the Supreme Court, which held that "it can hardly be argued that either students or teachers shed their constitutional rights to freedom of speech or expression at the schoolhouse gate" (p. 506). The Court, however, did not allow total freedom of student expression, instead adopting a balancing test that "in the absence of a specified showing of constitutionally valid reasons to regulate their speech, students are entitled to freedom of expression of their views"

(p. 511). The court held that constitutionally valid reasons would be found where the speech could be reasonably calculated to cause a "material disruption to class-work or involves substantial disorder or invasion of the rights of others" in the school environment (p. 513). Although *Tinker* signaled an important shift in think-ing about student expression, it is not the only case that a school administrator must consider when writing a student expression policy. In addition to traditional *Tinker* analysis, a school administrator must also understand forum analysis as it is applied to all curricular speech issues.

Forum analysis has become an important tool for school administrators today mainly due to the 1988 Supreme Court decision, *Hazelwood School District* v. *Kuhlmeier*. This case involved a school principal's deletion of two student-written articles from a school-sponsored newspaper. The court undertook a forum inquiry in *Hazelwood* and determined that the school newspaper was a nonpublic forum. In forum analysis, the type of forum that the school is considered to be is very sig-nificant because this determination dictates to what extent student expression in the public school is protected. Three main forum types have evolved in the courts: public forum, limited public forum, and nonpublic forum (see Exhibit 17.1). In determining the type of forum involved, courts traditionally have looked to the forum's characteristics, the usual activities that occur in the forum, and whether its historical dedication has been to exercise First Amendment rights. The Supreme Court in *Hazelwood* classified the newspaper as a nonpublic forum because the stu-dent-sponsored paper was tied to the school curriculum as a product of the school class and because the school had not by policy or practice created any type of open forum.

Because the school newspaper was deemed a nonpublic forum, all that was required for the censorship of the newspaper to be considered valid was that the

EXHIBIT 17.1   Three Main Forum Types

Traditional Public Forum: A state area that has immemorially been held in trust for use of the public and has been used for the purposes of assembly, communicating thoughts between citizens, and discussing public questions. This forum has generally been applied to areas such as sidewalks and parks. In this forum, free speech may not be withdrawn (even in a content-neutral fashion) unless a compelling state interest exists and if all restrictions are narrowly drawn to serve that interest.

Limited Public Forum: Property that the state intentionally creates or typically opens for public use. Schools, although not required to do so, may create limited public forums where school officials purposely open an area as a limited public forum or where there is evidence that wide access has been otherwise granted to that area. If a school is a limited-open forum, free-speech analysis is the same as in a traditional public forum.

Nonpublic or Closed Forum: Property that the state does not open for indiscriminate public expression. If a school or a portion of the school is considered a nonpublic forum, school officials can control access to the forum based on subject matter and speaker identity so long as distinctions drawn are reasonable in light of the purposes served by the forum and are viewpoint neutral.

principal's action be viewpoint neutral and reasonable under the circumstances. The Court found this test easily met in the principal's decision to remove the two articles from the newspaper. One article discussed teenage pregnancy and anonymously referred to three students whom the principal was afraid would be easily identified; the other discussed the effect of divorce on high school students, and the principal feared that the school could come under attack for not allowing the fathers upon whom the article was focused a chance to respond. The Court, therefore, upheld the principal's decision as constitutional.

A conscious distinction was recognized in *Hazelwood* between "an educator's ability to silence a student's personal expression that happens to occur on school premises," as in the *Tinker* situation, and "an educator's authority over school-sponsored publications, theatrical productions, and other expressive activities that students, parents, and members of the public might reasonably perceive to bear the imprimatur of the school" (*Hazelwood* v. *Kuhlmeier*, 1988, p. 217). Thus, the distinction between *Tinker* analysis and forum analysis for the public school falls on whether the student speech involved is tied to a curricular matter that is held out as school sponsored:

> *Educators are entitled to exercise greater control over (curricular) student expression to assure that participants learn whatever lessons the activity is designed to teach, that readers or listeners are not exposed to material that may be inappropriate for their level of maturity, and that the views of the speaker are not erroneously attributed to the school.* (Hazelwood School District v. Kuhlmeier, 1988, p. 271)

Although this language suggests that *Hazelwood* forum analysis can be applied to any speech tied to the school curriculum, the exact contours of the doctrine have not yet been determined.

Hazelwood provides clear precedent that school-sponsored newspapers can be created and administered as a nonpublic forum, thereby giving schools broad control over the paper's contents. In the wake of *Hazelwood*, there has been a tendency for schools to draft policies that made the school-sponsored newspapers into nonpublic forums, in many cases even where the paper had operated with broad editorial discretion enjoyed by the students. Principals consequently have broader authority to monitor and censor material in the school paper.

In spite of this tendency, schools have broad latitude to define the scope of their school-sponsored newspaper. It is instructive to review the actions of one school district that wrestled with its high school newspaper policy following the *Hazelwood* decision. After lengthy discussion, the district approved a policy that reaffirmed the paper as a limited open forum. The community that wrestled with this First Amendment policy issue is a small town and politically conservative. The school had, however, established a tradition of journalism excellence, recognized through a variety of state and national awards, with the efforts of a committed journalism teacher with over 20 years of experience in the district. Shortly after the *Hazelwood* decision, the board of education was engaged in a systematic review of district policies, and a serious discussion evolved about the school-sponsored newspaper policy. The journalism students and the newspaper advisor proposed amendments to the standard school-board policy on school newspapers that the district was considering. The first proposal stressed that the newspaper was meant to be a learning experience in the standards of journalism and to serve as a forum for public expression. The school board countered with the argument that the paper was a part of the school curriculum. Students, in arguing for the existing policy, emphasized the trust that this policy placed in them, and the responsibility they carried because of this trust.

Additional discussions were held about subsequent paragraphs of the policy. What were the student responsibilities for accuracy, objectivity, and making grammatical corrections? The school board insisted on a policy provision requiring students to "check and verify all facts and verify the accuracy of all quotations" that appear in the paper. The board also insisted that letters to the editor had to be signed. The name of the editorial writer might be withheld at publication, but a letter could not be accepted by the editorial board without a signature. Considerable debate occurred about the language prohibited from being published. The student editors proposed the policy language: "Students are prohibited from expressing, publishing or distributing materials that are obscene, lewd or libelous." The board members, with the strong encouragement of administrators, insisted that the phrase "inappropriate in the school setting" be added to this statement. Discussion also attended the responsibility of the faculty advisor for the content of the paper. The board wanted a statement of advisor responsibility, but the students countered that this would indicate that the students were not responsible for the content. The compromise was that the faculty advisor was responsible for monitoring the content of the publications and for teaching professional standards of English and journalism to the students and staff.

The superintendent who was involved in the discussions that shaped this school-sponsored publication policy had these observations about the process:

> *You can see that at first glance if you'd read other policies, this seemed very liberal. But by going piece by piece, you can see we wanted to give the kids—we trusted the kids, they did a good job—freedom to continue to enjoy and to understand and exercise this First Amendment right, but we tried to build in things that were reasonable for the school. . . . Ultimately, of course, we [the board and administration] are responsible for the content of any school publication. I guess that's my continued focus. I feel that a school can be an extremely positive element in the morale of every day life. . . .What scares me most is comments students can make about students. We're just very cautious about that. . . . We had our lawyer working with us [to craft this policy]. If we had not had the experience of 20 years of award winning journalistic publications, we would have probably not approached this as reasonably. And I don't know if that would have been fair to kids because ultimately, I think, there's a lot to be said about enjoying the freedom and expression of this, and really have the experience of newspaper publication. But the dangers are also tremendous. . . . So you're giving a tremendous amount of trust. Our lawyer was extremely cautious about this. We were getting legal advice that we could have gone 180 degrees on this and defended it. . . . Probably the best thing is, we*

have fewer surprises since this policy went into effect. This policy could be good or bad. It was a trade off based on trust and freedom to get responsible journalism. We took a risk and it has worked! (De Roche, 1994, pp. 191–193)

Clearly, *Hazelwood* forum analysis is applicable to any student expression that is student sponsored, as in a class, a student club, or a school activity. Gray areas exist in determining exactly where school sponsorship exists. Do financial support, faculty involvement, student involvement, and use of school premises trigger the title? A school administrator may follow the *Tinker* test when creating a blanket student speech policy, but that administrator should also attempt to determine what type of forum the school is in order to create a curricular student expression policy for the school.

Underground Newspapers

A school administrator is faced with a dilemma. She has heard reports and has personally witnessed a group of sophomores in her school distributing a "right to life" newsletter in the doorways of the lunchroom before and after each lunch hour. She calls one of the students in to question him about the newsletter, which appears to be commercially prepared, and the student tells her that the student group wrote and produced the newsletter themselves. The commercial appearance was achieved with the aid of one student's father who works in a publishing firm. The students raised money for the project, wrote the articles, typeset the newsletter on a home computer, and paid the student's father to produce it. The school administrator does not know what to do. She is afraid that other special-interest groups may organize and also attempt to distribute newsletters before and after lunch. Teachers have approached the administrator and discussed their beliefs that the students seem distracted by the newsletter and that too much time has been spent in class discussing its contents. The district has an editorial policy for the school-sponsored newspaper, and it has policies against commercial publication distribution, but it has no policy that exactly covers the facts of this case. What should the administrator do?

The administrator in this situation called her school attorney and asked if she could legally forbid the students to distribute the letter. After expressing a desire to ultimately develop an underground newspaper policy for the district, the school attorney explains the contours of the law as it currently exists so as to inform the administrator of options for dealing with the situation at hand. The attorney explains that the First Amendment, in addition to guaranteeing freedom of speech, guarantees freedom of the press, which has interesting implications in the school setting. This freedom applies both to student-sponsored (curricular) publications and to nonschool-sponsored (underground) publications. There is a presumption that any restraint on speech is unconstitutional, and school districts bear the burden of proving that such a restraint (editorial or distribution) on student publications is justified (*Perry Educational Association* v. *Perry Local Education Association*, 1983).

An underground newspaper is a nonschool-sponsored and nonschool-approved newspaper that is prepared by students. An underground newspaper is contrasted with a curricular newspaper prepared by students taking a journalism class who will receive credit from the school for their work and with a school-approved newspaper that is prepared by students who are members of a student organization and who work on the paper during nonschool hours on school property. Both the curricular and school-sponsored newspapers would be considered closed forums under *Hazelwood*. Thus, school administrators can control the content of such newspapers as well as the time, manner, and place of distribution so long as their regulations are reasonable in light of the circumstances and are viewpoint neutral (see Exhibit 17.2).

An underground newspaper, on the other hand, would probably be considered an open or limited open forum because it is not at all tied to the curriculum and is not school sponsored. Underground newspapers, therefore, may only be regulated for content where the regulation serves a compelling state interest, which is a much higher standard than "reasonable under the circumstances" (*Hazelwood School District* v. *Kuhlmeier*, 1988). The higher standard means that school officials can regulate underground newspapers far less than curricular or school-sponsored newspapers. Underground newspapers cannot be kept out of the school because of the viewpoint of the writer or because of the content unless the content is offensive to the extent that keeping it out of the school is a compelling state interest. Reasonable time, place, and manner of distribution restrictions may always be applied by schools to underground as well as curricular newspapers. These regulations have traditionally been viewed by the courts as monitors of school disruption instead of invaders of free press rights.

The administrator in the preceding hypothetical case has some concrete answers as to what she can do to deal with the right-to-life newsletter case. The administrator first needs to look to the manner in which she and other administrators have dealt with similar situations in the past. If other students have been allowed to hand out newsletters and papers outside the lunchroom, the administrator will likely need to allow the students to continue handing out their newsletter because the school will have created a limited open forum. (See *Thomas* v. *Waynesboro* [1987], where a school was held to have created a limited open forum due to the manner in which it previously dealt with student distribution and, thus, the school's prohibition on distribution of a religious newsletter was invalid.) Although time, place, and manner of distribution regulations may be imposed,

EXHIBIT 17.2   Time, Place, and Manner of Distribution of School Newspapers

Time, place, and manner restrictions to production or distribution of a publication may be made by an educational institution regardless of whether the school newspaper is considered an open, limited-open, or closed forum. Thus, it would be appropriate for an institution to specify the areas within the school building where publications may be distributed (*Eisner* v. *Stamford Board of Education, 1981*), or to ban distribution during a school fire drill (*Fujishima* v. *Board of Education*, 1972), or to require students to pick up any discarded copies of the newspaper from the school property (*Nelson* v. *Moline School District No. 40*, 1989).

they must be imposed in a manner that is neutral to the content of the underground newspaper. If no similar situation has ever been dealt with in the school, the administrator can create a precedent for the school, either allowing the distribution to occur or forbidding it due to some compelling state interest. In this example, the religious nature of the issue and of the publication could be argued as a nonproper topic for the public schools rising to the level of a compelling state interest.

Assuming that the administrator has successfully dealt with the right-to-life issue, she now sits down with her school attorney to develop a school policy dealing with underground newspapers so that this problem can be avoided in the future. The administrator's first instinct is to write a policy requiring students to give her materials for her approval before distributing them. The attorney explains that this type of approval is known as "prior restraint," and it is generally viewed by the court with a heavy presumption of unconstitutionality because it is thought to inhibit speech even more than does subsequent punishment. The majority of the courts, however, will not state that prior restraint is unconstitutional per se "so long as guidelines are explicit, narrowly written, and state the relationship between the prevention or curtailment of disruption that the policy seeks to remedy" (*Stanley v. Northeast Independent School District*, 1972). Using forum analysis, most courts considering underground newspaper fact situations have treated such distribution to be a nonpublic forum and upheld policies that require prior restraint so long as they are reasonable. The Seventh Circuit, for example, in *Muller* v. *Jefferson Light House School District*, upheld an elementary school policy that required presentation of the material at least 24 hours before distribution. The administrator will need to consider a time, place, and manner of distribution policy for underground newspapers. Such restrictions, where content neutral, will typically be upheld by the courts. In addition, the policy can spell out the prohibitions that will be enforced for underground newspapers—libel, slander, fighting words, and obscenity—and the sanctions that will apply to those who violate such standards.

Hate Speech

Many school districts have made decisions in the last few years of heightened political awareness to adopt hate speech policies for their elementary and secondary schools. Although open forum (see Exhibit 18.1) expression rights have clearly expanded to encompass "offensive speech,"* there are many questions as to the applicability of that expansion to student expression in public schools (limited public forum or closed forum).

Schools, as nonopen forums existing to educate children, clearly have more freedom in regulating expression than do open adult forums. As *Hazelwood School District* v. *Kuhlmeier* (1988) states, "First Amendment rights of students in the public schools are not automatically coextensive with the rights of adults in other

---

*See *R.A.V.* v. *City of St. Paul, MN* (1992), in which the Supreme Court held a city policy unconstitutional that banned certain symbols (i.e., burning cross or Nazi swastika) that are known to arouse anger, alarm, or resentment in others on the basis of race, color, creed, religion, or gender.

settings . . . and must be applied in light of the special characteristics of the school environment" (p. 266). For example, schools are permitted to restrict certain forms of student expression in their effort to maintain order and discipline. *Tinker* v. *Des Moines Independent Community School District* (1969) held expression to not be immunized by the constitutional guarantee of freedom of speech where it "causes, or reasonably could be expected to cause, material and substantial disruption of the school's operations or that 'invades' the rights of others. The latter criterion . . . presumably would permit prohibition of speech that defames others or invades their privacy" (p. 513). Schools have developed hate speech policies in the last decade, consistent with the reasoning of *Tinker* to protect students from having their rights invaded by others. Challenges to the protection rationale focus on the fear that hate speech policies will prohibit the free flowing exchange of ideas that can be the most beneficial component of education.

A typical hate speech policy prohibits behavior or expression by students or staff that insults, degrades, or stereotypes any race, gender, handicap, physical condition, ethnic group, or religion. Such a policy, although apparently consistent with the Constitution, as articulated in *Tinker* and *Hazelwood*, raises serious constitutional and enforcement questions. Constitutionally, the policy could be held invalid because it is vague. Vagueness doctrine invalidates policies, statutes, or laws that are too vague to provide notice to a person that his or her conduct violates the policy. The policy is vague because it prohibits speech that "insults," "degrades," or "stereotypes"—terms that in themselves can have different meanings to every person who reads the policy. Serious First Amendment challenges to this policy could also be raised, for this policy identifies certain kinds of speech as impermissible without requiring that the speech cause a substantial disruption within the school, as required by *Tinker*.

This type of First Amendment challenge to a hate speech policy was raised in *Pyle* v. *Hadley School Committee* (1994). The court held unconstitutional the school district's policy, which regulated clothing that "is directed to or intended to harass, threaten, intimidate, or demean an individual or group of individuals because of sex, color, race, religion, handicap, national origin or sexual orientation" (p. 163). The court stated:

> *The Constitution forbids a school from prohibiting expression of opinion merely because of an undifferentiated fear or apprehension or disturbance. It follows, that while a school can ban a T-shirt that causes a material disruption, they cannot prohibit one that merely advocates a particular point of view and arouses the hostility of a person with an opposite opinion. . . . It is impossible to avoid the conclusion that the harassment provision of the South Hadley dress code is aimed directly at the content of the speech, not at its potential for disruption or its vulgarity. . . . Under the current code, if a student wore a T-shirt to South Hadley High School containing a message expressing antipathy toward, or for that matter, sympathy with a particular group, the school could still ban the T-shirt, if it reasonably concluded that the message would cause a substantial and material disruption to the daily operations of the school.* Tinker *allows the school to do this. But the school cannot pick and choose; it may not prohibit antipathetic slogans but*

> *allow positive ones. The constitutional line is crossed when, instead of really teaching, the educators demand that the students express agreement with the educators' values. (p. 171)*

Although it is not yet clear that *Pyle* is the law, as it could be overturned in the appellate court or different circuits may decline to follow its holding, it does raise concern over the constitutionality of hate speech policies.

Of more immediate concern to many administrators is the difficulty in enforcement of hate speech policies. It is very difficult to know for certain whether many hate speech policies have ever been violated. Consider these questions:

1. When determining whether speech is offensive or demeaning, should the administrator focus on whether any complaining student found the speech to be offensive or demeaning or should the administrator instead focus on some objective definition of what is offensive or demeaning?
2. Should an administrator consider the source of the expression? For example, is the policy violated where two Hispanics are joking with one another in the hallway and one calls the other a "dirty spic"? Are the words themselves violative of the policy, or should the principal consider the source of the expression (a fellow Hispanic) and the joking tone in which it was uttered?
3. Suppose the violative speech is uttered in the course of an affirmative action debate by a student opposed to affirmative action. Should the student be given greater leniency because his speech occurred in a curricular project? Should he or she be given greater leniency because the subject matter is clearly controversial?

An administrator enforcing a hate speech policy is clearly in for some difficult decisions. Although public schools have the ability to regulate student speech, it is not clear how an administrator can create a constitutional and enforceable policy that protects both the students' rights to utter speech of their choosing and to receive speech that is nonoffensive.

First Amendment Religion Cases: Separation of Church and State*

The First Amendment provides that "Congress shall make no law respecting an establishment of religion, or prohibiting the free exercise thereof." The Fourteenth Amendment applies this to the states and their subdivisions. The precise meaning

---

*Defining the First Amendment boundaries between church and state in the public school context has consumed considerable Supreme Court attention. Following are a few of the cases in the area, which are beyond the scope of this chapter. Release time for instruction: *McCollum v. Board of Education* (1948) and *Zorach v. Clauson* (1952). Prayer in school: *Engle v. Vitale* (1962). Free transportation to parochial school students: *Board of Education v. Allen* (1968). Public aid to private schools, generally: *Meek v. Pittinger* (1975) and *Wolman v. Walter* (1977). State income-tax deductions for certain public and private school expenses: *Mueller v. Allen* (1983). Public school district providing sign language instruction at parochial high school under Individual with Disabilities Education Act does not violate Establishment Clause: *Zobrest v. Catalina Foothills School District* (1993).

given to these words has been the source of considerable litigation and numerous Supreme Court opinions. This litigation usually involves either the constitutionality of some religious practice in the public schools or the constitutionality of some public aid to parochial schools.

In 1963, the Supreme Court rendered an opinion, based on two different lower-court opinions, about whether the reading of the Bible and the Lord's Prayer at the beginning of the school day violates the establishment clause of the First Amendment. In one case, a Unitarian family challenged a Pennsylvania statute requiring Bible reading, without comment, at the opening of each school day, although any child could be excused with parental permission. In the other case, an atheist challenged a similar Baltimore rule requiring Bible reading or the Lord's Prayer. Both plaintiffs testified the Bible readings conveyed religious doctrines contrary to their own religious beliefs—the Unitarians about the literal meaning of the Bible purveyed in these exercises and the atheist about the emphasis on belief in God as the source of all moral and spiritual values.

The Supreme Court framed the following test for measuring whether a requirement violates the establishment clause of the First Amendment:

What are the purposes and primary effect of the enactment? If either is the advancement or inhibition of religion, then the enactment exceeds the scope of legislative power as circumscribed by the Constitution. That is to say that to withstand the strictures of the Establishment Clause there must be a secular legislative purpose and a primary effect that neither advances nor inhibits religion. (Abington School District *v.* Schempp, *1963)*

The Supreme Court held that both situations involved religious exercises because of the basic part the Bible plays in religious belief. These exercises violate the religious beliefs of the plaintiffs and are therefore unconstitutional. It is unimportant to the Court that the plaintiffs can be dismissed from the exercises, as that still imposes a religious burden. Nor is it important that these are relatively minor encroachments. The principle of religious neutrality must guide inclusion of practices in the public schools so as not to infringe on the religious beliefs of people attending the school. As stated in *Abington School District* v. *Schempp* (1963), "In the relationship between man and religion, the state is firmly committed to a position of neutrality."

During the late 1970s and early 1980s, many state legislatures enacted laws authorizing a "moment of silence" at the beginning of school. These statutes vary, some specifying that the moment of silence may be used for prayer and others specifying meditation. In *Wallace* v. *Jaffre* (1985), the Supreme Court considered the constitutionality of an Alabama statute that authorized a period of silence "for meditation or voluntary prayer." In earlier states of the litigation, not reviewed by the Supreme Court, an Alabama statute authorizing a one-minute period of silence in all public schools "for meditation" was upheld, but another statute authorizing teachers to lead "willing students" in a prescribed prayer to "Almighty God, the Creator and Supreme Judge of the World" was struck down as unconstitutional.

The period of silence for meditation or silent prayer was held unconstitutional because the intent of the sponsoring legislator was to advance religion. In a concurring opinion, Justice O'Connor stated that, in her view, a moment-of-silence law that permitted prayer, meditation, and reflection within the prescribed period should be considered constitutional so long as one alternative is not advanced over another.

In 1992, the Supreme Court, in a 5–4 decision (*Lee* v. *Weisman*), held unconstitutional a Rhode Island school policy providing for prayer at a junior high school commencement ceremony. The Providence School Committee had a policy permitting principals to invite members of the clergy to offer invocation and benediction prayers at school commencement exercises. The principals provided the clergy with a pamphlet recommending nonsectarian prayers. The father of a graduating student objected to having a commencement prayer and filed suit in federal court to prevent its delivery.

The majority decision, which held that the commencement prayer given pursuant to this policy was unconstitutional, was based solely on the second prong of the *Lemon* test (*Lemon* v. *Kurtzman* [1971] will be discussed later in this chapter), whether the challenged action "has the primary effect of advancing or prohibiting religion" (p. 612). The Court said the essential facts that established a state religion were that the junior high school principal made the determination a prayer should be given, selected and invited the speaker, and controlled the content of the prayer by giving the speaker a pamphlet on nonsectarian prayers. The majority determined that the principal, a state official, directed the performance of a formal religious exercise at the commencement.

The majority was concerned about the protection of the right of the students to be free from the subtle, coercive pressure to participate in the prayer. The Court was also bothered by the obligatory nature of the activity. Students who wished not to participate were not provided any alternatives to the prayer. The obligation to stand in silence might be perceived as being in agreement with the prayer.

In *Lee* v. *Weisman* (1992), Justice Scalia wrote a scathing dissent in which he criticized the majority for being too fact specific, limiting its holding to instances where the prayers are school sponsored. He objected to this result that reversed a tradition of government policies of accommodation and support for religion that have always been an accepted part of the political heritage of the United States.

The narrowness of the Court's decision in *Lee* v. *Weisman* is being tested in many school districts that have permitted prayer at commencement exercises where the prayer is initiated and chosen by students. There is a split of authority between the First and Ninth Circuit Courts of Appeals as to whether this is constitutional. The Fifth Circuit, in *Jones* v. *Clear Creek Independent School District* (Jones II, 1992), reaffirmed its 1991 decision (Jones I) about the constitutionality of student-initiated and student-sponsored prayer at a high school commencement exercise that had been remanded by the Supreme Court to be reconsidered in light of its *Lee* v. *Weisman* decision. The decision of the Fifth Circuit distinguished the facts of student-led prayer on all points of concern raised by the Supreme Court.

> *There is a deep public concern that radical efforts to avoid pressuring children to be religious actually teach and enforce notions that pressure the young to avoid all that is religious. . . . The* Lee *Court held that government-mandated prayer at graduation places a constitutionally impermissible amount of psychological pressure on students to participate in a religious exercise. . . . We think that the graduation prayers permitted by the [district] Resolution place less psychological pressure on students than the prayers at issue in* Lee *because all students, after having participated in the decision on whether prayers will be given, are aware that any prayers represent the will of their peers, who are less able to coerce participation than an authority figure from the state or clergy. (*Jones v. Clear Creek Independent School District, *1992, Jones II, pp. 965–971)*

The Fifth Circuit also argued that the older students, high school seniors, would find the prayer less coercive than the junior high students in *Lee* v. *Weisman.* The Fifth Circuit concluded, "The practical result of our decision viewed in light of *Lee,* is that a majority of students can do what the State acting on its own cannot do to incorporate prayer in public high school graduation ceremonies" (*Jones II,* 1992, p. 972). The Supreme Court denied certiorari to review this decision. Consequently the *Jones II* (1992) decision is good law for the Fifth Circuit and has been reaffirmed in *Ingebretsen* v. *Jackson Public School District,* 1996).

The Ninth Circuit Court of Appeals heard a challenge to student initiated prayer at graduation and held it unconstitutional, rejecting the logic of the Fifth Circuit. The Ninth Circuit in *Harris* v. *Joint School District No. 241* (1994) held that the school ultimately controlled the commencement exercise. The school allowed the seniors the opportunity to select the prayer, and the school covered expenses involved in giving the prayer during graduation. The court said, "School officials cannot divest themselves of constitutional responsibility by allowing the students to make crucial decisions" (p. 455). The Ninth Circuit was also concerned about the protection of religious views of the minority members of the student body. The disclaimer by the district that it neither promotes nor endorses the views of the students giving the prayers does not save the school's practice.

> *The student in the religious minority is well aware that the school has delegated authority over the prayers to the majority of her classmates while retaining ultimate control over the school-sponsored meeting. The student is also aware that the effect of the delegation is that her religious views are subordinated to the majority's. (pp. 455–456).*

In reviewing the school prayer decisions, Carter (1994) explains the public dissatisfaction with the long line of school prayer cases, the *Lee* v. *Weisman* decision being only a recent example. As Carter states, "Not every legal funeral leads to a political burial" (p. 60). Unlike many areas of constitutional law that were broadly criticized at the time of Supreme Court action (i.e., *Brown* v. *Board of Education,* 1954, holding segregated schools violated the Equal Protection Clause) and then generally settled into the nation's moral and political conscience, school prayer cases have been continually unpopular with a majority of the population for over 30 years. The Supreme Court continues to be badly split in finding an interpretation for the Establishment Clause. The three-part *Lemon* test (discussed later in this chapter) continues to be employed in most Establishment Clause cases, but it had no predictive value for the outcome of the case. There is a trend to allow greater access of religious materials into public schools. This access is being accomplished through First Amendment free speech interpretations that are given priority over more restrictive establishment clause interpretations. Before examining some of the developments in this area, it is important to review the Equal Access Act and the Supreme Court's 1993 *Lamb's Chapel* v. *Center Moriches Union Free School District* decision.

In 1984, Congress passed the Equal Access Act, which provided that any public secondary school that receives federal financial assistance and allows non-curriculum-related student groups to meet on school premises during non-instructional time may not deny access to any student "on the basis of the religious, political, philosophical, or other content of the speech at such meetings." The statute was passed to allow student religious groups to meet at the high school so long as the school officials maintained neutrality toward the content of the speech. In 1990, the Supreme Court decided a challenge to the constitutionality of the Act and a question of the Act's interpretation (*Board of Education of Westside Community Schools* v. *Mergens*, 1990). Mergens requested and was denied permission to form a Christian club that could meet at the same time and under the same conditions as other clubs at the school, except that it would not have a faculty sponsor. Permission was denied by the board of education because it did not have a faculty sponsor, which was a policy of the board, and it was believed to violate the Establishment Clause of the First Amendment. The Supreme Court affirmed the Eighth Circuit Court of Appeals decision that the Act did not violate the Establishment Clause.

The Court first interpreted the Act's applicability to this request. The critical phrase in applying the statute is "noncurriculum-related student group." As this phrase is not defined in the statute, the Court had to give it meaning. A majority of the justices interpreted this term to mean "any student group that does not directly relate to the body of courses offered by the school." Four factors are important in determining whether the group directly relates to the school's curriculum: (1) if the group's subject matter is actually taught, or will soon be taught, in a regularly offered course; (2) if that subject matter concerns the body of courses as a whole; (3) if participation in the group is required for a particular course; and (4) if participation in the group will result in academic credit. In applying these factors, the Court found at least one club, Subsurfers, for students interested in scuba diving that did not meet this criteria. Consequently, the school was in violation of the Act for discriminating against students desiring to meet based on the religious content of the students' speech.

The Court also found, although no five judges agreed on the analysis to be applied, that the Act did not violate the Establishment Clause. Four judges applied the tripartite *Lemon* test, holding that the Act has a secular legislative purpose, does not have the primary effect of advancing religion, and does not risk excessive entanglement between government and religion.

The Ninth Circuit has held that the Equal Access Act provides religious students a federal right and that state law must yield to this right (*Garnett* v. *Renton School District No. 403,* 1993, p. 646). The effect of this is to give students' religious rights a priority over a state constitutional provision that is more restrictive than the Establishment Clause. The Ninth Circuit in *Ceniceros* v. *Board of Trustees of San Diego Unified School District* (1997) held that the "no religious preference clause" of the California Constitution, which is more stringent than the Establishment Clause, cannot limit students' rights under the Equal Access Act. The court held that as some student groups were meeting during lunch hour when no classes were in session, another group of students could hold devotional meetings during this noninstructional lunch time. The court showed no concern about peer pressure (a focus in *Lee* v. *Weisman*) on other students during this lunch hour.

As secondary schools cope with complying with the Equal Access Act, they must first assess whether the Act applies and determine whether they allow any noncurriculum-related student groups to meet on school premises during noninstructional time. If so, these schools must allow other student groups to meet during this noninstructional time regardless of the content of their speech. This could, arguably, apply not only to religious groups, such as the Fellowship of Christian Athletes or the Campus Crusade, but also to student groups who espouse an abstract doctrine of racial or ethnic hatred (so as not to amount to a present danger) or student groups who want to discuss a topic such as homosexuality or lesbianism that may be viewed unfavorably by large segments of the community. Except for the specific prohibitions of the statute, schools would have authority under *Hazelwood* to regulate these curricular matters. But the Act provides very broad free-speech protections that may lead to serious controversy and a subsequent decision by school officials to deny access to all noncurriculum-related student groups to avoid this controversy.

The Supreme Court has not explicitly overruled the three-part *Lemon* test in analyzing Establishment Clause cases, but it has used First Amendment free speech grounds to circumvent the wall of separation between church and state, the metaphor that was historically used to explain why certain religious activities violated the Establishment Clause. In *Lamb's Chapel* v. *Center Moriches Union Free School District* (1993), the Court held that a school district could not deny school access to an evangelical church that wanted to show a film series on family relationships. Religious perspectives on family relationships had the same right of access to school facilities as other perspectives on family relationships. School-district enforcement of school-facility use policies cannot discriminate against a specific community group's viewpoint.

In *Rosenberger* v. *Rector and Visitors of the University of Virginia* (1995), the Supreme Court considered whether the University's refusal to use student activity funds to pay the cost of publishing a student group's religious literature violated the Establishment Clause. The policy of the University of Virginia amounted to viewpoint discrimination by eliminating religious views from the "diversity of views from private speakers" that the student activity funds were designed to subsidize. The *Lamb's Chapel* decision stands for the principle that religious viewpoints cannot be singled out for differential treatment in a limited public forum. This principle is extended in *Rosenberger* so that religious expression cannot be barred from a limited public forum; religious perspectives must be permitted on any topic that private individuals are allowed to address. *Rosenberger* requires governmental funding for religious viewpoints where other private parties and viewpoints were being funded. The decreased importance of the *Lemon* test is clear given the impact of *Lamb's Chapel* and *Rosenberger*. The extent to which this evenhanded approach for defining government and religion interaction is consistent with Establishment Clause principles is unclear and will likely be worked out in future case law (Mawdsley, 1996).

The priority given to free speech considerations over Establishment Clause concerns is being applied in several lower court decisions (McCarthy, 1996). In distribution of underground newspapers, for example, courts treat religious and secular materials the same (*Hedges* v. *Wauconda Community Unit School District No. 118*, 1993). The shift away from establishment clause analysis to free-speech analysis on religious topics promises to support school law attorneys for the next few years and make teachers and administrators think about how they view religious topics. The disagreement between the Fifth and Ninth Circuits on the constitutionality of student-initiated prayers at commencement exercises is but one example of the different policy interests being articulated.

Another fertile area where this free-speech right for religious expressions will likely receive considerable attention is in the classroom (Mawdsley & Russo, 1996). A 1995 decision of the Sixth Circuit Court of Appeals, *Settle* v. *Dickson County School Board*, provides an example of a religious challenge to teaching practice. A ninth-grade teacher assigned a research paper. One student submitted the topic of drama as the subject of her research paper, but after the deadline for topic submission had passed changed the topic and submitted an outline for a paper titled "The Life of Jesus Christ." The teacher rejected this topic and a subsequent one on "A Scientific and Historical Approach to Jesus Christ," and eventually the student received a 0 for the paper when the student refused to complete the assignment. The teacher told the student and the student's father that she would not accept a paper that dealt "solely with Christianity or the Life of Christ." The Sixth Circuit affirmed the district court in granting summary judgment for the teacher and school district. The authority of teachers over curricular matters was affirmed by the Sixth Circuit. Still, the teacher's refusal to consider a religious topic raises a red flag in light of the *Lamb's Chapel* and *Rosenberger* viewpoint discrimination cases. A concurring judge emphasized that, in this case, where a research paper assignment was involved, free-speech considerations were not implicated. The judge continued that "Had the assignment been to write a paper of opinion, and had [the teacher] rejected the paper on the ground of its religious content alone, [the student's] freedom of speech truly would have been violated" (p. 159). It is not hard to see how viewpoint discrimination analysis would apply to the legitimacy of religious subjects when students are allowed to write or discuss topics that they can choose or that allow personal opinion. It is doubtful that teachers can uniformly deny religious topics from being discussed merely because the wall of separation between church and state demands this type of neutrality. More litigation will be coming in this unsettled frontier between *Hazelwood* and *Lamb's Chapel*.

In the area of public aid to parochial schools, Rhode Island and Pennsylvania had statutes that provided aid to parochial schools. Simply stated, Rhode Island would pay up to 15 percent of the salaries of teachers of secular subjects in non-public elementary schools. In addition to certain limitations on the salaries and per-pupil expenditures not exceeding those in public schools, the law required teachers to agree by written oath not to teach a course in religion while receiving these salary supplements. Pennsylvania authorized the state superintendent of public instruction to buy certain secular educational services from nonpublic schools for the actual costs of teachers' salaries, textbooks, and instructional materials for certain restricted courses in mathematics, modern foreign languages, physical science, and physical education found in the curricula of public schools.

In considering the constitutionality of these parochial statutes, in *Lemon* v. *Kurtzman* (1971), the Court prescribed three tests. "First, the statute must have a secular legislative purpose, its principal or primary effect must be one that neither advances nor inhibits religion . . . finally, the statute must not foster 'an excessive government entanglement with religion.'" Although the Court accepted the legislation as having a valid secular intent, both statutory schemes were found unconstitutional because of excessive entanglement between government and religion.

In the Rhode Island and Pennsylvania programs, the Court was cognizant of the religious character and purpose of Roman Catholic elementary schools, which were the only beneficiaries of salary supplements. The Court emphasized the high percentage of nuns in these schools who, although they would not qualify for salary supplements, represent the pervasive religious atmosphere the legislation cannot avoid. In addition to concern over the substantial religious character of these church-related schools, the Court expressed fears of entanglement necessitated by attempts to enforce the legislation. It would be very difficult to know the extent to which a teacher was engaging in religious or secular instruction.

Two 1985 Supreme Court cases challenged the practice of utilizing public-school teachers in sectarian schools. The Grand Rapid, Michigan, public school had a shared-time program in which the supplementary classes were offered at private schools. These classes—including such courses as mathematics, reading, art, music, and physical education—accounted for about 10 percent of the class time of the students. The shared-time teachers were full-time employees of the public school district and moved from class to class in the private-school setting. The Supreme Court, in *Grand Rapids* v. *Ball* (1985), held that the shared-time program was unconstitutional because it advanced religion.

Given that 40 of the 41 schools in this case are thus "pervasively sectarian," the challenged public-school programs operating in the religious schools may impermissibly advance religion in three different ways. First, the teachers participating in the programs may become involved in intentionally or inadvertently inculcat-

ing particular religious tenets or beliefs. Second, the programs may provide cru-
cial symbolic link between government and religion, thereby enlisting—at least in
the eyes of impressionable youngsters—the powers of government to the support
of the religious denomination operating the school. Third, the programs may have
the effect of directly promoting religion by impermissibly providing a subsidy to
the primary religious mission of the institutions affected. (p. 385)

In New York City, federal Title I funds were used to pay the salaries of public-school employees who taught in parochial schools to meet the needs of education-ally deprived children from low-income families. Teaching assignments were made by the city, and teacher supervision was done by field personnel. The Supreme Court, in *Aguilar* v. *Felton* (1985), held that this use of federal money amounted to a violation of the Establishment Clause because of excessive entan-glement. The pervasive monitoring in the sectarian schools involved too great an entanglement. The frequent contacts between the regular and remedial teachers and the monitoring of the remedial teachers put the government and the school into too close a relationship.

In a 1997 decision, *Agostini* v. *Felton,* the Supreme Court, in a 5–4 decision, reversed the 1985 *Ball* and *Aguilar* cases. The high cost of providing remedial ser-vices off site to needy students at private religious schools brought criticism of the results of the 1985 decisions. In *Agostini,* the Supreme Court held that the Estab-lishment Clause does not prohibit a federally funded program that provided sup-plemental, remedial instruction to disadvantaged children on a neutral basis when the instruction is given on the premises of sectarian schools by government employees pursuant to a program containing reasonable safeguards. The basis for the Court's unusual action to reverse an earlier decision was that post-1985 deci-sions undermined *Aguilar* and *Ball,* thereby making them no longer good law. The Court abandoned the presumption in *Ball* and *Aguilar* that public employees placed on parochial school grounds will inevitably inculcate religion or that their presence constitutes a symbolic union between government and religion. Addi-tionally, the Court has departed from the rule relied on in *Ball* that all governmen-tal aid that directly supports the educational function of religious schools is invalid. The New York City program does not have the effect of advancing religion or creating an excessive government entanglement. The decision is significant beyond the issue of where Title I services can be provided. The decision will be closely analyzed for its implications for providing other types of public support to private religious schools.

The use of public funds to support student access to private religious schools has considerable support but is held up because of serious doubts about its consti-tutionality. New York City avoided the potential legal problem by getting dona-tions in the fall of 1996 to support the cost of allowing several hundred volunteer students from overcrowded public schools to attend parochial schools. A voucher program in Milwaukee approved and supported by Wisconsin law is tied up in the courts. Nonsectarian private schools are allowed to participate while the participa-tion of parochial private schools depends on the outcome of the constitutional challenges. Ohio passed legislation in 1995 authorizing vouchers of up to $2,250 for low-income parents of children in grades K–3 to pay for tuition at any participating private school or at public schools in adjoining districts. The constitutionality of the Ohio law has also been challenged. It is only a matter of time until the Supreme Court hears and decides on the constitutionality of voucher programs.

Legal Standards of Liability

Fear of potential liability is a powerful motivation for compliance with legal standards. This fear is not lost on public-school administrators, many of whom worry about their personal and organizational liability and many of whom use this fear to communicate legal responsibilities and obligations to teachers and staff. This section will briefly explore liability and consider the extent to which fear of liability is justified.

Liability generally refers to the negative consequences that can result from failure to satisfy a legal obligation. Although these consequences might broadly include demotion or dismissal for failure to perform the job adequately, liability specifically is concerned with the narrower topic of monetary consequences. What potential monetary liability does a principal or superintendent have for lawsuits filed?

Standards of liability differ markedly from one area of law to another. For the purposes here, it will be sufficiently instructive to consider potential liability for negligence and constitutional torts. The fourth element of the prima facie case of negligence is that there be real injuries (see the section titled Torts, earlier in this chapter). The injured person is to be compensated for the injuries resulting from the negligent behavior of others. These compensatory damages are intended to make the person whole from the injuries suffered. Punitive damages may also be available in negligence cases where the behavior of the defendant is so egregious, willful, or reckless that a strong message needs to be communicated to the defendant, as well as others, that such outrageous behavior will not be tolerated, and that there are extreme sanctions for those persons who engage in such inappropriate conduct. The purpose of punitive damages is to punish the offending party, and the measure of damages consequently is linked to the defendant's ability to pay rather than any actual relationship to costs associated with the injury.

A well-known example of a large punitive damages award is the McDonalds' (1994) coffee case, in which an 82-year-old Albuquerque woman was awarded $2 million in punitive damages for third-degree burns she sustained when the coffee she purchased at McDonalds spilled on her in her car. The jury reportedly arrived at the $2 million amount through estimates of McDonalds' daily profits from coffee sales. Before the appeal was heard, McDonalds settled the case out of court for an undisclosed sum.

There has been an evolution over several decades toward greater liability for school districts and their employees. As late as the 1950s, most states protected school-district employees from any tort liability through the doctrine of sovereign immunity. Although sovereign immunity has been eliminated in many states, vestiges of it continue in a variety of ways, ranging from placement of strict notice requirements for eligibility to file suit to limitation on the size and type of awards that can be claimed. These limitations vary widely from state to state.

A second source of liability is Section 1983 of Chapter 42 of the United States Code:

> *Every person who, under cover of any statute . . . of any state . . . subjects . . . any citizen of the United States or any person within the jurisdiction thereof to the deprivation of any rights, privileges, or immunities secured by the Constitution and laws, shall be liable to the party injured in an action at law, suit and equity, or other proper proceeding for redress.*

Section 1983 provides the jurisdictional authority to sue for constitutional torts, which are injuries suffered as the result of deprivations of federal constitutional rights. Federal case law developed over the past two decades provides guidance about liability under Section 1983.

Section 1983 is a popular cause of action upon which to base a complaint because of the robustness of the remedies available—injunctive relief as well as monetary damages. Injunctive relief provides the court authority to order parties to take certain actions separate from the payment of fines. Section 1983 also allows for attorneys' fees to be transferred to the defendant under the Civil Rights Attorneys Awards Act (1976). The cost of such attorneys' fees to school districts can be substantial, running to millions of dollars in federal desegregation suits.

Individuals and school districts are potentially liable for constitutional torts. A teacher, principal, or superintendent may be liable for depriving a person of a constitutional right. Liability applies to an individual only where the constitutional right was clearly established at the time the alleged improper conduct occurred (*Harlow* v. *Fitzgerald*, 1982).

The Ninth Circuit Court of Appeals decision in *P.B.* v. *Koch* (1996) provides an example of how individual liability is analyzed under Section 1983. Three students brought suit against Koch, a high school principal, for allegedly using excessive force and depriving them of their substantive due-process rights. One student claimed Koch slapped him in the face and grabbed his neck, another claimed Koch grabbed him by the neck and punched him in the chest, and a third claimed Koch grabbed him by the neck and threw him head first into the lockers. Koch disputes portions of the student allegations but does not dispute he used force. The Ninth Circuit, in considering Koch's claim for qualified immunity, weighs whether he violated clearly established constitutional rights. The court examined a number of factors in determining whether substantive due-process rights had been violated: (1) the need for the governmental action in question, (2) the relationship between the need and the action, (3) the extent of harm inflicted, and (4) whether the action was taken in good faith or for the purpose of causing harm.

> *In the instant case, there was no need to use force against the three students. Accordingly, the force Koch used—slapping, punching, and choking the stu-*

dents—bears no reasonable relation to the need. Because there was no need for force, one can reasonably infer that Koch took these actions not in good faith but for the purpose of causing harm. In this context, the deliberate and internional harm allegedly inflicted—causing pain, bruising, and emotional injury—is significant. . . . Whether we describe the "right" as the right to bodily integrity, the right to be free from unjustified intrusions on personal security, the right to be free from excessive force, or the right to be free from arbitrary and excessive corporal punishment, it is clear that a principal, who physically assaulted his students in the manner Koch allegedly did, has violated their clearly established constitutional rights. (p. 1302)

The Court, by denying Koch's claim for immunity, clears the way for the case against Koch to be tried.

Qualified good-faith immunity exists for individuals so that individuals are responsible only for those constitutional rights that are clearly recognized at the time of the alleged violation does not exist for school districts. School districts have absolute liability for a violation of a constitutional right, even if this is the first time that the court has determined that such a constitutional right exists (*Owen* v. *City of Independence*, 1980).

The school district, as a governmental entity, is also liable under Section 1983 for constitutional deprivations. This district liability is limited, though, to the official policies of the district. These official policies of the district include both adopted, written policies and the administrative actions that are repeated a sufficient number of times so that the school district can be presumed to have knowledge of the actions. The school district is not responsible for the isolated, insubordinate acts of its employees (*Monell* v. *New York City Department of Social Services*, 1978).

Punitive damages are not available against school districts (*City of Newport* v. *Fact Concerts*, 1982), but they are available against individuals. Punitive damages may be assessed under Section 1983 against an individual "when the defendant's conduct is shown to be motivated by evil motive or intent, or when it involves reckless or callous indifference to the federally protected rights of others" (*Smith* v. *Wade*, 1983).

As in the negligence area, the primary measure of damages for deprivation of a constitutional right is the compensation necessary to make the person whole for the actual injuries suffered (*Stachura* v. *Memphis Community School District*, 1986). The measure of compensatory damages awarded by the jury needs to be based on actual injuries, which could include pain and suffering as well as actual out-of-pocket expenses. Compensatory damages could not include a monetary value placed on a constitutional deprivation. Where no compensatory injuries are involved, the court may award nominal damages of $1, recognizing the deprivation of a constitutional right but no injuries meriting compensation. In the case of nominal damages, however, attorney fees could be awarded to the plaintiffs.

Potential personal liability for negligence and constitutional torts can be limited by carrying professional liability insurance. Even though this professional liability insurance can provide considerable peace of mind, there are broad protections from individual liability provided by state statute. Illinois, for example, identifies a different standard of negligence liability for employees who hold administrative or teacher certification than for those without certification. The presumption is that teachers and other certificated employees have received instruction in student management and safety as part of their educational programs and therefore deserve immunity from reasonable care liability. Noncertificated employees such as bus drivers and teachers' aides do not enjoy this level of protection. More significantly, many states remove district employees from personal liability that has occurred within the scope of employment. These statutes have the effect of making the district financially responsible for the tortious acts of these employees while committed in relation to the job. Statutes might also obligate the district to provide legal defense for employees being sued for allegedly tortious conduct committed during their employment. The district can cover these potential liabilities through its insurance coverage. In those circumstances where the misconduct occurred outside of the employee's scope of employment, however, the district has no responsibility. One example that courts have used in finding the teacher's conduct outside the scope of employment is the sexual abuse of a student.

Even though a substantial amount of money is paid to settle legal claims and to pay the attorneys who work both sides of these claims, this money is overwhelmingly paid by school district resources. Personal liability is relatively rare. Still, professional liability insurance is a good investment in most states, if for no other reason than peace of mind.

Formulating Policies in Unsettled Areas of Law

Student-to-Student Sexual Harassment

Some policies evolve through periodic reviews, others through the school improvement process, and some through a concern about potential legal vulnerability because of a case reported in the media or legislation that places new requirements on the district. For example, *Education Week* (Walsh, 1996) reported that a 14-year-old girl was awarded $500,000 by a jury in California that found school officials ignored her complaints of harassment from a male sixth-grade student. The *New York Times* ("Gay Man Abused," 1996) reported a $900,000 out-of-court settlement that a school district's insurer paid to a former student for the injuries he suffered as a homosexual from other students in school and the failure of district administrators to protect him from this repeated abuse. *Education Week* (Jacobson, 1996) reported a federal jury in New York state ruling against the claims of a former sixth-grade student who said that she had been sexually harassed by verbal attacks and inappropriate touching by boys in her class. The concerns this sort of information raises can often be satisfied by waiting for guidelines from the state or talking with the school district's attorney about the implications of the reported case. Still, emerging areas of the law can cause special problems because the law is dynamic and it is frequently impossible to know precisely the standard to which the school and district will be held accountable.

Administrators will want to seek advice from legal counsel, to have a certain level of understanding about the nature of the legal issues involved, and to have some sense of the implication of these matters for school policies. Thinking about the development of policy in areas of legal compulsion is important because most administrators will face it. In some instances, it can be quite easy. Lawyers provide standardized policy language that is added to the policy manual. Sometimes this is deceptive because implementation may not be as easy as the policy suggests. More significantly, there are often fundamental changes in the school culture necessary to respond to developing areas of the law, and simple changes in the policy are inadequate. The topic of policy development for student-to-student sexual harassment will be briefly explored here. It is an area of the law that is quite unsettled at the time of this writing. It is also an area of considerable litigation and of significant district liability. The legal dimensions of student-to-student sexual harassment will be considered and then responsive policy formulation will be explored.

Sexual Misconduct among Students as a Legal Issue

Title IX of the Education Amendments of 1972 mandates, with certain limited exceptions, that no person in the United States shall, on the basis of sex, be excluded from participation in, be denied the benefits of, or be subjected to discrimination under any educational program or activity receiving federal financial assistance. Title IX applies to all educational institutions that receive federal financial assistance, which includes most private and all public schools, and prohibits them from engaging in virtually all discriminatory actions on the basis of sex.

In *Franklin v. Gwinnett County Public Schools* (1992), the Supreme Court found that Title IX may be used as a basis for seeking damages where a student has been subjected to intentional sexual harassment. Sexual harassment may include abuse. In *Franklin*, a student alleged that she was sexually harassed by a male teacher/coach employed by the school district. Among her charges were that the teacher removed her from class and subjected her to coercive intercourse. It was further alleged that the school district was aware of and investigated the teacher's sexual harassment of the student and others, failed to take action to halt it, and even discouraged the student from pressing charges against the teacher. The investigation was ultimately closed by the school district after the teacher resigned.

As of December 1996, seven federal courts had decided student-to-student sexual misconduct cases, and the opinions were quite divergent.[*] None of the courts imposed liability on the defendant schools for failing to maintain a 100 percent harassment-free environment. There was also broad agreement that Title IX does provide a potential remedy for student sexual misconduct. The courts disagreed widely on what the applicable Title IX standard should be.

---

[*]Fifth Circuit: *Rowinsky v. Bryan Independent School District* (1996); Eleventh Circuit: *Davis v. Monroe County Board of Education* (1996); Ninth Circuit: *Doe v. Petaluma City School District* (1995); Utah: *Seamons v. Snow* (1994); Northern District of California: *Oona v. Santa Rosa City Schools* (1995); Connecticut: *Mennone v. Gordon* (1995) and Western District of Missouri: *Bosley v. Kearney R-1 School District* (1995).

In *Davis* v. *Monroe County Board of Education* (1996), the Eleventh Circuit Court of Appeals considered the liability of a school board for the sexual harassment of a fifth-grade girl by a male classmate. The plaintiff brought constitutional and Title IX causes of action against the school board. The constitutional claims alleged that the failure of school officials to restrain the male student's harassing behavior violated the female student's liberty interest to be free from sexual harassment and that the intrusions on her personal security violated her substantive due-process rights. The Eleventh Circuit affirmed the district court's decision dismissing the constitutional claims, but the three appellate judges reversed the trial court on the applicability of Title IX, holding that Title IX could provide a remedy to a student injured by peer sexual harassment. The three judges split on the applicable standard. The two-judge majority applied the hostile working environment standard used in Title VII cases prohibiting employment discrimination to Title IX. "We conclude that . . . Title IX encompasses a claim for damages due to a sexually hostile educational environment created by a fellow student or students when the supervising authorities knowingly fail to act to eliminate the harassment" (p. 1193).

The five elements that the plaintiff must prove to win this type of peer sexual harassment case are (1) that she is a member of a protected group, (2) that she was subject to unwelcome sexual harassment, (3) that the harassment was based on sex, (4) that the harassment was sufficiently severe or pervasive so as to alter the conditions of her education and create an abusive educational environment, and (5) that some basis for institutional liability has been established. The first three elements are relatively easy to identify.

The court suggested four elements to consider when determining whether the environment is hostile or abusive to the plaintiff: (1) the frequency of the abusive conduct, (2) the conduct's severity, (3) whether it is physically threatening or humiliating rather than merely offensive, and (4) whether it unreasonably interferes with the plaintiff's educational performance. These factors need to be viewed both subjectively and objectively. "If the conduct is not so severe or pervasive that a reasonable person would find it hostile or abusive, it is beyond Title IX's purview. Similarly, if the plaintiff does not subjectively perceive the environment to be abusive, then the conduct has not actually altered the conditions of her learning environment, and there is no Title IX violation" (p. 1194).

In determining the fifth element, whether some basis for institutional liability has been established, the majority applies agency theory that "holds employers liable for a hostile environment created by a co-worker where the plaintiff can show that the 'employer knew or should have known of the harassment in question and failed to take prompt remedial action'" (p. 1195). The majority found sufficient allegations to establish the prima facie case and remanded the case to trial at the district court. This ruling has been set aside, with the case to be reheard and decided *en banc* (by the full membership of the court).

The dissenting judge in *Davis* rejected the majority opinion's application of Title IX to make school boards liable for negligently failing to prevent one student from sexually harassing another student. He would limit the reach of Title IX to school boards only for their intentional actions. In addition, he would limit the remedy to injunctive relief only in those cases where the violations of the board were unintentional.

The Fifth Circuit Court of Appeals, in *Rowinsky* v. *Bryan Independent School District* (1996), rejected the legal analysis of the Eleventh Circuit. The plaintiff brought the suit under Title IX, claiming the district was liable for peer hostile environment sexual harassment for not taking appropriate action to intervene and protect her two eighth-grade daughters from repeated verbal and physical abuse of a sexual nature by three male students on the bus to and from school and while at school. The *Rowinsky* court refused to analogize the hostile sexual environment standard from Title VII as it applies to employer-employee relations to Title IX and student-to-student sexual harassment. The power relationship that is imputed between the employer and employee in Title VII hostile environment cases does not exist in the school setting.

> *In the context of two students there is no power relationship, and a theory of respondent superior has no precedential or logical support. Unwanted sexual advances of fellow students do not carry the same coercive effect or abuse of power as those made by a teacher, employer or co-worker. This is not to say that the behavior does not harm the victim, but only that the analogy is missing a key ingredient—a power relationship between the harasser and the victim. (p. 1011)*

The majority in *Rowinsky* examined closely the Title IX statute and its legislative history and concluded that Title IX imposed liability only for the acts of grant recipients, not of third parties. In affirming the district court decision, the majority opined that peer sexual harassment under Title could be demonstrated if it could be shown that the school district responded differently based on the sex of the students harassed. Thus, if a school vigorously investigated a male student's claims of harassment, but investigated a female students' claims less vigorously, a violation would be found. No such claim could be supported by the facts, and the summary judgment of the district court dismissing the claim was affirmed. These cases demonstrate the degree to which courts disagree on the appropriate standard of responsibility for peer sexual harassment, making it difficult for an administrator to get a handle on establishing a policy.

Developing a Policy Regarding Sexual Misconduct among Students

School administrators will have some trepidation about how to develop policy in this area of sexual misconduct among students. Even though there is disagreement across the various circuit courts of appeal about the applicable standard of liability for school districts and administrators, one of these cases will likely provide the guiding precedent for the jurisdiction of the school district. Reports of monetary settlements for student-to-student sexual harassment also appear periodically, providing the administrator with a sense of potential vulnerability in this area.

Two recent stories received national attention. A 7-year-old New York boy was punished for stealing a kiss that he called affection and teachers called harassment. The boy's five-day suspension was revoked after public criticism. A 6-year-old boy from North Carolina was censured for kissing a classmate and banned from attending an ice-cream party. School officials there also had a change of heart, dropping the ban and revising its policy on sexual harassment. These stories remind the administrator how sensitive policy development is in this area.

There are a number of questions administrators will need to ask in thinking about the scope of a sexual harassment policy that applies to students allegedly harassing one another:

1. Does the board want to have a strongly worded policy that speaks out against sexual harassment in the schools and states that the district will not tolerate sexual harassment? Will the same policy also provide a description of procedures that will be followed if someone wants to report an incident of sexual harassment? Such policies are common to refute hostile environment claims.
2. What definition(s) of sexual harassment are provided in the policy? Do the definitions allow for both subjective and objective determinations of harassment? Are the definitions narrow enough so that free-speech interests are not jeopardized? Who can make the complaint? How detailed and how well documented does the complaint need to be?
3. What sanctions are described for violating the policy? Who makes the decisions and what appeal avenues are open? Are the sanctions age appropriate, and do they provide room for discretion to be applied by the decision maker?
4. How proactive does the school want to be in dealing with sexual harassment? Will sexual harassment be discussed in the school, made part of the curriculum, or raised as a larger issue with parents and community members? To what extent is the enforcement of the policy to be supplemented by other means to affect the culture of the school?

Mawdsley (1994) recommends four different categories that need to be addressed in developing a sexual harassment policy: (1) writing a clear, concise policy; (2) informing students, parents, and staff about the policy; (3) instituting appropriate, effective procedures for managing and reviewing harassment complaints; and (4) crafting appropriate decisions and remedies. Attention to these areas will facilitate the drafting and implementation of the policy. The drafters of the policy still need to be guided by a clear sense of the scope of the policy and attention must be given to the details of communicating it to others.

References

Abington School District v. *Schempp*, 374 U.S. 203 (1963).

Agostini v. *Felton*, ____U.S.____, 64 LW 4524 (1997).

Aguilar v. *Felton*, 105 S. Ct. 3232 (1985).

Aurora East Public School District v. *Cronin*, 442 N.E. 2d 511 (Illinois 1982).

Bittle, E. H. (1986). *Due process for school officials: A guide for conduct of administrative proceedings.* Topeka, KA: National Organization on Legal Problems of Education.

Board of Education v. Allen, 392 U.S. 236 (1968).

Board of Education of Westside Community Schools v. Mergens, U.S., 110 S. Ct. 2356 (1990).

Bosley v. Kearney R-1 School District, 904 F Supp. 1006, 1023 (W. E. Mo. 1995).

Boykins v. Fairfield Board of Education, 492 F.2d 697 (5th Cir. 1974).

Brown v. Board of Education, 347 U.S. 343 (1954).

Bruin, L. L. (1989, November). School discipline: Recent developments in student due process rights. *Michigan Bar Journal, 68*(7), 1066.

Bush, R. A. B., & Folger, J. P. (1994). *The promise of mediation: Responding to conflict through empowerment and recognition.* San Francisco: Jossey-Bass.

Carter, S. (1994, December 5). Let us pray. *The New Yorker,* 60–74.

Ceniceros v. Board of Trustees of San Diego Unified School District, 106 F.3d 878 (9th Cir. 1997).

City of Newport v. Fact Concerts, 453 U.S. 247 (1982).

Civil Rights Attorneys Awards Act, 42 U.S. Code Section 1983 (1976).

Cleveland Board of Education v. Loudermill, 105 S. Ct. 1487 (1985).

Community Projects for Students v. Wilder, 298 S.E. 2d 434 (North Carolina App. 1982).

County of Macon v. Board of Education, 518 N.E. 2d 653 (4th Ill. App. 1987).

Davis v. Monroe County Board of Education, 74 F.3d 1186 (5th Cir. 1996); rehearing en banc granted, 91 F.3d 1418 (11th Cir. 1996).

De Roche, D. G. (1994). *Illinois school districts' response to Hazelwood v. Kuhlmeier.* Unpublished doctoral dissertation, University of Illinois at Urbana-Champaign.

Dicken v. Kentucky State Board of Education, 199 W.S. 2d 977, 981 (Kentucky, 1947).

Doe v. Petaluma City School District, 830 F. supp. 1560 (N. D. Cal. 1993), *reversed on other grounds* 54 F. 3d 1447 (9th Cir. 1995).

Eisner v. Stamford Board of Education, 440 F.2d 803 (2d Cir. 1981).

Engle v. Vitale, 370 U.S. 421 (1962).

Ewing v. Board of Equalization, 420 N.W. 2d 685 (Neb. 1988).

Franklin v. Gwinnett County Public Schools, 503 U.S. 60, 112 S. Ct. 1028, 117 L. Ed. 2d 208, 72 Educ. L.R. 32 (1992).

Freeman v. Case Corporation, 924 F.Supp. 1456, 1471 (W.D. Va. 1996).

Fujishima v. Board of Education, 460 F.2d 1355 (7th Cir. 1972).

Garnett v. Renton School District No. 403, 987 F. 2d 641, cert. denied 510 U.S. 819 (1993).

Gay man abused as student wins $900,000. (1996, November 21). *New York Times,* p. A12.

Girard, K., & Koch, S. J. (1996). *Conflict resolution in the schools: A manual for educators.* San Francisco: Jossey-Bass.

Givens v. Poe, 346 F. Supp. 202 (W.D. North Carolina 1972).

Goss v. Lopez, 419 U.S. 565 (1976).

Grand Rapids v. Ball, 473 U.S. 373, 105 S. Ct. 3216 (1985).

Hall v. Tawney, 621 F.2d 607 (4th Cir. 1980).

Harlow v. Fitzgerald, 457 U.S. 800 (1982).

Harris v. Joint School District No. 241, 41 F.3d 447 (9th Cir. 1994).

Harris, D. K. (1996). When things turn ugly: Threats in the student-teacher relationship. *Rethinking Schools, 11*(1), 18–19.

Hazelwood School District v. Kuhlmeier, 795 F.2d 1368 (8th Cir. 1986), rev'd on other grounds, 484 U.S. 260 (1988).

Hedges v. Wauconda Community Unit School District No. 118, 9 F.3d 1295 (7th Cir. 1993).

Herbert v. Livingston Parish School Board, 438 So. 2d 1141 (Louisiana App. 1st Cir. 1983).

Hill, P. T. (1994). *Reinventing public education.* Rand (DRU-690-IET/LE/GGF).

Hill, P. T. (1996, October). *School-centered reform and accountability.* Paper presented at the O'Leary Symposium on Financial Management, University of Illinois, Urbana-Champaign.

Hosea, S., Colwell, B., & Thurston, P. (1996). Increasing school district autonomy through waivers of legislative mandates: The Illinois experience. *Education Law Reporter, 107,* 443–458.

Illinois Revised Statute, Chapter 122, Article 10, Section 21.3 (1977).

Ingebretsen v. Jackson Public School District, 88 F.3d 274 (5th Cir. 1996).

Ingraham v. *Wright*, 430 U.S. 651 (1977).

Jackson v. *Chicago Board of Education*, 549 N.E.2d 829, 833-4 (Ill. App. 2 Dist. 1989).

Jacobson, L. (1996, December 4). District not liable for harassment of student by peers, court rules. *Education Week, XVI*(16), p. 12.

Johnson, D. W., & Johnson, R. T. (1995). Teaching students to be peacemakers: Results of five years of research. *Peace and Conflict: Journal of Peace Psychology, 1*(4), 417–438.

Joint Anti-Fascist Refugee Committee v. *McGrath*, 341 U.S. 123 (1951).

Jones v. *Clear Creek Independent School District*, 930 F.2d 416 (5th Cir. 1991) (Jones I).

Jones v. *Clear Creek Independent School District*, 977 F.2d 963 (5th Cir. 1992) (Jones II) Cert. denied 113 S. Ct. 2950 (1992).

Keller v. *Fochs*, 385 F. Supp. 262 (E. D. Wisconsin 1974).

Kiddie Korner Day Schools v. *Charlotte-Mecklenburg Board of Education*, 285 S.E. 2d 110 (North Carolina App. 1981).

Lamb's Chapel v. *Center Moriches Union Free School District*, 508 U.S. 384, 113 S. Ct. 2141 (1993).

Lawrence v. *Grant Parish School Board*, 409 So.2d 1316 at 1321 (Louisiana Ct. App. 1982).

Lee v. *Weisman*, 505 U.S. 577, 112 S. Ct. 2649 (1992).

Lemon v. *Kurtzman*, 403 U.S. 602 (1971).

Linwood v. *Board of Education*, 463 F. 2d 763 (7th Cir. 1972).

Madera v. *Board of Education*, 386 F. 2d 778 (2d Cir. 1967).

Mawdsley, R. D. (1994). Sexual harassment in schools. *Update on Law-Related Education, 18*(2), 39–44.

Mawdsley, R. D. (1996, March 21). Neutrality between government and religion. *Education Law Reporter, 106*, 453–470.

Mawdsley, R. D., & Russo, C. J. (1996, March 21). Religious expression and teacher control of the classroom: A new battleground for free speech. *Education Law Reporter, 107*, 1–14.

McCarthy, M. M. (1996, May 30). Free speech versus anti-establishment: Is there a hierarchy of First Amendment Rights? *Education Law Reporter, 108*, 475–488.

McCollum v. *Board of Education*, 333 U.S. 203 (1948).

McDonalds settles coffee case out of court. (1994, December 2). *Chicago Tribune*, p. 1.

Meek v. *Pittinger*, 421 U.S. 349 (1975).

Mennone v. *Gordon*, 889 F. Supp. 53 (D. Conn. 1995).

Minor v. *Sally Buttes School District 58-2*, 345 N.W. 2d 48 (South Dakota 1984).

Monell v. *New York City Department of Social Services*, 436 U.S. 658 (1978).

Mueller v. *Allen*, 463 U.S. 388 (1983).

Muller v. *Lighthouse School District*, 98 F. 3d 1530 (7th Cir. 1996).

Nelson v. *Moline School District No. 40*, 725 F. Supp. 965 (C.D. Ill. 1989).

Oona v. *Santa Rosa City Schools*, 890 F. Supp. 1452 (N. D. Cal. 1995).

Owen v. *City of Independence*, 445 U.S. 622 (1980).

P. B. v. *Koch*, 96 F.3d 1298 (9th Cir. 1996).

Perry Educational Association v. *Perry Local Education Association*, 469 U.S. 37 (1983).

Phay, R. E. (1982). *Legal issues in public school administrative hearings*. Topeka, KA: National Organization on Legal Problems of Education.

Prosser, W. (1984). *Handbook of the law of torts* (5th ed.). St. Paul, MN: West.

Pyle v. *Hadley School Committee*, 861 F.Supp. 157 (D. Mass. 1994).

R.A.V. v. *City of St. Paul, MN*, 505 U.S. 377 (1992).

Rosenberger v. *Rector and Visitors of the University of Virginia*, 115 S.Ct. 2510 (1995).

Rowinsky v. *Bryan Independent School District*, 80 F.3d 1006 (5th Cir. 1996), cert. denied 117 S. Ct. 165 (1996).

Seamons v. *Snow*, 864 F. Supp. 1111 (D. Utah 1994), Aff'd in part, Rev'd in part 84 F. 3rd 1226 (10th Cir. 1996).

Settle v. *Dickson County School Board*, 53 F.3d 152 (6th Cir. 1995), cert. denied 116 S. Ct. 518 (1995).

Smith v. *Wade*, 461 U.S. 30 (1983).

Stachura v. *Memphis Community School District*, 106 U.S. 2537 (1986).

Stanley v. *Northeast Independent School District*, 462 F.2d 960, 977 (5th Cir. 1972).

Ten lessons about regulation and schooling. (1992). *CPRE policy briefs: Reporting on issues and research in education policy and finance*. (No. RB-09-06/92).

Thomas v. *Waynesboro*, 673 F. Supp. 1397 (M.D. Pa. 1987).

Tibbs v. *Board of Education*, 114 N.J. Super. 287, 276 A. 2d 165 (New Jersey Superior 1971).

Tinker v. *Des Moines Independent Community School District*, 393 U. S. 503 (1969).

Title IX of the Education Amendments of 1972, 20 U.S.C. § 1681, 1682.

Valente, W. D. (1980). *Law in the schools.* Columbus, OH: Merrill.

Village of Lucas v. *Lucas Local School District*, 442 N.E. 2d 449 (Ohio, 1982).

Wallace v. *Jaffre*, 472 U. S. 38 (1985).

Walsh, J. (1996, October 16). Supreme Court declines to accept student sexual-harassment case. *Education Week, XVI*(7), p. 4.

Wolman v. *Walter*, 433 U.S. 308 (1975).

Zobrest v. *Catalina Foothills School District*, 509 U.S. 1, 113 S. Ct. 2462 (1993).

Zorach v. *Clauson*, 343 U.S. 306 (1952).

Chapter *18*

School Finance
Equitably Funding Schools for Excellence

Schools are big business in the United States. Over $240 billion were spent in fiscal year 1992 to educate public elementary and secondary school students in this country (Snyder, 1994). The value of an education can be measured in a variety of ways. The significant relationship between years of schooling and income levels as an adult are well documented (Bowen, 1977; Kosters, 1991; Kaminski & Adams, 1993). Beyond the significant economic value of an education are the quality-of-life considerations that accrue to an educated person and the societal benefits of an educated citizenry. Still, given the value that flows to individuals and the commonwealth from public education, there is considerable disagreement over how to and at what level to finance this educational system.

Determining the appropriate spending level for public education is a fundamental policy question as well as a continuing political issue at the national, state, and local levels. What are the appropriate sources of revenue to equitably support public elementary and secondary education? Do public schools need more money to realize higher levels of student achievement? Is more money necessary for public schools to adequately educate the citizenry at a level necessary for the United States to be economically competitive? Reich (1991), for one, argues that greater levels of public spending are necessary to realize the benefits of education. Others argue that more money is not the only answer to providing increased educational effectiveness. The Consortium on Productivity in the Schools (1995), for example, argues that given the competition for public dollars, there is little likelihood of significant increases in support for public education, and that attention needs to be focused on increasing the productivity of public schools instead of continually focusing on the need for more money. The financing of public schools involves complex political and personal choices that are inextricably intertwined with demographic and economic conditions. Thus, funding for education has to be considered within the social, economic, and political contexts. Demographic factors; competition for public resources among education, medical coverage, and military spending; and the general health of the economy all effect the level of educational spending.

Administrators are at the center of this policy debate on school funding because they prepare and manage the budgets under which the schools operate. They also communicate to parents, policymakers, and other citizens the stewardship of these financial resources. This chapter will consider the various revenue sources that support public education and how they are distributed, explore the various legal challenges that have been made regarding the alleged inadequacy and inequity of various state funding systems, and analyze some of the calls being made for tightening the link between funding and student performance.

Revenue Generation and Distribution

Financial support for public education comes from a mix of local, state, and federal governmental sources. Beyond the issue of adequacy of funding, there are a number of revenue issues focusing on tax policy and the generation of revenue for schools. Among these issues are the appropriate mix of taxes and the appropriate mix of governmental resources necessary to support education.

Total expenditures for public schools increased during the late 1980s through the 1993–94 school year, both in terms of current and constant dollars (Alexander & Salmon, 1995). The role of the federal government in supporting elementary and secondary education declined during the 1980s and then began to increase slightly during the early 1990s. Alexander and Salmon report that federal appropriations for elementary and secondary education, adjusted to 1992 constant dollars, fell from the equivalent of $27.1 billion in 1975 and $27.4 billion in 1980 to $20.1 billion in 1983 before rising to $23.7 billion in 1990 and to $28.3 billion in constant dollars (adjusted for inflation) in 1992. During the 1980s and early 1990s, there was a trend toward greater reliance on local taxation, with federal and state contributions declining.

Based on his campaign promises, it is possible that federal support for elementary and secondary education will increase during President Clinton's second term. Still, the revenues to support this increase have to be realized within the commitment to move toward a balanced budget and pressure from a number of other priorities. In order to better understand the implications of the sources for funding education, for purposes of equity as well as adequacy, it is necessary to consider the different revenue sources and their comparative strengths and weaknesses.

Income, Sales, and Property Taxes

The three most significant forms of taxation, based on the amount of revenue generated, are income, sales, and property taxes. Each has advantages and disadvantages, and all, to varying degrees, provide the major funding for elementary and secondary education.

Income Tax

The taxation of individual income is a significant source of revenue for the federal government and most state governments. The income tax is based on the principle that income earned—rather than wealth as measured by currently held assets as property—is subject to taxation. That is why interest earned on money in a savings account is taxed, whereas the principal in the account is not.

The concept of income tax is quite simple; however, the mechanism developed to determine one's income-tax liability is complicated because of tax and social policy considerations. Although a detailed examination of these complicating considerations is beyond the scope of this chapter, a few examples will be illuminating. For example, a number of deductions and tax credits are provided for expenditures ranging from business expenses and moving expenses to child-care costs. Each of these deductions or tax credits is based on the general principle that certain expenses are incurred as a necessary incident to the generation of income. A second example of the complicating effect that tax or social policy often has on the calculation of one's income-tax liability is the rule that interest on municipal bonds is not treated as income. This rule is designed to encourage the purchase of municipal bonds, which offer a lower rate of interest than other types of bonds.

For ease of administration, collection of state income taxes are keyed to collection of the federal income tax. Although most states tax the income of both individuals and corporations, states differ as to the existence of a constitutional limit on the extent to which the corporate tax rate can exceed the personal income-tax rate. States also differ widely regarding the progressivity of these state income-tax rates. In addition, some states give special income-taxing authority to municipalities.

Sales Tax

Another source of financial support for public education is the state sales tax. Most states have a general sales tax, and several states permit local governments to levy a local sales tax. New York City, for example, has a higher sales tax than the state of New York. A sales tax is based on the sale of a good or commodity at the retail level. The purchaser pays the sales tax, and the seller is responsible for transferring the tax revenues to the governmental taxing authority. States vary in what they include as taxable. Historically, costs of services, such as those provided by lawyers and doctors, have not been taxed. In addition, most states do not tax medicines and food and some states exempt clothing or other necessities.

Excise taxes are a type of sales tax, with direct charges or taxes being levied on particular items. The best-known excise taxes are those charged for gasoline, cigarettes, customs duties, and liquor. The purposes of these taxes range from trying to affect consumption habits to attempting to raise revenues. For example, gasoline taxes are presently used to provide maintenance and construction money for highways. With increased pressure for new revenue sources, more attention has been given to excise taxes. The federal government has increased excise taxes on several products. Many states have increased tax rates on liquor and cigarettes and some have placed excise taxes on other consumption items (e.g., long-distance telephone charges).

Property Tax

The property tax is a form of taxation on one specific classification of wealth: property. Typically, other forms of wealth have not been taxed, presumably because of the difficulty in administering the tax and the mobility of the wealth. A legal distinction exists between real property, which includes the land and any physical improvements upon it, and personal property, which includes any personal belongings, such as checking accounts or animals, not attached to the land. Some states assess and tax both personal and real property; other states assess and tax only real property. This scheme is further complicated by the distinction between individual and corporate property. One state may assess and tax corporate personal property but not individual personal property. Even though states vary considerably in what is included in their property taxation, a significant source of revenue comes from the individual real property tax.

Although the principle of taxing the value of real property is simple, the implementation of the principle is more difficult. Assessment provides the greatest problem. All real property has to be given an assessed valuation. The fundamental principle that all real property is unique necessitates the use of judgment in valuing property. The touchstone for valuing property is its real market value—the value of this property if it were to be sold today. Real market value is easier to determine when dealing with types of real property that are often sold. Some items, such as large industrial plants, are hard to value because the market for them is very special. In some circumstances, the determination of replacement cost can be used as an alternative method of valuation. With this method, the assessor asks what it would cost to build the property in question today.

The assessed value of property is usually pegged at a certain percentage of its real market value or replacement cost. For example, Illinois has assessed valuation pegged at 33 1/3 percent of real market value. Some states allow property of various types to be classified at different rates of full market value. For example, Arizona assesses utilities at 50 percent, commercial and industrial property at 27 percent, agricultural land at 18 percent, and residential property at 15 percent of full market value.

Uniformity of assessment is a central concern with any property tax. Any lack of uniformity is partly the result of the fact that many assessors are elected officials and are therefore anxious to avoid increasing assessments for fear of political reprisal. Consequently, assessed valuations tend to lag behind the rapid increase in real market values associated with inflation. Historically, this has not been a major concern, because as long as all property within the local government taxing unit—whether it be municipality, school district, or county—was treated the same, it was irrelevant how the property in another taxing unit was being assessed. However, with many states providing state aid to schools based to some degree on the assessed property valuation of each district, it becomes imperative that assessment practices be standardized on a statewide basis. As a consequence, some states have applied property assessment ratios in an attempt to standardize assessment-valuation practices throughout the state. In other states, citizens have filed lawsuits challenging assessment abuses and state legislatures have prepared legislation aimed at improving assessment practices (Harp, 1991).

With high rates of inflation in the late 1960s and 1970s, property value and property taxation increased at a much faster rate than other forms of wealth, such as personal income. As a consequence, taxpayer revolts occurred in many states. In California and Massachusetts, constitutional amendments were passed to limit the increased value of property to a certain annual maximum level, unless the property were transferred. Circuit-breaker provisions were passed in other states to relieve the regressive effect of a high property tax on persons of fixed income. Under such provisions, persons of fixed income pay a reduced income tax when their property taxes reach a certain proportion of their personal income.

During the mid-1980s and again in the early 1990s, certain types of real property in some parts of the country actually decreased in value when the rate of inflation decreased, with negative consequences for governmental bodies that relied on property-tax revenue. One example of such a decrease in value occurred with respect to farmland, which, because of the general depression in the farm economy in the mid-1980s, dropped in value as much as a third or half, depending on the location and productivity of the land. This drastically reduced not only the net worth of individual farms and the farmers' ability to borrow against those farms but also the property valuation of rural school districts dependent on property taxes for operating. Suburban school districts have experienced the same drop in revenue where property values have suddenly gone down.

The tax rate to be applied to the assessed value of the property is determined by state law, voter referendum, or a combination of both. For example, it is common for state law to allow a certain tax rate to be applied to the assessed valuation. Districts are allowed to tax at a rate equal to or lower than the maximum allowed by law. If the district wants to exceed this limit, approval of the voters in the district must be obtained.

Determination of the tax rate *(t)* is calculated by dividing the amount of money needed from local property taxes *(Mn)* by the local tax base *(B)* (the total assessed valuation of the district).

$$t = \frac{Mn}{B}$$

The tax rate is usually described as either a percentage or a millage. One mill equals 0.1 percent. Therefore, a tax rate of 245 mills is the same as a rate of 24.5 percent. If the tax rate calculated is higher than the maximum rate allowed by law, the district must fall back to the legal maximum. This tax rate is added to tax rates for other services, such as fire and police protection, and then charged against the property owners.

Table 18.1 tracks the changing levels of contributions that federal, state, and local governments made to supporting public elementary and secondary education between fiscal years 1950 and 1992. The major trends are the increasing involvement of the federal government through the 1950s, 1960s, and 1970s with declining levels of funding in the 1980s and a slight increase in the early 1990s. Local support declined steadily into the 1980s and then leveled off at the 47 percent level during the early 1990s. The level of state funding jumped from the 40 percent range to the 47 percent range during the 1970s, and it stayed at this level through the early 1990s. These national figures mask trends that may differ drastically from state to state. Still, these figures suggest the changing reliance on different forms of taxation, as the local revenue relies almost completely on property tax, the federal government relies to a large extent on income tax, and the state government relies on income and sales tax revenue.

Criteria for Evaluating Taxes

The variety of tax sources of revenue can be analyzed according to several criteria to provide a better understanding of their respective advantages and disadvantages. Equity and efficiency as criteria will receive the most attention, but other factors such as yield, simplicity, predictability, and ease of administration are also important.

Equity

Equity considerations can focus on the taxpayer from either the perspective of the benefit the taxpayer will receive or from the perspective of the taxpayer's ability to pay the tax. Monk (1990) provides a detailed description of the "benefit" perspec-

TABLE 18.1   **Percentage of Tax Revenue Receipts for Public Elementary and Secondary Schools by Level of Government for Fiscal Years 1950, 1960, 1970, 1980, and 1990–92**

Level of Government	1950	1960	1970	1980	1990	1991	1992
Federal	2.9%	4.4%	8.0%	9.8%	6.1%	6.2%	6.6%
State	39.8%	39.1%	39.9%	46.8%	47.3%	47.2%	46.4%
Local	57.3%	56.5%	52.1%	43.4%	46.6%	46.7%	47.0%

Source: From *Digest of Education Statistics* (p. 50) by T. D. Snyder, 1994, Washington, DC: National Center for Education Statistics.

tive of equity. Briefly, and from a purely theoretical perspective, individuals are free to pay for what they want, even social goods, to the extent they believe that, under a personal cost-benefit analysis, they receive a benefit from purchasing the good. This theoretical approach is difficult to apply, though, because most social goods are taxed to whole classes of people (e.g., tax-paying adults) and it is therefore impossible to know at the individual level how each person would have "costed-out" the benefit of a particular social good. For example, how much is a person willing to pay for the benefits received from national defense spending? How much for educational spending?

Because some individuals might take advantage of the spending of others for social goods and thereby receive, for example, free national security, taxes for social goods are allocated to all taxpayers. Still, the benefit analysis of equity is useful because it suggests that payment for social goods should be keyed, to a certain extent, to those who benefit from the service. Consequently, under this analysis, support for national parks, for example, would come largely from user fees generated from those who make use of the parks. The exact balancing of this payment through user fees and general taxes would depend on judgments about what the range of benefits are. Scrutiny on the benefit side of taxes can also be helpful in thinking about the appropriateness of the level of the tax paid for the amount of services provided. In a very rough way, some taxes, like highway usage charged as a gasoline tax, approximate this. Still, the match between tax source and perceived citizen benefit is not always so clear.

Equity considerations much more commonly focus on the fairness associated with one's ability to pay taxes. *Horizontal equity* is concerned with the equal tax treatment of equals. For Monk, 1990, this means that "two persons with the same ability to pay ought to pay the same tax." This rather straightforward proposition becomes difficult when one tries to identify a measure of one's "ability to pay." In fact, Monk identifies three different measures of ability to pay: income-based measures, consumption-based measures, and wealth-based measures. Obviously, different taxes are keyed to different measures of ability to pay.

Horizontal equity problems arise because of the variety of resources people have. For example, there may appear to be equity because two taxpayers with equal property wealth are taxed at the same level, yet because of quite different levels of income, each taxpayer's ability to pay the property tax may differ markedly. It is possible that, because of the mix of taxes that utilize various types of resources, a form of horizontal equity will occur in the aggregate. Still, taxing decisions are often made by different levels of government, often utilizing different measures of resources, and there is little systematic, overall attention to horizontal equity.

Vertical equity values the equal treatment of unequals (i.e., people in different financial circumstances should be treated in appropriately different ways). The debate with regard to vertical equity turns on the meaning to be given to "appropriately different" treatment. For example, should a person who has twice the ability to pay be required to pay twice as much tax? Or should the level of payment depend on where comparable persons are placed in terms of their actual ability to pay?

Vertical equity is often considered in terms of the regressivity or progressivity of a tax. The critical variable is the tax paid as a percentage of income. If the tax paid as a percentage of income increases, the tax is said to be progressive; if it decreases, the tax is said to be regressive; and if it remains unchanged, the tax is said to be proportional. Figure 18.1 provides a graphic illustration of this relationship. There are three beliefs built into the concept of vertical equity. First, one's ability to pay is used as a principle for equalizing the taxation load. Second, as income increases, less of the money is used for consumption of necessities, and more can be saved or used for nonessentials. Third, someone using money for savings or the purchase of nonessentials is in a better position to pay taxes than is someone paying for essentials.

Although progressivity is valued generally, it is nonetheless difficult to agree on the precise relativity to apply to different taxpayers. This difficulty is further complicated because, even within a tax, it is hard to tell the precise relationship between taxpayers. For federal income tax purposes, an individual with a small amount of income may pay at only a 5 percent rate, while one with a larger income may pay at a 28 percent rate. Yet, on closer analysis, the person who paid the 28 percent rate may have reported a lower income than actually enjoyed because of deductions for real estate taxes or charitable contributions, which the other taxpayer may not have had available to him or her through the standard deduction.

In addition, it is often hard to identify those taxpayers who bear the burden of a particular tax. For example, there is debate about whether the property tax paid by an apartment owner is borne by the apartment owner, and is therefore progressive, or whether it is paid by the renter, and is therefore regressive. Finally, because of overlapping taxes that have different degrees of progressivity or regressivity, it is often difficult to calculate the overall degree of progressivity of a particular tax.

Efficiency (Neutrality)

The efficiency or neutrality criterion is concerned with the possibility that the imposition of a tax will artificially distort the economic scene. The open market-

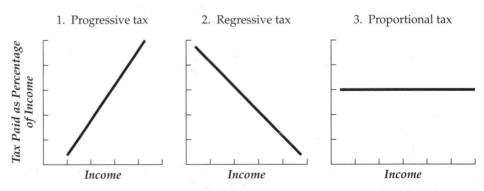

FIGURE 18.1   Relationship between Tax Rate and Income for Progressive, Regressive, and Proportional Taxes

place should dictate the appropriate allocation of resources, and the perfect tax would not affect this allocation. A tax should not affect spending patterns, work incentives, or anything else. Abstractly, taxes can reach a high degree of neutrality if they are broadly based and uniform. Excise taxes on cigarettes and alcohol are probably most clearly "unneutral" to the extent that states differ in levels of taxation and that they encourage utilization of other items that are not taxed. The other types of taxes are neutral by general definition, but they may not be neutral in their effect. For example, the definitions of what can be counted as deductions and credits for federal income-tax purposes affect the way people spend their money.

The neutrality standard often conflicts with lawmakers' attempts to achieve certain social objectives in the process of raising tax revenues. An excise tax on liquor is a prime example of how a state might have a high tax rate to discourage consumption, while also hoping to generate revenues to fund state products.

Elasticity

A tax should be dependable. With the budget process requiring long periods of planning and projection, the dependability of tax revenue is an important factor in matching projected expenditures. One index of dependability is elasticity. A tax is said to be elastic if it grows more rapidly than the gross national product.

Elasticity refers to the willingness of people to spend increasing amounts of revenue for a product as they have increasing amounts of disposable income. The demand for an item is inelastic if it is largely unaffected by increases in price. Gasoline and alcohol are examples of products with relatively inelastic demands.

A tax that does not influence the supply or demand of a product is preferred. The effect on behavior may be because of differences in tax rates across jurisdictions, like neighboring states charging different gasoline tax rates. Or the tax may influence the demand for the product. This is the elasticity effect.

Other Factors

Beyond equity, efficiency, and elasticity, several other important aspects of a tax should be considered when evaluating that tax. Among these additional aspects are the tax's yield, simplicity, and ease of administration. For example, with regard to ease of administration, excise and sales taxes are easy to pay and relatively simple to administer. On the other hand, a property tax requires significantly more resources to administer—there is cost both in maintaining the property tax rolls and in collecting the revenues.

Nontax Sources of Revenue

Hentschke's (1985) observations that school and district administrators are alert to the need to generate new revenues continues to be true today. Administrators no longer passively wait to see how much money is allocated to their district through the traditional revenue sources. Rather, they assume some of the characteristics of their private-sector counterparts in ferreting out additional revenue sources. For example, revenue can be raised and/or costs can be cut by selling items to individuals and organizations; charging tuition for nonresident students; renting some facilities; accepting donations, such as gifts from foundations; participating in business/school partnerships; and contracting for services (e.g., hiring services) from outside the district when such services are provided at lower cost by outside providers. Many school districts are also trying to pass certain expenses on to the students in the form of student fees, which has been characterized as a *hidden tax* (Bouman & Brown, 1996). School administrators will likely continue to look for additional revenues to support their districts and school. Some of this revenue will come in the form of grants or aid made available by a range of funding agencies, and some will be sought from new revenue sources.

Distribution of State Revenues

The contributions by state and local levels of government to support public elementary and secondary education are about equal. These macroeconomic generalizations mask important issues of how this money is distributed. The way the state distributes money to the school districts influences greatly the extent to which horizontal and vertical equity are realized. The distribution of educational revenues can be held up against a standard of fiscal neutrality. The distribution of educational services would be determined by preferences of the taxpayers for education, and not by their ability to pay, as measured by wealth, income, or some broader measure. Fiscal neutrality is realized when three objectives are achieved: differences in wealth among local school districts is neutralized, differences in taxing efforts to support education among local districts is permitted, and differences in educational needs of students among local school districts served is accommodated. The following section will briefly describe a range of state educational funding mechanisms with attention given to their effect on fiscal neutrality.

Methods of Disbursement

A wide range of options for disbursing revenues to local school districts are available to the states. These options include full state funding, voucher plans, equalization formulas, flat grants, and categorical aid. The choice of a distribution mechanism has a profound effect on the equity—both vertical and horizontal—by which local districts are treated.

Full state funding, under which a state would assume primary responsibility for funding education and funding all children in the state at the same level, would—by definition—guarantee equity. A *voucher system* would presumably allow for increased equity because it would provide some educational choices that would not currently be available. The precise nature and range of these choices would be defined in the particular voucher plan. Although there is some interest nationally in voucher plans, it is unlikely, for political reasons, that large amounts of money will be distributed through a totally centralized finance scheme such as the use of vouchers or full state funding. Consequently, one must be attentive to the equalization effects that a formula distribution system has when combined with flat and categorical grants.

Formulas can be used to allocate state moneys to supplement locally generated taxes and to realize the equalization of support for students across the state, thereby minimizing wide disparities in property-tax wealth across districts. Use of fixed-unit equalizing and percentage equalizing formulas are two different approaches to realizing this equity objective.

The principle at the heart of the *fixed-unit equalizing grant*, or foundation plan, is that a certain minimal level of support, or foundation, will be provided each student in the state so long as the taxpayers are willing to be taxed at some minimum qualifying level. The state will pay this guaranteed foundation level, beyond what the local district can raise, through imposition of the qualifying tax rate.

$$Dd = Nd[\ f - r(Vd)]$$

where

> Dd = dollars received by district from state
> Nd = number of pupils in district
> f = dollar level of foundation, constant for all districts
> r = qualifying tax rate, constant for all districts
> Vd = valuation of tax base of district

Assume that a state has set a foundation level of $500 per pupil and a qualifying tax rate of 1 percent. Assume that two districts, A and B, each have 1,000 students. District A has a tax base of $20 million and district B has a tax base of $40 million. Both districts will receive $500,000 in total, although the amounts from state and local sources will differ. District A will receive $200,000 from local and $300,000 from state sources, and district B will receive $400,000 from local and $100,000 from state sources. Under this formula, districts can generate additional money by taxing at rates higher than the qualifying tax rate. Note the differential impact that has for districts of different tax bases. Using the same districts A and B, assume they are both taxing at 1.5 percent. District A will receive $600,000 ($500,000 from the fixed-unit equalizer computation plus $100,000 from additional 0.5 percent times $20 million), whereas district B will receive $700,000 ($500,000 as figured above plus $200,000 from additional 0.5 percent times $40 million). As this example shows, considerable disparity can exist between wealthy and poor districts (measured by property wealth) under fixed-unit equalizing, particularly when the foundation level and the qualifying tax rate are kept at low levels.

Fixed-unit equalizing has been a popular system for distributing revenues—by the late 1970s, 34 states utilized it. Since then, the formula has declined in popularity because of its inherent tax and spending inequalities. These inequalities exist to the extent that a state is not able to adjust the foundation level to cover the cost of educating students. Once the foundation level gets too low, there is wide disparity between districts in per-pupil expenditures because of the willingness and ability of citizens in wealthy districts to supplement school revenues through local property-tax revenues. Still, if the foundation level is kept at a reasonably high level, the fixed-unit equalizing plan is attractive because it allows for some local initiative in providing greater resources for education than the state provides. This allows certain districts to innovate in ways other districts cannot and also allows taxpayers some choice in the level of education they desire.

The use of *percentage-equalizing grants* guarantees all districts, regardless of their variation in property wealth, equal access to equal dollars. Percentage equalizing equalizes per-pupil expenditures across districts. Such equalizing is accomplished by guaranteeing each district the same equalized assessed valuation support for each student. Under this system, different tax rates will generate different levels of support, but a tax rate in one district will generate the same support as the same tax rate in another district, regardless of the wealth differences between the two districts.

Equalization is a matter of both political feasibility and will power, not technical knowledge. *Flat grants,* which provide financial support at a per-pupil level (often with a weighting factor included to compensate for level of schooling), and *categorical grants,* which provide money according to specific program categories (e.g., special education, transportation, and summer school), are not equalizing.

The two fundamental finance questions are those of adequacy and equity. One must look at both the level of funding and the mix of funding sources in order to better understand the financial support (both in terms of gross resources and level of effort) and the equity among districts in distributing this support.

In attempting to realize an adequate and equitable level of funding for public schools, several sensitive issues should receive considerable attention (see Giertz, 1990; Juday, 1990). The following issues deserve brief consideration, based on the salience in your state:

- Is it politically feasible to increase equalization of financial support among districts without large increases in state aid? Historically, equalization occurred when large amounts of money were injected at the state level, with a general leveling up of all districts. With stiff competition for additional resources, this leveling up is more difficult to accomplish. When political will for providing new funds is not forthcoming, pressure on the legislature can come in the form of a constitutional challenge to the state finance system. Such challenges are discussed in more detail in the next section of this chapter.

- Property taxes come under a variety of criticisms, yet they are a critical source of revenue for public schools. As a consequence, it is difficult to imagine a state income or sales tax generating sufficient revenues to replace a property tax as the main source of tax revenues. A property tax, being relatively stable, also serves to buffer school budgets during periods of recession, when shortfalls occur from projected sales tax and income-tax revenues.

- At a more technical level, there are questions about whether realistic, minimal property tax rates must be charged at the local level in order for a district to qualify for state aid. This is a question of equity in balancing wide disparities in property wealth and levels of effort. One proposal to equalize property wealth would give the state access to local property wealth—at least from certain types of property— and revenues generated from a minimum tax on this property would be distributed across the whole state, or at least across regions larger than individual school districts. A variation on this proposal would treat certain types of property—such as power plants and shopping centers—as being regional or statewide for taxing purposes. A more extreme variation would treat all corporate and real property, except for residential real property, as being taxed at a regional or state level.

- Such a categorizing of property would leave some property taxed at a state or regional level, while other property would be taxed at a local district level. The purpose of such a system would be to better equalize property values across the state. It is possible, when pursuing this logic, to sever the financial and governance responsibilities that almost all boards currently enjoy. School districts or even school buildings could receive money under a formula calculated on the basis of regional property wealth supplemented by state funds, yet there could be a governing board for the school district or school building that would have fiscal oversight of the budget and authority over the educational program, but no, or quite limited, authority to raise or lower taxes.

- A fundamental question facing state policymakers when deciding on the appropriate mix of tax sources to fund public schools is whether the aspiration is to provide an adequate or a uniform education to every student in the state. The answer to this fundamental question has significant implications for the taxes utilized and the degree of local autonomy allowed. If uniformity is the standard for equalization, then it is difficult to allow local districts, particularly property-wealthy districts, to choose to tax themselves at a higher rate to provide a slightly better education for their students. But shouldn't citizens have the liberty to choose to provide a better education, particularly if they pay for it? Yet, if adequacy is the measure of equalization, with every student being provided a basic, adequate education, what are the criteria for defining adequacy? Is it measured by inputs or by the results of the school system? Where wide disparities exist in funding levels, all arguably above the level of adequacy, would you be satisfied if your children attended the basic, "adequate" school?

- Increasing attention is being given to the relationship between accountability and educational funding. Fiscal accountability—attention to financial inputs—is the common way of thinking about equalization. An increased focus on program accountability exists, and states are attempting to develop mechanisms to better evaluate how schools and school districts are utilizing their financial resources.

Finally, a related issue is the extent to which program improvement should be rewarded in the funding system. Should there be incentives for improvement in student performance or some other factor? In order to provide incentives, it is attractive to think about linking increased state support for education with demonstrated increases in student performance. But attempts to implement this rationale bump into a multitude of tough measurement questions: What are the appropriate standards of performance? How does one fairly measure these standards across disparate schools with different student populations? How can discretion be given to local school authorities to meet meaningful state goals?

These funding questions are political as well as technical. Where these political questions were at one time solely the domain of state legislators, state judiciaries have become increasingly involved through authority derived from state constitutions.

Constitutional Challenges to Funding Public Education: Three Waves of School Finance Litigation

Since the early 1970s, litigation has been a popular vehicle for attempting to reform state systems for financing public education. This litigation is described as proceeding through three waves (Thro, 1990). The first wave of decisions utilized the Equal Protection Clause of the Fourteenth Amendment to challenge the disparity of wealth among school districts in a state. This wave covers the relatively short period in the early 1970s between the decisions of *Serrano* v. *Priest* (1971) and *Rodriguez* v. *San Antonio Independent School District* (1973).

California's system of financing public schools, with its heavy reliance on property wealth, was challenged under the equal protection clauses of both the United States and California Constitutions. Table 18.2 illustrates the property-wealth disparities that existed between certain California school districts. Notice, for example, the two Kern County schools. Because of the tremendous disparity in property wealth among districts, residents of Rio Bravo could tax themselves at about one-third the amount that residents of Lamont could tax themselves, yet Rio Bravo students received almost triple the per-student expenditures received by Lamont students.

Such disparity between wealth and effort, and the effect that disparity has on determining the quality of education students receive, are the heart of the constitutional challenge in *Serrano*. Relying on both the Equal Protection Clause of the Fourteenth Amendment of the United States Constitution and a similarly worded Equal Protection Clause in the California Constitution, the California Supreme Court ruled in the *Serrano* case that, as a matter of law, reliance on a property tax that had such a disparate effect on per-pupil expenditures was unconstitutional.

The *Serrano* decision had a dramatic effect throughout the United States because all states except Hawaii relied on a property tax in basically the same fashion as California did. A flurry of cases followed, all using the arguments found in *Serrano* to challenge state finance formulas. School-finance schemes in Kansas (*Caldwell* v. *Kansas,* 1972), Michigan (*Milliken* v. *Green,* 1972), Arizona (*Hollins* v. *Shofstall,* 1973), New Jersey (*Robinson* v. *Cahill,* 1973), Texas (*Rodriguez* v. *San Anto-*

TABLE 18.2   Comparison of Selected Tax Rates and Expenditure Levels in Selected California Counties, 1968–1969

County	ADA*	Assessed Value per ADA	Tax Rate	Expenditure per ADA
Alameda				
Emery Unified	586	$100,187	$2.57	$2,223
Newark Unified	8,638	6,048	5.65	616
Fresno				
Colinga Unified	2,640	$ 33,244	$2.17	$ 963
Clovis Unified	8,144	6,480	4.28	565
Kern				
Rio Bravo Elementary	121	$136,271	$1.05	$1,545
Lamont Elementary	1,847	5,971	3.06	533
Los Angeles				
Beverly Hills Unified	5,542	$ 50,885	$2.38	$1,232
Baldwin Park Unified	13,108	3,706	5.48	577

Source: Serrano v. *Priest,* 487 P.2d 1241, 1252, fn. 15.

*Average Daily Attendance

nio *Independent School District,* 1973), and Minnesota *(Van Dusartz* v. *Hatfield,* 1971) were declared unconstitutional.

The Texas decision, *Rodriguez* v. *San Antonio Independent School District,* was based exclusively on the Fourteenth Amendment Equal Protection Clause. On appeal, the United States Supreme Court reversed the federal district court decision on the grounds that the Court could find neither a suspect classification nor a fundamental interest involved. Where the *Serrano* court and Texas federal district court had found differential levels of school-district property wealth to be a suspect classification, the Supreme Court could not find a connection between the property wealth of the district and the individual wealth of persons living in the district. Individual wealth (or poverty) had been found to be a suspect classification for purposes of equal protection in earlier cases (e.g., in striking down a poll tax), but here the Court could not find the connection between property wealth and individual wealth.

In *Rodriguez,* the Court also refused to declare education to be a fundamental interest. Specifically, the Court refused to declare that a per-pupil expenditure in one district that was lower than that in another district was a deprivation of a fundamental interest. Left open was the question whether the failure of a state to provide any education would amount to a deprivation of a fundamental interest. This analysis, combined with the historical role the state has played in controlling and funding public education, persuaded the Supreme Court to uphold the Texas school-finance scheme as constitutional.

The effect of the *Rodriguez* decision was to make state courts the exclusive forums for school-finance challenges. The history of this approach to challenging school-finance systems is well documented (Camp & Thompson, 1988; Connelly & McGee, 1987; Franklin et al., 1987, 1990; La Morte, 1989).

The second wave of cases is marked by independence from the United States Supreme Court decision in *Rodriguez*. A number of states showed their independence by interpreting their state constitutional provisions—typically a state Equal Protection or Education Clause—as placing limits on funding disparities between school districts. The West Virginia Supreme Court, for example, in its 1979 decision in *Pauley* v. *Kelley,* held that education is a fundamental right guaranteed by the West Virginia Constitution and that any discriminatory classification found in the educational financing system would be reviewed under the strict scrutiny standard. The following year, the Wyoming Supreme Court, in *Washakie County School District* v. *Herschler,* also held education to be a fundamental interest under the Wyoming Constitution's Equal Protection Clause and struck down the state's system for financing schools. Like the first, the second wave of cases focused on horizontal equity matters. Attention in these cases was given to funding disparities and traditional input measures, such as per-pupil and overall spending levels for education.

The third wave of school finance cases differs in two important ways. First, the Education Clause of the state constitution, and not the state Equal Protection Clause, is the predominant legal authority for challenging the finance system. Second, and most important, the focus of the challenge shifts to the sufficiencies of funds provided to schools—from equity toward adequacy (Heise, 1995b; Underwood, 1995). Attention shifts from inputs to outputs, toward achievement and student outcomes. The most significant adequacy case, *Rose* v. *Council for Better Education, Inc.,* was decided in 1989 by the Kentucky Supreme Court and effectively shifted the nature of debate in the constitutionality of school finance across the country.

Language in the Kentucky Constitution obligates the Kentucky General Assembly to "provide for an efficient system of common schools throughout the State." In 1989, the supreme court of Kentucky declared the state's school funding scheme unconstitutional for not meeting this efficiency standard. The court found the funding system deficient for numerous reasons:

> *Kentucky's system of common schools is underfunded and inadequate; is fraught with inequalities and inequities throughout the 177 local school districts; is ranked nationally in the lower 20–25% in virtually every category that is used to evaluate educational performance; and is not uniform among the districts in educational opportunities.* (Rose, p. 197)

The Kentucky Supreme Court said the responsibility for remedying the deficiency lies with the legislature and provided a rich description of what is included in the meaning of an "efficient system," thereby articulating a standard for the legislators to meet. First, the court opined that an efficient system must provide, minimally, an equal opportunity for every child to have an adequate education:

> *The system of common schools must be adequately funded to achieve its goals. The system of common schools must be substantially uniform throughout the state. Each child, every child, in this Commonwealth must be provided with an equal opportunity to have an adequate education. Equality is the key word here. The children of the poor and the children of the rich, the children who live in the poor districts and the children who live in the rich districts must be given the same opportunity and access to an adequate education. This obligation cannot be shifted to local counties and local school districts. (Rose, p. 211) (Emphasis in original.)*

Local tax initiatives designed to supplement state resources for education were deemed acceptable so long as they would not substitute resources for the provision of an adequate education:

> *Having declared the system of common schools to be constitutionally deficient, we have directed the General Assembly to recreate and redesign a new system that will comply with the standards we have set out. Such system will guarantee to all children the opportunity for an adequate education through a* state *system. To allow local citizens and taxpayers to make a supplementary effort in no way reduces or negates the minimum quality of education required in the statewide system. (Rose, p. 212) (Emphasis in original.)*

The court then proceeded to describe the elements of a minimally adequate education:

> *A child's right to an adequate education is a fundamental one under our Constitution. The General Assembly must protect and advance that right. We concur with the trial court that an efficient system of education must have as its goal to provide each and every child with at least the seven following capacities: (i) sufficient oral and written communication skills to enable students to function in a complex and rapidly changing civilization; (ii) sufficient knowledge of economic, social, and political systems to enable the student to make informed choices; (iii) sufficient understanding of governmental processes to enable the student to understand the issues that affect his or her community, state, and nation; (iv) sufficient self-knowledge and knowledge of his or her mental and physical wellness; (v) sufficient grounding in the arts to enable each student to appreciate his or her cultural and historical heritage; (vi) sufficient training or preparation for advanced training in either academic or vocational fields so as to enable each child to choose and pursue life work intelligently; and (vii) sufficient levels of academic or vocational skills to enable public school students to compete favorably with their counterparts in surrounding states, in academics or in the job market. (Rose, p. 212)*

The court concluded that the whole system—not merely the financing system—was unconstitutional, and that legislation would have to be used to develop a new system of public schools. The opinion called for the broadest overhaul to date of any state educational system.

The *Rose* decision proved to be a turning point in the way school finance cases are conceptualized and argued. Plaintiffs have been successful in overturning state funding systems in nine other states since 1989: New Jersey, Massachusetts, Alabama, Tennessee, Missouri, Texas, Vermont, Ohio, and Montana (Underwood, 1995, pp. 501–502). In 1997 alone, the Supreme Courts of three states held their state school aid formulas as unconstitutional: Vermont (*Brigham* v. *State*, 1997), Ohio (*DeRolph* v. *State*, 1997), and New Jersey (*Abbott* v. *Burke*, 1997). Even with success in these states, plaintiffs in six other states have been denied relief: Kansas, Illinois, Virginia, North Dakota, Minnesota, and Wisconsin. The explanation for this lies not so much in significant differences in the constitutional provisions among the states as in differences in attitudes about the extent to which changes in the funding formula is appropriately resolved by judicial decree rather than as a political matter best left to the political system.

What difference do these judicial decisions make in the way schools are funded? An implicit assumption exists that judicial intervention will lead to a remedy that provides more money for schools. This assumption is hard to test empirically because it is difficult to know what the level of funding would have been in the state if the judicial decree had not been issued. The limited amount of research that does exist, although mixed, does caution one about whether the assumption is warranted. A 1992 study by Hickrod and colleagues, based on the coincidence of increases in the growth of educational spending in states where supreme court decisions have declared the state school finance systems unconstitutional, supports the assumption that increases in the growth of educational spending and school finance litigation are causally connected. Still when another researcher went beyond the Hickrod study to test the assumption for individual court decisions in the educational funding levels in those states, he could not support the assumption. Heise (1995a) used a time regression model to test this assumption for Wyoming and Connecticut, and he concluded that "Court decisions in both states are associated with declines in educational funding" (p. 1761). This research led Heise to determine, at least for these two earlier school finance decisions, "that the cumulative effect of these results challenges the general assumption that successful school finance litigation will lead to increased educational spending" (p. 1761). This assumption could not be tested for Kentucky because insufficient time lag existed following the decision to fit into the model he was using.

Joondeph (1995) analyzed per-pupil expenditures in five states where the states' highest courts, in decisions prior to 1984, held the school financing schemes unconstitutional. The five states were Arkansas, California, Connecticut, Washington, and Wyoming. In all five states, a more equitable distribution of educational resources was achieved. In four of the five states, all but Connecticut, educational funding grew at a rate below the national average. Joondeph also found that, "as a general matter, those states that reduced disparities the most increased educational funding the least" (p. 774). The results from California were most disturbing. Despite improved equalization between poor and wealthy districts, the per-pupil expenditures in the poorest districts grew more slowly than the national average. Joondeph speculates about the potentially troublesome relationship between equalization and expenditures.

> *It may be that forces unrelated to school finance reform have undermined these states' commitment to funding public education. Nevertheless, four of the five states conformed to the negative correlation. These results, combined with the credibility of the plausible explanations for the relationship, should give reformers reason to carefully reexamine whether school finance litigation is truly an efficacious means to expanding educational opportunities. (p. 823)*

One major attraction of the third wave of school finance litigation is the promise it holds for providing significant amounts of new money for public elementary and secondary education. The Kentucky Education Reform Act (1990), passed to remedy the constitutional infirmities identified in *Rose*, provided an increase of 38 percent in combined state and local support for public school between fiscal years 1990 and 1992. All Kentucky school districts experienced a significant increase in spending during this period: Some property-poor districts experienced a 39 percent increase while wealthier districts rose 18 percent. The new legislation put $490 million in new funds into local school districts in fiscal year 1991, 77 percent of which came from state funds (Trimble & Forsaith, 1995).

New money has come to the Kentucky schools as a result of *Rose*, but the consequences of the high-stakes assessment system, where financial rewards or sanctions for schools depend on student performance on standardized tests, is not clear. Some commentators worry about the impact that the funding system, potentially tied too narrowly to the assessment system, might have in causing the instructional process to narrow its curriculum inappropriately.

> *High stakes accountability has imposed new pressures and responsibilities on both the assessment and instructional process. Within this environment, student assessment cannot be designed and implemented without confronting the impact that these assessments will have on the daily instruction and on the educational experiences of students.... A statistically well-designed assessment conceived to run efficiently in terms of time and financial costs still may be indefensible and too expensive if it causes the instructional process to narrow its curriculum inappropriately. Such an assessment may be too expensive if it results in an instructional program that does not cause teachers to challenge all students to reach for high levels of performance or to apply and communicate their academic achievements. In the end, any assessment and accountability system that puts at risk our ability to produce the quality students we seek is a system that is too expensive (Trimble & Forsaith, 1995, p. 653).*

Still, the financial commitment that Kentucky made to its public schools following *Rose* has caught the attention of school finance scholars and educational policymakers. The traditional equity lawsuits have been replaced with adequacy lawsuits (Grossman, 1995). In spite of school finance litigation in many states, it remains clear that meaningful school finance reform is basically a political matter, and that school finance litigation provides one avenue to leverage public and legislative attention, but it by no means guarantees an optimal solution for public education. Tax policy and public commitment to public education need to be battled, to a large extent, in the political arena. The challenge of school finance reform in the dawning of the twenty-first century is to link finance reform with systemic educational reform (Hirth, 1996).

Striving for Equity and Excellence: Financing Schools in the Twenty-First Century

Equity continues to be an important issue today as U.S. society becomes increasingly differentiated by wealth. Educational quality and school improvement will also continue to be important, and thus attention will continue to be given to the relationship between money and educational quality. Just as school finance litigation has moved to issues of adequacy, and as states wrestle with ways to connect state funding systems with systemic reform, school finance will continue to be occupied with leveraging higher levels of student academic achievement from existing financial resources.

One way of talking about the relationship between financial resources and student achievement is through the lenses of economists. Production is an economic concept that studies the relationship between resources and outputs. Educational production functions have been developed by economists who apply statistical regression analysis to better understand the relationship between a range of inputs (e.g., certain aspects of family background like income level and parental education and certain school factors such as teacher qualifications and class size) and outputs (e.g., student performance on standardized tests) (Hanushek, 1986, 1991; Levin, 1976; Monk, 1992). Fierce methodolgical battles rage over the appropriate ways to perform such production functions. Rather than review the methodological disagreements, the remainder of this chapter will briefly review the findings of salient production function research and explore the implications of this debate for the funding of public education and the allocation of resources within schools.

The production function research of Hanushek is important because he raises questions about the relationship between money and student performance on standardized test scores. He finds little agreement on what school inputs, if any, systematically affect student performance on standardized test scores. He argues that a number of public school inputs—such as teacher/pupil ratios, certain attributes of teachers (i.e., advanced education and years of experience), and administrative expenses—do not systematically influence student performance on standardized tests (Hanushek, 1986, 1991, 1995). He goes beyond this work to cast serious reservations about the effectiveness of school spending. "The rapid increases in expenditure on schools in the past three decades have simply not been matched by measurable increases in student performance. Moreover, detailed studies of schools have shown a variety of inefficiencies that, if corrected, could provide funds for a variety of improvement programs" (Hanushek, 1995, p. 24).

Greenwald, Hedges, and Laine have in a series of articles reviewed a number of educational production function studies (Hedges et al., 1994; Laine et al., 1995; Greenwald et al., 1996). After applying a different methodology than Hanushek to the variety of research studies on school inputs, they conclude that "school resources are systematically related to student achievement and that these relations are large enough to be educationally important" (Greenwald et al., 1996, p. 384). They point specifically to global resource variables such as per-pupil expenditures, the smaller size of schools and classes, and the resource variables that describe the quality of teachers (teacher ability, teacher education, and teacher experience) as all being strongly related to student achievement. A 1995 study by Ferguson and Ladd concluded that money did matter in the performance of fourth-grade Alabama students. They concluded that four school-input variables, three related to teachers and class size, appeared to affect student learning. They found these inputs to be connected to student learning, particularly in low-spending districts.

The production function studies do not provide easy answers on how to effectively allocate resources. In spite of the disagreement among production function researchers about the power of various educational inputs, there is, nonetheless, a general, almost commonsense, belief that money does make a difference. The challenge is how to increase the productivity of education. The Consortium on Productivity in the Schools (1995) argues that schools have to become more productive in the future.

> *Changing the way education is delivered to increase its productivity is directly within the control of policy makers and educators and is our one best hope for increasing student learning across the system.* The nation's need for an educated labor force in the 21st Century cannot be met unless the institution on which we depend to educate us finds ways to increase its productivity. *(p. 16) (Emphasis in original)*

Odden and Clune (1995) explore the topic of improving educational productivity. Their research indicates that wasteful administration and higher teacher salaries are not to blame for low productivity. Instead, one problem affecting productivity is poor resource distribution. Funding differs drastically across districts within states and often between schools in the same district, and the funding differential is significant enough to influence the level of education provided. Another problem is that money is not used in ways that directly raise student achievement. New money tends to be allocated to hire more teachers or provide more out-of-classroom services, which do not demonstrate gains in student academic achievement. Money is also often allocated to special student populations, again with little showing of increased achievement. There is a tendency in districts to engage in a number of practices that drive up education costs but do not necessarily lead to higher student achievement: responding to new issues by adding programs rather than honing the existing program, adding administrative staff for new categorical programs, and changing workplace norms for teachers by reducing teaching loads or lowering class size without being attentive to effect on increased levels of student performance.

Three broad areas that influence productivity deserve attention. The first is an examination of current expenditures to determine appropriateness of current spending levels. The second is to focus on the school as the unit of analysis for determining effectiveness in the delivery of instruction. Information can be collected and analyzed at the building level, and it is also a level where responsibility can be placed and high-involvement management encouraged. Finally, new approaches to teacher compensation continue to be explored.

A critical aspect of productivity is to be knowledgeable about the variety of resources that are available and to explore the extent to which these resources contribute to student achievement. One area of increasing attention is the amount of money spent on special education services. It is clear that a significant part of increased educational expenditures over the past two decades has come in special education, and that the number of students being served in special education has steadily risen (Barnett, 1994). With the unique federal legislative status of special education, and its treatment as an entitlement, there is little attention to whether special education is more effective than regular education. Many states are concerned about the costs of special education and are exploring how to change the way it is paid for. New York state provides an example of this increase in special education. Between 1983 and 1996, statewide special education enrollment increased from 266,000 to 363,000. Between 1992 and 1996, the percentage of special education students in the student population has increased from just over 9 percent to just over 11 percent. The state estimates that special education consumes nearly a quarter of the total state expenditure on instruction (Schnailberg, 1996). With these increasing special education costs, Richard Mills, the New York State Commissioner of Education, has called for changes in the way special education is paid for.

The quality of information available on educational resources and how they are budgeted can be a significant issue in making informed decisions to improve productivity. Part of the problem lies in being able to trace educational expenditures in meaningful ways at the building level. Speakman and colleagues (1995) address this issue in analyzing expenditures in New York City to allocate costs to the classroom level. This involves taking district-level financial information and organizing it in a variety of frameworks to better understand what money is used to support instruction. Once information is available for a variety of expenditures at the building level, this information can be compared with similar expenditures in other buildings in the district or other buildings in the state. There is need for better comparative information on which to make judgments about the appropriateness of particular expenditures. Such comparisons can provide a beginning place for inquiring why one building's expenditure may be so high compared to that of other buildings. There may be a justification for it, but there also may be an opportunity for reducing certain expenditures by examining the practices involved (Cooper et al., 1994).

A second area of considerable interest is school-based decision making, with the focus being on the school site as the locus of authority and control. Wohlstetter and Van Kirk (1995) argue that high-involvement, decentralized management is desirable for schools. Such schools will realize improved organizational effectiveness and productivity if four key resources are decentralized: power, information, knowledge, and rewards. The model is basically a school improvement model that emphasizes high levels of professional involvement from teachers, parents, and noncertified staff to realize high levels of student achievement. Good information is necessary to be able to track student achievement and parent satisfaction as well as to track expenditures at the school level. Accurate, appropriate information will not only provide the opportunity for professional leadership but it will also provide the basis of an accountability system for parents and the larger community (Guthrie, 1995).

Currently such reliable student assessment information and budget information is hard to find at the building level. A few schools have moved toward improving the budget information that exists at the school level, but few schools provide models for having broad autonomy over how to allocate this money in significantly different ways. Part of the problem in utilizing this discretion at the school building level is that teachers do not have experience in making personnel decisions, particularly as they affect colleagues. Many personnel matters are still tied up in district-level contract agreements, and it is difficult to obtain authority to make certain types of decisions delegated to the building level. In current conditions, with 70 to 80 percent of expenses tied up in personnel costs, there is relatively little room for meaningful control of resources given to the organization and structuring of instruction.

It has become increasingly common to use a pull-out model of instruction. Students are pulled out of regular classrooms for special education and for certain Title I services. This practice, obviously, has consequences for the size of regular classes. In a provocative article, Miles (1995) explores the matter of teacher allocation. Although there are a number of regulatory and contractual constraints that exist, a difficult challenge is changing how teachers, students, and administrators work in schools. Miles recommends four strategies to reduce the specialization and fragmentation of teaching resources that collectively limit a school's flexibility to best match its teaching resources to student needs. These include:

- *Increasing the portion of teachers who serve children in regular classroom settings while reducing the segregation of students with special needs*
- *Considering new ways of providing for teacher planning and professional time and redeploying teachers now used to cover this time to reduce average teacher-student ratios*

- *Eliminating age grading or combining grades and programs within schools to reduce the unevenness in class sizes . . . and*
- *Rethinking school schedules to reduce the number of students each teacher has responsibility for. (pp. 489–490)*

Thinking about the total staff of the school and utilizing the full array of resources to meet student academic needs is a significant challenge that could probably be best attacked at the school level. Decreasing the use of specialized teachers and organizing resources around a larger view of regular education seems to be a potentially powerful way of thinking about how to use significant resources in new ways.

The topic of teacher incentives and rewards is still raised, but there is no longer a discussion of merit pay and career ladders. Discussion of teacher incentives now focuses on connecting teachers with systemic reform to improve student academic performance. One approach to teacher incentives is to recognize the potential motivating nature of the work in its own right. Mohrman and Lawler (1996) argue for a high-involvement model where teacher participation and expertise are valued. Presumably, an incentive for participating in this environment is knowing that meaningful changes are being made that contribute to increased levels of student learning. For many people, the creative aspect of working with colleagues to accomplish something is also motivation. Such attention to intrinsic motivation does not minimize the importance of appropriate wages and working conditions.

Odden and Clune (1995) also emphasize the relationship between teacher pay and incentives with the broader goals of the organization. They propose two types of teacher compensation that move beyond the traditional single-salary schedule that awards teachers on the basis of years of experience and education units. First, they propose a salary schedule that awards teachers on the basis of their knowledge, skill, and competency. Odden and Clune suggest that subject-matter knowledge of teachers will be important as well as classroom management and pedagogical expertise. There is also a question of how much reliance to place on external assessment measures such as the National Board for Professional Teaching Standards (1994) and how much to place on internal assessments at the district or school level.

A second performance award could be given to groups of faculty members or teams in recognition of their collaborative work in improving schoolwide student performance. Student achievement in academic subjects would be the anchor performance indicator. These two proposals are not worked out in operational terms, but they do provide a conceptual framework for thinking about new approaches to teacher compensation. The broad conceptual framework is to link pay incentives to student academic achievement while encouraging teacher cooperation. Significant issues of measurement and assessment need to be worked out before they can be successfully implemented.

Efficient, productive resource allocation is a significant educational challenge for today and the future. Attending to it will require focus on realizing higher levels of student academic achievement, information sources able to track expenditures and student achievement, and an environment committed to continuous improvement. Increased productivity holds promise for increasing student performance with current levels of resources and the basis for asking for additional resources to accomplish even more.

References

Abbott v. *Burke*, 693 A.2d 417 (New Jersey 1997).

Alexander, K., & Salmon, R. (1995). *Public school finance.* Boston: Allyn and Bacon.

Barnett, S. W. (1994). Obstacles and opportunities: Some simple economics of school finance reform. *Educational Policy, 8*(4), 436–452.

Bouman, C. E., & Brown, D. J. (1996, December). Public school fees as hidden taxation. *Educational Administration Quarterly, 32,* 665–685.

Bowen, H. R. (1977). *Investment in learning.* San Francisco: Jossey-Bass.

Brigham, v. *State,* 692 A.2d 384 (Vermont 1997).

Caldwell v. *Kansas,* Civ. No. 50616 (Dist. Ct., Aug. 30, 1972).

Camp, W. E., & Thompson, D. C. (1988). School finance litigation: Legal issues and politics of reform. *Journal of Education Finance, 14*(2), 221–238.

Connelly, M. J., & McGee, J. (1987). School finance litigation in the 1980s. *Journal of Education Finance, 12*(4), 578–591.

Consortium on Productivity in the Schools. (1995). *Using what we have to get the schools we need: A productivity focus for American education.* New York: Institute on Education and the Economy, Teachers College, Columbia University.

Cooper, B. S., Sarrel, R., Darvas, P., Alfano, F., Meier, E., Samuels, J., & Heinbach, S. (1994). Making money matter in education: A microfinancial model for determining school-level allocations, efficiency, and productivity. *Journal of Educational Finance, 20,* 66–87.

DeRolph v. *State,* 677 N.E.2d 733 (Ohio 1997).

Ferguson, R. F., & Ladd, H. F. (1995, April). *Additional evidence on how and why money matters: A production function analysis of Alabama schools.* Paper prepared for the "Performance-Based Approaches to School Reform," Brookings Institution Conference held in Washington, DC.

Franklin, D. L., Hickrod, G. A., Frank, L. E., Lenz, R. J., & Hubbard B. C. (1987). *The constitutionality of the K–12 funding systerm in Illinois. Volume I. Legal Issues.* (MacArthur/Spencer Series No. 3). Normal: Illinois State University, Center for the Study of Educational Finance.

Franklin, D. L., Hickrod, G. A., Frank, L. E., Lenz, R. J., & Hubbard, B. C. (1990). *The constitutionality of the K–12 funding system in Illinois. Volume II: 1990 Supplement.* (MacArthur/Spencer Series No. 15). Normal: Illinois State University, Center for the Study of Educational Finance.

Giertz, J. F. (1990, December). Tax policy and revenues for education. In *Education Policy Assembly on School Finance and School Improvement.* Symposium conducted at the University of Illinois at Urbana-Champaign.

Greenwald, R., Hedges, L. V., & Laine, R. D. (1996). The effect of school resources on student achievement. *Review of Educational Research, 66*(3), 361–396.

Grossman, M. S. (1995). Oklahoma school finance litigation: Shifting from equity to adequacy. *University of Michigan Journal of Law Reform: Adequacy Litigation In School Finance Reform, 28*(3), 521–557.

Guthrie, J. W. (1995). Implications for policy: What might happen in American education if it were known how money actually is spent? In L. O. Picus (Ed.), *Where does the money go: Resource allocation in elementary and secondary schools* (pp. 253–268). Newbury Park, CA: Corwin Press.

Hanushek, E. A. (1986, September). The economics of schooling: Production and efficiency in public schools. *The Journal of Economic Literature, 24,* 1141–1173.

Hanushek, E. A. (1991). When school finance "reform" may not be good policy. *Harvard Journal on Legislation, 28,* 423–456.

Hanushek, E. A. (1995). The quest for equalized mediocrity: School finance reform without consideration of school performance. In L. O. Picus (Ed.), *Where does the money go: Resource allocation in elementary and secondary schools* (pp. 20–43). Newbury Park, CA: Corwin Press.

Harp, L. H. (1991, January 16). Property assessments loom as key issue in education finance. *Education Week,* pp. 1, 21.

Hedges, L. V., Laine, R. D., & Greenwald, R. (1994). Does money matter: A meta-analysis of studies of the effects of differential school inputs on student outcomes. *Educational Researcher, 23*(3), 5–14.

Heise, M. (1995a). State constitutional litigation, educational finance, and legal impact: An empirical analysis. *The University of Cincinnati Law Review, 63* (Summer 1885): 1735–1765.

Heise, M. (1995b). State constitutions, school finance litigation, and the "third wave": From equity to adequacy. *Temple Law Review, 68* (Fall 1995): 1151–1176.

Hentschke, G. C. (1985). Emerging roles of school district administrators: Implications for planning, budgeting and management. *Public Budgeting and Finance, 5*(1), 15–26.

Hickrod, G. A., Hines, E. R., Anthony, G. P., Dively, J. A., & Pruyne, G. B. (1992). The effect of constitutional litigation on education finance: A preliminary analysis. *Journal of Educational Finance, 18*(2), 180–210.

Hirth, M. A. (1996, December). Systemic reform, and school finance reform: Essential policy linkages. *Educational Policy, 10,* 468–479.

Hollins v. *Shofstall,* Cir. No. C-253652 (Arizona Super. Ct., June 1, 1972), rev'd, 515 P.2d 590 (1973).

Joondeph, B. W. (1995). The good, the bad, and the ugly: An empirical analysis of litigation-prompted school finance reform. *Santa Clara Law Review, 35*(3), 763–824.

Juday, S. L. (1990, December). The politics of Illinois school finance: "We have met the enemy, and he is us." In *Education Policy Assembly on School Finance and School Improvement.* Sympo-

sium conducted at the University of Illinois at Urbana-Champaign.

Kaminski, R., & Adams, A. (1993). *Educational attainment in the United States: March 1993.* Washington, DC: U.S. Department of Commerce, Bureau of the Census.

Kentucky Education Reform Act of 1990, ch. 476, 1990 Ky. Acts 1208 (codified as amended in scattered sections of KY. REV. STAT. ANN., chs. 156-65 and other scattered chapters).

Kosters, M. H. (1991). Wages and demographics. In M. H. Kosters (Ed.), *Workers and their wages* (pp. 1–32). Washington, DC: AEI, 1-32.

La Morte, M. W. (1989). Courts continue to address the wealth disparity issue. *Educational Evaluation and Policy Analysis, 11*(1), 3–15.

Laine, R. D., Greenwald, R., & Hedges, L. V. (1995). Money does matter: A research synthesis of a new universe of education production function studies. In L. O. Picus (Ed.), *Where does the money go: Resource allocation in elementary and secondary schools* (pp. 44–70). Newbury Park, CA: Corwin Press.

Levin, H. M. (1976). Concepts of economic efficiency and educational production. In T. Joseph, J. T. Froomkin, D. Jamison, & R. Radner (Eds.), *Education as an industry* (pp. 149–191). Cambridge, MA: National Bureau of Economic Research.

Miles, K. H. (1995). Freeing resources for improving schools: A case study of teacher allocation in Boston public schools. *Educational Evaluation and Policy Analysis, 17*(4), 479–493.

Milliken v. *Green,* 203 N.W.2d 457 (1972), vacated, 212 N.W.2d 711 (Michigan 1973).

Mohrman, S. A., & Lawler, III, E. E. (1996). Motivation for school reform. In S. H. Fuhrman & J. A. O'Day (Eds.), *Rewards and reform: Creating educational incentives that work* (pp. 115–143). San Francisco: Jossey-Bass.

Monk, D. H. (1990). *Educational finance: An economic approach.* New York: McGraw-Hill.

Monk, D. H. (1992). Education productivity research: An update and assessment of its role in education finance reform. *Educational Evaluation and Policy Analysis, 14,* 307–332.

National Board for Professional Teaching Standards. (1994). *National board certification: Prin-*

ciples of successful implementation. Detroit: Author.

Odden, A., & Clune, W. (1995). Improving educational productivity and school finance. *Educational Researcher, 24*(9), 6–10.

Odden, A. (1996). Incentives, school organization and teacher compensation. In S. H. Fuhrman & J. A. O'Day (Eds.), *Rewards and reform: Creating educational incentives that work* (pp. 226–256). San Francisco: Jossey-Bass.

Pauley v. *Kelley*, 255 S.E.2d 859 (W. Va. 1979).

Reich, R. B. (1991). *The work of nations.* New York: Knopf.

Robinson v. *Cahill*, 287 A.2d 187, supplemented in 289 A.2d 569 (1972), aff'd as modified, 303 A.2d 273 (New Jersey 1973).

Rodriguez v. *San Antonio Independent School District*, 337 F. Supp. 280 (W.D. Texas 1971), rev'd., 411 U.S. 1 (1973).

Rose v. *Council for Better Education, Inc.*, 790 S.W.2d 186 (Kentucky 1989).

Schnailberg, L. (1996). States rethink how to pay for special ed. *Education Week, 16*(13), 1.

Serrano v. *Priest*, 487 P.2d 1241 (California 1971).

Snyder, T. D. (1994). *Digest of education statistics.* Washington, DC: National Center for Education Statistics.

Speakman, S. T., Cooper, B. S., Sampieri, R., May, J., Holsomback, H., & Glass, B. (1995). Bringing money to the classroom: A systemic resource allocations model applied to the New York City public schools. In L. O. Picus (Ed.), *Where does the money go: Resource allocation in elementary and secondary schools* (pp. 106–131). Newbury Park, CA: Corwin Press.

Thro, W. E. (1990). The third wave: The implications of the Montana, Kentucky, and Texas decisions for the future of public school finance reform litigation. *Journal of Law and Education, 19*(2), 219–250.

Trimble, C. S., & Forsaith, A. C. (1995, Spring). Achieving equity and excellence in Kentucky education. *University of Michigan Journal of Law Reform: Adequacy Litigation in School Finance Symposium, 28,* 599–653.

Underwood, J. K. (1995, Spring). School finance adequacy as vertical equity. *University of Michigan Journal of Law Reform: Adequacy Litigation in School Finance Reform, 28,* 493–519.

Van Dusartz v. *Hatfield*, 334 F. Supp. 870 (D. Minnesota 1971).

Washakie County School District v. *Herschler*, 606 P.2d 310 (Wyo. 1980).

Wohlstetter, P., & Van Kirk, A. (1995). Redefining school-based budgeting for high-involvement. In L. O. Picus (Ed.), *Where does the money go: Resource allocation in elementary and secondary schools* (pp. 212–235). Newbury Park, CA: Corwin Press.

Index

A

A Nation Prepared: Teachers for the 21st Century, 3
A Nation at Risk, 2, 3, 12, 86, 245, 276, 283
Accountability, 7, 9, 15–18
  value-added, 7, 18
Administration (*see also* Administrative work;
    Metaphors in administration; Models of
    administration):
  as applied science, 145–146
  choices in, 1
  compared with leadership, 58–59
  compared with management, 60–65
  compared with policy, 56–58
  complexity in, 165–166
  constraints in, 1
  critical responsibilities in, 60–65
    cultural patterns, 60
    external adapting, 63
    goal attainment, 63
    internal integration, 63
  defined, 58, 60
  demands in, 1
  ethical behavior, 163–165
  evaluation, 65–70
    principals, 67–68
  knowledge base, 92, 93, 97
  metaphors (*see* Metaphors in administration)
  models of (*see* Models of administration)
  as moral craft, 148–151, 162–163
  need for, 55–56

nonrational, 136–140
organizational culture, 140–141 (*see also* Models
    of administration)
preparation programs, 83–85
  reforming, 86–91
  standards for, 95, 96
processes in, 69
profession of, 80–91
  criticisms of, 80, 91–95, 100
  history of, 81
  reforming, 86–93
  as source of authority, 26–28
  standards for, 106–112
as reflective practice, 147
reforming, 86–91
roles in, 72–74
skills in, 70–72
values in, 146
women in (*see* Women in administration)
Administrative Science Quarterly, 157
Administrative theory (*see also* Leadership;
    Models of administration):
  challenge to, 159–160
  community, 144
  human relations, 129–130, 132
  human resources, 130–132
  institutional, 149
  and practice, 156, 158
  social system, 130
  theory movement, 157

Administrative theory *(continued)*
Theory X, 131
Theory Y, 131
work activity school, 168
Administrative work:
administrative processes, 69
as applied science, 145
characteristics of, 179
as moral craft, 148–151
as professional, 147
reflective practice, 147
roles in, 169–177
decisions, 170, 173
international, 170, 173
interpersonal, 169
skills in, 70–72
as technical, 147
time in, 181–182
variation in, 177, 198–200
Agostini v. *Felton*, 347
Aguilar v. *Felton*, 347
Alexander, L., 279, 287
Allen, J. D., 188
"America 2000," 277
American Association of Colleges of Teacher
Education (AACTE), 88, 96
American Association of School Administrators
(AASA), 81, 82, 84, 85, 95, 96, 98, 118
American Association of University Women, 98
American Civil Liberties Union (ACLU), 238
American Federation of Teachers (AFT), 85, 86,
240–242, 279, 282, 291
American Vocational Association, 282
Annie E. Casey Foundation, 46
Antos, R. L., 190
Appleby, P. H., 57
Argyris, C., 60, 130
Arizona State University, 82
Association of California School Administrators,
85
Association of School Business Officials
(ASBD), 85
Association for Supervision and Curriculum
Development (ASCD), 85, 96
Astuto, T. A., 277
Athos, A. G., 143
Auburn University, 85

Authentic pedagogy, 10
Authority:
bureaucratic, 25–27
democratic, 28–29
professional, 26–28

B
Baldridge, V., 135
Ball, S., 192
Barnard, H., 118
Bates, R., 141
Bell, C. S., 98, 217, 220
Bell, T. H., 275
Bennett, W. J., 8, 279
Bennis, W., 75, 130, 142, 143
Berliner, D., 8
Biddle, B., 8
Bill of Rights, 22
Blase, J., 151
Blumberg, A., 76, 148, 149, 162, 163, 217, 218, 219,
220
Bobbitt, F., 118, 122
Bossert, S. T., 76
Boston University, 85
Bower, J., 145
Boyer, E. L., 276
Breaking Ranks: Changing an American Institution,
95
Brookover, W. B., 75
Broudy, H., 146
Brown v. *Board of Education of Topeka*, 243, 271, 301,
342
Bureau of Indian Affairs, 278
Bureaucracy, 20, 24 (*see also* Models of
administration)
bureaucratic "bloat," 8, 9
bureaucratic teaching, 24, 26
and efficiency mode, 126–128
nature of, 164
Bush, G. W., 277, 281, 283

C
Caldwell v. *Kansas*, 372
California State University System, 86
Callahan, R., 214
Campbell, M., 98
Canaan, J., 189

Capper, C. A., 53
Carlson, R. O., 217
Carnegie Corporation, 244
Carnegie Forum on Education and the Economy, 3, 86
Carol, L. N., 34, 37
Carter, J., 275, 278
Carver, F. D., 100
Casteen, J. T., 25
Cavazos, L., 279
Ceniceros v. *Board of Trustees of San Diego Unified School District*, 344
Center for the Advanced Study of Educational Administration, 82
Chamber of Commerce, 244
Change:
    agency theory, 33
    human nature and, 31
        constrained view, 31, 33–34
        unconstrained view, 31–33
    rational choice theory, 32
    strategy for, 35
    theory of, 31
Charter schools, 30
Chase, S., 98, 217, 220
Children's Defense Fund, 282
Cioci, M., 104, 105
Civic virtue, 34
Civil Rights Act of 1964, 272
Civil Rights Attorneys Awards Act, 349
Clark, D., 88
Clark, D. L., 277
Clemin, L. A., 83
Cleveland Board of Education v. *Loudermill*, 328
Clinton, W. J., 86, 277, 282, 283, 287, 360
Clune, W., 379, 382
Cohen, D. M., 139
Coladorci, T., 158
Collective bargaining, 262
Colorado Association of School Executives, 85
Community Projects for Students v. *Wilder*, 317
Connelly v. *Gibbs*, 303
Consortium on Productivity in the Schools, 359
Cookson, P. W., 30
Coons, J. E., 29
Cooperative Program in Educational Administration (CPEA), 81, 82

Council of Chief State School Officers, 81
Council for Exceptional Children, 282
Creative experience, 129
Crim, A., 86
Cuban, L., 149
Cubberty, E., 118, 119, 123, 126
Cultural perspective, 140–144 (*see also* Models of administration)
Cunningham, L. L., 34, 37
Curcio, J. L., 255
Cusick, P., 37, 137, 193
Cyert, R. M., 137

D
Dahl, R., 236
Danforth Foundation, 86, 88
Darling-Hammond, L., 25, 26
Darwin, C., 32
Davis v. *Monroe County Board of Education*, 353
Deal, T. E., 143
Demographics and education:
    condition of children, 46
    educational achievement, 49
    educational attainment, 47
    population changes by 2000, 45
    poverty levels, 46
Department of Defense, 278, 279
Department of Health and Human Services, 278, 279
Department of Justice, 278
Deutsch, K. W., 63
Dubin, R., 132
Dwyer, D., 202, 205, 207

E
Economic Opportunities Act of 1994, 272
Edmonds, R., 75
Education for All Handicapped Children Act, 273
Education Commission of the States, 3, 276
Education Leadership, 102
Education Week, 351
Educational Administration Quarterly, 157
Educational Administration: The UCEA Document Base, 97
Elementary and Secondary Education Act (ESEA), 272
Elliott, E. C., 118

﹖ore, R. F., 4
﹖ngle v. *Vitale*, 275
Ewing v. *Board of Equalization*, 316

F
Far West Laboratory for Educational Research
    and Development, 202
Fayul, H., 123, 124
The Federalist: The Administration of Government, 57
Finn, C., 82, 83
Firestone, W. A., 143
Follett, M. P., 75, 129, 151
Ford Foundation, 86, 244
Fordham University, 84, 85
Forsyth, P., 85
Fortune, J. C., 255
Franklin, B., 8
Franklin v. *Gwinwett County Public Schools*, 352
Fredericksen, N., 103
Fuhrman, S., 296

G
Gamoran, A., 10
General Accounting Office (GAO), 281
George, R. G., 190
George Peabody College for Teachers, 81
Gibboney, R. A., 87
"Goals 2000," 277
Goldhammen, K., 77
Goodlad, J., 21, 26, 76, 77, 276
Goodnow, F. J., 56, 57
Goss v. *Lopez*, 305, 326
Grand Rapids v. *Ball*, 346
Great Society, 6
Greenfield, J. B., 142
Greenfield, W., 76, 143
Greenwald, R., 379
Griffiths, D. E., 87, 103
Gross, N., 103
*Guidelines for the Preparation of School
    Administrators*, 84
Guthrie, J., 83
Guttman, A., 239

H
Hall v. *Jawney*, 325
Haller, E. J., 92, 164

Halpin, A., 207
Hamilton, A., 57
Hansot, E., 117, 119
Hanushek, E. A., 378
Harris, D. K., 330
Harris v. *Joint School District No. 241*, 342
Harsanyi, J. C., 235
Harvard University, 81, 85
Hawkins, H., 310
Hazelwood School District v. *Kuhlmeier*, 332, 344, 346
Head Start, 278
Hedges, L. V., 379
Heise, M., 376
Hemphill, J. K., 58, 103
Hentschke, G. C., 367
Herscher v. *Kawkakee*, 303
Hickrod, G. A., 376
Hobbes, T., 31
Hofstede, G., 140
Hofstra University, 85
Hoge, R. P., 158
Hollins v. *Shofstall*, 372
The Holmes Group, 3, 86
Homans, G. C., 172
Homeless Children and Youth Act, 301
Houston Chronicle, 16
Howe, H., II, 23
Hoy, W., 97
Hunter, F., 236
Hunter, M., 194

I
Iannaccone, L., 159, 218, 292
Illinois State University, 85
Improving American Schools Act of 1994, 273
*Improving the Preparation of School Administration:
    Agenda for Reform*, 88
Indiana University, 88
Individuals with Disabilities Education Act of
    1995, 274
Ingebretsen v. *Jackson Public School District*, 342
Ingraham v. *Wright*, 325

J
Jackson, J., 243
Jacksonian democracy, 9
Jennings, M. K., 217, 218, 254

Johnson, L. B., 6, 11, 272
Jones v. *Clear Creek Independent School District*, 341
Joondeph, B. W., 376

K
Katz, R. L., 70
Kean, T. H., 3
Kellog Foundation, 81
Kennedy, A., 143
Kennedy, J. F., 272
Kentucky Education Reform Act, 377
Kiddie Korner Day Schools v. *Charlotte-Mecklenburg Board of Education*, 316
Kirst, M., 21, 27, 29
Kiwanis, 244
Krant v. *Rachford*, 303

L
Laine, R. D., 379
Lam, D., 98
Lamb's Chapel v. *Center Moriches Union Free School District*, 343, 344, 345, 346
Lanter, J., 86, 87
Laswell, H. D., 36, 181, 225
Lau v. *Nichols*, 280
Lawler, III, E. E., 382
Leaders for Tomorrow's Schools, 87
Leadership:
    compared with management, 73
    cultural, 140–144
    defined, 32, 72
    educational, 72, 76–78, 202–203
    qualitative, 74–76
    theories of (*see also* Administrative theory):
        constrained, 32
        high-performance, 14, 23, 34
        moral, 14, 15
        pyramid, 13, 34
        railroad, 13, 34
        unconstrained, 33
Lee, V. E., 104, 105
Lee v. *Weisman*, 308, 341
Legislated learning, 20, 24
Lehr, A., 299
Lemon v. *Kurtzman*, 341, 345, 346
Levitt, T., 72
Lewin, K., 130

Lezotte, L., 75
Lieberman, A., 75, 191, 203
Lightfoot, S. L., 200, 204, 206
Likert, R., 130
Lindblom, C., 139, 231
Lions Club, 244
Lipham, J., 58
Lipsitz, J., 76, 143
Local School Council, 239
Lortie, D., 191, 192
Louis, M. R., 140
Lundberg, C. C., 143
Lutz, F. W., 159, 218

M
MacArthur Foundation, 86
Magnet schools, 30
The Man in the Principal's Office, 198
Mann, H., 118, 212
Marshall, C., 225, 290
Maslow, A., 130
Mayo, E., 129, 130
McDonnell, L. M., 4, 27
McGregor, D., 130, 131
Meskin, J. D., 102, 103
Metaphors in administration:
    artisan, 148
    craft, 148, 162
    factory, 126
    garbage-can decision making, 139
    mechanistic, 127
    muddling through, 139, 231
    organic, 128
    production, 126
Metz, M. H., 208, 209
Miami University of Ohio, 85
Milgram, S., 186
Miller, L., 75, 191, 203
Milliken v. *Green*, 372
Mills, C. W., 236
Mills, R., 380
Mills, T. M., 63
Mintzberg, H., 169, 173, 174, 176, 180, 181, 182
Mitchell, D., 225, 290
Mitos, K. H., 381
Models of administration, 120–122
    culture, 140–144

Models of administration *(continued)*
  community, 140
  corporate, 143
  defined, 140
 definition of, 115
 efficiency, 122–128, 160, 214–216
  bureaucracy *(see* Bureaucracy)
  Cubberly, E. P., 119–120
  neoscientific management, 125
  scientific management, 119, 122–124, 160, 214
  strengths of, 127
 person:
  criticism of, 132, 134
  Follett's views, 129
  human relations, 129–130
  human resources and human relations,
   130–133
 politics and decision making, 134–140
  conflict, 135
  nonrational view, 136–140
  open systems, 134
Mohram, S. A., 382
Morrill Land Grant Act, 271
Muller v. *Jefferson Lighthouse School District*, 337
Murch, J. G., 137, 145
Murks, H., 10

N
Nanus, B., 75, 143
National Academy for School Executives (NASE),
  82
National Association for the Advancement of
  Colored People (NAACP), 215, 224, 243
National Association for Bilingual Education,
  282
National Assessment of Educational Progress
  (NAEP), 49
National Association of Elementary School
  Principals (NAESP), 85, 95, 96, 100, 101,
  106, 282
National Association of Rural Superintendents, 81
National Association of Secondary School
  Principals (NASSP), 85, 95, 96, 106
National Board for Professional Teaching
  Standards, 3, 86
National Catholic Education Association, 243
National Center for Education Information, 98
National Center for Education Statistics, 101

National Commission on Excellence in Education,
  3, 85, 86, 276
National Commission on Excellence in
  Educational Administration, 86
National Conference of Professors of Educational
  Administration (NCPEA), 81
National Congress of Parents and Teachers, 239
National Council for Accreditation of Teacher
  Education (NCATE), 96, 106, 118
National Council of Administrative Women in
  Education, 101
National Defense Education Act (NDEA), 272
National Education Association (NEA), 85, 129,
  240–242, 275, 282, 291
National Education Goals Panel, 49, 51
National Institute of Education, 279
National Policy Board for Educational
  Administrators (NPBEA), 88, 89, 90, 96,
  106, 118
National School Boards Association, 282
National Science Board, 276
National Society for the Study of Education, 82
New York State Education Department, 102
New York Times, 351
New York University, 87
Newman, F., 10
Nieto, S., 53
Northern Illinois University, 85
Northwest Ordinance of 1787, 271
Northwestern University, 84
Nova Southeastern University, 84

O
Odden, A., 379, 382
Office of Management and Budget (OMB), 281,
  282, 283
Ohio State University, 81, 82, 214
Olsen, J. P., 139
Ouchi, W., 143

P
Parsons, T., 60, 63
Pascale, R. T., 143
Pauley v. *Kelly*, 374
P.B. v. *Koch*, 349
Pennsylvania State University, 82
Perry, A., 103
Peshkin, A., 61, 63, 210

Peters, T. J., 143
Peterson, K. D., 66, 82, 83
Peterson, P. E., 214
Plyer v. *Doe*, 301
Pohland, P., 97
Policy (*see also* Administration; Models of
    administration; School finance; School law;
    School reform):
  centralized, 295
  classroom, 248–249
  contrasted with administration, 56–58
  decentralized, 295
  definition of, 230
  dissatisfaction with, 232
  evaluating, 234
  federal role in, 20
    Congress, 280–281
    current trends, 278–280
    history of, 270–278
    national goals, 277
    presidential politics, 275–278
  implementing, 232
  interest groups, 282–283, 291–293
  levels of, 250
  local role in, 7, 9, 21, 249–254
    school boards, 254
  local, state, federal relations, 293–297
  policy in use, 56–58
  public confidence in, 37
  state role in, 21, 285
    chief state school officers, 289–290
    function of, 290–191
    governor's rule, 287
    state boards, 288
    strengthening of, 286, 290–291
  values in, 11–13, 20, 225
    choice, 6, 9, 29–31
    democratic choice, 10, 228–230
    market choice, 10
    efficiency, 6, 8, 226, 366
    equity, 6, 8, 52, 226, 274, 364
    equity and equality, 43, 51–52
    excellence, 6, 10, 226, 274, 276, 285
    reconciling differences, 227–230
Politics:
  business interests, 243–244
  definition of, 225
  minority interests, 243

model of, 159–160
Power, 235–236
  community, 236–240
The Preparation of School Administrators: A
    Statement of Purpose, 90
Principals:
  diversity among, 201
  educational leaders, 72, 76–78, 202–203
  effective, 77, 200–202, 204–210
  evaluation of, 65–70, 198–200
  standards for, 95, 106–112
Principles of Scientific Management, 122
Professional Standards for Superintendents, 95
Professionalism:
  in administration (*see* Administration)
  in teaching, 26, 214
    standards for, 86
Proficiencies for Principals: Kindergarten through
    Eighth Grade, 95
Project Head Start, 245
Proposition 13, 9, 293
The Public School System of the United States, 213
Pyle v. *Hadley School Committee*, 338

R
Rainbow Coalition, 243
Reagan, R., 275, 283
Reich, R. B., 359
Reynolds, W. A., 86
Rice, J. M., 213
Riley, R., 279, 283
Robbins, T., 299
Robinson v. *Cahill*, 372
Rockefeller Foundation, 244
Rodriguez v. *San Antonio Independent School*
    District, 372, 373
Roethlisberger, F., 129
Rose v. *Council for Better Education, Inc.*, 374, 376,
    378
Rosenberger v. *Rector and Visitors of the University of*
    Virginia, 344, 345
Rotary International, 244
Rowinsky v. *Bryan Independent School District*, 354

S
Sayre, W., 145
Schon, D., 147
School Administration as Craft, 162

School-based management, 22, 263–264, 381
School boards, 253–260
   collective bargaining, 262
   concerns of, 256
   demographic overview, 255
   electing, 256–260
   referenda, 264–267
School as community, 144 (*see also* School culture)
School culture, 142–144, 185
   concept of, 186
   defined, 140
   student culture, 188–191
   teacher culture, 191–195
School finance:
   block grants, 294–295, 370
   categorical grants, 294
   equalizing grants, 369–370
   federal, state, local expenditures, 294, 394
   full state funding, 368
   general revenue sharing, 294
   generating revenue
      income tax, 360–361
      property tax, 360, 362–364
      sales tax, 360–361
   production function research, 378–380
   school finance litigation, 372–378
   values in taxing, 364
      efficiency, 366
      elasticity, 367
      equity, 364–366
School law:
   administrators' responsibility, 304–305
   delegation issues, 315–318
   federal constitution, 324
      Fourteenth Amendment (due process),
         324–331
      freedom of speech, 331–334
      church and state, 339–348
   federal jurisdiction, 305–309
   judicial precedent, 302
   legal standards, 301
   litigation, 309
   residency policies, 302–303
   sexual harassment, 351–355
   standards of liability, 348–351
   state boards, authority of, 319–320
   state jurisdiction, 304–305

   torts (negligence) issues, 320–324
School reform:
   and culture of teaching, 192–196
   strategies, 4, 5
   waves of, 3–5, 21, 252, 278, 286
Schools:
   autonomy versus control, 20
   bill of rights for, 22–23
   as community, 144
   as cultural system, 185 (*see also* School culture)
   culture building in, 142–144
   evaluating, 68
   public confidence in, 142–144
Scientific management, 119, 122–124, 160, 214–216
Seattle University, 84
Selznick, P., 142, 149
Sergiovanni, T. J., 144
Serrano v. *Priest*, 285, 372
Servicemen's Readjustment Act (GI Bill), 271
Settle v. *Dickson County*, 345
Shanken, A., 86, 87, 241
Shirley, R. C., 22, 23
Simm, H. A., 57, 136, 137, 139
Sizer, T. R., 276
Skakeshaft, C., 98, 100, 103, 104, 105, 106
Smircich, L., 140
Smith, J. B., 104, 105
Smith, J. K., 151
Smith-Hughes Act, 271
Soltis, J. S., 164
Southern Christian Leadership Conference
      (SCLC), 243
Spaulding, F., 118
Speakman, S. T., 380
Sproul, L. S., 179, 180
Stacy, D., 224
Stanford University, 81, 84, 85, 118, 119, 214
Stake, R., 10
Starratt, R. J., 73, 74
Steffens, L., 213
Strauss, G., 134
Strayer, G., 118, 119, 120
Strike, K. A., 92, 164
Superintendency:
   conflict in, 217–219
   future of, 220–221
   historical overview, 212–217

scientific management, 214–216
women in, 220–221
Syracuse University, 57

T
Tarazi, G. J., 255
Taylor, F., 119, 122
Teachers College, Columbia University, 81, 82, 83, 84, 118, 119, 214
Texas A&M University, 84
Texas Assessment of Academic Skills (TAAS), 7, 16
Texas Education Agency, 15, 96
Theory X, 131
Theory Y, 131
Thompson, S. D., 90
Tinker v. *Des Moines Independent Community School District*, 331, 333, 338
Tomorrow's Teachers: A Report of the Holmes Group, 3
Toward High and Rigorous Standards for the Teaching Profession, 86
Trask, A. E., 103
Trinity University, 84
Turner v. *Board of Education*, 303
Twentieth Century Fund Task Force, 276
Tyack, D., 117, 119, 212
Tyler, R., 147

U
U.S. Constitution, 2, 22, 239, 270, 299
First Amendment, 331–348
Fourteenth Amendment, 324–331
U.S. Department of Education, 271, 278–280
U.S. Department of Health, Education and Welfare, 98
U.S. Office of Education, 271, 279
University of Buffalo, 85
University of Chicago, 81, 84, 85, 119, 214
University of Cincinnati, 85
University Council for Educational Administration (UCEA), 82, 84, 85, 86, 87, 88, 96, 97
University of Illinois at Urbana-Champaign, 84, 85
University of Michigan, 85, 214
University of Missouri, 82

University of Orgeon, 81, 82
University of Texas, 81
University of Toledo, 85
University of Wisconsin, 118
Urban League, 243

V
Vaill, P. B., 142
Van Dusartz v. *Hatfield*, 373
Van Kirk, A., 381
Vanderbilt University, 84 (*see also* George Peabody College for Teachers)
Village of Lucas v. *Lucas Local School District*, 318

W
Wallace v. *Jaffre*, 340
Walton, J., 92
Washakle County School District v. *Herschler*, 374
Waterman, Jr., R. H., 143
Weber, M., 126, 231
Western Electric Company, 129
What Next? More Leverage for Teachers, 3
Wilson, B. L., 143
Wilson, W., 57
Wirt, F., 225, 290
Wise, A., 24, 25, 26, 27, 96
Wohlstetter, P., 381
Wolcott, H., 198
Women in administration, 98–106
androcentrism, 100
principalship, 100–103
and professionalization, 106
status of, 98–100
styles of, 103–106
superintendency, 220–221
Women in Educational Administration, 104

Y
Yale University, 118
Young, E. F., 128, 129

Z
Zaleznick, A., 58, 73, 92
Zeigler, L., 217, 218, 254
Zheng, H. P. Y., 94, 104